A GOOD BIRTH, A SAFE BIRTH

"It would . . . do hospital administrators, doctors in general, and obstetricians and pediatricians in particular, a world of good to read *A Good Birth, A Safe Birth* and take to heart, mind, and practice the wise words of the authors."

—Ashley Montagu, Ph.D., author of
Touching and
The Natural Superiority of Women

"Diana Korte and Roberta Scaer have done a beautiful job of writing warmly and personally to the reader, and they have also presented information in a most professional and easily read academic manner. It is enjoyable and very informative reading—a must for every woman, whether she is of child-bearing age or not! Women *must* be informed on the level this superb book depicts, and hopefully this and other similar works will be the catalysts for major changes in our obstetrical and pediatric fields."

—Ruth D. Rice, Ph.D.
perinatal psychologist and
director, Cradle Care Company

"BRAVO! How well I remember my first clumsy questions and answers concerning childbirth, bonding and breastfeeding. What a welcome guide this would have been. Too many books judge . . . too few impart information."

—Mariette Hartley,
actress

P9-ELR-673

A GOOD BIRTH, A SAFE BIRTH

A GOOD BIRTH, A SAFE BIRTH

"Women have the right to enjoy the full pleasure potential of their own bodies that comes through their unique gifts of birthing, breastfeeding and mothering. This clear and interesting book is full of useful suggestions about how to make childbearing a really good experience."
—Niles Newton, Ph.D.,
professor of behavioral sciences,
Northwestern University Medical School

"I strongly recomend this well-written and researched book for parents who wish to be informed enough to join the professionals in the decision-making process for their own infant's birth."
—Marshall Klaus, M.D.,
author of *Parent-Infant Bonding*,
adjunct professor of pediatrics,
University of California, San Francisco

"The book everyone's been waiting for. I wish I could give it to every pregnant woman."
—Barbara Seaman, author of
Women and the Crisis in Sex Hormones
cofounder, National Women's Health Network

"A marvelous teaching tool for childbirth educators written without fear or hostility. It helps put to rest many of the myths and mysteries surrounding birth."
—Rhondda Evans Hartman, R.N., M.A.,
Bradley Childbirth instructor

"Physicians truly concerned with the well-being of mothers and their infants should read this book, because it so deeply reflects the heart of women and their justifiable resistance to hospital-based obstetric care."
—Doris Haire, president,
American Foundation for
Maternal and Child Health

"Diana Korte and Roberta Scaer are mothers who are not handicapped by medical training. They are able to understand that an easy birth is safer than a difficult one. They are able to understand that the priority, for every birth, should be an environment which disturbs as little as possible."
—Michel Odent, M.D., author of
Birth Reborn

A GOOD BIRTH, A SAFE BIRTH

REVISED EDITION

••

Diana Korte & Roberta Scaer

BANTAM BOOKS
New York • Toronto • London • Sydney • Auckland

A GOOD BIRTH, A SAFE BIRTH

A Bantam Book
Bantam trade edition/March 1984
Bantam revised updated paperback edition/June 1990

Library of Congress Cataloging-in-Publication Data

Korte, Diana.
  A good birth, a safe birth.

  Bibliography: p. 352
  Includes index.
  1. Childbirth. 2. Childbirth—Psychological aspects.
  3. Pregnant women—Family relationships. 4. Hospitals,
  Gynecologic and obstetric. I. Scaer, Roberta. II. Title.
RG652.K67 1984   618.2   83-20008
ISBN 0-553-28612-9 (pbk.)

Published simultaneously in the United States and Canada

PRINTED IN THE UNITED STATES OF AMERICA

RAD   0 9 8 7 6 5 4 3 2 1

With affection, to all the women
we know in La Leche League
who helped us toward the good
births, breastfeeding, and
mothering of our children.

▪ CONTENTS ▪

▪ ACKNOWLEDGMENTS TO THE FIRST EDITION ▪

We're both grateful to our husbands, Gene Korte and Bob Scaer, and all eight of our children—Kathy, Mike, Andy, and Amanda Scaer . . . and Neil, Drew, Aren, and Juliana Korte. They encouraged us, while putting up with our joint, all-consuming passion to write this book.

Many others helped, too. Mary Ann Fitzharris, our Boulder editor, not only cleaned up our copy before we submitted it but kept encouragement flowing. We're grateful for the advice and feedback our manuscript readers gave us: Renee Chalfant-Bednark, Darleen Eide, Donna Ewy, Pat and Michael Fritsch, Jan Graham Lippitt, Pam Novotny, Barbara Pfeifle, Karen Pryor, Judy Sanders, and David Stewart, among others.

Local March of Dimes Director Becky Messina was invaluable. She launched the M.O.M. Survey with financial support from the Northern Colorado chapter of the March of Dimes–Birth Defects Foundation. We thank the forty-two volunteers who helped us with the Boulder survey. Our special appreciation goes to Shannon Pope in Wenatchee, Washington, and The COMA Committee (Bobbi Seabolt, DeSales Beling, Linda Levy, Mary T. Maher, Linda Schummers, Susan M. Treanor, and Cheryl E. Wood) in Baltimore, Maryland, for sharing their survey results and enthusiasm with us. Thanks also go to the thousands of women who participated in all three surveys and others who responded to us in workshops or told of their concerns in phone calls and letters.

We can't forget Boulder's Community Hospital—its administrators, doctors, nurses, and trustees who worked with us and other consumers to give women the maternity care they want. The process was often heated, but the job was well done and something for all of us to be proud of. Special thanks to the late Patrick Cussen, then director of nursing at Community Hospital, who guided the maternity-care changes through the morass of hospital bureaucracy.

Dozens of health professionals provided us with interviews and copies of research findings. Many are cited throughout the book, and others are listed in the references. A special nod goes to those who didn't agree with us but cooperated anyway. We must give credit to those matchless sources of information David and Lee Stewart, the directors of the National Association of Parents and Professionals for Safe Alternatives in Childbirth (NAPSAC), and Madeleine Shearer, editor of the journal *Birth*.

The following are our major influences and forerunners, listed alphabetically: American Society for Psychoprophylaxis in Obstetrics (ASPO), Suzanne Arms, Robert Bradley, Adelle Davis, Donna Ewy, Ina May Gaskin, Doris Haire, Rhondda Hartman, International Childbirth Education Association (ICEA), Marjorie Karmel, Sheila Kitzinger, John Kennell, Marshall Klaus, La Leche League International, Ashley Montagu, Niles Newton, and Karen Pryor.

And, finally, special mention goes to Toni Burbank, our Bantam editor, who gave us the freedom to write the book that we knew had never been written before, and to our agent, Lynn Seligman, who believed in us.

INTRODUCTION TO THE
REVISED EDITION

Six years ago when the first edition of this book was published, we told you that the two trends in childbirth were moving in opposing directions. They still are. One trend is the growing number of hospitals providing homelike accommodations, including Jacuzzis and microwaves, plus the more than 130 out-of-hospital birth centers, which numbered only in the dozens a few years ago.

The other trend is high-tech childbirth. We've had routine IVs, labor induction, and cesareans for years. Now there's a growing emphasis on tests and procedures of all kinds. It starts early in pregnancy in many parts of the country with the encouragement of genetic testing for pregnant women of all ages, not just women past age thirty-five. It continues with the use of the electronic fetal monitor during labor for all women, (and before labor for some) as well as ubiquitous ultrasound for all, offered routinely in at least three ways (scans, Dopplers, and external monitors). And in the last six years, the cesarean rate has increased from one in five births to one in four.

What about home births, that bastion of all-natural, no interference pregnancies? They have shrunk even more in the last six years from 2–3 percent of all births to less than 1 percent today, based on a 1989 report from the National Center for Health Statistics. But high tech is present in some home births, too, with the use of the ultrasound Doppler instead of the traditional fetoscope, a stethoscopelike, hand-held device used to listen to the fetal heart.

Which trend is growing the fastest? No doubt about it: In the United States, high tech has taken over childbirth. If you're like most pregnant women, it's as much a part of your pregnancy and birth today as is your big belly. Birth centers, both out of hospital and particularly those that are in hospital, may not use as much high tech as a traditional maternity unit, or may not use it as soon, but it is not unusual for the electronic fetal monitor and the Doppler to be offered to you during your stay at an in-hospital birth center, and Pitocin and painkilling drugs are not far behind. In contrast, out-of-hospital birth centers seldom use technology.

Though there are more choices in the United States for birth attendant and place of birth than probably anywhere else on this planet, nearly all women give birth one way here—with a doctor in a hospital. And over the last six years, some things have become more, not less, rigid.

Birth plans with their list of mothers' preferences during labor, birth, and hospital stay were designed to help many women get what they want. But today birth plans carry little punch except for a few women whose requests match their physicians' usual obstetrical routine. And the change in insurance coverage for most of you who have insurance to prepaid plans with limited choice of health-care providers and hospitals may curtail your options unless you're willing to pay out of pocket.

Each nation's culture is reflected in how women experience birth. High-tech childbirth is our dominant style of birth as we enter the 1990s, in part because most American women expect labor to be painful and anticipate using a variety of drugs to reduce the pain. And both expectations are met. In spite of what we think might happen, however, there are great differences among women in the "normal" amount of pain they experience, just as there is great variation in the "normal" length of labor and the "normal" number of days in each pregnancy.

A 1988 study comparing labor pain experienced by women in teaching hospitals in Holland and the United States found that the Dutch women, in contrast to the American women, did not expect to experience much pain and used far fewer drugs for pain relief. "There is in Dutch birth participants a deep-seated conviction that the woman's body knows best and that, given enough time, nature will take its course, whereas birth in America was characterized as much more of a 'medical event,'" noted one of the authors. In Holland most women are cared for by midwives, and nearly 40 percent of births still occur at home. As old-fashioned and unscientific as that sounds to many of you, more babies survive in Holland than they do in the United States, because the Dutch infant mortality rate is superior to ours even when racial differences are considered.

But we don't live in Holland, we live in the United States, where there is much fear and anxiety about birth. And women are threatened with comments like, "If you don't get going on your labor, we're going to give you Pitocin (or a cesarean)," which increases your discomfort and pain, sometimes leading to panic and your body's total shutdown of labor.

High tech, not Mother Nature, is the norm. For most of you, the question is not, Are you going to use high-tech tools? The question is, Which tools are you going to use when? For instance, the use of ultrasound has doubled since our first edition, and the electronic fetal monitoring of United States labors is nearly universal. Your decision making about high tech for a hospital birth is likely to be when and for how long you will use either of these tools, not whether you'll use them at all.

Six years ago we told you that many women, based on surveys of two thousand mothers, weren't satisfied with their birth experiences. What about today? The hundreds of you who sent us your completed questionnaires from the back of the first book, or who phoned us or spoke to us in person, are more satisfied than not. Though satisfaction is hard to measure, some research in this country and England shows that most of you like high-tech pregnancy and birth. Obviously: Why else would most of you use it? (Though British birth researcher Ann Oakley reminds us that physician satisfaction, not mother's satisfaction, determines what most women get.)

Most of you like the feeling of giving your baby the best with "state-of-the-art" tools, and many of you no longer believe that so-called "natural" childbirth is best, though you like many of the accoutrements associated with the early days of natural childbirth, such as help from the staff during labor and your setting the pace for contact with your baby and other children after the birth.

However, many of you also simultaneously worry about the effects some of these tests and machines may have on your infant. And the older your child gets, the more critical you may become. For those of you who were looking forward to an unmedicated birth, you may feel guilty or defensive about erroneously believing that you "flunked" childbirth because you used drugs for pain relief.

We've heard from readers in thirty-eight states, six Canadian provinces, and seven other countries, and some of your comments are included in this new edition. We apologize for not being able to add more, due to space constraints. Some of you have even written with several birth stories, and we thank all of you, and invite you again to write after you've read this edition. Either one or both of us have replied to each letter, though some of you moved and our notes were returned.

A few of you have bought many books to give to friends, and others enjoy passing around the same dog-eared copy. There are many childbirth educators and La Leche League leaders (and a few nurses and doctors) who keep copies in their libraries. And this book is offered in dozens of mail-order catalogs and has been placed on many recommended reading lists.

Several dozen of you wrote early on to say that you were interested in organizing surveys or consumer groups. More often than not, those plans changed, and the women who wrote us decided on a new direction, one often related to birth, either in childbirth education or midwifery.

Some of you have found particularly helpful birth attendants, and most of these helpers are midwives. But some are physicians who buck the trend of obstetrics today. Many of you liked the idea of the doula, in particular, and if you didn't have one at your last birth, you plan to the next time. Some of you said you couldn't afford a doula. We still think you don't have to spend money to hire this helping woman, though the concept has caught on around the country, and many doula services have sprung up in the last six years. (See "Doulas—Birth Assistants and Mother Helpers," in your List of Helpers.)

Your stories have told us that birth's hospital routines are remarkably the same in the United States, whether you gave birth in California or Maine. Like the rest of pregnant women in this country, most of you gave birth in hospitals with the help of an obstetrician, and have many routine interventions, though questionnaires in the last year or two show a big jump in the use of midwives. In spite of your preference for hospitals and obstetricians, your letters have also made it clear that you do not all want the same options, and your preferences may vary from pregnancy to pregnancy.

> I had two very different experiences with childbirth. My son (number-one child) was a twenty-seven-week preemie. I am still grateful that the interventions used were available. I feel all were necessary, and I have

nothing but praise for the hospital, nurses, doctors, and technologists who contributed to saving our son. Three years later I gave birth to a healthy full-term baby girl. Same doctors, hospital, nurses, etc. Also same interventions. It was a nightmare. I felt so helpless. I checked myself and my daughter out of the hospital against medical advice thirty-six hours after her birth because of all the interferences.

—CANADIAN MOTHER

Just as one woman's Dr. Right is another woman's Dr. Wrong, one woman's good birth experience is another woman's misery.

I was amazed how my body took control. With the first push or two, my water broke (I even got to do that myself!) while I squatted. A couple more pushes and I could see her head in the mirror. I reached down to touch my baby! Minutes later, she was nursing at my breast. The feelings of joy and awe at the experience of a natural delivery are hard to describe. But I can tell you that it was worth all the months of preparations, discussions with the doctors, and two days of contractions.

—OHIO MOTHER AFTER THIRD BIRTH, FOLLOWING
TWO PREVIOUS CESAREANS

The information on anesthesia was extremely one-sided. You've pointed out only the negative aspects of it without giving examples of times when it is beneficial. I know from experience that an epidural can be a sanity saver, and turn what would otherwise be a nightmare of prolonged, unbearable, uncontrollable pain into a calm, happy, positive birth.

—CONNECTICUT MOTHER

Most of you have attended childbirth education classes, and though you were satisfied overall, nearly all of you had suggestions for more information you wish had been offered. Many of those suggestions had to do with information about pain relief ("realistic discussion of pain, not fairy tale") or discovering what options were really available ("not just what doctors want us to hear"). Many readers thought that classes "pushed drugs," and "didn't tell us about risks vs. benefits of *anything*."

Reminiscent of our comments in the first edition, most of you found the best advice about breastfeeding came from friends, La Leche League, childbirth educators, midwives, and books. Now you also can have the help of more than 1,000 lactation consultants. (See "International Lactation Association") Family members still tend to give advice that falls either in the "really helpful" category or the "really terrible." Hospital nurses, obstetricians, and pediatricians fared the worst in the advice category overall, though there were some exceptions, and family practice doctors tend to be more helpful than not.

This book, as did the first edition, provides information about options other women want and about the seldom-discussed sexual pleasures of pregnancy, birth, and breastfeeding. Birth attendants (midwife and doctor) and places of birth (hospital, birth center, and home) are compared. We present a demystified view of doctors and nurses so that you understand why they do what they do. From pubic shaves, to cesareans, to newborn jaundice phototherapy, the risks and benefits of modern American childbirth interventions are discussed. And as your best guarantee of having a normal vaginal birth once you're in the hospital, we suggest that in addition to having your mate with you, you have a doula (a special helper) and perhaps a monitrice (your personal ob nurse).

We've extensively revised nearly all chapters to reflect many of the changes in the childbirth world during the last six years, as well as your suggestions and comments about wanting more consumer information. Examples are the added section on circumcision and an expanded appendix, including many more organizations and other resources for consumers. Nearly every chapter has new research confirming the conclusions we made in the first edition about a good birth being also a safe birth. We've added a section on prolonged pregnancy because of the relationship between the increasing number of cesareans and women who have been induced because they've gone past their due dates.

And we're also more sensitive to the fact that "husband" doesn't compute for the 25 percent of you who are single when you give birth. Unless the research specifically mentions husbands, we've used "mate" or "partner." However, we've kept masculine pronouns to refer to doctors throughout this edition, just as we did in the first book, because most practicing physicians are men, though there are many more women doctors in practice today than there were six years ago.

We've listed our names alphabetically again, with each of

us revising our own half of the book. And because many of you asked which one of us wrote what, we provide the following: Roberta wrote chapters 1, 3, 6, 7, 8, 9, 12, the "Reader Questionnaire," and "The Three Surveys." Diana wrote the "Introduction," chapters 2, 4, 5, 10, 11, 13, 14, "How to be a Changemaker," and "Your List of Helpers."

Most of you who read this book will be working outside the home throughout your entire pregnancy and returning to your job within three to six months. Some of our suggestions may seem to be far too much bother for the amount of time that you have, especially when you're interested in making your pregnancy and birth as easy as possible, not more complicated. We think the issue remains choice, not what you pick. We don't always agree with each other either. Do what works for you, take what you want from this book, and ignore the rest.

ONE

WHAT WOMEN WANT

I believe the best environment in which to deliver a baby would be within the ob wing, but in a more casual, homelike setting. I think a new mother should be allowed to have as much interaction with family members as she feels up to—including other children, parents, spouse. . . . The new baby should be allowed in the patient's room during these family gatherings if the parents so wish. I would also encourage as much mother-infant interaction as possible during the stay, interaction hopefully commencing immediately after delivery. I also feel "standing orders" for medication prior to and following delivery should be replaced with individualized recommendations. . . . Congratulations for caring enough to conduct this important survey.

—SURVEY MOTHER*

As health-care consumers, we have the right to have a big say in those services that affect our welfare so critically and that cost us so dearly. But instead of finding out what people want and need in their health care, doctors and other health-care providers too often tell us what we'll be getting. So far, that's worked because hospitals and doctors have had a monopoly in their business. In at least one area of health care—childbirth— the situation is changing.

Today more and more women know what they want to have happen in their childbirth experience. Really, they've known all along, but no one ever asked them what they wanted.

*All quotes from women throughout the book are from the three maternity-preference surveys cited, unless otherwise noted.

In the late 1970s, three unique studies took care of this oversight. More than 2,000 women were asked to rate hospital maternity options in three different cities. They represented the Northwest (Wenatchee, Washington), the Mountain States (M.O.M. Survey, Boulder, Colorado), and the East Coast (COMA Survey, Baltimore, Maryland)—a cross-section of the nation.

Women of very diverse educational and economic backgrounds came up with virtually the same results: 2,067 women agreed that there are five major needs in maternity care.

- They want the baby's father present for the labor, delivery, and recovery, and to have unrestricted visiting rights.
- They want cooperation and assistance from the hospital staff—doctors and nurses—in using prepared childbirth techniques.
- Women who breastfeed want effective help from nurses and doctors.
- They want a lot of contact with their babies, immediately after birth and throughout their entire hospital stay.
- They want their other children to visit them and to see and hold the new baby.

ISSUE NUMBER ONE:
FATHERS' PRESENCE

The battle to have the husband present at labor and a vaginal birth has been won at most American hospitals. But there are still places where a "significant other" is not allowed with the woman. In the case of cesareans (at least one in four of all births), the fathers often are made to wait in a waiting room.

The women in the three surveys were in strong agreement on this issue: nearly all of them believe that the father's presence at all times, during labor and delivery and after the birth of the baby, is the most important issue to them. Here's what some of them said:

The only change I would make in my childbirth experience would be that my husband could be with me during labor, even if he doesn't attend a childbirth class . . . just for comforting purposes. I was scared and lonely during labor.

The presence of the father throughout labor and delivery is of uppermost importance. After all, having a baby is a combined and most rewarding experience for both parents.

WHAT RESEARCH SAYS
ABOUT FATHERS' PRESENCE

Research supports women who want to have their husbands present during labor and delivery. Deborah Tanzer, Ph.D., was the first researcher to study husband participation in childbirth. She found that when the birth was unmedicated, and the husband was present, the marriage was strengthened. The husband appeared stronger and more helpful, more masculine, and more competent in his wife's eyes. One third of these women describe their births in such blissful terms that Dr. Tanzer concluded that they had what psychologists call a "peak experience," one of transcendent ecstasy. In contrast, none of the women who were alone in labor reported a peak experience. Apparently, the husband's presence was required for women to experience that kind of intense joy, and for women to view their husbands more positively after the birth than before.

One of the most likely times for severe strain in a marriage is in the first months after the birth of a baby, especially the first baby, studies show. Jane and James Pittenger, family counselors and childbirth educators, describe how the routine practices of doctors and hospitals contribute to an absent and disinterested father, an overwhelmed and dissatisfied mother, and confusion and ambivalence for them as a couple and as new parents. Often a woman looks to her doctor for the kind of support her husband could give. The pregnant woman's growing attachment to her doctor is at the expense of her feelings toward her husband. The foundation of the marriage, which combines both pleasure and commitment, is greatly weakened by a birth experience that makes them feel alienated from each other and from their baby.

However, the Pittengers also found that some couples were more satisfied with their marriages after the birth of their baby and found great pleasure in their new roles as parents. The differences between them and dissatisfied couples was that the satisfied parents took time to study together about birthing and parenting. They chose doctors who assisted and supported them, rather than took over. They were together in labor and delivery. Mothers in this group breastfed their babies for many months after birth.

ISSUE NUMBER TWO: INFORMATION AND HELP FROM DOCTORS AND NURSES DURING LABOR AND BIRTH

Nearly 98 percent of American babies are born in hospitals. Mothers go to hospitals to get what they believe is the best care for themselves and their babies. We were not surprised, then, to find that mothers believe strongly in getting informed, positive help from the hospital staff and doctors. A major concern of the mothers is having doctors and nurses trained in prepared childbirth techniques to help them in their labor and delivery.

Voluntary comments from mothers about staff help (or lack of it) during labor and birth were abundant.

The nurse needs to know when to help the husband help his wife or when to help directly—an art.

I will not have another birth in that hospital. Women want and need to be in charge of their whole childbirth experience. There is nothing more frightening for someone having a first baby than to be strapped down in bed, stuck with needles, examined by ten different people, experience terrifying pain and have no one explain it to you, and have absolutely no control over your body whatsoever. At this time a woman needs friendly advice, comfort, and warmth.

Many comments in this section had to do with the use of *anesthesia* (drugs that block sensation) and *analgesia* (drugs used to relieve pain).

I did not have a private ob. The ob that delivered my child was on staff at [X] hospital. I was very displeased with him. He kept trying to push drugs on me when I was in labor. The nurses were very helpful, very kind and understanding.

* * *

My last birth I almost had a natural childbirth, but I was too afraid not to have the spinal. I would like to see the hospital teach more about natural childbirth rather than push their own method of delivery. I figure natural childbirth has got to be better than that awful head and neck ache I had for a full week.

Women expect their childbirth education to reduce or eliminate the need for drugs in labor and delivery. But it doesn't work that way for many women, often to their dissatisfaction. The Baltimore survey found that fully 66 percent of the women who were given anesthesia felt that it was *not* necessary for them to deliver in comfort.

Several possibilities come to mind for why this is so. During the stress of labor women may ask for or accept analgesia or anesthesia and then later regret it. Some women tell us that they believe they could have avoided drugs if they'd had more human support and encouragement at crucial moments when relaxation and breathing techniques seemed to fail. Also, the lack of preparation for resisting the routine use of analgesia or anesthesia for almost all deliveries is another possible reason women get unnecessary drugs. Even a woman who may have decided to avoid drugs, if possible, could find herself in hard labor trying to explain to a doctor or nurse why she's different from other women in refusing "something for the pain."

WHAT MEDICAL RESEARCH SAYS ABOUT DRUGS DURING CHILDBIRTH

Medical research strongly supports the preference of women for staff help in using prepared childbirth techniques to reduce or eliminate analgesics and anesthesia that are risky for mothers and risky for babies.

There is a delicate physical balance between mother and baby during labor and birth that can be disrupted by drugs, with the result that labor may be prolonged. Folklore from individual women and doctors holds that anesthesia has sometimes helped a woman finish dilating quickly after she seemed stuck at 5 or 6 centimeters for several hours. But no research shows that analgesia and anesthesia shorten labor. On the contrary, the slowing effect, particularly of anesthesia, has been documented in the medical literature. In fact, the drug Pitocin is often ordered to accompany anesthesia to offset the labor slowdown.

Analgesia and anesthesia may cause a drop in the mother's blood pressure, which may affect the amount of oxygen the unborn baby receives. Anesthesia often interferes with or eliminates the ability to bear down, requiring the use of forceps in delivery. There is often considerable transfer of the drugs from the mother to the baby, which can cause respiratory distress in the newborn, requiring resuscitation. The transfer of drugs causes short- and long-term effects on the baby. These effects are described in chapter 7, "The Obstetrician's Black Bag of Interventions."

ISSUE NUMBER THREE: EFFECTIVE HELP FROM NURSES AND DOCTORS WITH BREASTFEEDING

Getting good breastfeeding help from the hospital staff was the third major preference of women. And from their comments it was clear that negative comments about breastfeeding were especially unwelcome.

The nurses were very helpful. They offered suggestions to make breastfeeding more comfortable for me and answered my many questions without making me feel dumb.

I feel all doctors and nurses and pediatricians should do further study on breastfeeding and not rely on ineffective theories about it.

In 1961 only 18 percent of newborns in the United States were breastfed. By 1989, nearly 60 percent of newborns started out being breastfed, reported La Leche League International. Many of these newborns, however, go home from the hospital already receiving bottles of formula or water or nursing through a breast shield placed over the mother's nipple. These kinds of nursing problems are the responsibility of poorly informed doctors and nurses. Most mothers want to breastfeed their newborns, but are not receiving support and information from the staff that will help them nurse successfully.

WHAT MEDICAL RESEARCH SAYS
ABOUT BREASTFEEDING

As far back as 1967, Niles Newton, Ph.D., and Michael Newton, M.D., reported in the *New England Journal of Medicine* that failure in breastfeeding can often be traced to the doctor or the hospital experience. The surveys and our readers confirm this is still true. Drugs given to mothers during labor affect the ability of the infant to suck readily at the breast. Also, regulated, restricted, short breastfeedings advocated by many nurses in hospitals lead to reduced milk yield, poor weight gain, more nipple soreness, and greater likelihood of ending the breastfeeding altogether, according to the Newtons.

"The babies of our human ancestors were probably carried and nursed frequently for over 99 percent of our species' existence," says pediatrician John Kennell, M.D. In those cultures where successful breastfeeding continues for an average of two years, the mother and infant are inseparable from birth, and breastfeeding is so frequent that it appears to our eyes to be almost continuous. Dr. Kennell compares the fat and protein content of human milk to other animals', and concludes that human milk was designed for babies to be almost continuous feeders.

If breastfeeding results in more contact with the baby, it also means a larger time commitment on the part of the mother. In this modern world of fast-paced living and lots of demands on our time, why do it? Because hundreds of studies attest to the biochemical superiority of breast milk. New York researcher of pediatric infectious diseases, Jane Pitt, M.D., says, "There is hardly an antiinfective mechanism I can think of that we know of in the body that does not show up in breast milk."

"Formula-fed babies have 80 percent more infections than breastfed babies," says Mark Thoman, M.D., Iowa pediatrician and toxicologist. Only one quarter of breastfed babies "needed to be seen by a doctor even once in their first six months because of illness," reports La Leche League. But almost all (97 percent) of formula-fed babies needed doctor visits for illness in the first six months. And the sick formula-fed infants made more visits to the doctor than the sick breastfed infants. Dr. Thoman also points out that bottle-fed babies have an 80 percent greater chance of developing allergies. And for every nursing baby that succumbs to Sudden Infant Death Syndrome (SIDS), twenty formula-fed babies die of SIDS.

Formula itself is deficient in the more than one hundred components of breast milk that have been identified, with more added to the list as research continues. Formula cannot duplicate these as-yet-undiscovered elements. But our breast-fed babies are getting them, even though we can't yet give them a label. In addition, breast milk composition varies so enormously from woman to woman that some scientists speculate an individual woman's milk may be especially suited to her own baby's nutritional needs and age. It's not just a matter of your breastfed baby getting Formula A or Formula B, but of getting milk unique for him, and that changes appropriately as he grows older. According to Dr. Thoman, "Mama-lac is still the best."

However, simply breastfeeding because of a sense of duty to the baby isn't sufficient to keep most mothers breastfeeding very long. Dr. Niles Newton, La Leche League, and most successful nursing moms point out the physical and emotional pleasure to the mother that is a natural part of breastfeeding. This pleasure bond between mother and infant is what keeps the mother breastfeeding her baby in the face of difficulties.

The Pittengers describe the advantages of breastfeeding to the father, noting that fathers do not need to express their love for their baby by putting a bottle in its mouth. "In exchange, fathers gain an active, more responsive, sweeter smelling, and healthier baby, a wife who is more apt to be content in her role as mother, and exposure to the breastfeeding style of parenting with its frequent parent-child interactions, touching, and play," say the Pittengers. Almost all men whose wives have success-fully nursed feel that the support and protection they give their wives is essential to the success of the nursing relationship.

Again, women are right on the button in their strong preference for breastfeeding help from doctors and nurses. For most mothers to be successful, positive information and support are essential. With an outside network such as La Leche League, many mothers are able to overcome breastfeed-ing difficulties that begin in the hospital. But the issue remains. Moms want doctors and nurses to give the very best informa-tion available on breastfeeding.

ISSUE NUMBER FOUR: CONTACT WITH BABY

A fourth vital concern of women is the contact they have with their babies. They want their babies with them from birth, so that the mother's body warms the baby, in preference to an incubator; so that the mother can start breastfeeding as soon after delivery as possible; and so that the mother can become acquainted with her new baby as soon as it is born.

I wish I had been more assertive about my wishes. I wanted my baby with me immediately after delivery and I was not allowed to see her until six hours later. I still don't know why. She was a normal, healthy, term baby.

When my second child was born, I was barely able to touch her tiny hand and quickly kiss her cheek before she was whisked away from me. I would have liked to have put her on my stomach. I had a hard labor and wanted to be close to her right away.

During their hospital stays, the mothers want a great deal more contact with their babies than is now possible in many American hospitals. Many mothers want their babies with them night and day, with the choice to use the nursery for short intervals. Hospitals call this "rooming-in." Significant numbers of mothers want no separation at all from their babies.

WHAT MEDICAL RESEARCH SAYS ABOUT MOTHER-BABY CONTACT

The strong desire of mothers to stay close to their newborn babies is nothing new. Ashley Montagu, Ph.D., was one of the first scientists to zero in on the critical importance of mother-baby contact immediately following birth. In his book *Touching,* he describes the benefits of uterine contractions during labor for the baby. "The stimulation the baby receives from the contractions of her uterus tone up his sustaining systems— respiratory, circulatory, digestive, eliminative, nervous and endocrine—for the functions they will be called upon to perform after birth." He believes "these uterine contractions of labor constitute the beginning of caressing of the baby in the right way—a caressing that should be continued in very special ways in the period immediately following birth and for a substantial period of time afterward." After the somewhat trying time of birth, both mother and baby "clearly require the reassurance of the other's presence," he says.

A usual hospital routine is for the newborn baby to be removed to a heated bed or incubator to warm him. Mothers who have wondered why their own bodies cannot warm their newborns will be reassured by nurse Celeste Phillips's research on heated cribs versus mothers' arms at Watsonville and Santa Cruz, California, hospitals. She found that newborn body temperature was as well maintained when babies were wrapped and held by their mothers as by the incubator. Because she noted cold delivery rooms during her research, Mrs. Phillips further suggests keeping the babies warmer by raising the delivery-room temperature regardless of whether babies are in their mothers' arms or an incubator.

After the baby was born we didn't get to spend much time with him. I would have liked to keep him with me longer and to nurse him. As it was, it was eight hours until I got to hold him and nurse him for the first time. They said his temperature had to stabilize and had him under a heat lamp. Wouldn't my body heat do the same thing?

Mothers say they prefer having their babies with them so they can immediately offer the breast when their newborn awakens. This avoids the painful breast engorgement common with mothers who feed their babies on a schedule. "Another very, very exciting and interesting thing we have found regards weight gain by the newborn," says Mayer Eisenstein, M.D., a home-birth physician in Chicago, writing in *Safe Alternatives in Childbirth*. "I was trained that it takes seven to ten days for a newborn to regain its birth weight, and I believed it. But we found our homebirth babies gaining very well, usually exceeding their birth weight by one-half to one pound by one week of age. We interpret this to be the result of no maternal separation."

Many mothers who have experienced this kind of complete contact with their baby during their hospital stay report they do not have the difficult adjustment from hospital to home described by other mothers whose babies spent long periods of time in the nursery. Research supports women in this also.

For years mothers accepted as inevitable the adjustment problems from hospital to home. Staying up all night with a crying baby the first night home seemed to start the awful, constant fatigue that wears down new mothers. "She's asleep when I'm awake, and I want to sleep when she's awake," became the common new mother's complaint. Every new mother and baby need time to adjust to each other. Sleep and nursing patterns that are mutually satisfying to mother and baby develop fastest when mother and baby are together from birth on, reports psychiatrist Muriel Sugarman, M.D., from Brookline, Massachusetts. Multiple caretakers, different nurses on changing shifts who care for newborns left in nurseries, interrupt the progress of the mother and baby adjusting to each other. In fact, from her comprehensive review of the literature on maternal-infant attachment, Dr. Sugarman suggests that multiple caretakers of the newborn prolong the period of time needed by mother and newborn to adjust. New mothers and babies need lots of uninterrupted time to be with each other.

The current practice of routine drug prescriptions, day and night following normal childbirth, interrupts maternal-infant attachment, mothers tell us. Women feel too drugged at night to care whether they see their infants or not. One woman reports she was told by a nurse that she was the only woman during her three day hospital stay who refused the routine pain killers during the day and sleeping medication at night. Women may not know they can refuse such routine medications or that normal childbirth does not require them.

What is this age-old experience of maternal-infant bonding that mothers have always been aware of and scientists have just begun to study? This attachment is a unique, intense, learned relationship between two people, a long-term commitment between mother and child. It begins when their eyes meet at birth, and just may be the strongest kind of link we have with one another. Babies arrive with their bonding antennae well in tune. A newborn loves to look at a face. It seeks out the mother's eyes, and may mimic an act, such as sticking out the tongue. As its body is cradled by mother, the baby hears the heartbeat it has known for months. The child feels warmth and softness, detects mother's scent, and recognizes her voice. Brought to the breast often, the alert baby takes the warm sweetness of its mother's milk. The infant is secure and content. No more are babies looked upon as passive, unresponsive creatures who should be relegated to newborn nurseries.

Certainly the research on maternal-infant attachment most widely influencing doctors and hospital routines and supporting women's ideas is that of Marshall Klaus, M.D., and John Kennell, M.D. In one of their studies they compared two groups of women, all bottle-feeding mothers. One group had traditional contact with babies: glimpse after birth, brief contact between six and twelve hours, then thirty-minute visits for feeding every four hours. The other group had more contact. They enjoyed their new babies for one hour within the first three hours of life, and also had five extra hours of contact each afternoon on the first three days after birth, a total of sixteen extra hours of contact beyond the traditional amount given to the first group.

Observed at one month, one year, and two years, the mothers with extended contact fondled their babies more, were more soothing, gave fewer commands, and were more reluctant to leave the baby with someone else. "Incredibly," report Klaus and Kennell, "at five years of age these children had significantly higher I.Q.s and more advanced scores on language tests." Their early bonding studies were stimulated by knowledge of a high rate of child battering among children who spent their first weeks in premature nurseries separated from their mothers. Welcoming mothers into the nurseries and encouraging as much contact as possible between mother and child seemed to prove to be a successful abuse preventive for many premature babies.

Once again, mothers have been right all along. Doctors, nurses, and hospital administrators need to listen when women say it is vital to have their babies with them from birth, rooming-in, with the choice to use the nursery for short intervals.

I was made to feel that the baby was mine—not the hospital's property. I needed no permission, nor did my husband, to have access to our baby at any time.

I was not allowed to touch the baby, only look, although my delivery was uncomplicated, the baby was fine, and I had had no medication. I did ask the ob if the baby could be brought to me to hold after I was back in my room—he said, "Yes," but that he didn't believe in "all this bonding business," and he laughed at the idea that early mother-baby contact could be beneficial. I strongly believe the hospital could become the best place to deliver a baby if normal, uncomplicated deliveries were to take place in a homelike environment where the mother could be with her family. In this way, medical help and medical facilities would be close by, if needed, and yet birth could still be a normal, natural, family event.

ISSUE NUMBER FIVE: VISITS WITH OTHER CHILDREN

The desire of women for a strong family unit at the time of birth extends to their other children. Mothers want their other children to see the baby, and the mothers want to be able to see their other children, not waving through a window from a distance, but up close so they can talk to them, hug them, and reassure them.

I enjoyed having our two older children (ages three and five) visit me and the baby in the hospital. There were no traumatic spells of crying because they got to see the new baby and they were with both my husband and me as a family unit.

I think it's very important that your children are allowed to visit you. It was very hard to be able to see my children standing outside the maternity door when I couldn't go out there to hug them and they couldn't come in.

Those visits from their other children is the fifth crucial concern to women in their hospital experience. They strongly agree that they want their other children to visit them in the hospital, and they want their other children to see the new baby. Though the two other surveys asked women if they wanted to see their other children, the Baltimore survey was the first to ask moms whether they wanted their other children present soon after birth. An overwhelming 88 percent of the mothers want their other children there in the period following birth, during the recovery time.

I feel sisters and brothers should be able to hold the newborn as soon as possible after the birth, and that restrictions on family visitations be eliminated. After all, family means more to a baby than a nurse who works in a nursery.

WHAT MEDICAL RESEARCH SAYS ABOUT VISITS FROM OTHER CHILDREN

Again, mothers are way ahead of professionals in perceiving that there is a crucial time for beginning sibling attachment to the baby; very few research reports compare the reactions of siblings who have been present at birth with those who have not.

Sandra Anderson, R.N., and Leta Brown, R.N., of the University of Arizona College of Nursing in Tucson, contributed a much-needed survey of the reactions of children present for a sibling's birth, compared with children who were not present. The positive reactions of the children seeing their sister or brother born continued in the months following the birth. The children who were present showed less regressive behavior (for example, fewer accidents in recently toilet-trained children) and less abusive behavior toward the new baby. In their book *Children at Birth,* Marjie and Jay Hathaway, through photos and prose, show the intense interest of brothers and sisters in their newborn sibling.

"What we're seeing," says David Stewart, Ph.D., of NAPSAC, "is that there is a biological prime time for attachment for all those who are present, regardless of age." Mothers whose other children are present at the birth or come in immediately after birth and see and hold their new sibling report that their older children have a deep concern for the baby's welfare.

In *Parent-Infant Bonding,* Klaus and Kennell refer to several studies showing that children who do not visit their mothers in the hospital are very distressed. These children showed "emotional distance" when their mothers tried to hug them after coming home: the children "either stiffened or turned away." Children who had visited their mothers were happy to see them at the end of the hospital stay. "Surprisingly, even one short visit seemed to allay some of the children's anxieties," said the authors.

WOMEN'S WANTS ARE ALL BACKED BY RESEARCH

It is abundantly clear that research strongly supports women's preferences. As health-care consumers demand change, they can have great confidence in their feelings about what is right for them and their families. Says Shannon Pope, who spearheaded the Wenatchee survey, "Never for a moment allow yourself to feel that, because you are a layperson, your viewpoint in childbirth is any less accurate or less valid than that of the person you are trying to influence. If you are a woman, you will be discounted on the basis of your 'obvious inability to separate the emotional aspects of childbirth from the factual.' But you have the advantage of recent scientific studies and *common sense* on your side! If you are a woman who has already experience childbirth, you have the advantage of first-hand knowledge, and unless the person you are dealing with is also a person who has experienced childbirth, you are unique in possessing this area of knowledge."

ARE WOMEN SATISFIED WITH THEIR CHILDBIRTH EXPERIENCE?

Many women are satisfied, and their survey responses glow with their pleasure:

Beyond the joy of giving birth, I found another satisfying experience while in the hospital. The staff was consistently gracious, involved in my care and my excitement over childbirth. The best way to describe it is that I felt loved and "mothered" by the nursing staff.

I don't believe I would change anything. I had a very positive experience with the birth of my last child. All the hospital personnel were pleasant, efficient, and supportive of breast-feeding, prepared childbirth, rooming-in, sibling visits, fathers visiting anytime. All families should be lucky enough to have such a positive experience.

However, the above women are in a minority! Many women are not satisfied, concluded the three independently done surveys. Only 18 percent of the women would make no changes in their last birth experience, according to the Baltimore survey. (This was the only one to ask that specific question.)

I would not use the fetal monitor again—it really interfered with my relaxation positions and my breathing.

Labor experience went smoothly until the "rush" to the delivery room. During this time my husband was not allowed to be with me. I worried about him missing the delivery and I missed his coaching support. This interruption in our experience together was very disturbing to both of us.

Although the clinic had been highly recommended by family and friends, I found the doctors' attitudes toward me as an intelligent person very disgruntling—the problem was that they assumed I was not informed about my body or my birth and made no effort to change that assumption. There was no individualization of the care regime.

I would change a great deal. I would not have an obstetrician, but a nurse-midwife team. I would have no prep, no episiotomy (unless needed). I would like a Leboyer delivery in a homelike atmosphere. I would also room-in and would like my husband and the children to visit whenever they wished. I would never have another baby in the manner and atmosphere that I had my last child in.

Whether women would choose an alternative to the traditional hospital delivery, if available, is another measure of dissatisfaction. Twenty percent of the Boulder women said their first choice was a home delivery. Fifty percent of the Wenatchee women gave, as their first choice, home, birth centers, or birthing room. A whopping 76 percent of the Baltimore women said they would "choose to labor and deliver in the same bed, with a homelike environment, if it were available."

WHY HOSPITALS AND DOCTORS DON'T ALWAYS SUPPORT WOMEN'S WANTS

At this point many of you may be thinking, If research supports what women want, why in the world don't hospitals and doctors just give it to them? Why do I have to make an effort to get what I want? We've thought about that question a lot.

The only satisfactory answer seems both simple and complicated, and it took writing this book for us to answer it for ourselves. *Hospitals and doctors think that what they are doing is best, is right, is safe for the majority of women and babies.* Doctors' beliefs about what the best care is determine hospital policies.

Women's preferences in childbirth include a very broad view of birth; the *social*, the *psychological*, and *spiritual* aspects are as important to women as the *physical* act of giving birth. The doctor's viewpoint is different. He focuses on the *physical* act of giving birth. In other chapters we will examine the belief system of the doctor and how the way he views birth determines how it must be treated. A key issue in understanding doctors and in getting what you want is how the word "safe" is used. How is "safe" measured? How do you define "safe"? Doctors feel free to act as they do because of the way they use maternal mortality and infant mortality figures to measure safety.

Because of what doctors believe about childbirth and how they view safety, they intervene in most births. To intervene means to get in there and get that baby out by applying technology. The doctor takes decisive action to speed or to end the labor and get the baby delivered. Intervention procedures are being carried out on a massive scale that most women do not believe is necessary. They are beginning to understand that one intervention leads to another, and the doctor may find himself on a treadmill he cannot stop without doing a cesarean delivery.

INTERVENTIONS AND SATISFACTION

Because of my last experience, I am convinced that the majority of gyn doctors are not the least bit interested in the mothers' preferences in childbirth. They seek the safest and quickest way to immobolize you and pull your baby out, regardless of your insistence that you are experiencing no discomfort and wish to have no drugs. I was not permitted to labor and deliver in the same bed, to have my hands free, or to nurse my child immediately following delivery. There was no medical reason for denying me these things, especially after we had talked about these very points before my delivery, and the doctors had all agreed. My doctor was able to harass me into having a spinal, which was being administered under my protests as my new son slipped into this world. I was in the hospital exactly forty-two minutes before my child was born, and it was filled with tears and loud arguing between my doctors and myself. Thank God it was not my first pregnancy, for if it were, I would surely not have another.

The Baltimore researchers measured the rates of medical-surgical intervention, and the mothers' opinions of them. The intervention level is so high that a typical woman having her baby at a Baltimore hospital will have a fetal monitor and IVs during her labor. She will have anesthesia for her delivery. Her chances are greater than one in two that she will have either a forceps vaginal delivery or a cesarean delivery. There is also a strong possibility (one chance in three) that her labor will be started or speeded up by a drug. And while the rate of intervention was very high, many women did not believe it was necessary.

My last baby was born after my doctor induced labor. I would definitely not allow that again, unless there was a definite medical need. My baby was two weeks early and he didn't even look ready to be born. My first labor I was home except for the last half hour. I just made it into the delivery room. Because I had two very different labors, I believe that in most cases the following are totally unnecessary: prep, enema, induced labor, stirrups. I also believe doctors should be more supportive to the women who do not want pain relievers.

When my last child was born, an internal monitor was used and I don't feel that it is entirely safe since it pierces the baby's scalp. If I had known then what I know now, I would not have allowed them to use it.

* * *

Of the Baltimore women who had medical-surgical interventions such as fetal monitors, anesthesia, or induction, one-half to three-quarters of the women (depending on the intervention procedures they had) believed these interventions were unnecessary, less than best, or risky for themselves or their babies. The Baltimore authors said, "We can conclude that women are seeking less use of current routine obstetrical procedures and less anesthesia."

Something is very wrong here. Women are wondering why there is so much intervention. They are wondering, "Why me? I didn't want it. There could have been less intervention. I would have been more satisfied and the birth would still be safe." These women are right! In other chapters we will show again and again that research is on the side of the mother. The less intervention there is, the safer it is for mother *and* baby.

Women are right to take a broad view of the birth experience, to consider the social, psychological, and spiritual aspects as important as the physical act of giving birth. Meeting women's preferences makes the birth *more* safe. When a woman's preferences are met, she needs *less* intervention and has fewer complications for herself and for her baby. Chapter 3, "If You Don't Know Your Options, You Don't Have Any," demonstrates over and over that a good birth is a safe birth.

"The challenge for all of us—childbirth educators and advocates, parents and concerned providers—is to give birth back to mothers," wrote Beth Shearer, MEd, M.P.H. and codirector of C/Sec. "Words I wrote for ICEA's 25th Anniversary seem even more relevant today: 'Perhaps it is time to change the emphasis from "family-centered" birth to "woman-centered" birth. When women feel in touch with their own needs, free and strong enough to ask for them, and confident they will be met, the needs of their babies and their families will be met at the same time, regardless of the method of delivery.' The choice between mothers' and babies' 'rights' is a false choice. If mothers are taken care of well, they will take care of their own babies better than the 'experts.' " The needs of the mother, father, and other siblings can all be met in a safe birth. Where you have your baby, who your birth attendant is, what options you have, and what interventions the doctor uses are all negotiable. You can have your baby the way you want to.

TWO

THE PLEASURE PRINCIPLE

Biologically, you are designed to receive great pleasure from your body not only during lovemaking and intercourse, but in birth and breastfeeding, too. This pleasure—*not duty*—is the best glue for happy families.

Are you stumbling on the word *pleasure?* Maybe you thought the birth process at its best was one of incredible exertion and stoic acceptance mixed with much pain—but a process that women have to put up with to get that longed-for baby. Yes, birth will be exertion, pain, and acceptance, but that pain and exertion will cause your body to release large amounts of endorphins, body chemicals that trigger feelings of euphoria and well-being.

And Mother Nature built in another payoff. Birth offers sexual pleasure on a continuum from pleasant sensations (felt while your uterus rhythmically contracts in early labor if you're relaxed and feeling secure) to an intense birth climax (yes, just like an orgasm) as your baby slithers into the world of your waiting arms.

Does this sound like a fairy tale and not much like the Bible, which says that women will bring forth children in pain and suffering? Our North American cultural view of birth provides some reasons for that. Even today, most women and their mates, plus doctors and nurses—in spite of the so-called sexual revolution—are not aware of the birthing woman's pleasure potential. But it's there. As world-renowned sex researcher, Virginia Johnson-Masters, said in a Saint Louis interview, "The whole cultural message—subliminal if not direct—is that you shouldn't be sexual."

Niles Newton, Ph.D., is both a professor of behavioral sciences at Northwestern University Medical School and a researcher who frequently writes of the pleasure potential of all of women's sexual functions. In 1979 she said, "Duty is a recent invention in human relationships. Basic pleasure may be the foundation of family life. Pleasure in birth may be the starting point for optimal family relationships. Our knowledge of reproduction suggests there may be a biological reason for connecting pleasure in birth with the best outcome for the baby." Women who put great emphasis on the quality of their childbirth experience may well be intuitively seeking the kind of birth experience that enhances family stability.

If childbirth is supposed to produce sexual pleasure, why are so many women dissatisfied with their birth experiences? Standard hospital birth practices, from the shaving of your pubic hair to routine episiotomies (the "unkindest cut"), destroy much of this pleasure potential. Another reason women may not experience pleasure in birth is because we've not been taught that *all* of our reproductive functions are designed to give us pleasure—physically, emotionally, and spiritually.

Sexually, women are not carbon copies of men. Our sexuality involves far more than just making love, important as that is. Part of it can be the increased sexual energy a woman may feel before menstruation, the relaxing spurt of milk from her breasts when her milk lets down, and the sensitive tug of her baby's rhythmic sucking on her nipple.

But nearly all sex research has been done by men, so it is not surprising that most sexual research concentrates on the study of intercourse. Women's other sexual functions have been less fully examined. But we can describe some of the similarities between sexual arousal and women's reproductive functions and the sexual bonus nature bestows on women who give birth.

SEXUAL AROUSAL AND PREGNANCY

Sexual arousal and pregnancy have strong bodily similarities. In both states, breasts enlarge and nipples become sensitive. There's also extra blood flow and lubrication in the vagina. Hormone production soars in both instances. And, according to Masters and Johnson and others, masturbation is common during pregnancy, even if never experienced before. However, not all pregnant women are hovering in a permanent state of sexual arousal. Many other influences—such as fatigue, nausea, worry, or just plain being busy—can affect a pregnant woman's sexual desires.

Your sexual interest during pregnancy probably resembles one of the following four descriptions:

- Your sexual desire hasn't changed at all during pregnancy.
- You've felt tired and nauseated from day one. Now that you're past the first few months, you're not prostrate anymore, but you're not much better. Though you need your partner to hold and comfort you, sexual intercourse is not a priority. In fact, you'd prefer to do without it.
- Even though you were sleepy and sometimes nauseated in the first trimester, now in the second trimester you marvel at your energy . . . and you feel wonderful. Surprisingly (because no one mentioned this as a pregnancy bonus), your desire to make love suddenly grows and is greater than ever before.
- You are vibrating with good health and have felt that way since the beginning of the pregnancy. Your senses are more acute than ever. Food is appetizing, and you've never had a moment's queasiness. Your desire to make love with your mate continues to increase right up to the time of birth.

Whichever description most closely matches your own experience, you're in lots of good company. Other women have felt the same. An unchanged sexual response is the least likely, while increased desire in the middle trimester is the most common. But whether you're turned on or turned off, whether you want an orgasm or not, your feelings are normal, and may vary from pregnancy to pregnancy.

OXYTOCIN—THE CAREGIVING HORMONE

A seldom-studied hormone, oxytocin, flows in the woman's body during intercourse, during birth, and again during breast-feeding. (Though oxytocin can be found in men, too, even less is known about how their bodies use it.) In intercourse, orgasm triggers this hormone's release; in labor, the onset of contractions find oxytocin in the body; and in breastfeeding, it is liberated with each letdown of milk. This hormone acts on the uterus, as well as the breasts, causing the uterus to contract rhythmically during breastfeeding.

Unlike many other hormones, oxytocin is generated in sporadic bursts rather than in a steady stream. With orgasm or milk letdown, it usually produces a euphoric sensation, a relaxing sense of well-being. Its release is easily inhibited. Just as orgasm in lovemaking can be prevented by sudden noises, many a labor's progress has been stopped by an inhibiting hospital environment. Nursing mothers sometimes report their milk letdown slowing or stopping altogether when they're criticized, fatigued, or unhappy.

Oxytocin is very much involved in the bonding process. This hormone's presence in your body may actually make you want to take care of your baby. Breastfeeding often increases a mother's attachment for her baby; and the mother, in turn, has a physical need for her infant. Her breasts fill with milk, and it's a pleasurable relief to have the breast emptied by the baby's sucking. And the baby's sucking gives rise to the gentle and prolonged stroking of one of the most sensitive parts of the female body—the nipple.

This caregiving hormone also bonds you with your mate through the pleasure of lovemaking and orgasm. People care both physically and emotionally for each other in nearly all human societies when they live together. Caregiving which is stimulated by the hormone oxytocin, is essential for human survival.

PARALLELS BETWEEN THE BIRTH PROCESS AND SEXUAL INTERCOURSE

During sex, women do not want their concentration disturbed. In undrugged and uninhibited labor, they also do not want to be disturbed. In both intercourse and labor, Dr. Newton states, breathing is both deep and erratic, sometimes with grunts, gasping, and sucking. Social inhibitions decrease as climax nears, and again as unmedicated labor progresses. In both instances, a tense (almost tortured) look appears on the face. (Research with weight lifters shows that grimacing affects the brain's supply of blood and may release endorphins, thus reducing the pain.) And great effort is required, either to push out the baby or to sustain the intensity of orgasm. In both, the uterus rhythmically contracts.

Masters and Johnson data demonstrate that the uterine

contractions in orgasm have the same recorded pattern as those of the first stage of labor—differing only in intensity. The cervical plug loosens and, for some women, the clitoris engorges. In fact, caressing the breasts can get a slowed labor going again by stimulating uterine contractions.

British natural-childbirth pioneer, Grantly Dick-Read, M.D., pointed out more than thirty years ago that anesthesia and analgesia inhibit the joy that often comes after the hard work of producing a baby. Medicated women remember the pain experienced before sedation but fail to have the compensation of elation that often follows the physical sensations of birth—feeling the arrival of a beloved baby.

Some women experience intense emotion at birth especially when they are undrugged and have a supportive environment. Passionate emotions are released and sensory perceptions are heightened. Regardless of how much pain is endured, once into the second stage of labor, the pushing stage, many women report extraordinary pleasure *if* they are well supported and not fearful or anxious. A few report a birth climax at the moment the head and shoulders slip through the vagina.

Some women describe giving birth, one month after the event, as being "like an orgasm," according to Deborah Tanzer, Ph.D. Most women who experience natural childbirth as Tanzer defines it (no sedation in labor and delivery and consciously participating during the entire pregnancy and birth process) report feelings of triumph, and enormous satisfaction. They may or may not have experienced a lot of pain. That seems to be a separate issue. The euphoria following an unmedicated birth in a supportive environment can last for months. And that memory helps many a weary mother cope with a fussy baby months later.

THE ROLE OF YOUR PC (PUBOCOCCYGEUS) MUSCLE

Your PC muscle surrounds and supports your sexual organs. The strength of this muscle not only enhances your sexual response during lovemaking, but it can enhance your physical sensations when you give birth.

In the 1940s gynecologist Arnold Kegel, M.D., emphasized the need for women to exercise their PC muscle to prevent unwanted urine leaking. (Hence, these exercises have ever since been known as "Kegels.")

Bradley childbirth instructor Rhondda Hartman, RN, MA, says, "There's a misconception about the PC muscle. It isn't birth that weakens it. Rather, it's the weak PC muscle that creates complications in birth, such as tearing, and gynecological problems later in life.

There still aren't many doctors who suggest that pregnant women do their Kegels. For the last thirty years, childbirth educators have been the ones to spread the news. If your childbirth instructor hasn't already described these "tighten and relax" exercises, ask her to tell you.

THE NATURAL EROTICISM OF BREASTFEEDING

Breastfeeding also has similarities intercourse. In both, the uterus contracts, the nipples become erect, and the breasts receive extensive stimulation. The skin flushes. Soon after a baby is put to the breast, a letdown sensation brings the milk to the baby. As she or he sucks, the milk comes from the back of the breast, down into the nipple, and into the baby's mouth. While oxytocin, the pleasurable caregiving hormone, is responsible for this milk ejection reflex, nursing mothers don't usually have orgasms when their milk lets down (though some occasionally report they do). However, nearly all nursing moms describe a feeling of well-being. For a first-time mother, however, it may take a couple of months before she can recognize the letdown sensation.

As a nursing mother, you will spend many more hours breastfeeding your infant than in either sexual intercourse or childbirth. By the time your baby is three months old, she or he will have been put to the breast more than seven hundred times. This constant contact with the nipples often has unexpected advantages for you. For many, it reduces a sense of false modesty about not exposing or touching your breasts. Breastfeeding also enhances the response of your erogenous zones, especially if you occasionally nurse the baby skin to skin, unclothed. It is even common for breast milk to leak from a mother during lovemaking. Some mothers then worry that there won't be enough milk for the baby's next feeding (but there will be). Some couples find milk-filled breasts an added sexual pleasure, and others don't. Of course, either reaction is normal. Breastfeeding's enhancement of your sexuality probably won't be noticeable until you have weaned the baby. While you're in the midst of nursing, you become accustomed to the constant breast stimulation.

> Sometimes I just ache to be nursing a baby again. We hear so much about pain in birth, the discomforts of pregnancy, or the inconveniences of nursing in our fast-paced world, but rarely does anyone speak on the physical pleasure one can experience with these.
>
> —WISCONSIN MOTHER

Masters and Johnson report that many nursing mothers resume lovemaking with their husbands sooner than bottle-feeding mothers. For other mothers, the nearly constant body contact with their babies, and unavoidable fatigue, postpone their sexual desire whether these mothers are breastfeeding or bottle-feeding. It's probably part of nature's survival plan for you to be mostly interested in your baby during her or his early months. In fact, it is normal for estrogen levels to be lower than usual in new mothers, causing vaginal dryness for a few months. When you do desire to have intercourse after your baby's birth, consider using extra lubrication. Sexual desire will vary in any mother who has recently given birth, but all new mothers have an unusually strong need to be held and comforted. Just as in pregnancy, there's a wide range of sexual interest. Whatever you feel, whatever you want, is right for you.

MOTHER NATURE'S SEXUAL BONUS

Perhaps as a biological message to make sure that women keep having babies, our capacity for sexual pleasure grows with each experience of birth and breastfeeding. M. J. Sherfey, M.D., reports that in all women (as long as obstetric damage doesn't intervene), pregnancy will bring an increase in the volume of blood flow in the pelvis, enhance the capacity for sexual tension, and improve your orgasmic intensity, frequency, and pleasure. With increasing sexual experience and childbirth, your capacity for sexual pleasure unquestionably grows. Unmedicated birth that you feel *you* accomplished, with your own exertion, further enhances your erotic response.

Nature offers a double insurance policy of pleasure, to

ensure a bonding of mother to baby. Even if you couldn't experience the pleasure of childbirth because your lower body sensations were numbed by anesthesia, you will still enhance your attachment to your child through the pleasure of breast-feeding.

If you are still breastfeeding as your baby gets close to a year old, you'll see that the baby adores the breast (much as you've seen bottle-fed babies at this age adore the bottle). This adoration of the breast is normal, and is another source of pleasure to the mother. For more than 99 percent of our human existence, our ancestors' babies were probably carried and nursed frequently. Mutual bodily enjoyment, both mother's and infant's, is instinctive in humans. This pleasure conditions a mother to respond to her baby's needs. Sexual pleasure makes us want to take care of the partner—whether an adult partner in lovemaking, or the baby in birth and breastfeeding. Your sexuality, your pleasure in yourself as a woman, are natural, biologically determined forces.

VULNERABILITY—A NECESSARY INGREDIENT FOR CAREGIVING

All three sexual functions—intercourse, birth, and breast-feeding—share the quality of vulnerability, which is essential to bring a pair-bonded couple closer together. Your vulnera-bility increases both physically and psychologically during pregnancy and birth, just as it does during sex. It's a mixture of risk, trust, and personal growth. During the process of birth, your body and emotions want to open up as surely as they do in lovemaking.

In pregnancy it's likely you'll experience the full gamut of feelings, from high spirits to low. Though your mate, or your boss may criticize you for being "too emotional," these feelings are a necessary preparation for your caregiving role. Experiencing increased emotions changes you. It makes you more receptive and opens you to respond to your baby. This period of special vulnerability helps you get in touch with what is deeply important to you.

As your pregnancy progresses, and you more closely approach the moment of birth, you look more and more for calm reassurance and support from those who care for you.

Many career women, normally accustomed to assertively managing their lives, amaze themselves by this need for support. It's unexpected, perhaps, but normal. You feel that you don't want anyone to bother you; while simultaneously you don't want to cause anyone any trouble. Perhaps more than at any other time of your life, you now feel that you want someone to take care of you.

As birth approaches, you withdraw and turn inward. You marshal forces to give birth and care for your baby.

THE IMPORTANCE OF TOUCH DURING LABOR

As we approach the time for labor and birth, we start to become aware that the reassurance and support that we want also come from being touched. We sometimes forget how rewarding it can be to accept the comfort of touch when we're under stress. And labor surely is a stress. A tender, caring touch during labor can be sympathetic and restorative, as well as pleasurable. Research shows that laboring mothers cope better with the pain when there is constant support that includes touch.

Our hesitation to touch each other is unknown in many other parts of the world. In other societies, mothers carry babies in their arms, or on their hips, or slung around their backs until they're two or three years old. This pleasure of intimate touching continues throughout childhood between the children and both parents. Raised this way, men, for example, feel comfortable touching other males.

Many of us are painfully inhibited about touching and being touched by other people—even those we love. Often we fail to realize how this separates us from those who share our lives. As a matter of fact, as you read this, you may recoil at the thought of others touching you in labor besides your mate.

Just as foreplay does in sex, touch enhances the physical sensations and the joy the birthing mother feels. A laboring mother in pain may recover her equilibrium through a sympathetic touch. A hand on her arm, a caress of her hair may blunt the stress of a contraction and imbue a sense of strength.

Negative emotions leave their effects, too—increased pain, a slowed labor, a tightened cervix. But positive emotions can work to aid the mother's body to open up to the birth process and experience pleasure, if a woman's confidence is enhanced, and not shattered with anxiety. The chief obstacle to pleasure in all of its forms is fear. The fear of pain, of ridicule, of embarrassment is common among women who have their babies in hospitals. Ensure that your vulnerability will be met by loving support—and touch. Have not only your mate with you in labor, but a doula (a supporting woman), too. (See chapter 11.)

A NEW WAY OF EXPERIENCING BIRTH

There's a new consciousness of birth, emanating from the home-birth movement. "Despite the fact that almost all of the people now alive in the world were born at home, the home-birth movement in the United States . . . is completely revolutionary," wrote midwife and childbirth instructor Rahima Baldwin. She described three ways in which the new home birth is different. First, women who have home births today choose to feel, to know their bodies in the birth process. Second, these women "assume active responsibility for their bodies, their lives, and their birth experiences." Third, they recognize birth's spirituality. These parents demand "from the moment of birth, the recognition that their child is a whole and sensitive person, to be treated with care and respect."

Though less than 1 percent of babies born in the United States are now born at home, the needs and experiences of these parents have influenced hospital maternity care policies around the nation. You don't have to give birth at home, however, to feel pleasure. Women experience birth pleasure in hospitals and particularly out-of-hospital birth centers, too. This is especially true, research shows, when the birth attendant is a midwife rather than a physician.

In this new way of giving birth, women want active responsibility for their bodies. They choose to feel their body sensations. Feeling body sensations includes feeling the pain— not to be masochistic, but rather to experience a sense of endurance and triumph much like a long-distance runner's. Just as in a marathon race, labor, like a long race almost over, can cause excruciating pain. But would the runner want an epidural to finish, when she can see the finish line only yards away? Or would she want to use those reserves of physical, mental, and emotional energy with which she had primed herself to finish the race with her full senses? Biologically, our bodies want to finish labor and give birth triumphantly . . . with our senses intact.

Nature offers endorphins, too. Hard exercise, whether in labor, vigorous walking, or tear-provoking laughter, increases levels of these natural, narcoticlike painkillers in your blood. Endorphins are found in the placenta and are released in both mother and baby through labor, nursing, and skin-to-skin contact. One researcher has found that the mother's endorphin level after a cesarean birth is lower than after the exertion of an unmedicated, vaginal birth.

No matter how much you know or don't know about the process of birth itself, you are right to want to experience the pleasure of birth. Make the most of this information. It's meant to broaden your knowledge about your sexual self and, we hope, expand your appreciation of your body, your birth, and your baby. When you are the center of your birth, instead of the hospital and its impersonal routines, you enhance and expand yourself, strengthening the quality of your own life as well as that of those you most love. And remember, your own perfectly normal reaction will vary from other women's along the continuum of pleasure.

THREE

IF YOU DON'T KNOW YOUR OPTIONS, YOU DON'T HAVE ANY

> No one can tell a woman how to make the choice that
> is best for her. There is no one *right* choice. Today
> there are more choices and more support for trying
> than ever before in American history, which also leaves
> women with the burden of choice.
>
> —GAIL SHEEHY, *PASSAGES*

For every one of you reading this chapter there is the strong possibility that within a fifty-mile radius of where you live you can find both a place for giving birth and a birth attendant that you will like. Change has come and is still coming, so fast it is difficult to keep up with the new possibilities. Find out what's available in your area.

The movement to humanize hospital maternity care started in the 1950s. The two main thrusts of this movement—called "family-centered maternity care"—were to keep mothers and babies together while in the hospital and to ensure the father's presence before, during, and after birth. In the late 1960s, childbirth education had reached enough birthing women so that they began to "vote with their feet"—that is, they started going to those doctors and hospitals where the fathers were not only allowed, but encouraged to be present. This was the crack in the door to change in hospital maternity policies.

Today, while acceptance of the father's presence at a vaginal delivery is *almost* universal in American hospitals, there are still hospitals that deny single women support persons during labor and delivery. Many cesarean mothers are denied the father's presence at delivery. And while it is easier in many hospitals for mothers to get their babies on demand, interference in family togetherness is still widespread. So, more and more, demand for change has accelerated, and women continue to "vote with their feet" and go to those hospitals where they *can* get what they want.

Some women with their babies due *now* see changes in hospitals as turtle slow. They see their only choice as voting the hospital out altogether and opting for an out-of-hospital birth, either at home or in a birth center. Because childbirth is an annual $15 billion business in the United States today, there is a strong economic motivation for hospitals and doctors to keep you as a customer. While the actual percentage of out-of-hospital births is small, it is growing fast, and the threat of many women opting for out-of-hospital births is one of the most important reasons why hospitals have made changes demanded by consumers.

Getting accurate, out-of-hospital birth statistics is difficult. Enriqueta Bond, Ph.D., research scientist with the National Academy of Sciences, estimates 70,000 to 130,000 out-of-hospital births a year. She bases her estimate on national government figures for the low figure and home-birth figures for the state of Oregon for the high figure. Oregon is one of the very few states to have accurate data on home birth. Because Oregon has several established home-birth services and most states do not, using Oregon's data to estimate national figures may result in an overestimate of home births, according to Dr. Bond.

NAPSAC, the National Association of Parents and Professionals for Safe Alternatives in Childbirth, was founded in late 1975 by Lee and David Stewart, Ph.D., at a time when there were very few alternatives to the traditional hospital delivery. Interviewed in December 1988, the Stewarts said the national NAPSAC office receives five hundred requests a month for literature and information. "The most frequent question we get—in the hundreds every month—is 'Where can I get a competent midwife or doctor for a home birth?' " said Dr. Stewart.

He estimates 1–2 percent of all births are planned home births. "The difficulty in getting accurate figures probably comes from the lack of registration of home births," he said. "Parents just don't want to call attention to themselves by registering a home birth. They fear harassment of themselves or the direct entry midwives they tend to use."

One to 2 percent is 40,000 to 80,000 planned home births a year. Although the numbers encourage home-birth advocates and frighten most obstetricians, home births barely twitch birth statistics. The numbers are tiny compared to three-and-three-quarter million or so babies born each year in hospitals in the United States.

WHERE TO HAVE YOUR BABY

There are five different places where you may choose to give birth:

- In a traditional hospital with labor, delivery, and recovery rooms
- In a hospital with single-room maternity care
- In a hospital alternative birth center
- In a birthing center outside the hospital
- At home

One way of evaluating where to have your baby is to look at the likelihood of intervention for each place of birth. The fewer interventions there are, the less risk there is to mother and baby. With fewer interventions there will be fewer problems as a result of intervention, fewer c-sections, and, we believe, a safer birth for the normal mother and baby.

Another way of evaluating where to have your baby is to look at how satisfied women have been with each option. That satisfaction can be measured in three ways—by how the family is kept together; by how much pleasure is involved; and by how much a woman's self-esteem is enhanced by the experience.

With less intervention, mother, baby, and father are more likely to have a strong attachment to each other, and this fragile new family will have the mutual loving start they need. The pleasure principle, the full expression of a woman's sensuality in birth, operates best with the least intervention. And finally, with less intervention a woman feels more that she has "given birth" rather than that she has been "delivered." Her enhanced self-esteem from this achievement helps the woman in her new role as a mother. "The sense of achievement from a good birth experience is the strongest stimulus I know to greater self-esteem and effective functioning," said nurse-midwife Ruth T. Wilf, C.N.M., Ph.D., Philadelphia.

In contrast to this, the greater the amount of intervention the more likely the mother will not have her preferences met, which can lead to regrets about the birth and lowered self-esteem.

PLACE OF BIRTH: TRADITIONAL HOSPITAL

Birth in a traditional hospital will often resemble the birth described by Jenny in chapter 7, "The Obstetrician's Black Bag of Interventions." Birth there will be organized according to the obstetrician's belief that birth is a physical procedure with significant risks.

The laboring woman is first put to bed in the labor room, then moved to the delivery room. Delivery is often a surgical procedure (vaginal delivery with episiotomy and use of forceps, or a cesarean delivery) following an actively managed labor. She is then moved to a recovery room before being transferred to the postpartum room, where she will stay for the remainder of her time in the hospital. Her baby is removed from her at birth and placed in a central nursery.

The traditional hospital is where millions of American babies are born each year at a typical cost of four thousand dollars, including the doctor's charges and the average two-day stay after birth. A cesarean delivery averages six thousand dollars. These figures include no newborn complications. The choices a mother may make in her labor and delivery vary greatly among hospitals. Some hospitals offer a great deal of flexibility; in other hospitals, almost all mothers experience the same routine. You *can* get what you want if you act ahead of time by choosing the hospital where policies are very flexible, and by negotiating with your doctor for agreement on those options most important to you. The second key to getting what you want in a traditional hospital is to have labor support from a woman friend (your doula) as well as the baby's father.

The satisfaction of women delivering in a traditional hospital can be high when the staff is committed to a family-centered birth. As an example, only one out of every eight women was satisfied with her birth experience in the eighteen hospitals of the Baltimore metropolitan area surveyed by the COMA researchers. However, one out of three women giving birth at one particular Baltimore hospital was completely satisfied with the birth. A woman reported of this hospital:

I would like to take this opportunity to praise the staff and my obstetrician for making my childbirth experience the best of my life. The care I received was excellent. During the delivery I received so much praise and encouragement from the doctor and the attending nurses, it made things easy to do with no medication at all. We were even able to avoid an episiotomy. Also my hospital is a very flexible place that goes to great lengths to keep childbirth a family experience. My husband was with me the entire time. I also had rooming-in on a twenty-four-hour basis, with the nursery taking the baby for about one-and-a-half hours a day for bathing and pediatrician's rounds. Any questions I had or assistance I needed was thoughtfully attended to by the staff. I wouldn't have my next baby anywhere else.

The rate of intervention at most traditional hospitals is very high. The following chart shows the average rate of each intervention for all of the eighteen hospitals covered in the Baltimore COMA survey. The second column shows the highest rate of intervention recorded at any one hospital. The third column shows the lowest rate for any one hospital.

Intervention	Average Rate for All Hospitals	Highest Recorded Use	Lowest Recorded Use
Induction	22%	34%	14%
IV fluids	81%	95%	62%
Prep	83%	96%	57%
Enema	57%	78%	41%
Fetal monitor	67%	94%	47%
Anesthesia (general, spinal, or epidural)	65%	88%	44%
Lithotomy position for delivery	63%	74%	50%
Episiotomy	71%	80%	57%
Forceps used	33%	52%	19%
C-section (1987 rates)	26%	32%	22%

High rates of intervention in a traditional hospital setting carry a great risk of complications for mother and baby. Yet very little research has been done to document this risk. Lewis

Mehl, M.D., Ph.D., director, Institute for Childbirth and Family Research, Berkeley, completed one study of safety in home versus hospital birth. In his study, Dr. Mehl found the incidence of complications to mother and baby in a hospital birth was far greater than in a home birth. Because the rate of intervention is likely to be extremely low where the choice is for an unmedicated birth at home, and because the COMA survey data shows intervention to be very high in a traditional hospital setting, we agree with Dr. Mehl that it is the high rate of intervention that results in the greater risk of complications to mother and baby.

Dr. Mehl compared matched populations of 1,046 women planning home births to 1,046 women planning hospital births, with all the women defined as "low risk."* The home-birth mothers include those who needed a hospital delivery though a home birth was planned. The hospital-birth women were more likely than the planned home-birth mothers to have had the following: high blood pressure during labor (five times more likely); severe perineal tear (nine times more likely); postpartum hemorrhage (three times more likely); and a cesarean (three times more likely).

The babies born to the hospital-birth women also had a higher complication rate than the babies born to home-birth women. In the hospital, the infants were six times more likely to have had fetal distress before birth, four times more likely to have needed assistance to start breathing, four times more likely to have developed an infection. There were no incidents of birth injuries at home, yet there were thirty infants in the hospital with birth injuries.

Traditional Hospital

To sum up:

- Insurance coverage available.
- Birth takes place in several different rooms: labor room, delivery room, usually a recovery room, and a postpartum room (for the hospital stay after birth).

---

*A "low risk" designation means that these mothers had no complicating factors of age, medical history or socioeconomic problems that might lead to difficulty with childbirth. For a more complete discussion of the somewhat controversial "low risk" and "high risk" designations, see chapters 5 and 6.

- Baby is taken to a central nursery.
- Immediate availability of emergency equipment.
- No one-to-one nursing care because nurses are responsible for several patients.
- High possibility of medical intervention.
- High risk of complications for mother and baby, regardless of a predetermination of "low risk."
- Most babies are born in a traditional hospital.

PLACE OF BIRTH: HOSPITAL SINGLE-ROOM MATERNITY CARE

Wherever hospitals are being rebuilt, administrators are switching to single-room maternity care. Using this option, a woman labors, delivers, recovers, and often stays for postpartum care all in the same room. This choice pleases hospital personnel, doctors, and many consumers.

Costs to the hospital are greatly reduced by more efficient use of space, equipment, and staff. Multiple-use rooms are more often full than rooms that can be used only for labor, delivery, recovery, or postpartum care. Fewer rooms are required. Expensive equipment is moved from room to room as needed. Nurses are cross trained for all stages of care. Depending on her shift, a nurse can stay with a woman through labor, delivery, and recovery, something both nurses and patients appreciate.

Rooms are homelike, but emergency equipment is immediately available. The bed is convertible and can be broken away to place the women in a lithotomy position (on back, with legs in stirrups). Doctors find the rooms adapt easily to the use of interventions and technology. Because doctors feel comfortable that the setting allows them to use any intervention except for a cesarean, women with all levels of risk can use single-room maternity care.

Single-room care is also clearly a response to women's demands. Family-centered care and individual choice is much more easily met in this setting than in a traditional hospital. Women get the feeling that they have more control over what happens to them because their care can be individualized.

Consumers can be confused when they look for this option. Barbara Harness, spokesperson for the American Hospital Association, told us that 75 percent of hospitals giving maternity care offer "a combination labor/delivery unit with a homelike setting for couples who have completed special childbirth courses." But only one-third of those hospitals have all single-room maternity care. Most hospitals with this option have traditional areas and one or more rooms labeled "birth rooms."

Many hospitals have strict screening for birth rooms that acts as a deterrent to women who want to and could use them. For example, we know there are some hospitals that do not permit laboring women into their birth rooms until they're at least three centimeters dilated (one good reason for staying home as long as possible), but the women are admitted to the regular floor.

Usually this strict screening is instituted because the doctors are not committed to providing a real alternative to a traditional birth. Ross Planning Associates reports that "birthing rooms were good public relations tools, but they had low rates of use because they were not, in general, supported by the medical staff." When you are investigating your own hospital options, go beyond the words, for example, "birthing rooms" you are given. Ask for a detailed description of that hospital's services, using our description as a starting point.

In 1969, Manchester Memorial Hospital in Manchester, Connecticut, became the first hospital in the United States to open a birth room. Obstetrician Philip Sumner, M.D., was responsible for initiating the changes at Manchester Memorial Hospital. He describes what happens when a woman gives birth in one of the birth rooms.

> "Celebration" is the theme of birth in the birthing room. When possible, rheostated dim lights are used as the baby emerges, with the mother herself reaching down and lifting her baby to her breast. In almost every instance the umbilical cord is long enough to permit her to determine her infant's sex for herself, and thus immediate bonding is encouraged. After the parents share the first 60 minutes, the family is transferred together to the newborn nursery where the baby is examined. If the mother or baby have no complications, they may then be transferred directly to a family unit. Breastfeeding, rooming-in, and sibling visitation are encouraged.

The satisfaction level of women giving birth in the birth rooms at Manchester Memorial Hospital is very high. They see the staff as giving support rather than trying to take control of the birth. This is one mother's story:

> One of the things that surprised me was that by my lifting her out, she was facing toward me and the doctor said, "Well, what do you have, a boy or a girl?" And I remember thinking, "Oh, my gosh, what a switch, the obstetrician asking the mother the sex of the baby. Usually it's the other way around." This time I got to tell him. It was a very nice tone of things. I wanted to reach down after the head was out and pull my baby out the rest of the way, which the doctor and monitrice helped me to do. I was a little unsure as to just when was the right time to reach down, but the monitrice guided my hands, and I reached under Tara's hands and I remember thinking, "What do I do now?" and just then the doctor said, "Now lift and push." Then it all made sense to me. So I pushed once and lifted her out and put her right up on my chest. That was a beautiful feeling.
>
> —MOTHER, QUOTED IN *BIRTHING ROOMS*

Research is needed to see if single-room maternity care reduces complications, including cesareans. The only research comparing hospital policies with the use of interventions was reported in 1987. Researchers Judith Lumley, Ph.D., and Brian Davey, Ph.D. surveyed thirty-six Australian hospitals in which forty-four thousand babies are born every year. The survey compared intervention rates with hospital policies regarding family-centered maternity care and flexibility of options. The study showed no relationship between a hospital's flexibility and the rates of intervention. The researchers stated "that it is clearly possible for a hospital to have implemented family-centered maternity care and still have very high intervention rates. There is no guarantee that changing hospital policies toward flexibility or sensitivity to parents' wishes will do anything at all about the use of oxytocin, forceps or cesarean delivery. A commitment to minimal intervention is necessary."

That kind of commitment was made in 1976 when obstetrician Richard Stewart, M.D., and the certified nurse-midwives with him in a group practice changed the whole maternity unit of Douglas General Hospital in Decatur, Georgia. Single-room maternity care and low intervention are the standards of care. Women are admitted regardless of risk factors except for excessive prematurity. Women in labor before the thirty-second week of pregnancy are transported to a regional neonatal intensive-care hospital. All others, women with diabetes, hypertension, twins, the need for induction, previous cesareans (many are delivered vaginally), receive the same low-intervention care. In 80 percent of all the births the midwife is the birth attendant (and is with the laboring woman from admission). If the birth turns out to be complicated and needs the obstetrician's presence and expertise, as in twin or breech births, he comes in, but the midwife often completes the birth.

The expectant couple comes to the hospital when labor is well established. Women are encouraged to walk and assume any position giving the most comfort. Solid food in early labor and drinks as labor progresses are encouraged. Preps are not done. Enemas are given only if the laboring woman asks for one. Amniotomy (breaking the bag of water around the baby) is not done. The cesarean rate is 13 percent (including repeat cesareans); forceps use is 2 percent. Of the vaginally delivered women 25 percent had analgesia, 10 percent had anesthesia, and 27 percent had episiotomies. Maternal and infant outcomes are excellent.

"Babies do not need to be delivered by obstetricians," Dr. Stewart told us. "Babies *need* to be delivered by midwives who give absolutely superior care." So sold on midwifery care are Dr. Stewart and his wife that when their daughter was born in 1982, the Stewarts had the midwife on call as their birth attendant. "The obstetrician has been the star of the show too long," Dr. Stewart emphasized. "That's why childbirth is handled the way it is. The star of the delivery is the mother. Although many women want alternatives, they are uncomfortable questioning their doctors. Women are going to have to work to get what they want," he concluded.

Hospital Single-Room Maternity Care

To sum up:

- Insurance coverage available.
- Labor, delivery, and recovery in the same bed.
- Immediate availability of all emergency equipment.
- An alternative accepted by many doctors.
- Almost all women can use single-room care.

- Satisfaction of women is often high; the family unit is kept together.
- One-to-one nursing care is possible in some hospitals, especially if parents hire a private nurse.
- High possibility of medical intervention.
- No research available measuring complication rates.
- Some hospitals offer birth rooms but prevent most women from using them.

PLACE OF BIRTH: ALTERNATIVE BIRTH CENTER IN HOSPITAL (ABC)

These homelike, low-key birth settings are being built to lure into the hospital those women who might otherwise choose a home birth. In alternative birth centers, birth is considered a normal process. The atmosphere is relaxed. Routines are absent; flexibility is the watchword for everyone. And intervention is greatly reduced. The woman can participate as an equal partner with her doctor in decision making. Many mothers with their newborns leave for home within hours of birth.

The disadvantages of an ABC have to do with the screening required to ensure that only low-risk women are admitted, and with the resistance of most doctors and many nurses to using the alternative birth center. This resistance has led to the closing of many ABCs, especially when hospitals convert to single-room maternity care.

Women who use these ABCs are highly satisfied because they feel in control in a homelike setting, yet they are in a hospital where they feel safer. A regular double bed, conventional furniture, hidden medical equipment, wallpaper, plants, and rocking chairs all contribute to the feeling that the woman is not in a hospital. However, it is the medical staff's attitudes of flexibility and support for whatever the woman wishes to do in her labor and delivery that contribute most to her feeling of control. The relaxed setting encourages her to walk, stand, or sit as she wishes during her labor, and to assume any delivery position she feels comfortable with. The father-to-be can lie on the bed with the mother to comfort her, as can any other support person present. The mother's other children can be present for the birth. In these ABCs, birth becomes a family affair, and often includes several close friends as well.

Because the alternative birth center is structurally separate from, though very close to, the ob floor, an ob nurse comes to the birth center when the mother arrives and follows her through her labor, delivery, and recovery, giving her one-to-one nursing care the whole stay. Some centers have that same nurse make a home visit at both twenty-four and seventy-two hours after birth to give medical follow-up to mother and newborn.

In the ABC, intervention and drug use is minimal or absent. Instead, the relaxed setting is an encouragement to all to wait out a difficult or prolonged labor and, instead of intervention, to offer the mother support by word and touch. About one mother in ten finds that pain remains the least-liked part of the alternative birth center experience, according to a 1980 report from Stanford University Hospital. Using an alternative birth center requires a commitment from the woman that no anesthesia, except for a local for episiotomy repair, will be used.

Only women considered at low risk for complications may use an alternative birth center. Strict screening for problems is done during pregnancy, to rule out women who have pre-existing medical problems such as heart disease, who have had previous severe delivery problems such as a stillbirth or a cesarean, or who have developed complications during pregnancy such as high blood pressure or premature labor. That still leaves most women eligible.

The flexibility and relaxed atmosphere of the alternative birth center, while it enhances the woman's control, reduces the control of the doctor. His role becomes one of lifeguard of the birth, not manager. Careful record keeping from alternative birth centers shows that, because of this, obstetricians do not like to use this alternative, according to Madeleine Shearer, editor of *Birth*. British-trained midwife Linda Nelson, S.C.M., of Roosevelt Hospital in New York City, explained why obstetricians tend not to use the alternative birth center at her hospital. "Obstetricians view the use of the birthing room as more time-consuming, since they would have to be available for longer periods," said Nelson. "The births, although normal, do not entail the use of the various monitoring devices and other procedures with which obstetricians have trained and are comfortable."

When alternative-birth-center mothers and their babies are compared to low-risk women and their babies in traditional labor and delivery rooms the differences are nothing short of spectacular. The few studies of alternative birth centers give strikingly similar results. One 1980 report of five hundred births in an alternative birth center comes from Robert C. Goodlin, M.D., of the University of California Davis Medical Center. The alternative birth center offered little obstetrical intervention. Mothers ate and drank as they desired (most took only fluids). No IVs were used. No anesthesia was given. No electronic fetal monitors were used. Only 6 percent of the mothers had minimal doses of analgesia during labor. In comparison, interventions were high among the five hundred low-risk women who delivered in the traditional labor and delivery areas of the same hospital. All had IVs; 81 percent had the electronic fetal monitor; 70 percent had moderate-to-high doses of analgesia; and 30 percent had epidurals.

The following chart shows the difference in complications between the two groups.

Complications	Regular Birth (%)	ABC (%)
Mother		
Failure to progress in labor	18.3	5.2
Labor augmentation	21.2	3.1
Cesarean section	9.2	2.8
Infant		
Fetal distress	5.3	0.3
Meconium-stained fluid	11.9	2.3
Meconium aspiration	.2	1.2
Scalp infection	1.2	0
Jaundice	12.6	2.4
Neurological abnormalities	0.6	0.2

Mothers delivering in the traditional area were three times more likely than mothers delivering in the alternative birth center to have their labor diagnosed as "failure to progress," and seven times more likely to have their labors speeded with oxytocin. In the traditional area mothers were over three times more likely to have cesarean section. Before they were born, the babies delivered in the traditional area were fifteen times as likely to experience fetal distress and six times more likely to have meconium-stained fluid, another indication of possible distress. After birth, the infants born in the traditional area were three times more likely to have neurological abnormalities. They were six times more likely to have jaundice, a growing problem in pediatrics, possibly related to the much higher rate of Pitocin and other drug use in the traditional area. (See chapter 14, "Your Baby Doctor.")

Just over 1 percent of the traditionally delivered babies got scalp infections from the use of electronic fetal monitors. Because the monitor was not used in the alternative birth center, there were no scalp infections. Follow-up for an average fifteen months after birth showed that 2.4 percent of the infants born in the traditional area were victims of child abuse, while none of the infants born in the alternative birth center were abused. The babies born in the ABC were more likely to breathe in meconium, a potential problem. Dr. Goodlin believes this reflects the absence of drugs in the ABC babies, who were more vigorous. Out of the six significant labor or birth complications for infants, the ABC babies did much better than the traditional-area babies in five complications.

Many professionals who use alternative birth centers believe that a better outcome for mother and baby is the result of two important factors. The first is the greatly reduced use of intervention. The second is the homelike setting itself, which results in a less anxious and more effective labor. Dr. Goodlin suggests that low-risk women benefit from a "service which seeks to reduce apprehension and insure tranquillity."

Alternative Birth Centers

To sum up:

- Insurance coverage available.
- Emergency delivery area readily accessible.
- Only low-risk pregnant women admitted.
- One in five women admitted is transferred to the regular delivery area.
- Most homelike setting in the hospital; relaxed, flexible setting and staff.
- One-to-one nursing care.
- Intervention rate very low.
- Risks of complications very low.
- Resistance to use by most obstetricians and some family practitioners; most midwives use readily.

- Satisfaction of women is very high; they feel control over the birth experience.

PLACE OF BIRTH: OUT-OF-HOSPITAL FREE-STANDING BIRTH CENTER

In 1975 there were 5 free-standing birth centers in the United States. By 1989 there were 130 centers according to data from the National Association of Childbearing Centers (NACC). Birth centers outside the hospital are similar in many ways to alternative birth centers within the hospital and have the same homelike environment and relaxed, flexible atmosphere. The birth process proceeds with little intervention, and the outcomes for mothers and babies are excellent. The birth center concept was developed by midwives who believe that it is the best alternative to both home and hospital deliveries.

Free-standing birth centers are unique in many ways. A healthy woman gives birth outside the acute-care setting of the hospital. Birth is viewed as a normal process to be respected but not feared. Most free-standing birth centers are several minutes away from the hospital that serves as backup for complicated deliveries. To ensure safety for women who wish to use their services, birth centers are strict in screening for health problems or complications during pregnancy that may require a hospital birth. Birth centers have emergency equipment available for the birth attendants to resuscitate a baby at birth or to stop a maternal hemorrhage, the two most frequent serious complications at birth.

About one out of five women who apply to an out-of-hospital birth center will be ineligible, either at the first prenatal visit or sometime during the pregnancy. "Horrendous emergencies can always be linked to risk factors predictable before labor and delivery," said Linda Ross, C.N.M., nurse-midwife of the Denver Birth Center. This strict screening pays off for the pregnant women and for the birth center. During labor only one woman in eight requires transfer to a hospital—usually for delayed progress in her labor. When transfer is needed, the midwife or doctor accompanies her to the hospital to deliver the baby, thus maintaining continuity of care. Check your chosen birth center to confirm whether this is done.

Birth centers are unique in that the woman in active labor has the constant attendance of the midwife or doctor. Continuity of care throughout the childbearing cycle is part of the birth-center philosophy. All care, from early pregnancy through labor and delivery, postpartum and baby care, is given by the midwife in the same place where the woman will deliver.

Education of the parents is another crucial element of birth-center philosophy. "Maternity care is viewed as a process of education to promote a healthy, safe, and satisfying birth outcome in which there is a high value on the feelings and wishes of the family during childbirth," said Ruth Watson Lubic, C.N.M., Ed.D., director of the Childbearing Center, Maternity Center Association, New York City.

Because birth is viewed as a normal process and as an important beginning to a healthy family, the mother-to-be is encouraged to take responsibility for her health care during her pregnancy and delivery as a first step in taking care of her baby. Educating the parents to be responsible for their baby's birth is viewed as the best preparation for assuming the responsibility of raising their baby. "Knowledge is power," said Kittie Ernst, C.N.M., M.P.H., speaking at the *Birth* journal conference in 1989. "The more parents understand, the more powerful, in control, and confident they are going to be."

All free-standing birth centers are characterized by "parent power," says Ruth Wilf, C.N.M., Ph.D., a nurse midwife with The Birthing Suite, Pennsylvania Hospital, Philadelphia. Families are not only encouraged but expected to design their own highly personalized birth plan. Parents are encouraged to make all the decisions about who will be present at the birth, what the labor and delivery positions will be, and when they will be discharged. They are told to bring to the birth center anything they want to eat (many birth centers have kitchen facilities), and to do just about anything they want to do during the birth experience.

Unmedicated childbirth is advocated by free-standing birth centers. "We guarantee you won't have an epidural unless it's absolutely needed," Kittie Ernst told us. "We practice midwifery, not obstetrics. An epidural allows the woman to escape from the birth experience. For many women we see, a midwife-assisted, natural delivery may be the first success a woman has had."

"You are designed to give birth without drugs," Loretta Ivory, C.N.M., nurse-midwife of the Denver Birth Center tells her clients. She also encourages women to remain at home as long as they want to. "Women at term pregnancy, including women having their first babies, know when to come to the birth center if they have been encouraged by their birth attendant to listen to their own feelings." She describes how she handles the question of when a woman should come to the birth center. "When a woman calls me and says, 'Should I come in?' I say, 'Do you want to?' and if she says, 'Well, I don't know, I thought you'd tell me,' then I say 'Stay home.' However, when she calls and says, 'I want to come in,' then it's time to come in."

Although intervention is very low in all free-standing birth centers, most provide analgesia for those women who request it. All women who choose The Natural Childbirth Institute in Culver City, California, have unmedicated births, nurse-midwife and co-owner Robin Ozerkis, M.S., C.N.M., told us. (A numbing injection is given after birth for suturing an episiotomy, if needed.) Intervention and complication rates are very low. Fewer than 3 percent of births are augmented with Pitocin. (Pitocin is given only after transfer to the hospital.) Fewer than 3 percent of the deliveries need forceps or vacuum extraction; under 50 percent of the women have episiotomies; and the primary cesarean rate is under 7 percent.

Many of the babies born at The Natural Childbirth Institute have their sisters and brothers present at their birth. Founders of the institute, obstetrician Vic Berman, M.D., and Salee Berman, C.N.M., encouraged the presence of siblings from the time the institute opened in 1975. (The Bermans have since left the birth center.) The institute was one of the chief sources of photos for the Hathaways' book, *Children at Birth*.

The American College of Obstetricians and Gynecologists (ACOG) and The American Academy of Pediatricians have issued statements opposing all out-of-hospital births "because of a lack of information to support out of hospital births," according to the organizations. After a literature review the Institute of Medicine of the National Academy of Sciences reported in 1982 that "reliable information about the safety of all birth settings is lacking." We have no evidence to say that the hospital is safer or as safe as an out-of-hospital birth.

In 1982, the same year the institute report came out, Anita Bennetts, C.N.M., Ph.D., and Ruth Watson Lubic, C.N.M., Ed.D., of the Childbearing Center of the Maternity Center Association, New York City, reported an evaluation of two thousand births from 1972 to 1979 in eleven free-standing birth centers. The authors were denied information on low-risk women delivering in hospitals as a source of comparison "primarily for political reasons," the authors report. They settled for evaluating the centers.

Intervention rates were low and include the women transferred to a hospital. The only women who had anesthesia were the 5 percent who had cesareans. Five percent of the deliveries were assisted by forceps or vacuum extraction. Outcomes were excellent. The neonatal death rate for birth-center infants *including transfers* was 4.6 per 1,000 births. Paul Branca, M.D., of Thomas Jefferson Medical College, Philadelphia, said "the outcomes for the birth centers studied were at least as good (maybe even slightly better) as outcomes for hospitals for a comparable group of mothers."

"Safety, satisfaction, and savings characterize free-standing birth centers," reported Kittie Ernst, director of the National Association of Childbearing Centers. At the 1989 *Birth* journal conference she presented the results of a national, descriptive study of 11,814 women giving birth in eighty-four centers, the largest study ever done of free-standing birth centers. This first report of the data from the study showed low intervention rates and good outcomes for mothers and babies.

Midwives managed three-fourths of the births, physicians the rest. Monitoring was almost always done by portable Doppler or fetoscope rather than by electronic fetal monitoring. Nipple stimulation (7.7 percent) was used in preference to oxytocin (1.4 percent) for labor enhancement. Twelve percent were transferred to hospitals in labor, primarily for delayed progress. Pain-relieving medication was not withheld if the mother asked for it (57 percent of the women had it at some point in labor), but other comfort measures were used more often. During labor 95 percent of the women ate or drank, 43 percent took showers or baths, and 35 percent had body massages.

Women were encouraged to assume positions of choice during labor and delivery. Eighty percent delivered in positions other than lying down on the back (the lithotomy position was not used). Sitting and sidelying were the most common choices. Twenty-two percent had episiotomies.

The overall cesarean section rate was 4.4 percent (one-third of those transferred to hospitals). The neonatal death rate, *including transfers*, was 1.27 per thousand births, comparable to the best results for deliveries of low-risk women in hospitals, according to Ms. Ernst.

Satisfaction with the birth centers was so high among the women in the study that virtually all of them (99 percent) said they would recommend the birth center to friends. Although costs varied from center to center, Ms. Ernst reported that they are often half that of a traditional hospital delivery and 30 percent below hospital single-room maternity care. In response to the cost-effectiveness of free-standing birth centers, insurance coverage is now widespread.

The Department of Defense includes free-standing birth centers in *Champus,* a program that allows dependents of armed-services personnel to get civilian medical care. A nonavailability statement is not needed; that is, the dependent can still use the birth center even if military childbirth care is available.

Some readers of this book are members of an HMO, a health maintenance organization, in which members prepay a fixed amount to the HMO for all medical care and must use the health-care providers employed by the HMO. Depending on the local HMO, birth centers can be included on the approved list of childbirth providers. In some areas, doctors on the boards of the HMOs have kept birth centers run by midwives off the list.

Free-Standing Birth Centers

To sum up:

- Insurance coverage available.
- Labor, birth, and recovery in a regular bed.
- No separation of mother, infant, and father.
- Equipment available for most common obstetrical emergencies; hospital backup provided.
- Very strict screening for admission.
- Complete pregnancy, birth, postpartum care, and pediatric care given at the birth center.
- Highly individualized and personal care, usually by nurse-midwives.
- Interventions nearly always absent; birth viewed as normal.
- 12 percent transfer during labor to regular hospital for delivery.

- Risk of complications very low.
- Parents educated and guided to take responsibility for their own health care.
- Satisfaction is very high.

PLACE OF BIRTH: HOME

> Should babies be born at home? What a question! Where else should they be born, if not in the home? The hospital? But I had thought that a hospital was a place where one went for relief from sickness or injury. I would not have thought, had I not known it to be a fact, that the most important event in the life of a family, the birth of a child, was celebrated away from home, away from the family, in a hospital.
>
> —ASHLEY MONTAGU, PH.D.,
> QUOTED IN *THE HOME BIRTH BOOK*

Home birth isn't seriously considered by most North American and European women today. This is not true in the rest of the world, where the vast majority of babies are born at home. However, there is a small but growing percentage of women who believe, as Ashley Montagu does, that the home is the best place to give birth, a place of celebration in the midst of one's family, with the hospital a place of medical refuge if needed.

The number of babies born at home in the United States, though small in relation to the millions born in hospitals, is growing. In many states, the percentage of babies born at home is about 1 percent. In a few states, the percentages are much higher. In Oregon, for example, 4.4 percent of all births take place at home. In some counties of California, estimates range as high as 15 percent.

The cost of home birth is minimal compared to a hospital birth. Almost all of the cost, in fact, is the birth attendant's fee, which varies from nothing or very little, to six hundred dollars or more. Very few state insurance regulations cover the cost of home birth.

People who choose a home birth vary widely in their life-styles and economic levels. Their reasons for having a home birth almost always have to do with a strong desire to have a self-directed rather than doctor-directed experience, to enhance family unity, and an inability to get what they want at a hospital. These parents see childbirth as a normal process. They believe that the addition of a new family member should take place in a way that is most conducive to acceptance of the new baby. The parents embrace full responsibility for decisions they make. The child is theirs forever, wherever it is born; the responsibility for the best outcome is theirs.

Most families who choose home birth do so in an atmosphere of widespread disapproval, so that they are often forced to carefully examine the reasons for their decision. In the area of safety, they see two key hazards of the hospital they are unwilling to accept: the risk of infection and high rates of intervention in normal births. They are willing to accept the risk of not having surgical delivery immediately available because they believe screening for risk can be effective. They believe that home birth is safer for a normal mother and baby than a hospital birth.

No one knows for certain whether it is safer today for a woman having a normal pregnancy to have her baby at home with a skilled birth attendant or for her to use a hospital or free-standing birth center. The report of the Institute of Medicine of the National Academy of Sciences described in detail the research needed to evaluate birth settings and safety for mother and baby. In order for research to be done, the cooperation of doctors and hospitals is required so that comparisons can be made between out-of-hospital and in-hospital births. So far, that cooperation is sadly lacking. Many obs are so convinced any kind of out-of-hospital is unsafe, they will not sanction any research.

What research there is suggests that home birth is as safe or safer than hospital birth when women are attended by skilled birth attendants. Lewis Mehl, M.D., Ph.D., a family practitioner and statistician, carried out the first study comparing a group of women who gave birth at home to a similar group of women who gave birth in a hospital. The results appear earlier in this chapter. This 1976 study suggests a much better outcome for the home-birth group.

During a decade of work that extended into the 1980s, English research statistician Marjorie Tew compiled the strongest evidence supporting the safety of home birth. Ms. Tew used British birth data covering hospitals, planned home births, and "general practitioner units" (GP units) similar to free-standing birth centers. Data was available to classify 16,328 births into risk categories of very low, low, moderate, high, and very high. The perinatal mortality rate (PNMR) is the number of deaths of babies during and around the time of birth per thousand births. The PNMR was used to compare outcomes for hospital births and planned out-of-hospital births, including home and GP units.

At each level of risk, perinatal mortality was lower out of hospital. Except for very high-risk births, the differences in PNMR were what statisticians call statistically significant, meaning the differences are great enough that we may assume with confidence they reflect real differences. At the very low and low level of risk, hospital births had a two-to-three times higher rate of perinatal mortality. At a moderate level of risk, the hospital PNMR was more than eight times greater than out-of-hospital PNMR. Even at a high level of assigned risk to the birth, the hospital PNMR was over three times higher.

Rona Campbell, a lecturer at the University of Ulster in England, reported on her survey of British home-birth research (including Tew's research) at the International Homebirth Conference in London in 1987. Campbell was meticulously careful to phrase her conclusions with scientific accuracy. She said that an experiment called a randomized control trial (see a description of RCT in chapter 6) was needed to be able to say with certainty that one or the other place of birth was the safest. She summarized the evidence to date:

> "There is no evidence to support the claim that the safest policy is for all women to deliver in hospital. For women having a planned homebirth, the risk of perinatal death appears to be low, particularly for women who have already had one child. Morbidity (illness, infection or other complications) is higher among mothers and babies cared for in hospital. Most women with experience of home and hospital delivery prefer home delivery."

Marsden Wagner, M.D., an official with the World Health Organization spoke at the same conference:

> The World Health Organization supports the more traditional forms of health practices such as home birth. Just for the record, let me read to you out of the WHO publication *Having a Baby in Europe:* "It is important to remember that it has never been scientifically proven that the hospital is a safer place than the home for a woman who has had an uncomplicated pregnancy. Studies of planned home birth in developed countries with women who have had uncomplicated pregnancies have shown morbidity and mortality rates

for mothers and babies equal to or better than hospital birth statistics. These studies have also found significantly fewer interventions used in home births."

A unique experiment in home birth continues to take place in rural Tennessee in a spiritual community of families called The Farm. Over 1,700 babies have been born at home, on The Farm or in the surrounding area. All were attended by Farm midwives who learned their skills through practical experience and apprenticeship (called empirical midwifery). Statistics for these births (including the 4.7 percent of all births transferred to hospital during labor) contradict most hospital obstetrical statistics. Intervention is almost nonexistent. Ninety-eight percent of the women gave birth with no analgesia or anesthesia; 28 percent had episiotomies, and less than 1 percent were given Pitocin to stimulate labor; less than one-half of 1 percent of deliveries required forceps; and the cesarean rate was 1.8 percent. Complications are usually managed at home. Nine out of eleven sets of twins and two-thirds of the breech babies (thirty-three of forty-nine) were born at home.

Ina May Gaskin, The Farm's head midwife wrote "unless home birth is considered by a society to be a valid option worthy of social support, it is easy to lose the knowledge that birth is a normal process. When all maternity care is in the hospital, it becomes fragmented, and caregivers lose their skills and the knowledge of how women's bodies function in pregnancy and labor. The cost in human lives and suffering is uncounted but catastrophic."

Home

To sum up:

- Insurance coverage unlikely, but costs low.
- Parent responsibility is high for finding a skilled birth attendant and for ensuring hospital backup.
- Screening essential to reduce risks.
- Approximately 15 percent transfer to the hospital during labor (one out of four first-time mothers).
- Interventions absent.
- Complication rates extremely low.
- The risk of infection is low because the mother is not in an alien environment.
- The birth experience is directed by the parents.

- Mothers may feel more relaxed in their own territory.
- Siblings can easily participate in the birth at their own pace.
- The baby is part of the family from the beginning.
- Satisfaction very high.

THE CHOICE OF YOUR BIRTH ATTENDANT

You have four choices for a birth attendant: an obstetrician, a family practitioner, a certified nurse-midwife, or a direct-entry midwife. For the few parents who are unable to find a birth attendant they are satisfied with, a fifth choice is possible: themselves.

OBSTETRICIAN

Whether a woman expects to have a healthy normal pregnancy, or whether she has been labeled "high risk," most American women choose obstetricians as their birth attendants. Obstetricians—surgeons trained to handle any gynecological or obstetrical problem—deliver more than four out of five American babies. Many women like the idea of having a specialist for their baby's birth, believing that, because the obstetrician can handle any complication that may develop, they have the best care available at all times.

In chapter 4, "Understanding Doctors," we describe the obstetrician's training and practice. In a three-year residency the ob/gyn-to-be spends sixteen months on obstetrics. The rest of the time is spent mostly in gynecology, with some months in anesthesia, pathology, and endocrinology. He becomes a surgical specialist in diseases of the female reproductive system.

Most obstetricians believe birth to be a time of highest risk to the baby and that they are obliged to get the baby out as quickly as possible. They view a woman's birth canal as dangerous to the baby and believe that intervention is necessary in almost all births.

FAMILY PRACTITIONER

Family practitioners, who deliver under 15 percent of American babies, are medical doctors who have taken an additional three years of residency after medical school.

A family practitioner chooses his specialty because he wants to treat the whole family. This is often the main reason some women prefer to go to a family practitioner for obstetrical care. They like the fact that he already knows the whole family, and they prefer the continuity of care that they receive by having the same person care for them and their newborn baby. Because the family practitioner's philosophy is to give primary care to the whole family, many family practitioners have a policy of delivering their obstetrical patients whether it is their night on call or not.

Family practitioners view birth as a normal process. Because they take care of newborns just as pediatricians do, they often see the complications from interventions. They view intervention in labor and delivery as risky and see themselves as skillfully using interventions only when necessary.

CERTIFIED NURSE-MIDWIFE

Certified nurse-midwives deliver roughly 3 percent of American babies. They are registered nurses with an additional two years of midwifery training. During this time, the student midwife participates in over one hundred normal deliveries. "The new nurse-midwife has more experience in normal childbirth than the average family practitioner," says Silvia Feldman, Ph.D., author of *Choices in Childbirth*. "She rapidly accumulates so much experience thereafter, working full time with normal births, that she soon knows more about managing normal pregnancies and childbirths than the average obstetrician."

The nurse-midwife's practice is limited to managing the maternity care of mothers whose progress through pregnancy, labor and delivery, and postpartum is normal. During training a certified nurse-midwife is taught to recognize an abnormal situation in pregnancy or birth, and to refer, or seek consultation with, a specialist. Education of the pregnant woman is a basic part of the philosophy of certified nurse-midwives. They view this education as helping the woman to participate in her own health care.

"Historically, midwives have viewed themselves as experts in the normal birth, skilled assistants to the birthing woman's efforts, trusting her body's own powerful ability to give birth naturally and safely," said Rebecca Barber, C.N.M., with the

Denver Birth Center. Because they share this viewpoint, certified nurse-midwives believe intervention risky, and prefer a more "hands-on" approach, with the skillful avoidance of drugs. What some see as a disadvantage of the midwife, that she is not trained to do the surgery necessary in complicated deliveries, others see as the main advantage. Her primary effort is to assist the childbearing family to have a normal delivery. "She is better equipped to give complete care to the normal [woman] than is her obstetrician physician colleague," said Ruth Lubic, nurse-midwife and director of the Maternity Center Association of New York City.

DIRECT-ENTRY MIDWIFE

Direct-entry midwives enter training directly without having first qualified as a nurse. Commonly known as lay midwives, they deliver 1–2 percent of babies in the United States each year, reports David Stewart, Ph.D., of NAPSAC. The training of direct-entry midwives varies. Some have completed midwifery and licensure programs in England. Others have trained at a birth center run by direct-entry midwives, such as the Casa de Nacimiento (House of Birth) in El Paso, Texas. Still others have learned through a short training program and apprenticeship to experienced midwives.

Licensure and legality of practice varies also. As of this writing no Canadian province has legalized the practice of direct-entry midwifery. "The practice is definitely illegal in nine states in the U.S., and in twelve states it is legal," Terra Palmarini, midwife and coauthor of *Pregnant Feelings,* told us. "In the rest no legislation deals with direct-entry midwifery, putting its practice in a 'grey' area of legality." Ms. Palmarini suggested that women contact the Midwives Alliance of North America (MANA) or their local health department for their state or province's status and referral.

Direct-entry midwives have the same commitment to normal birth as certified nurse-midwives. The word "mid-wife" means "with woman." All midwives give continuous one-to-one care through all stages of labor and birth. Direct-entry midwives almost always deliver at home, though many hospitals permit the midwife to accompany a woman to the hospital when a complication arises, and to remain with her through the delivery by a doctor. Direct-entry midwives are also being used as labor assistants for women choosing hospital births.

YOURSELVES AS BIRTH ATTENDANTS

Very few American women choose to deliver their own babies without a birth attendant. When they do, it's usually because they are unable to find a birth attendant who will give them the kind of birth they want either at home or in a hospital. Gregory White, M.D., a home-birth practitioner in Chicago, reports hearing from a registered nurse whom he had attended for her first three home deliveries. After she moved to Florida, she went to thirty different doctors, by actual count, to try to find a home-birth attendant. None would do it. Finally, she gave up and decided to have a do-it-yourself birth.

A number of do-it-yourself births are done by preference. Marilyn Moran of Leewood, Kansas, is the spokeswoman for this choice, believing that birth is a spiritual and sexual experience between husband and wife that should not be intruded upon if the pregnancy and labor are going normally. Believing it inappropriate for a woman to give birth into a stranger's hands, Moran suggests that a woman give birth into the waiting hands of the baby's father. For those who choose a do-it-yourself birth, Moran says it is crucial to have prenatal care to give the parents continuing information on the woman's risk status, and for the parents to study as much material about birth as they can, so they know the signs indicating a possible complication requiring hospital assistance.

MEASURING THE SAFETY OF
A BIRTH ATTENDANT

The best way to look at safety is to compare mother and baby death and complication rates for the different kinds of birth attendants. Obstetricians point to dropping maternal and perinatal mortality rates as proof of how well they are attending births. In chapter 6, "Obstetricians' Beliefs about a 'Safe Birth,'" we point out that overall death rates don't prove that what one is doing is safe; only evaluations of each intervention used could prove or disprove that. But death and complication rates can be useful in *comparing* birth attendants by specialty.

Maternal mortality is based on the number of deaths of women per one hundred thousand live births. Maternal mortality rates in the United States are so good that it is difficult to distinguish any significant differences by specialty. The maternal mortality rate is less than one maternal death for every ten thousand live births. For comparison, you have a far greater chance (more than twenty times greater chance) of becoming pregnant after your husband has had a vasectomy than you have of dying in childbirth.

There are reported differences in *infant* outcome by specialty that can be useful in comparing birth attendants. The best outcomes for mothers and babies in the industrialized countries of the world are, with the one exception of Japan, those countries where many or most of the babies are delivered by midwives. As an example, highly ranked Sweden has almost universal midwifery. Drug-free childbirth and 100 percent hospital births are also basic to Swedish maternity care.

One of the very few direct comparisons of neonatal mortality rates for babies delivered by either midwives or doctors was presented in the *American Journal of Obstetrics and Gynecology* in 1971. The neonatal mortality rate is the number of infant deaths per one thousand live births during the first twenty-eight days of life. For about three years, beginning in 1960, state funds were used for a nurse-midwifery demonstration project at Madera County Hospital in California. During the program, midwives managed "the vast majority of pregnancies and 78 percent of the hospital deliveries," according to the report. From mid-1963 on, doctors again handled all prenatal care and deliveries at the hospital. The program was terminated, despite the good results, because of opposition from the California Medical Association.

This was a rare opportunity to compare birth attendants, all caring for the same kind of maternity population with the same mixture of low- and high-risk patients. The safest birth attendants were the midwives. During the period of time midwives practiced at Madera County Hospital, 1960 through 1963, neonatal mortalities were more than halved, dropping from 23.9 in 1959 to 10.3 neonatal deaths per one thousand live births. The prematurity rate decreased by 40 percent, dropping from 11 percent to 6.6 percent. These neonatal mortality and prematurity rates were better than the average rates for the whole state of California.

The dramatic difference came, however, when the midwifery program was ended and doctors again became the birth attendants. During the next two-and-one-half years, the neonatal death rate more than tripled under doctors' care, averaging 32.1 neonatal deaths per one thousand live births. The prematurity rate increased by almost 50 percent, rising to 9.8 percent, a lower rate than in 1959, but much higher than during the midwifery program. Midwives gave the best care at Madera County Hospital.

Published reports of home-birth and direct-entry midwifery care in Kentucky, North Carolina, Missouri, and Arizona are available, showing excellent outcomes. For example, in the North Carolina study by the Center for Disease Control, planned home-births attended by direct-entry midwives had a neonatal mortality rate of four per one thousand live births. In the same time period, the neonatal mortality in hospital births in North Carolina was twelve per one thousand.

Marjorie Tew, whose work we referred to earlier in this chapter, has analyzed the most complete data on place of birth and birth attendant. The same data that showed birth safer at home or in a general practitioner unit than in a hospital can be used to compare birth attendants. Almost all births in hospital at the time of the study were attended by obstetricians. Yet the perinatal mortality rates were higher at every level of labor risk for the obstetrical units than for home-birth with midwives or birth centers with general practitioners. Again in their careful, scientific way, Rona Campbell and Alison Macfarlane, social policy analysts, looked at Tew's data and analysis and reported that there was no proof that the obstetricians were responsible for the higher mortality rates. They did agree that there is some evidence that complications are higher among mothers and babies delivered in hospitals and cared for by obstetricians.

The most comprehensive review of the literature on midwifery is given by David Stewart, Ph.D., editor of *The Five Standards for Safe Childbearing*. His historical review shows that midwife-attended deliveries have neonatal death rates well below national averages. In many, if not most, of the studies the midwives were attending the poor and high-risk client, where one could expect *higher* neonatal death rates.

He cited the outstanding example of North Central Bronx Hospital in New York City, reported in a public hearing of the National Institute of Health Task Force on Cesarean Birth in 1980. More than 30 percent of the mothers were labeled medically at high risk of complication. Another 30 percent

were considered at risk because of socioeconomic consider-
ations. Nevertheless, 83 percent of the births were completed
by midwives. In spite of the risk status of many of the women
delivered by the midwives, the neonatal mortality rate, which
included many low-birth-weight babies, was a low 4.2 deaths
per 1,000 live births. At that time no reports of doctor-attended
births of women with similar risks showed as good outcomes as
this low neonatal mortality rate achieved by midwives.

Maternity systems based on midwifery have better mother
and baby outcomes according to the literature. "The data base
for these figures is in the millions, is global in scope, and spans
almost a century, up to and including the present," said
Stewart. He estimates that if all the women delivering between
1940 and 1980 had had a birth attendant with a midwife
philosophy, mother and baby mortalities would have been
halved and the rates of brain-damaged children and other birth
defects would have been reduced by at least three-fourths.
According to his estimates, 30,000 mothers died in childbirth
who should not have died; 1.5 million children were severely
brain damaged because of medical procedures; and 45 million
children suffered minimal brain damage who would have
been normal, had unnecessary intervention in normal deliveries
been avoided.

In 1985 the World Health Organization held a conference on
the "Appropriate Technology for Birth." WHO adopted a
series of recommendations that follow a "careful review of the
knowledge of birth technology." WHO recommends that
"the training of professional midwives or birth attendants
should be encouraged. Care during normal pregnancy, birth,
and afterwards should be the duty of this profession." Normal
pregnancy care includes 80 percent or more of all births. WHO
recommends that professional midwives, certified nurse-
midwives, or direct-entry midwives care for all those women.

David Stewart agrees that it is the philosophy of care and
not the title of the birth attendant that determines safety for
mother and baby. This philosophy of care involves:

- Prenatal education and screening
- Continuous one-to-one labor support by a skilled labor
  attendant, who may also be the birth attendant
- The view that a woman's body is designed to give birth
  safely to her baby in her own unique way

- The belief that intervention should be used only when the need is greater than the risk

This philosophy is common among midwives, but can be found among some family practitioners and obstetricians, too.

Women at low risk for complicated deliveries have much greater rates of intervention and complication for themselves and their babies in hospitals than in alternative settings, either within the hospital or outside of the hospital. Your chance of a normal birth is related to your choice of a birthplace and a birth attendant.

If you are willing to look, you have a great chance of finding a place of birth fairly near you that will satisfy your needs in childbirth. Many hospitals have eased their policies to allow flexibility in their routines. With your coach, a woman friend, and an agreeable birth attendant, you can have a good and safe birth in many hospitals today.

FOUR

UNDERSTANDING DOCTORS—WHY THEY DO WHAT THEY DO

I'm proud of what I do. I'm proud that I've gone to school and become an educated person. I don't think I'm better than anyone else. We doctors are not pillars of society. We are part of society. Who's a pillar? The guy who sweeps out a gas station, pays taxes, doesn't commit any crimes, goes to church, loves his wife. Isn't he a pillar of society?

—OBSTETRICIAN*

Most of you will have a doctor, probably an obstetrician, as your birth attendant. To get a good and safe birth, you need to understand your doctor. He's a unique person, with his own background, training that has shaped his thinking and beliefs, and his own pressures and successes.

Many doctors-to-be know from their early years that they want to go into medicine. And after four years of college, plus another four years of medical school, the doctors-to-be begin the next step—internship and residency.

INTERNSHIP

Internship is a year in which new doctors sample all the medical specialties and choose one for themselves. Because

*This anonymous doctor's comments follow throughout this chapter.

nearly all doctors specialize, most will enter a residency program. Many hospitals have eliminated the year of internship, and students progress directly into a residency. This internship, or combined internship-residency, is a world in which single-minded dedication to medicine is mandatory, mostly because of the demanding work schedule.

In *Hospital Management Quarterly,* Julie C. Donnelly, Ed.D., reports on the stresses that face interns:

> The first year of postgraduate training is significant in that the individual is now an actual M.D., may legitimately be addressed as "Doctor," is now earning a salary for the first time, is now in a supervisory position over medical students, and has primary patient responsibility. At the same time, the intern is at the bottom of the medical training hierarchy and bears a workload of 70 to 100 hours per week. This typically includes an on-call schedule that demands being in the hospital every third night and weekend and often going without sleep for 36 hours.

In the late 1980's, both major newspapers and medical journals voiced concern over the health effects of such a schedule, not just for the intern-resident, but also for patients who were being misdiagnosed and treated inappropriately due to the physician's poor mental and physical functioning.

RESIDENCY

In the usual residency the working hours and the elimination of a life outside the hospital hardly get any better. Michelle Harrison, M.D., author of *Woman in Residence,* describes her ob residency training: "Medical training works like brainwashing. Two major components are sleep deprivation and isolation from one's support system." The hospital becomes the entire focus. Home is just a place to go to sleep occasionally. This is true of all residencies, but it is especially true, and accentuated, in surgical residencies such as ob/gyn.

I was in surgery seven hours from seven A.M. until two in the afternoon. Usually there were a half dozen or more operations, and I'd make rounds in between or after. The afternoons and evenings were for admitting new patients, performing physical exams, writing up charts, and prescribing tests or medications.

Typically, 75 percent of an ob/gyn's training is in surgery. Surgeons at their best are finely trained technicians. Learning to use technology is crucial for them, so that they can intervene automatically and quickly in lifesaving situations.

Obstetrics is the least scientific of all specialties. Traditionally in the past, the bottom half of the medical class went into obstetrics.

When I was in training, we still listened with a headscope. That was the state of the art. We were afraid to do a c-section and we knew nothing about the fetus. Now in fifteen years there has been an explosion of technology in obstetrics.

In the 1970s technology was added to the ob/gyn training program, making it a more challenging residency to new doctors. But it's more than the magic of science. "A lot of medicine is drudgery and trivia," one doctor told us, giving his opinion why doctors so readily accept new technology in their practice. "Medicine is often like an assembly line [a common complaint of the patient also]. New techniques and technology are exciting. They are like new toys, and you think you are doing things better. You become part of relentless progress."

Unless residents are trained to keep technology in perspective, I can see where they would get on a treadmill and rely upon machinery too much. Nurses are the same way. I was trained in the in-between era, where I saw both worlds. There is a place for technology, but people tend to rely on it too much. Doctors and nurses who are trained at high-tech centers have to make a conscious effort to not allow high-technology procedures to be their only tools. That's not easy. If that's the way you were trained, you'll be uncomfortable changing.

The most important skill for most ob/gyns, from their point of view, is not delivering babies; it's surgery. This is an emphasis that is often not in women's best interests. Sociologist Diana Scully wrote in her book, *Men Who Control Women's Health: The Miseducation of Obstetricians and Gynecologists,* "Most of a doctor's training in obstetrics and gynecology focuses on surgery and on gaining expertise in diagnosis and treatment of acute and pathological conditions. The majority of cases that a resident sees, however, do not require these skills." She concluded that in order to get enough surgical experience residents found patients whose problems might or might not indicate the need for surgery and then persuaded these patients to have surgery. Research since then and women's experiences show that this emphasis on surgery and intervention has not lessened.

Residents are eager to do surgery. There is pressure on residents to find surgery because there is never enough to go around. I don't think I'm overtrained for surgery. I don't think you can ever be surgically overtrained. But you can very easily be undertrained. You can quickly get in the habit of doing surgeries that don't need to be done when there are alternatives, too.

Ob/gyn residents, like other specialists, treat low-income women almost exclusively. These women are the most likely in our culture to be high risk, and the least likely to ask questions. This treatment, plus the normal vulnerability of pregnancy, labor, and birth, guarantees that many of these women will not object to any procedure done to them. An ob/gyn resident is not encouraged to discuss with a patient what she wants; his daily training reinforces the belief that only he knows what's best.

I tell residents that they are going to find a different world when they go into private practice. Nobody ever told me that when I was a resident. If I said to a patient during my training, "You need a hysterectomy," she never said, "Why?" She said, "Yes, doctor, thank you, doctor." Well, that's not the real world. In my practice, there is a lot of consumer interest. And questions . . . and more questions.

Doctors who specialize in family practice treat the whole family—not just the pregnant woman. Like family practitioners, pediatricians in their three-year residencies often will see the same child and that child's family for many visits. A family-practice doctor contrasted his own residency training for us with the training he saw in ob/gyn: "I had fifteen patients of my own that I took care of from the very beginning of their pregnancy to their labor and delivery, and then I took care of their babies until I finished my three-year residency. That kind of follow-through in patient care is something you don't get at all in the standard ob/gyn training." Patients at major medical centers usually see a different ob/gyn resident for each visit and yet another stranger at the birth.

As a resident, I used to see forty to forty-five people in a three-hour clinic. I might have seven patients in labor at one time. All I could do was make a snap judgment, a quick decision. I couldn't really sit down and talk to people. There just wasn't enough time. I have a real easygoing practice now. I see about half the patients that the average obstetrician does.

I've made it a point not to treat my patients in my private practice the same way we treated women during my training. A doctor can change just like everybody else. It just depends on how human he is.

The resident obstetrician typically believes that he will learn all he needs to know about childbirth in his residency. That may leave him suspicious of any ideas that are different from what he learned.

I delivered two thousand babies in my residency. If the patients didn't get medication, it was a rare exception. In fact, I was told that I failed in my duty if I did not provide the patient with medication. I trained in a big-city ghetto hospital. There the women wanted and needed medication. There was no prenatal education, no Bradley or Lamaze classes. Most of the women were not married and didn't want to be pregnant. They didn't want pain. There was no reward for them to have that child, and so in that situation, if I didn't provide them with anesthesia, I wasn't doing my job. That's what I was there for.

Many an obstetrician feels that if an unmedicated birth was good for the baby and the mother, he would have been taught that in his training. If good communication skills were essential, they, too, would be taught in residency. If understanding women's need for the biological pleasure of birth was thought significant, that also would be part of residency training. However, these topics are seldom mentioned, if at all, in ob/gyn residencies.

I am way overtrained to deliver a perfectly healthy woman who is having her third child, who is going to go into spontaneous labor. She doesn't need a board-certified and surgically trained obstetrician for that delivery, nine out of ten times. One out of ten she might. My training makes it hard for me to sit on my hands and just wait and watch.

One obstetrician described the transition from training to private practice to us by saying, "Physicians are trained in a high-pace setting and have to unlearn rigidity, haste, and intensity." Asking an ob to "sit on his hands" and wait for nature to take its course goes against his beliefs, training, and experience.

"The exuberant years of medical research have set loose on an unsuspecting public a large number of physicians who are in command of highly complex, cost-intensive technologies of uncertain value, which they then proceed to implement," said Stanford University economist Victor Fuchs in 1978. "They understandably want to practice medicine in the style to which they have become accustomed."

And that style definitely affects the care your physician gives you.

SPECIAL INFLUENCES ON DOCTORS

FEAR OF MALPRACTICE SUITS

Malpractice is more than a specter for many obstetricians. It's a reality. Your physician knows colleagues who are being sued and may have been sued himself, since 70 percent of ob/gyns have been sued at least once, according to a 1988 report of the American College of Obstetricians and Gynecologists. That strongly influences what your doctor may or may not do during your pregnancy and birth.

I talk to other doctors, and they are worried. This is especially true when I'm doing an ob consultation. I've read in the newspapers about doctors who deny that the fear of malpractice influences their decisions. Well, that's not true. Privately, we know a very large portion of an ob's decisions are based on the legal implications. It gets worse every day. The agencies that handle our malpractice policies come and give risk-management seminars for doctors.

The anxiety level about malpractice suits among most

obstetricians is high. "The shadow of malpractice falls over our every act," states surgeon Ralph S. Emerson, M.D., in the *Bulletin of the American College of Surgeons*. And some lawyers encourage "defensive medicine." James J. Pagliuso, J.D., in his article, "Situations to Avoid If You Don't Want to Be Sued," in *Contemporary Ob/Gyn,* stated: "I believe obstetricians and hospitals are taking substantial medicolegal risks if they don't undertake at least external monitoring from the outset of active labor." And when doctors are sued, judges hold physicians liable when they don't use technology.

I have people who come into my office and they say, "Why haven't you done the ultrasound yet?" and I say that I don't think it is indicated, and they say, "Well, my girlfriend had an ultrasound, and I want an ultrasound; I want to see the baby." "You'll see your baby in six months," I say. "Well, I don't want to wait," she tells me. She'll get her ultrasound. And strictly because if ever there was an anomaly or the slightest thing wrong, she is going to say to me, "Why didn't you do the ultrasound when I asked you to?" So I am pressured to do it. I don't do everything that a patient demands, but those kinds of pressures I cooperate with because I don't want to lose my practice. I have to earn a living, and I like what I do. I'm basically just like everybody else. If you work in a factory, and the guy down the line does something wrong and gets fired for it, you are not going to repeat his mistake. It's the same with obstetricians.

Who's the least likely to get sued? The doctors who listen and talk to their patients. The fear of a malpractice suit in your doctor's mind might cause you to receive unnecessary interventions, from extra office tests to a cesarean. Prevent "defensive medicine" from interfering with your pregnancy and birth by doing your part in developing a partnership with your doctor.

INSURANCE COMPANIES REINFORCE YOUR DOCTOR'S URGE TO INTERVENE

About 85 percent of Americans have health coverage. Nearly all hospital bills and two-thirds or more of doctors' fees are paid by insurance. Health insurance allows most patients to buy services from both doctors and hospitals without concerning themselves about price, though this is starting to change. In a turnaround from only five years ago, now most of you who have insurance belong to a prepaid health plan that offers comprehensive medical care for a fixed fee. And these plans do not always cover all the expenses once paid for by the choose-your-own-physician plans.

When a hospital buys ultrasound machines and electronic fetal monitors, the administration is counting on insurance companies to pay the tab—and that means using the machines. Insurance (ultimately the consumer) pays for all those other extras in the hospital, too–from IV bottles and Pitocin, to epidurals and anesthesiologists, nursery fees and baby bottles, sleeping pills and dry-up shots. Although your doctor doesn't get a cut of the insurance company's payment to the hospital, insurance companies reinforce the inclination of the ob/gyn to *do* something by virtue of what procedures they choose to pay for. (Some physicians, however, get a finder's fee from certain hospitals for bringing in new ob clients.) Costs for cesareans, a surgical procedure, for instance, are usually reimbursed 100 percent. This is not always so with vaginal births.

Obstetricians have incentives to use technology during pregnancy, too. Insurance companies routinely pay for prenatal tests. Critics of the American medical industry point out that physicians with diagnostic equipment in their offices use that equipment more than physicians who use independent labs to do the work. You'll get more tests of all kinds if they can be done in your doctor's office. This is not to say that your doctor doesn't believe these procedures are necessary, but their use is likely a habit, rather than thought out specifically with you in mind.

Knowing your physician's incentives to use technology during both your pregnancy and birth, perhaps, when the question of tests, ultrasound, or hospital procedures comes up, you can discuss the pros and cons *for you,* with a clear explanation of the risks/benefits before automatically agreeing with your doctor's suggestions.

WHAT ABOUT DOCTORS' DRUG EDUCATION?

There continues to be controversy over the drug education that physicians receive. Some say that doctors receive more information than is appropriate from drug companies. These companies offer endless free samples to doctors, starting when they are medical students and continuing through their private practice years. Robert Seidenberg, M.D., Clinical Professor of Psychiatry at Upstate Medical Center, State University of New York at Syracuse, told a hearing of the House Select Committee on Narcotics Abuse and Control that "physicians do not understand what conflict of interest means—that you don't get educated by your suppliers."

"Last year $215 million worth of advertisements were placed in the 150 leading medical journals, and that represents only the smallest part of the typical drug promotion campaign," reported *Time* magazine in 1982. "Hundreds of millions more go into snappy exhibits at medical meetings, glossy brochures presented to doctors by company 'detail men,' and educational videotapes for physicians."

Others say that pharmacology takes up one-seventh of a physician's national board exam, and many doctors work hard to keep up with drug information.

Regardless of who's right about where doctors get their information, many physicians continue to prescribe drugs widely known to be ineffective or dangerous.

PHYSICIAN INCOME

The typical ob/gyn in 1988 netted (after expenses, including the payment of a malpractice insurance premium, before taxes) $149,104. This income has increased 50–100 percent, depending on the individual physician, since 1980. This figure is based on a 1988 report of the American College of Obstetricians and Gynecologists, though the American Medical Association placed ob/gyn income higher for the same year at $163,000. (A high-earning midwife may make as much as $30,000 per year, and the typical nurse makes $25,000.)

I know a lot of doctors who drive Chevrolets and Toyotas, have modest homes, and don't play golf every day. And they have a hard time paying their bills. I am under the same pressures as everyone else, so I want to make more money, too. Until I was into my thirties, my top yearly income was $18,000. That's not a lot of money. I was married early and had two children. I had $25,000 in loans to pay back, and it cost well over $50,000 to *start my practice. Right there is a lot of incentive to make some money and make it fast. Many physicians think they deserve it. I don't know how to argue with that, because this is a money-oriented society, and that's status and that's America.*

THE DOCTOR SURPLUS—HOW IT HAS CHANGED YOUR MATERNITY CARE

The predicted doctor glut has come to pass, with the number of doctors having grown proportionately faster than the population. Some ob/gyns managed to increase their income dramatically by dropping obstetrics and concentrating on gynecology, which is more lucrative and has better hours.

Ob/gyns have also increased the number of medical tests they perform. How many women do you know, who, during the course of their pregnancies, have several ultrasound scans, routine Doppler use, a variety of genetic tests, and several uses of the electronic fetal monitor (stress tests and nonstress tests) before they go into labor—plus additional tests and procedures during the birth process? It is likely that it is many of the pregnant women you know.

Ob/gyns have also raised prices and, as much as possible, eliminated the competition.

I believe the demand for obstetricians in society will rapidly decrease. I think it should. We have too many specialists. There are women who do want an obstetrician, and they would no more go to a midwife or a family practitioner than they would live in an underground sod shack. I mean, they want an epidural; they want me; and they want to tell their friends that I'm a specialist and I'll deliver the baby. There will always be that demand. But that is going to be decreasing in the future, and what are all those extra twenty thousand obstetricians going to do? I've already lost some referring doctors because I have a nurse-practitioner in my office and I work with nurse-midwives.

Although obstetricians have made it hard for some family-practice doctors to get hospital privileges and virtually impossible for most certified nurse-midwives to get these same hospital privileges, the best example of the obs' efforts to eliminate competition is their battle against home births. Midwives who assist at home births have been harassed and accused of crimes. Some parents who've had their babies at home have been reported to state authorities and accused of child abuse. And doctors who participate in home births—or who give prenatal care to these women—are often hounded by their peers. These doctors are threatened with loss of hospital staff privileges; their malpractice insurance policies are usually dropped; and they are often treated like outcasts among other physicians.

Obstetricians are motivated strongly by their belief, learned in those training years, that all births should occur in a hospital, but there's no doubt that an economic incentive is at work. If birth can take place safely with a family practitioner or midwife in attendance, then fewer obstetricians are needed. With more obstetricians being trained, there is bound to be increasing conflict of interest.

PRESSURES OF MEDICAL PRACTICE

Doctors are trained to believe that their job is to take over and cure. But the reality of medical practice is not that simple. Sometimes not much can be done for patients, yet many patients demand that the doctor do something.

I spend hours on the phone every week trying to talk women out of using Bendectin [a drug prescribed for nausea, which was removed from production in June, 1983]. "Do you understand there has been a lawsuit on Bendectin?" "Yes," she says. "Do you understand that we cannot guarantee the safety of any medication or substance you take during pregnancy?" "Yes," she says. "Do you understand that I don't prescribe the drug routinely?" "Yes," she says. "Do you understand that it has a package insert that says it's to be used only in unusual circumstances?" "Yes," she says. "So I prefer you take crackers and watch your diet and stay away from food," I tell her. "Doctor," she says, "I want Bendectin." These women are nauseated. I wouldn't want to be nauseated and not feel good. They say that I have to have something to give them. All I can give them is what they know already; that's all I have. So I get pressure from them.

Consumers complain that doctors aren't like they used to be, that they are always in a hurry and they don't want to listen anymore. In the Baltimore COMA Survey, the most important quality women looked for in their obstetrician was communication skills. Other research confirms that. Yet most doctors are still trained to believe their job is to treat the physical problem, not listen. In *Medical Economics* one doctor expressed his frustration with "just" listening by stating, "But by and large, it's patients who do the most to fray a doctor's nerves. And pregnant patients are the worst. One of the most recurrent and annoying phone calls I get is from the patient in labor asking for instructions."

People expect more of doctors now. They don't expect mistakes. They are more aware of the shortcomings and faults that take place in medicine. And there's been another attitude change, too. If a woman delivers a baby that has a defect, people are much more surprised. In the past, people understood that there wasn't much we could do about it.

Patients have high expectations of physicians, and so do other physicians. Doctors expect all their peers to practice medicine much the same way.

There are fads—new, unproven techniques—in medicine, and they come and go. Its easier to go with these fads, no matter how unscientific they might be. You can buck the trend better if you are an established authority in a large medical center. It's a lot harder to do that when you are just an ordinary workaday obstetrician. You have no credentials and no research to support your viewpoints. Therefore, you are compelled to practice what is called the "standard of care," that is, what is reasonable in the community, what other obstetricians do. That's the threat, that's the problem. If you are outside the "standard of care," you are potentially leaving yourself open for liability, criticism, and loss of license.

The medical profession has always regulated itself. Now it's just beginning to be held accountable to different segments of society. Doctors believe they should be the only ones to regulate themselves. Self-regulation is always an invitation to abuse, especially when so much power and money is involved. But many doctors set that idea aside and believe it doesn't apply to them. Government regulation is perceived as an invasion of their privacy and an attack on their integrity.

We don't police ourselves nearly as well as we could. We've got a long way to go, but I think attitudes are changing. The older doctors resent any policing of hospital procedures, because they've been God so long. Nobody ever questioned them before. "Medicine is not fun anymore," they say. "Everyone is telling us what to do and what not to do." I think the younger physicians coming up are going to practice in an era of peer review. People are going to know what doctors are doing. Due to liability concerns and consumer demands, hospitals and doctors are going to have to protect themselves through self-regulation.

Although many other professionals put in as many years of schooling and work as many hours in a week as physicians do, there remains a difference. Only physicians make life-and-death decisions though nurses often feel that responsibility, too. And this is perhaps the greatest pressure of all. To add to the stress of making these decisions, patients willingly give that power to doctors. Often we want the doctor to decide, thereby adding to his pressure to perform without error.

Physicians do want the best medical care for you. However, your doctor is trained to believe that, of the two of you, he's the best judge of what that is. It probably won't be any easier for your doctor to change his ways than it is for the rest of us to change our unrealistic expectations. He not only is trained to believe he's always right, he also has peer pressure from his colleagues to not rock that boat called "the status quo."

But there is a right birth attendant for you. Our next chapter describes how to find your "Dr. Right," a person who will be your health care partner—not your boss. The search is yours, because ultimately you, and only you, are responsible for your health and well-being.

FIVE

FINDING DR. RIGHT

> Women must realize first that they do have a right to
> say how they want their babies delivered, with whom
> and where. . . . Like everything else—one must care
> to have things a certain way. If there is no strong
> desire, then the doctor, as most people do, will follow
> whatever practices that are convenient for him. We
> need to educate women who will then demand proper
> services from doctors and hospitals.
>
> —BALTIMORE MOTHER

Knowing what birth options you want is no guarantee that
you'll get them or that you'll experience all birth's potential
pleasure. But it's a step. Understanding your doctor's point of
view based on his training and background is also a necessary
step. Next in getting the birth you want is not only choosing the
right birth attendant, but establishing a relationship, based on
thorough communication, that works in the best interests of
you, your baby, *and* your doctor.

This chapter tells you one step at a time how to find Dr.
Right, what to do once you're in his office, what to say/do/ask
when you're face-to-face with him, what questions you need
answered, what's in it for him to work with an informed
consumer, your legal rights, and, of course, what his responsibility is to you and what your own responsibility is in your
health care. To know where you're starting from, compare
your attitude to the following list:

1. You want your doctor to take over and be totally in
   charge.
2. You want the doctor to keep you informed, but you
   want him to make all the decisions.

3. You want to be informed, and when it comes to making medical decisions, you do it in partnership with your doctor.
4. You consider a doctor your consultant only and will make all decisions regarding your health care, except in a life-and-death emergency.

If your choice is #1 or #2, you are in the mainstream of American medical consumers who prefer "take-charge" physicians, 1988 research shows. Doctors are most accustomed to and comfortable with working with people like you. If your choice is #3 or #4, you are a pioneer in developing the partnership between pregnant women and their doctors. Like a pioneer anywhere, you're preparing the way for others, while risking criticism for yourself.

You may find that some doctors will be most unreceptive to your questions, particularly if your attitude is #3 or #4. However, these attitudes are your best chance of getting the birth you want, and when you do find Dr. Right, the search will have been worth it.

HOW TO FIND DR. RIGHT

Let's take it from the beginning. You think you're pregnant and you start to look around for the right doctor for you. You look at your current doctor. Your friends also make suggestions. The Baltimore COMA researchers asked women to list all the reasons for choosing their ob. Nine out of ten women put at the top of their list these two reasons: he already was her gynecologist, or he was referred by a friend or relative. (The other most important reasons were his ability to communicate and his hospital affiliation.) Effective communication was the most important reason why Lamaze-prepared parents chose their obstetrician according to research published in *Research in Nursing and Health* by Monica Brien and others in 1983.

Because nearly all of you will choose a physician, we call your birth attendant Dr. Right. For most of you, he is an obstetrician; for others, a family practitioner, or for a few, an osteopath. If your search is for a midwife, you can still follow the same process.

MAKING A LIST

I am again shopping for a doctor, a doctor who delivers at a hospital with practices I agree with. I would like to have a doctor who has a midwife working with him or her. I definitely know what I want and don't want next time and I will try not to get myself into an undesirable situation again. I plan to find out what I can about the doctor even before I see him or her, and then, during the first visit, make sure our ideas are in accord.

Start with the recommendations of others and make a list. When getting names, ask why this person is being recommended. You'll soon discover that many of the reasons aren't sufficient for a well-informed consumer like yourself. The key is to know what you want and find the person who will give it to you. Would you choose your partner in your health care for these reasons?

- He goes to my church and lives in the neighborhood. (He may even vote the same ticket, but that doesn't mean he's familiar with a Leboyer gentle birth or that he will help you avoid drugs in labor.)
- Your Aunt Sally says he has a wonderful bedside manner. (Your doctor probably won't get to the side of your bed until you're ready to deliver the baby.)
- She's the only woman doctor in town. (If your number-one priority is a woman, and your town doesn't have midwives, then this is obviously a valuable piece of information to add to your list. But if one of your reasons for having a woman doctor is that she's more likely to give you what you want because she's a woman, don't count on it. Women doctors experience the same medical training that men do. Chances are though, according to some research, a woman physician will pay more attention to your personal relationship with her than her male colleagues might. Since 51 percent of ob residents are now women, your chances of finding a woman practitioner increase all the time.)

Some people also look in the yellow pages or their town's medical directory (available at the public library). That can help you get a geographical fix on the doctors in town. But mere names and locations don't tell you enough.

Physicians often suggest to consumers that a hallmark to look for when doctor-shopping is board certification. This term means that a doctor has completed the required years of medical training and, in addition, has passed a series of professional competency exams in his specialty. Board certification, in the case of obstetricians, however, may work against your having your baby your way, unless you're having a cesarean. Those who put in that extra effort may be even more likely to want to use the interventive skills they've learned in their training. Board certification is no guarantee that your doctor will listen to your preferences, or that he has experience or interest in assisting you with your birth, free of unnecessary interference.

CHECKING IT TWICE

There are three valuable groups of people who can help you double-check your list: nurses who work on hospital ob floors; childbirth educators; and La Leche League leaders.

Before you call any of these, though, make up a list of key issues for your birthing experience, in order of priority. (If having your other children visit you after the birth is crucial, ask that question first—not last.) If you've never had a baby before, talk to your friends who might qualify as informed consumers and read a few books to help you think about what you want. Just because you've never had a baby doesn't necessarily mean you won't have strong preferences when the time for your labor and birth arrives.

Hospital nurses are proud of their ob units and are generally happy to help pregnant women who call for information, though some refuse to comment. The nurse can tell you which doctors are likeliest to help mothers with unmedicated births; what the hospital's cesarean rate is and which doctors do the fewest cesareans; who doesn't routinely have laboring women hooked up to IVs and fetal monitors throughout labor; who's the most enthusiastic about fathers in the delivery room; and more. These hospital ob nurses can also give you the phone numbers of local childbirth educators and La Leche League leaders.

Most women giving birth in the U.S. today attend childbirth-education classes in the last trimester of pregnancy.

Increasing numbers also go to early pregnancy classes. If you are in one of these classes now, talk to your teacher. If you aren't currently in a class, you can still call a childbirth teacher. She'll be glad to help you. Also, consider contacting La Leche League.

Both of these groups of women, La Leche League leaders and childbirth educators, are very knowledgeable about birth and caring for babies. They offer monthly meetings that attract large groups of women—pregnant or, in the case of La Leche League, new mothers, too. Though they may not give you direct physician or midwife referrals, they'll answer your questions about the reputations of the doctors on your list, and about the care that individual hospitals in your area give to new mothers. Be specific with them about your preferences. If you want your baby with you immediately after birth, with your body, not an incubator, warming your baby's body, say that. Don't ask which doctors believe in "bonding." That's too vague. You'll quickly zero in on those doctors most willing to give you your preferences.

DON'T FORGET THE HOSPITAL

Next time I will shop for a hospital as well as a doctor. Next time I definitely want rooming-in; I definitely want my first child to be able to visit me in the hospital, and to see her new brother or sister; I would really like to have a Leboyer delivery; I would really like to have the baby with my husband and me in recovery; I want to be able to feed my baby after its birth and have a period of closeness with it. To me the issue of bonding is much more important than whether I have an enema, prep, or an episiotomy.

You need to find "Hospital Right" as surely as you need to find Dr. Right. One mother who lived in a town without its own hospital found the right one by sending a questionnaire to ten hospitals within a fifty-mile radius of her home. All but one administrator responded, and her decision was easy, based on the replies. However, those of you who have prepaid medical plans that confine you to specific health-care providers and hospitals will not have that luxury. Your choices are more limited, and you may need to be more creative. See "How to Be a Changemaker," page 300. Then convert those suggestions for changing hospital practices for all women into getting those changes for yourself.

What about those local advertisements you've seen that show a nurse at a phone and a number you can call? Or better yet, what about the hospitals that advertise a "birth planner"? Yes, the women who answer the phones can give you a referral, but it will be for someone on their staff because its their staff that is paying for the phone-referral service. And, yes, the "birth planners" can talk to you about your preferences, but like all other birth plans, it will have to fit into that particular hospital's "menu" of services.

Some of the questions you will ask about hospitals may be the same ones you'll ask of prospective doctors. Following is a sampling:

1. *Do you have a birth room?* If so, who can use it? (Regulations vary from hospital to hospital.) Is the birth room always staffed? (Some hospitals do not have nurses in birth rooms all the time. It is possible to have your doctor plan to use this facility, but when you get there in labor, no one may be available for nursing duty.)

2. *How many nurses are available at a time for how many women in labor?* If the hospital has a shortage of nurses throughout the ob unit, but in every other respect is the right hospital for you, you might want to consider hiring a private-duty nurse (a monitrice) for your labor. (More on that later.)

3. *If a cesarean becomes necessary, can your partner stay?* If they say yes, ask which doctors (including anesthesiologists) arrange for partners in the cesarean operating room. Though the mate's presence in the operating room is more common than it once was, that arrangement is not automatic, especially if you are a single mom.

4. *When is the baby separated from the parents?* Pursue specific details. If you're told babies can be with parents all the time, ask, "You mean for twenty-four hours a day? There's no routine taking the baby back to the nursery for a newborn check or pediatrician visits?"

5. *What's the average cost?* Costs vary from hospital to

hospital. Even if you have insurance, most policies do not pay 100 percent of hospital maternity costs.

6. *Can fathers visit twenty-four hours a day?* In some hospitals dad can not only be there all the time, but the hospital will provide a bed for him in your room. In other hospitals, he's confined to visiting hours. Hospitals vary just as much in their policies about siblings visiting mom and the new baby.

It's essential that you know every hospital maternity floor has two sets of rules—one written and one unwritten. It's possible that any rule you might want to break has already been broken at least once (if only by a doctor's wife).

The written rule is the policy determined by the ob committee of the hospital—and includes rules about being able to labor and give birth in the same bed or not having your other children with you during labor and birth. Policies are hard to break, but not impossible.

On the other hand, the unwritten rule is the doctor's protocol—his routine recommendations for his patients. All hospital ob nurses know each doctor's routine. (That's why the ob nurses you called could answer your questions, not only about what the hospital rules are, but about what options individual doctors offer.) Examples are: routinely ordering a prep (shave of the perineum) or an IV on admission, an epidural at eight centimeters, or water for your baby in the nursery.

Issues like these are almost always doctors' routines, not the hospital's. Protocols vary tremendously from doctor to doctor in the same hospital, even for doctors who are partners in a practice together.

You will have difficulty getting information on rates of intervention in your local obstetrical unit unless a consumer group or childbirth educators have surveyed for this information. An exception is the state of Massachusetts. There the law requires that hospitals provide information about the rate of cesareans, so that consumers have a basis for comparison. (For information about some other states, see the "Public Citizen Health Research Group," listing, Your List of Helpers.) It's easier to find out about individual doctors than hospitals. One way to get information on intervention in general at any one hospital is to contact the head nurse or director of nursing and ask what percentage of mothers avoid episiotomies or do not

have analgesia or anesthesia or do not use a fetal monitor. Turn
the figures around to estimate intervention rates.

ASKING THE INITIAL QUESTIONS

After you've talked with friends and relatives, scoured the
yellow pages, consulted with hospital nurses (not only about
doctors, but about hospital options, too), childbirth educators,
and LLL leaders, you'll be able to narrow down the list to the
two or three doctors who you believe will meet your preferences. The next step is to find out all you can on the phone
before you have that first appointment for a consultation. Call
the doctor's office and ask for the following information. In
some offices, nurse/receptionists freely offer these answers on
the phone; in others, you'll have to get some of them directly
from the doctor himself.

1. *How much does maternity care cost?* In most places,
   the obs charge the same fee. Family practitioners
   often charge somewhat less, as do midwives. Out-
   of-hospital birth centers usually have a package fee
   for both the birth attendant and the place of birth.
2. *What is the scheduled length of the appointments?*
   The closer appointments are (ten to fifteen minutes
   apart, rather than twenty to thirty, for instance), the
   more likely it is you'll do a lot of waiting, as well as
   be rushed through your appointment when you do see
   him. Ask how long patients wait. (If it turns out that,
   for other reasons, he's Dr. Right, find out when you
   should schedule an appointment to reduce waiting—
   perhaps first thing in the morning, or just after
   lunch.)
3. *Does he deliver babies at more than one hospital? If
   so, which ones?* Doctors in metropolitan areas usually deliver babies at more than one hospital. As
   mentioned earlier, each hospital has its own set of
   maternity options. Some arrange twenty-four-hour
   rooming-in, for example; most don't. Some have
   labor and delivery beds or birthing chairs; most don't.
   You'll already have some idea of what each hospital
   offers from the calls you made to hospital ob nurses.
   (In your search for the best birth attendant and best
   hospital, you may have to resolve the dilemma of Dr.

Right not being on staff at what could be "Hospital Right.")

4. *How many babies does he help birth in a month?* If it's fewer than ten, he's more likely to give you more of his time and interest. If his number is closer to thirty, beware. Remember, babies aren't born an average of one a day. He may assist as many as five or six mothers on a single day. If you are one of the five or six, you might rightfully be concerned whether you'll get adequate attention from him.

5. *What percentage of his patients does he help birth himself?* If you hire an ob, you naturally assume he'll help birth your baby. But many a woman has a rude awakening when someone else is there. Now he may say (and many have), "Of course, I'll deliver your baby, except if I'm not on call or if I'm out of town." At first hearing, it sounds as though he'll be there. Check further. Ask, "Well, about what percentage of your patients do you personally help birth—75 percent, 50 percent, 30 percent?" He'll have some idea. We know from our Boulder M.O.M. Survey how important it is for the majority of women to have their own doctor there—especially if you've gone to a lot of trouble to choose him. In a look at obs in our survey, the chance of any one of them being there was only about 60 percent. Most of the obs we've discussed this with were surprised that women found this issue so important. And it continues to be important. In 1986 research, women reported more satisfaction when their regular physician was there for the birth.

After all, how many obs have ever had a baby? Even many of the women doctors delivering babies today have not given birth. They do not know from personal experience how crucial it is to have familiar, nurturing birth attendants present. There are enough strangers (nurses and other hospital employees) to cope with as it is. Also, if the doctor you're talking to is an obstetrician, it was part of his training to be at births on a potluck basis, that is, only if he was on duty. He probably never saw any woman twice at his residency hospital during any part of the prenatal, birth, or postpartum period. From his point of view, it's just not a big deal.

If your doctor delivers fewer than ten babies a month, our research shows that the chances are good he'll be there for your birth. If he's part of a joint practice with other doctors (and most obs are), then the chance of his being there decreases as the number of partners goes up. If you are a member of a prepaid medical insurance plan, you may have no control over who will be there for your baby's birth. However, many family practitioners and most midwives help their own clients give birth even when they are not on call—it's part of their philosophy of continuity of care.

In spite of knowing your ob may not be there, you may still decide that a particular doctor is Dr. Right. If so, tell him that you would like to meet all the doctors who might cover for him when your baby is born. There may be more than just his partners. (There literally can be a dozen or more doctors who might be on call for you when you are in labor. In some HMOs the number of doctors has been as high as sixteen.)

When you do meet these other doctors, review with them the agreements that you and Dr. Right have made about maternity options.

My other complaint is obstetricians who have partners with ideas incompatible with their own. If it's your chosen obstetrician's night off, nine months of planning can go down the drain because the partner pushes anesthesia or just goes along with the routine.

If you specifically do not want a particular associate of Dr. Right to deliver your baby, find out if you can request someone else, if the doctor you don't want is the one on call. Sometimes you can, sometimes you can't. If you can't, make extra sure he and the nurses know what you want.

A special problem occurs for women in small towns with only one or two doctors to choose from. What do you do if Doctor #1 always delivers babies with spinals, and Doctor #2 usually induces labor—both options you don't want? As with women who have limited-choice insurance try to negotiate the best you can with what you've got. Or look farther afield if you're not limited by your insurance plan or income.

FACE-TO-FACE NEGOTIATIONS

When you've made your list of possibilities and gathered what information you can by phone, then make an appointment. Traditionally, initial visits for pregnancy include an internal exam to confirm pregnancy. Just because it's office routine, however, doesn't mean you have to do it that way. You do not need to have a particular doctor examine your body to find out if he is the right one for you.

Step One: Schedule a "Clothes-On, Sit-Up" Consultation

One mother confided, "The worst part in finding a new doctor when I was pregnant was going through an exam with yet another stranger. I didn't realize until my fourth pregnancy that I didn't have to do it that way. I could just schedule a consultation." Pelvic exams often make women feel humiliated. Why have more than you need?

This is very important: schedule a "clothes-on, sit-up" consultation. Tell the receptionist that you want a consultation first with Dr. X so that you can become acquainted and discuss the maternity options you want. Usually doctors charge for this, some occasionally do not.

The receptionist may say, "Fine." But perhaps she'll say, "We don't do that here; all initial visits include an exam."

Try saying, "I know this is not what you usually do, but it's very important to me." Repeat yourself, calmly, until she budges. (It usually doesn't take more than three times.) If you can't get a "clothes-on, sit-up" appointment, we suggest you scratch that doctor off your list.

Here's why. If you go ahead with the exam first, one of two outcomes is likely: you will find changing doctors extremely difficult even if the one who examined you is *not* Dr. Right; or, after he's examined you, the doctor is more likely to become angry at your questions, your taking your time to make up your mind, or your decision to change doctors. Remember, you are negotiating first whether this doctor is Dr. Right.

Some doctors (or more likely, office nurses) may argue that your pregnancy must be confirmed first by an exam before you do any talking. Let's say you have your consultation first, and then you decide he *is* Dr. Right. Now you have your physical exam, only to find out you're not pregnant, for heaven's sake. You may be embarrassed, but it's an honest mistake. It does happen. Know that you are that much farther along in your search for the right medical care when you do get pregnant.

Persistence in pursuing the consultation first generally gets you past even the best gatekeepers. Those are the folks who help the doctor run the office. Their goal is office efficiency through tried-and-true methods called the "routine." That is their job, and it is appropriate for them to want to fit you into their way of doing things. It is also appropriate for you, the paying customer, to have some say in how you and the doctor will work together.

Step Two: Conducting Your Interview

The time arrives for your "clothes-on, sit-up" appointment. Take your mate with you if you can. An increasing number of partners go to prenatal visits. Your mate may often have more questions than you do.

If your mate is unavailable, take another adult with you. More attention is paid to patients (whether in the doctor's office or in a hospital) if they are accompanied by another adult. The other person is effective whether he or she says one word. It's especially helpful if the person appears to be taking notes— even if he or she is only writing a grocery list. Doctors, like the rest of us, are more careful when others are writing down their words.

So, you and your companion arrive at the doctor's office. Now it may all go according to plan, and the two of you may be ushered into the doctor's office for your consultation.

Or what might happen is that the receptionist may invite you into an examining room and ask you to disrobe. Remind her that you're there for a consultation, and repeat your phone conversation until things go your way.

Perhaps at this point, you'll think to yourself, it's not worth making a big deal about this. Sooner or later, I'll need to be examined anyway, you say. Go over in your mind why it's important to consult first, examine last.

- It's difficult to change doctors after that initial exam.
- You give the impression to the doctor that you will be his patient when what you need is information and time to decide.

• Many women find it difficult to meet a new doctor while flat on their backs, their legs in stirrups, counting the dots on the ceiling tile to pass the examination time.

These are some possible reasons. You may have others. So stick by your goal. This is a consultation appointment.

Now you're in the doctor's office. You've introduced the other adult by saying, "So-and-so is here because this is a very important appointment for me and he [or she] will make sure I don't forget any major questions I have." Most doctors don't mind this; they want patients to understand their explanations, and they know that two sets of ears are better than one.

THE PROBLEM OF NAMES

Our intent is to help you train your ob to listen to you differently. It's well established that similarity in how we address each other encourages equality. The words you choose, in this instance, are not a matter of etiquette—they are an indication of power. So, now for that special problem—what do you call each other? If you call him "Doctor" and he calls you by your first name, you have several choices:

a) *Call him by his first name.*

A mother at one of our workshops told us, "It was easier for me to call him by his first name than to get him to call me by my last name. He was startled when I first called him 'Bob,' but after that we were both comfortable. It helped our rapport."

If this first-name basis shocks you and makes you feel disrespectful, remember this: it's common in employer-employee relationships that the boss addresses his employees by their first names, but he remains "Mr." It helps maintain a respectful distance. Your doctor is not your boss. You're paying him.

b) *Tell him you'd prefer to be called Mrs. (Or Ms. or Miss) Smith.*

If the idea of calling your doctor by his first name appalls you, why not suggest he address you by your last name?

All of us have anxious moments when we try new things. That's only normal. But it doesn't have to stop us from doing things we never have done before. The anxiety will pass. It really does get easier with practice.

c) *Make no changes.*

It's not a big deal, you say to yourself. Names are not the only sign of equality.

IT'S TIME FOR THE QUESTIONS:
WILL HE OR WON'T HE?

Following is a sampling of questions to ask prospective doctors:

Can my partner be with me during the labor and birth?

For some women, if the doctor, or hospital, doesn't allow their mates to be present during labor and birth, that's the end of the interview. But let's say you're willing to discuss the issue further.

If this person can't be present all the time, when would this person have to leave?

Some doctors encourage mates to be there all the time, even for cesareans. Others want mates to leave for all procedures, including progress checks (to see how far along labor is) or insertion of an IV needle. Chances are good you'll want your partner there all the time. If this person is asked to leave, you can just insist that your supporter stay, but that's a hassle you don't need. You should negotiate *in advance* whether he or she ever has to leave, so that if you run afoul of hospital routine, you can say, "Dr. X said my partners never have to leave. If you have any questions, ask Dr. X."

How many other people can be with me during labor and delivery?

In some hospitals (and in out-of-hospital birth centers and home births) many mothers invite others to be present for the labor and birth, for both moral support and companionship, as well as specific help in breathing techniques and relaxation. Some want their children, too. However, your doctor may say that the hospital has a policy that only allows your mate to be present. Well, maybe yes, maybe no. This rule is almost always doctor-decided. It may be easier for him to "blame" the hospital, but he and his peers have made the decision. How does this information help you? Well, perhaps you can negotiate a special arrangement for yourself. Try saying:

Dr. X, it's really important to me that my best friend be there with me during labor.

His answer could be that the room is too small for additional people, or that it's distracting to the nursing staff. Or he may laugh and say, "Do you want me to put up bleachers and sell tickets?"

What do you do? You keep repeating the same phrase:

Dr. X, it's really important to me that my best friend be there with me during labor.

Repeat it in the same calm way until you're satisfied, one way or the other.

Example:

DOCTOR: "Your friend can stay, but if she gets upset or interferes with nursing routine, I may ask her to leave." Or, "That's absolutely out of the question."

You may accept the first reply as a reasonable compromise. The second reply may lead you, however, to find another doctor. It depends on how important it is to you. If part of your fact-finding early on was talking to hospital ob nurses, then you'll have a good idea which doctors do arrange for other people in the labor room, as well as which hospitals encourage or discourage it.

YOU: *I want you to hand me my baby as soon as it is born, and I don't want it to leave my arms for at least two hours.*

DOCTOR: You want that messy baby? We'll clean him up before we give him to you.

YOU: *I want you to hand me my baby as soon as it is born, and I don't want it to leave my arms for at least two hours.*

DOCTOR: Sure, but we must check the baby for vital signs, weigh him, and clean him up first.

YOU: *I'm perfectly agreeable to your checking him while I hold him. I have no objection to your cleaning and weighing him. I'm just asking you to do it later, at least two hours later.*

DOCTOR: It will take only five minutes to check your baby to see if all is normal. We can do it in the delivery room. Except for that five minutes, your baby will be in your arms.

You decide if that's reasonable. If not, keep talking or look for someone else.

YOU: *I want to see my other children immediately after the baby is born, either in my own room or in the recovery room. I want them to see and hold the baby, too.*

DOCTOR: Our hospital policy prevents children from coming into the recovery room.

YOU: *It is very important for me to see my children immediately. They could be brought up to my private room where I could go with my baby straight from the delivery room.*

DOCTOR: The nursing staff doesn't like children on the floor.

YOU: *I'll see to it that the adult caregiver with my children makes sure they move quietly through the halls and enter only my room. I agree with you that children should be respectful of others, but it's still very important to me that I see my children immediately after the birth.*

DOCTOR: If your birth is normal, I can arrange for you to go immediately to your postpartum room instead of the recovery room. Your children can visit you there if, indeed, there is an adult caregiver with them.

You decide if that's reasonable. If not, keep talking or look for someone else.

What's your policy about the use of ultrasound?

It's a rare pregnant woman in the United States and Europe today who doesn't use at least one form of ultrasound, but more likely at least three. Most pregnant women like the reassurance that ultrasound gives them, though British research shows that the uncertainty over its safety makes most of them worry. Obstetricians use ultrasound the most, midwives use it the least.

Following is a description of the four instruments that use prenatal ultrasound:

1. *Ultrasound scan.* This works by bouncing sound waves off the abdomen to determine the shape and position of the fetus. It allows doctors to "see" the fetus, and is used to determine your baby's age, though several studies show that scans are no more accurate in determining your baby's age or your due date than the old-fashioned way of dating from your last menstrual period. Scans are also used to detect ectopic pregnancies (those outside the uterus) or for the diagnosis of unexplained vaginal bleeding and some fetal anomalies. When ultrasound is used for these purposes, several scans are required because of the difficulty in diagnosis and, therefore, high error rate. Scans are also used to determine the presence of two or more babies, though the scans are not always accurate. More importantly, the outcome of these multiple babies is not improved by the use of ultrasound during pregnancy.

2. *Doptone or Doppler*. This is a hand-held fetal stethoscope used to detect fetal heartbeat. Nearly all physicians, but not midwives, use this routinely in monthly prenatal visits. The Doptone, it's believed exposes your baby to many times the exposure used in a scan, because the sound waves of a Doptone are continuous, not pulsed as they are in the scan.

3. *External electronic fetal monitor*. This records fetal heartbeat and sometimes fetal movement during labor. The Doppler device is contained in the belt that goes around the mother's abdomen.

4. *Vaginosonographic scan,* a newer version of prenatal ultrasound, scans the vaginal area instead of your abdomen to determine early pregnancy.

Although there is obvious widespread use of ultrasound, there's much concern about the possible side effects. According to a 1982 report from the American Medical Association, "Until physicians can say with assurance that ultrasound does not produce subtle or delayed harmful effects, it should be used only when medically indicated." In 1980 Marion Finke, M.D., director of the FDA's New Drug Evaluation Division stated: "There's increasing concern regarding the fetal safety of widely used diagnostic ultrasound in obstetrics. Animal studies have been reported to reveal delayed neuromuscular development, altered emotional behavior, changed brainwaves, abnormalities and decreased survival. Genetic alterations have also been demonstrated."

Concern over ultrasound use has continued since then, though actual use of ultrasound has doubled in the same time period. The U.S. Food and Drug Administration (FDA) ultrasound consent form, which you may be asked to sign before using any ultrasound, states in part: "I understand that the question of subtle and/or latent effects of prenatal and intranatal exposure to diagnostic ultrasound remains unanswered."

Most researchers believe that whatever damage there may be from ultrasound is dose related and probably subtle. The more exposure your baby has, however, the greater the risk for side effects. It also depends on the baby's age at exposure (early on may have more effects than later in pregnancy), the accuracy of the machine's adjustments, and whether ultrasound is used in a scan or in the Doppler.

How often and what version of ultrasound is safest is the typical kind of decision today's pregnant women make. And since there's no standard of care regarding ultrasound, that is, no universal rule among physicians about appropriate use, some of you will be asked to have ultrasound many more times than other women. When you're considering using ultrasound, you may want to ask yourself if the results of it will change anything about your pregnancy or your treatment.

What is your definition of "high-risk" pregnancy?

According to authors Roger K. Freeman, M.D., and Susan C. Pescar of *Safe Delivery: Protecting Your Baby During High-Risk Pregnancy,* the following conditions are high risk: diabetes, hypertension, heart disease, Rh incompatibility, kidney disease, some thyroid disorders, severe asthma, incompetent cervix and uterine malformation, a sexually transmitted disease, cancer, or some other disease that could affect the pregnancy's outcome.

A lesser list includes a history of any of the following: miscarriage, premature birth, stillbirth, bleeding problems, a previous abnormal child. Or you've been exposed to rubella and you are not immune, certain toxins, extensive radiation, certain chemicals, specific drugs. Other factors: a family history of hereditary disease or genetic disorder, smoking cigarettes, chronic alcohol consumption, taking unnecessary or potentially damaging drugs and being seriously overweight or underweight. Add women who have had three previous births or who are past age thirty-five to the high-risk group, as most doctors do, and it's no wonder that Dr. Freeman estimates that "20 percent to 25 percent of pregnant women are probably in the high-risk group."

So how does that affect you? "The term 'high-risk pregnancy' means something different to everyone," state Freeman and Pescar. Just as with the terms bonding and rooming-in, there's no uniform accepted definition. But if you are labeled "high risk," you automatically will be exposed to many pregnancy and birth interventions, though your pregnancy and birth may be as uneventful as any so-called "low-risk" pregnancy.

What can you do? Get a second opinion. And don't assume that if you, for instance, have a history of miscarriage, that means you automatically need amniocentesis, or that you'll need to be monitored electronically throughout labor, or have your labor induced. Always pursue specific answers to your questions about you. Ask what your options are, what the risks/benefits are.

Your line of questioning is seldom going to be answered with a simple yes or no. A doctor's replies are based on his own standard of care—his belief about what good medical care is—and his belief system maybe different from yours. His own personal experience affects every answer he gives you. Do not expect a doctor to be enthusiastic about something he has never tried before (allowing several people to be with you during labor and the birth, for instance, or letting you give birth in a supported squatting position).

GETTING IT ALL IN WRITING

Perhaps after your first interview you'll be satisfied that this, indeed, is Dr. Right. So you can tell him right then. Or you can let the doctor know later.

Whether you're sure he's Dr. Right or not, thank him for his time and tell him that you'll call the office with your decision. Don't pressure yourself to make a decision while you're sitting there. He doesn't need to know instantly. If you're not sure he's Dr. Right, interview the next doctor on your list.

I have a very progressive doctor, and he asked me for a list when I was pregnant of what I wanted in my childbirth experience, in terms of anesthesia, enemas, preps, stirrups, the whole bit. I wrote it all out—including the labor, the delivery, the postpartum experience. He took my list, we went over each item. He said okay to everything that was on my list. It became part of my chart, and I never had any problems with anybody.

Now your doctor may not ask you for a list, but that's no reason why you can't give him one.

Somewhere about the sixth or seventh month of pregnancy, after you and your doctor have had several chances to talk over your desired options, it's time to get it in writing. It may seem that asking your doctor for his signature shows a lack of trust on your part, but your doctor will not be with you all the time you're in the hospital. This signed paper takes your doctor's place. It also helps your health-care provider focus on you in particular.

Summarize your options on paper. Get your doctor's signature on it, in case he's not there at the labor and birth or, more likely, doesn't get there until some hours after you do. Give a copy to each of the possible substitute doctors when you meet with them. Have Dr. Right's partners sign the agreement, and leave a copy with each possible substitute. When there's a question about this or that being different from the routine, just wave your paper and say, "My doctor has agreed to this. If you have any questions, ask him." Incidentally, if he refuses to sign the paper, write down his verbal agreement and use the paper anyway.

Does that mean that your labor and birth will follow your birth plan to the letter? No. We don't want to mislead you. There are no guarantees for your birth plan, though you'll increase your chances of its effectiveness enormously by having a doula. (See chapter 11.) That's because once you're in labor, you're not likely to argue about birth-plan items if you're told that your child is "in danger." And forget about discussing an unplanned cesarean in a calm manner. You'll be in the throes of labor, likely feeling much pain, and worried about your baby because of the comments that have been made to you.

> It is somewhat misleading and unrealistic to imply that you are, or could be, in complete control in an environment that's set up to protect doctors and hospitals. Even when you have worked out all the bugs and are informed as to what your options are, there is always that gray area where no one is completely responsible.
>
> —MISSOURI MOTHER

> During pregnancy #2 I spoke to my obstetrician many times about my preferences. He assured me that "if" all went well I could "probably" have a delivery with no interventions. Too many ifs and probablys.
>
> —CANADIAN MOTHER

However, your job is not done after you've passed out the list. You have to continually reinforce it. Repeat every visit: "Remember, I'm the one who wants . . ."

CHANGING DOCTORS MIDPREGNANCY

During my first visits, my ob was thorough, very nice, and talked about her kids. She had been my gynecologist for years. When I was seven months pregnant, my husband and I took in our birth plan. The interview was a complete disaster. We wanted no routine Pitocin; she threatened us with possible infant brain damage if we didn't use it. When I said I didn't want medication, she said, "You can hurt as much as you please and you will." It went from bad to worse. When I said I didn't want a routine IV, she said she'd be "sloshing in my blood which would be all over the floor." Brain damage, agony, and death? Hardly the image of joyous childbirth I had imagined. I knew I had to change doctors and discovered it wasn't as difficult as I thought it would be. I was welcomed by the birth center I transferred to and thrilled with my birth there.

—COLORADO MOTHER

What if you get this far—or even farther—in your pregnancy, and you discover this is not Dr. Right? You realize you can't compromise as much as he wants you to. Should you change doctors? The natural vulnerability and dependency of pregnancy work to keep women from switching, but some women do change doctors. From our experience interviewing many women, those who have changed are very satisfied. The new Dr. Right will welcome you. You will find cooperation much easier to get because you have gone to the trouble of changing doctors in mid- or late pregnancy. Although it doesn't happen often, some doctors—when faced with your requests—will dismiss you as a patient. They'll send you your records and tell you to go elsewhere. Count your blessings. He or she obviously wasn't Dr. Right.

Sometimes when pregnant women decide they must change doctors, they will agonize unnecessarily over how and what to tell the first doctor. You don't owe him a lengthy explanation, certainly not an apology. Your new doctor will handle the request for a transfer of your records, or he will ask you to call your former doctor's office and request that your records be transferred. You can let your former doctor know why you're transferring, but a brief letter is adequate. Most of the time, this will be the end of it. Don't expect him to agree with your decision or even to be civil about it. That's okay. It's your decision, not his.

WHAT'S IN IT FOR YOUR DOCTOR
TO NEGOTIATE WITH YOU

When a doctor answers a woman's questions, explains pertinent facts, and offers choices, the doctor gets an informed patient, less likely to call anxiously at all hours with fearful questions. That means fewer time and energy demands on him.

And, as pointed out previously, doctors who have trusting relationships with their patients have far fewer malpractice suits. Besides, consumers have a right to good communication, some doctors say. They believe it's the birth attendant's role to educate patients about their bodies so they can be informed partners in health care. It's like getting a warranty. Education goes with the product.

Also, doctors who are partners, not bosses, have less pressure on them to be godlike. Doctors know in their hearts that medicine is an inexact science. All of us can, and do, make mistakes—including physicians. Inviting a doctor to be your partner ultimately allows him to function at his best.

But let's also be frank. The doctor makes his living from helping women give birth. The more women he helps, the more money he makes. The doctor wins economically if you buy his services. And the word will get around very quickly (probably from you) that this doctor is one who supports women's preferences.

RESPONSIBILITY—HIS AND YOURS

You have a right to an explanation of, and the reasons for, any procedure that might be done to you by your doctor or the hospital. You also have the right to refuse any procedure. You have the right to be informed of the probable consequences to you and your baby and of any alternative to that procedure. The patient must have a chance to weigh the benefits against the risks.

The New York state legislature established a law that "requires that a physician or nurse-midwife must provide expectant mothers with information regarding the possible risks of obstetric drugs to the mother and her baby." While this specific, informed-consent law is on the books in New York, all doctors are certainly expected to inform their patients adequately enough to enable them to make decisions—or else they risk malpractice liability.

You have to do your part, too. It's your responsibility, not the doctor's, to ask for plain English when you don't understand medical terminology. It's also your responsibility to keep notes during your pregnancy of your conversations with your doctor, regarding explanations of procedures and descriptions of drug side effects. Don't rely on memory alone, no matter how good a memory you have.

Communicate your preferences clearly, frequently, and repeatedly. If you don't, no one will read your mind. Doctors are as poor at mind reading as the rest of us. Doctors have repeatedly told us that their patients don't tell them what they like and don't like. How can you blame your health-care provider for not giving you what you want if you haven't asked?

YOUR LEGAL RIGHTS

Stuart and Susan McElhinney, J.D., reported that the issue of the rights of birthing parents is really an unclear area of the law.

> Generally, however, any patient has the right to refuse any treatment. Because the law in most states has refused to recognize the fetus as a person, separate from the mother, the mother may be entitled to refuse treatments—including sonograms [ultrasound], fetal heart monitors and cesarean sections—which directly affect her fetus. However, we all must be aware that this rule is changing and that in many instances the fetus is held to have separate rights which the court may act to "protect." Of course, we note that this "protection" usually takes the form of orthodox medical actions.

In the same article the authors describe a case at a Denver hospital in 1980. A woman was in labor and her electronic fetal monitor registered what appeared to be severe fetal distress. Hospital staff urged her to have a cesarean. She refused. The staff called in a judge who declared that the fetus was endangered and the woman had to submit to having a cesarean. And she did. Although the staff had expected an infant in severe fetal distress because of the EFM readout and the time that had elapsed (nine hours after the recommendation of a cesarean), the actual outcome of the baby was good. Nevertheless, the staff and attorneys felt they had taken proper action.

During the rest of the 1980s, cases of "forced" cesareans spread to ten more states. Most of these women were black, Asian, or Hispanic, about half were single, about one-fourth did not speak English as a primary language, and all were on public assistance. Like the results in the Colorado case, when the fetal monitor was used to diagnose the problem, none of the babies showed signs of fetal distress after they were born. Though the American College of Obstetricians and Gynecologists said in 1987, "resort to the courts is almost never justified," about half of surveyed obstetricians in 1988 said it's okay to have court-ordered cesareans.

You can avoid confrontations like this at your hospital by discussing with Dr. Right all issues important to you (including when and why he does cesareans) ahead of time, while you're still pregnant.

All of the steps we suggest may not apply to your situation or you may be reluctant to try every one. However, even doing one thing differently in your contact with your doctor is a sure sign of success. One step leads to another, and each time you try something new, it gets easier the next time. A woman in labor is in no condition to fight with her doctor or the hospital staff. She must negotiate her options ahead of time. We also believe that a true partnership with your health provider accomplished carefully visit by visit, question by question—is an important step toward personal satisfaction with the whole birth process.

SIX

OBSTETRICIANS' BELIEFS
ABOUT A "SAFE BIRTH"

No doubt about it, if ten women went into the jungle to
have a baby, nine would walk out with healthy babies.

—AN OBSTETRICIAN IN PRACTICE FOR TWENTY YEARS

I think I should practice the best medicine. All of my
patients are hooked up to fetal monitors and IVs during
labor.

—THE SAME OBSTETRICIAN

Why is it so difficult to get what you want? Why do you have
to negotiate with your physician for what surely is a perfectly
normal experience? In these modern times, why can't you just
go to the hospital and have your baby your way? You've read
articles in magazines that paint a beautiful picture of giving
birth: the mother labors with her partner's assistance, nurses'
help, and the doctor's encouragement. She delivers with great
joy and immediately gets to hold her baby. Then mother,
father, and infant spend the first few minutes after birth getting
acquainted. Isn't that the way it always is? No, it isn't.

Of your four friends who just had babies, one had a
cesarean, two had drugs to start or speed their labors, and also
regional anesthesia they had hoped to avoid. Only one had her
baby the way magazine articles describe as typical.

You may have wondered as you read the two quotes by the
same obstetrician at the beginning of this chapter how he could
say two things that seem so contradictory. Easy! Most obstetricians say they believe anywhere from 80 percent to 95
percent of births are "normal." Turning that around, they also
believe that from 5 percent to 20 percent of births will have

problems. One obstetrician told us, "Five percent of the time there are problems that arise, and these are the problems that we are here for." Yet most physicians believe those kinds of labels can only be put on a birth *after* the birth is over. As an eminent pediatrician wrote to the *Denver Post*, "There is no such thing as normal childbirth except after the fact." A prominent obstetrician said, "Normal pregnancy is really a retrospective diagnosis." Obstetricians believe that at the time they are handling your birth, they are handling a very dangerous situation.

Confirming our statement that most obstetricians believe that birth is a dangerous, high-risk procedure was a *McCall's* magazine report on a national survey of 243 obstetricians. *McCall's* stated, "The majority of obstetricians continue to picture childbirth as an event fraught with danger best left to the hands of an expert." Individual survey responses expressed that view: "The consumer ideas aren't going to decrease mortality and that's what it's all about." And another: "Some patients are trying to tell doctors how and when to deliver. That's ridiculous." And another: "The majority of pregnancies are high risk."

WHAT IS HIGH RISK?

Women who are high risk are simply more likely to have problems in their pregnancy or with their childbirth or baby than those who are low risk. The words "high risk" applied to a pregnant woman mean that she should be watched carefully for complications that may affect her or her baby. The factors that make a pregnant woman high risk are medical and social. The social factors known to make her high risk include being unmarried or poor, for example. Medical factors include high blood pressure, toxemia, or other serious diseases in the mother.

A high-risk labor includes women who have been labeled medically at high risk during pregnancy and all premature and induced labors. (Some doctors see augmented labors as high risk also.) These labors can result in a normal birth, but they are more likely to require the birth attendant's intervention for the best outcome for mother or baby. High-risk deliveries include cesarean and breech births.

A high-risk designation does *not* mean a woman or her baby

will have problems. One of the drawbacks with labeling is that the doctor or the pregnant woman may forget that. Once a woman is labeled high risk, the doctor and woman may act as if she or her baby *will* have problems. Unnecessary interventions to end the pregnancy may then take place. For example, a doctor may tell a woman he wants to deliver her breech baby by cesarean section a week before her due date. That presumes that the woman or her baby will have problems if she is allowed to go into spontaneous labor and deliver vaginally. The doctor and woman have forgotten that the high-risk label is a decision made in the minds of those who use the words, and it may or may not really exist for that particular woman.

Over half of dead, injured, or defective babies are delivered by the 20 percent or so of pregnant women who are labeled high risk. "The bulk of unsatisfactory outcomes of pregnancy derive from a relatively small proportion of the obstetric population," said Richard Aubry, M.D., writing "ACOG's Standards for Safe Childbearing." By intensifying care for these women, by applying high-quality, prenatal care and high-technology childbirth care to them *when needed*, many doctors believe the greatest gains can be made in reducing the number of dead or damaged babies.

MANY DOCTORS BELIEVE ALL BIRTH IS HIGH RISK

The words "high risk" are so widely applied today that most obs look at most of their patients this way. "We'll take [high-risk or difficult birth] patients the community hospitals can't, and we should," said William Clewell, M.D., of University Hospital of Denver, interviewed in 1982. "But the term 'high risk' gets kind of muddy. What some are calling high risk is not what we're calling high risk."

Most obs believe they are handling a dangerous situation with all births, including the low-risk woman. She's the healthy, married woman who has carried her baby to term, who has no serious medical problems, and who has started labor spontaneously. "You never know which woman will have complications or which baby will need intensive care; therefore, we need to treat all women as high risk," is the belief. Doctors point out that 30 percent of the admissions to neonatal intensive care units come from babies born to low-risk pregnant women. And more than half of the complications of childbirth occur in low-risk women.

"This seems to be a *damning defense* of the present system of obstetric care," said author Doris Haire, D.M.S., president of the American Foundation of Maternal and Child Health. "It compels one to ask what proportion of these complications, which had their onset *during* labor and birth, are the direct result of aggressive obstetric procedures." She quotes Professor G. T. Kloosterman, M.D., chairman of the department of obstetrics at the University of Amsterdam, Netherlands: "The spontaneous labor in a healthy woman is an event marked by a number of processes which are so complex and so perfectly attuned to each other that any interference will *only* detract from their optimal character. The doctor, always on the lookout for pathology and eager to interfere, will too often change true physiologic aspects of human reproduction into pathology."

WHERE DOCTORS' BELIEFS COME FROM

Doctors certainly do not believe that what they are doing causes complications in births and problems in the babies. "It is threatening to be told that what you are doing is not good, that you may have been hurting people," obstetrician Vic Berman, M.D., told us. "Doctors simply can't say what they have been doing for twenty years is wrong. If it were wrong, *they* were hurting babies. That's a totally unacceptable idea."

The obstetrician's training and his peers tell him that what he is doing is right. And his everyday experience with complications in birth shows him he needs to get in there and do more, not less. Besides, interventions and technology make an obstetrician's practice more interesting. "Every doctor enjoys his intervention," obstetrician John Franklin, M.D., told writer Alice Lake. "That's what his skill and training are for. Some think that nature is in constant need of improvement and others that nature can't be trusted, but one kind of intervention leads to another and then the doctor is kept busy seeking remedies for his own actions." The doctor's definition of "safe" is decided by his training, his peers, and his personal experiences—all of which tell him that all childbirth is high risk.

A SAFE BIRTH

If all childbirth is seen to be dangerous, the overriding concern of the obstetrician, naturally, becomes "a safe birth." Those are "buzz" words we find obstetricians using frequently: "I can't do that because it's not *safe*." "I find an epidural is a *safe* way to deliver a baby." "The delivery room is the only *safe* place for your baby to be born."

Women are very vulnerable when the doctor uses the word "safe" or "unsafe." *Of course* you are going to do what you are told will ensure your baby's safety. But you will come far in the art of negotiating to have your baby your way if you understand what "a safe birth" means to many obstetricians. There are six key elements; a "safe birth"

- Is actively managed
- Is predictable
- Is controlled by the obstetrician
- Takes place in the hospital
- Is attended by an obstetrician
- Is solely measured by a live baby and a live mother

A "safe birth" is actively managed. Among themselves, obstetricians call this "the aggressive management of parturition," writes Sandra Anderson, R.N., M.S., an instructor in community health at the University of Arizona College of Nursing. "In an effort to decrease maternal and infant mortality, modern obstetrics has developed its intervention to the point of 'active management' of not only the high-risk group but almost all labors and birth." But why active management of all labors and births? In *Patient Care* magazine, George Ryan, M.D., Professor of Obstetrics and Gynecology, University of Tennessee, Center for Health Sciences, is quoted: "A short obstetric hospital stay is a retrospective accomplishment. All patients require the same facilities and services during labor and delivery." But why all? An obstetrician explained to us, "You have to understand that we look at things virtually 180 degrees differently from you [consumers]. You are all saying this would be very pleasant and nice. Unfortunately, in medicine we have to do things for the minority situation, which is 5 percent of the time when things go wrong. We'll never have a meeting of minds on this issue because you look at things from the opposite standpoint. We are doing things and setting up rules and regulations for the small number of cases that are going to be bad, not for the large number that are going to be good."

Obstetricians honestly believe that all women, and babies about to be born, deserve the very best in technology. A West Coast family practitioner described to us what it was like to work with obstetricians: "The impression I got was that if you didn't do all these fancy things for the mother and the baby, somehow you were not providing optimal care. Optimal obstetrical care was that which used all the new technology." Technology is essential to the active management of labor and delivery.

A "safe birth" is predictable. When a birth is actively managed, it is quite predictable. The obstetrician knows the risks of his procedures, and he has faith that he can handle them with another procedure, if necessary. For instance, if the epidural he's given to a mother slows her labor, he can speed it up with Pitocin. If that same epidural prevents her from pushing, he can use forceps.

His basis for measuring whether your labor is going "normally" comes from a generally accepted medical standard called the "parameters of normal labor." For instance, if a woman's bag of waters breaks, it is expected that she will soon start to labor, and will deliver within twenty-four hours. Whenever labor begins, the woman is expected to deliver within twelve hours. When a woman is in what is called "active labor," after three or four centimeters dilation, obstetricians expect her cervix to dilate at least a centimeter an hour. In the second stage of labor, the delivery, the belief is that a woman shouldn't have to push for more than one or perhaps two hours, less if she has already given birth. For the third stage, or the delivery of the placenta, it's generally agreed that the woman should be given about a half hour before the birth attendant begins to extract the placenta. However, as one doctor told us, "Nobody waits that long. Everybody starts pulling on the cord sooner."

If your labor and delivery do not follow the above timetable, the obstetrician's belief in the active management of labor requires that he do something to bring your labor within the "normal" range. Using his tools of intervention carries some risk to the mother and the baby, but the obstetrician believes he can handle any complications that result from his own procedures. For example, two of the most common complications of "intensive obstetrical care" reported by Madeleine Shearer, R.P.T., editor of *Birth*, are newborn scalp infections (from fetal monitors) and maternal intrauterine infections. Both of these complications the obstetrician believes can be handled easily with antibiotics.

A "safe birth" is controlled by the obstetrician. Your doctor believes that he is giving you a safe birth and protecting your baby's interests when he denies you a part in the medical decision-making process. At the Northwest Regional International Childbirth Education Association convention in 1981, author and lecturer Suzanne Arms spoke to this issue when she said, "Society now has experts who believe we must leave important life decisions to them, that they know best." Doctors still hold to the view that they really do know what is best for you. As one doctor told us, "You do have to give us some credit for knowing technically what is best for the situation." Believing that he really does know what is best for you, he also supposes that you then have total trust in him.

This control by the obstetrician is the toughest issue to face in negotiations. He believes he knows what is best. You need to know what "best" means to him. You need to find out how your doctor handles childbirth.

In her book *The Hidden Malpractice*, Gena Corea writes that physicians consider it a misguided effort to inform women because it only leads to anxiety and loss of confidence in the physician. The prevailing attitude is, Don't confuse women by asking them to make decisions that are beyond their comprehension. Because obstetricians do not believe that women should make important decisions about their own deliveries, doctors sometimes become angry with inquiring pregnant women. The *McCall's* survey mentioned earlier analyzed responses from obstetricians across the country. The results "suggested a widespread disinterest in basic change and considerable irritation that accepted routines are being questioned at all."

You may have already experienced your obstetrician's irritation. Certainly a lot of women have. No one is necessarily immune. Suzanne Poppema, M.D., a family practitioner herself, was pregnant with her first baby when she had this experience. She was seeing an obstetrician substituting for her regular doctor. He spoke of using the fetal monitor on all of his patients. When she questioned him, suggesting that she didn't want to be attached to a machine, he became irritated with her. She later said, "I got the distinct impression that somehow I cared less about my baby than a woman who would have agreed that monitoring was the best way to go. When I shared with him the information that a very good study showed no evidence of benefit to monitoring low-risk labors, he said he didn't believe in the study. The impression I came away with was that, somehow, I wasn't quite as concerned about my baby as I should have been."

Where do the mother's preferences for her delivery fit in with a "safe birth"? Family Centered Maternity Care is a label that has been applied to maternity care that takes into account the social and psychological aspects of birth as well as the physical ones. The obstetrician's belief system does not give much value to the psychological and social dimensions of birth. Richard Schmidt, M.D., while president of the American College of Obstetricians and Gynecologists (ACOG), held a press conference to clarify ACOG's position on family-centered maternity care. Reported in a *NAPSAC News* editorial, Dr. Schmidt said that ACOG was not in a position to dictate policy in obstetrics to United States hospitals and that ACOG would be reluctant to "box hospitals in with rigid recommendations based more on human feeling than on scientific data." During the course of our negotiations with our local hospital, we came up against this belief system many times. In one session, a local obstetrician told us, "You need to understand our point of view. We are interested in medical safety, not TLC [tender loving care]."

The experience of childbirth for the woman is too often unimportant to the doctor. As one pediatrician told us, "It's okay for the doctor to follow the wishes of the patient when it doesn't make any difference one way or the other. But we need to communicate to the patient those things she wants to do that are dangerous." When we discussed the result of our M.O.M. survey with a surgeon, he unknowingly summarized the belief system of obstetricians in terms of control when he said, "You may know what women want, but it may not be what they need."

If the experience of childbirth for the woman is too often unimportant, the doctor's comfort is. Since he controls the situation, he becomes the key person in the whole experience.

The kind of bed or delivery table used, the labor and delivery position of the woman, the temperature of the delivery room, are all designed to contribute to his convenience and comfort, not that of the mother-to-be or the newborn infant. A nurse who has worked in newborn intensive care units was discussing with an obstetrician whether the cool delivery room could be contributing to breathing distress in the newborn. She asked him who he felt was the most important in terms of comfort in the delivery room, the infant or him. He replied, "I am."

Obstetricians believe very strongly that their control of the decision making for the birth process is an important key to a safe birth. The titles of two articles in *Patient Care* magazine clearly distinguish the dichotomy that doctors believe there is between what women want for their birth and what doctors believe is best. The first article is entitled "Mother's Wishes Vs. Doctor's Duties." The second is entitled "U.S. Experts: Safety Vs. Sentiment." An underlying assumption in both articles is that doctors care more about safety than mothers do.

Some doctors go much further and call all women's preferences "gimmicks" and "risky." Marsh Steward, Jr., M.D., wrote an editorial in 1981 for the California Association of Obstetricians and Gynecologists in which he said:

> It is even more frightening if, in addition, we also consider the fact that obstetrics has become almost totally consumer dominated. This "consumerism" has resulted to a large degree from the extensive media exposure given to an extremely vocal but misguided minority. It has panicked some hospitals into providing some poorly thought-out gimmicks in an effort to be seen as responding to these demands, i.e., the practice of "bonding," of putting the baby to breast on the delivery table, the "ABC Room," the birthing chair and other cult rituals. If we are to avoid being done in by the malpractice problem we must reassert our control over the patient and insist that we exclusively make the decisions relative to patient care, putting an end to nonpatient interference in this process.

A "safe birth" takes place in the hospital. If you believe that the active management of labor is best for all mothers and babies, then the associated risks of intervention are much too great to take place anywhere other than in a hospital. In this and other countries, midwives and doctors who deliver women at home or in birth centers are doing sophisticated screening of patients to identify those who are likely to develop complications requiring regular hospital care. However, because of their own personal experience with sudden emergencies in the hospital, most obstetricians do not believe that successful screening is possible. Therefore they reject any kind of out-of-hospital delivery, whether in a free-standing birth center or at home. One of the "Standards for Safe Childbearing" of ACOG is that all births occur in hospitals. Warren Pearse, M.D., when executive director of ACOG, authored the extreme opinion shared by obstetricians that "home delivery is maternal trauma—home delivery is child abuse!"

A "safe birth" is attended by an obstetrician. Accepting the assumption that birth is a dangerous procedure that must be actively managed with risky interventions, you can understand why obstetricians feel they are the only ones qualified to attend the birth, not midwives or family practitioners.

While a small number of hospitals have certified nurse-midwives on their staffs, and growing numbers of health-care consumers are lobbying hospitals to give certified nurse-midwives delivery privileges, most obstetricians are unaware of the high quality of care given by midwives. When we called the Washington, D.C., ACOG office to request some information on certified nurse-midwives, we were told that the information was not readily available since "we put midwives together with home birth; we don't separate nurse-midwives into their own file." In a speech to family physicians at their annual meeting, Dr. Pearse referred to the growing trend toward midwifery as a "serious problem" and as "worrisome."

Obstetricians feel uneasy about family practitioners, too. In the United States today, 85 percent of births are attended by obstetricians, less than 15 percent by family practitioners. In fact, the percentage of babies delivered by family practitioners has been steadily decreasing—down from 1968, when 31 percent of the babies born in the United States were delivered by family practitioners. Believing that the care that they give is superior to that of other birth attendants, obstetricians are passing around a catchy phrase that best describes their feelings toward family practitioners and midwives: "Why settle for a Ford when you can have a Cadillac?"

A "safe birth" is measured solely in terms of whether or not there is a live mother and a live baby. We all certainly agree with doctors that a live mother and baby are foremost in our minds, too. When everything reasonable has been done and death still occurs, there is some solace in knowing that every safety precaution was followed. That's the reason we are going to the doctor in the first place. Obstetricians, however, justify their interventive measures on the basis of improved maternal and perinatal mortality rates. "It has been the sophisticated medical technology afforded by the fetal monitor and the cesarean section that has vaulted this country's [perinatal] mortality rate to the best in the world," said William A. Cook, M.D., to an interviewer. Proclaimed Clayton T. Beecham, M.D., in 1981 at a Philadelphia meeting of the ACOG: "By tolerating or encouraging "natural childbirth" methods and the escalating use of midwives, American gynecologists and obstetricians could jeopardize the impressive decline in maternal mortality rates achieved in the past fifty years, which is directly linked to the spread of modern medical techniques in childbearing."

The obstetricians' keys to a "safe birth" (i.e., the birth is managed, predictable, and controlled by them; takes place in a hospital; and is attended by an obstetrician) are all justified because obstetricians believe their technology and interventions are the reasons for improved maternal and perinatal mortality rates. Improved maternal and perinatal mortality is their overriding concern, their measure of success, and the justification for their belief in their activity as scientific. We will look closely at that claim.

MATERNAL AND PERINATAL MORTALITY— CAUSES FOR THE DECREASE

The maternal mortality rate is measured by the number of deaths of women per one hundred thousand live births. The maternal mortality rate has gone down steadily since the beginning of this century, when more than seven hundred women died out of every one hundred thousand live births.

Year	Maternal Deaths per 100,000
1940	376
1950	83.1
1970	21.4
1980	9.2
1987	6.6

Perinatal mortality includes the deaths of fetuses from seven months of pregnancy through birth and to seven days of age of the baby. In other words, perinatal mortality measures deaths of babies around the time of birth. Perinatal mortality is so much higher than maternal mortality that it is measured per one thousand births.

Year	Perinatal Deaths per 1,000
1960	28.9
1970	23.2
1980	12.8
1987	10.0

Obstetricians tend to claim most of the credit for the steadily decreasing maternal and perinatal mortality rates. Because the decreasing death rates are so impressive, obstetricians' feeling that "what I'm doing must be the reason" might be easy to accept. But it's just not that simple.

The falling rates are due to complex interrelated factors having little to do with what obs believe are the keys to a safe birth. For example, dramatic falls in the maternal mortality rates in the 1940s were aided by the development of antibiotics, which controlled infection, and by the development of blood banks, which allowed needed transfusions for the mother to survive a severe postpartum hemorrhage. It wasn't until 1950, according to Herbert Ratner, M.D., former director of public health in Chicago, that birthing women were free from pelvic bone abnormalities caused by rickets, which had been a major problem complicating births. With better nutrition—especially the addition of vitamin D to milk, which started in the 1930s—this was the first generation of women who could give birth without the complications of rickets and other diseases of malnutrition.

In those years, too, obstetricians were in the forefront of changing maternity care. Then, as now, most births were normal, that is, uncomplicated vaginal deliveries. Then, as now, complicated births (both vaginal and cesarean deliveries) resulted in the highest rates of maternal and perinatal mortality. Obs made a major contribution to reducing mortality rates by starting to use—and by setting high standards for training in the use of—analgesia, anesthesia, forceps, and IVs in the care of those complicated births. Dr. Ratner paints a dramatic picture of the ob's role in reducing maternal mortality: "The actual fact is, and it must not be forgotten, that if it weren't for the contribution of obstetrical specialists, some of your mothers, and some of your grandmothers, would have died in childbirth and some of you in this audience would not be here today. . . . These specialists played an important role in the continuing reduction of preventable maternal deaths by reforming correctable professional and hospital practices." Obstetricians took the lead, and still do, in changing the care of complicated deliveries to make them safer for women.

Right up to the present many factors having nothing to do with labor and delivery affect maternal mortality rates, such as falling birthrates and the availability of family planning. "Some may argue that the improved statistics are due more to improved availability of family planning and abortion services," said Richard Aubry, M.D., codirector of the Perinatal Center, State University of New York, Syracuse. "However, it should be noted that a major part of the reduction in maternal mortality occurred before effective family planning was widely available [the sixties] and clearly well before the availability of abortion services [the seventies]." That's right. As shown in the maternal deaths chart, the giant drop occurred in the forties—long before the spread of technological interventions came to the ob floor.

The drop in perinatal mortality is also complex. The greatest cause of perinatal mortality in the United States today is the same as it has always been: respiratory distress syndrome, most often found in premature or low-birth-weight babies. Specialized pediatricians, called perinatologists, have reduced perinatal mortality by saving more babies born with complications, and by saving smaller and smaller babies. "That newborn intensive care can lower mortality in low-birth-weight infants is widely accepted," reported Nigel Paneth, M.D., M.P.H., et al., in a special article for the *New England Journal of Medicine* in 1982.

Low birth weight remains the most significant factor, far outweighing all others affecting perinatal mortality. The major reasons for perinatal mortality in the United States were traced by researchers J. David Erickson, Ph.D., and Tor Bjerkedal, M.D., who compared perinatal mortality in Norway and the United States and reported their findings in 1982. A high number of low-birth-weight babies born into economically deprived families is the major reason for the United States' perinatal mortality rate, "poor" in relation to Norway's, say the authors. They concluded that any major improvement in the United States' rate will await a reduction in the births of low-weight babies.

INTERNATIONAL COMPARISONS

Many factors affect mortality rates, so the rates by themselves can't be used to justify the way a baby is delivered. The mortality rates are useful in looking at differences in obstetrical care between countries.

The infant mortality rate is a different measure from perinatal mortality. Infant mortality measures the death of a live-born baby within the first year of life. For international comparisons it is the measure commonly used. The relative standing of the United States in comparison to other countries tells us how well we are doing. Though the infant-death rate for 1987 in the United States was the lowest in history—10.1 deaths per 1,000 live births—population experts call the rate high for an industrialized nation. The United States rate was higher than rates in most Western European countries.

The U.S. Commission to Prevent Infant Mortality invited American pediatrician and epidemiologist Marsden Wagner, M.D., representing the European office of the World Health Organization, to testify before it in 1988. Wagner outlined for the commission the major findings of the WHO regarding the successful efforts of the European countries with the best record for lowering infant mortality.

Universal access to prenatal care is one of the four interrelated findings. The two factors during pregnancy most associated with low birth weight are smoking and a lack of social support for the woman. When prenatal care includes help for these factors, perinatal mortality is improved. Maternity protection is the next element in pregnancy and birth care in Europe. Protection includes pre- and postnatal paid maternity leave, regulations regarding working conditions, and nursing breaks for breastfeeding mothers.

Obstetrical interventions are much fewer in the countries with the best records. Wagner quoted other WHO officials: "Countries with some of the lowest perinatal mortality rates in the world have cesarean rates of less than 10%." He noted that "the excess cesarean sections in the U.S." mean that "the U.S. is paying a considerable human price."

The final link in lowering infant mortality is midwifery. "In every European country practicing midwives far outnumber obstetricians," he testified. "Fundamental to the entire perinatal care system is that midwives provide the majority of pre- and postnatal care as well as being the principal birth attendant at uncomplicated births." The midwife has "a more social, non-interventionist, supportive approach. The physician's role is more interventionist and medical in nature. These two styles nicely complement each other."

Wagner summarized, "What is needed is less money spent on medically oriented prenatal care, more resources shifted to social and financial support and maternity benefits for families, far less money spent on interventionist obstetrical care and more resources put into building up a large, strong, independent midwifery profession."

RANDOMIZED CONTROLLED TRIALS— THE ONLY MEASURE OF WHAT OBS DO

What we know from looking at mortality rates is that obstetricians can't measure what they do in labor and delivery by using mortality rates (called "crude mortality rates"). They cannot say the dropping maternity and perinatal mortality rates are due to interventions such as using fetal monitors, Pitocin, cesareans, or other procedures. The active management of all births is an invention of the seventies, long after the greatest decreases began and continued in maternal mortality. Perinatal mortality was decreasing before the seventies too, and the decrease has many different reasons behind it. Current research clearly shows, however, that any major decreases in perinatal mortality will now come from prevention—reducing the large numbers of low-birth-weight babies in the United States.

Obstetricians call their tools beneficial, but can they prove it? They need to show the benefits, risks, and safety of each intervention by testing it separately. For the most part, research to evaluate the interventions of obstetricians on the basis of whether or not the interventions are better for the mother and baby than not using them has simply not been done.

Iain Chalmers and Martin Richards, British medical researchers, examined the tendency of obstetricians to claim their activities cause the falling maternal and perinatal mortality rates. Chalmers and Richards say:

> One is left wondering how a profession which has always thought of itself as scientific could have remained complacent in the face of such haphazard changes in practice. Certainly the relative research design has been available for many years: Johnston and Sidall in 1922 allocated alternate women to experimental and control groups in a prospective study which failed to demonstrate any beneficial effect of perineal shaving prior to labor. The fact that these findings, although confirmed by subsequent research in 1965, do not seem to have a major impact on actual practice, raises the question of whether well-conducted research influences practice to a greater extent than opinion and anecdote.

The evaluation that the authors refer to is called "randomized controlled trial" (RCT), which shows whether or not a new way is better than the old way, and whether doing nothing is better than either the old or new way.

In the example given, women were assigned on a chance, or random, basis to either of two groups. In the first, "the experimental group," the perineal area was shaved. In the second, "the control group," the women were not shaved. The reason usually given for the perineal shaving is that it reduces infection. There was a slightly higher infection rate for the experimental group (with perineum shaved). From several RCTs involving thousands of women, we know perineal shaving does not reduce infection, so there is no reason for shaving the perineal area of a woman in labor.

The use of randomized controlled trials of the various interventions of the obstetrician would tell us whether any one intervention was of any benefit and what the risks were. A doctor can only claim to be scientific if he uses the scientific method in his practice; if he either carries out research using RCTs, or in his practice uses only those interventions that have been evaluated and proven beneficial. "What constitutes science is the use of scientific method and not the status or the hopes of its practitioners," says author M. D. Riley in *The Benefits and Hazards of the New Obstetrics*.

Senators at a health subcommittee hearing on obstetrics were appalled to discover that there has been no systematic evaluation of the interventions used by the obstetrician. Former senator Jacob Javits said that many routine activities and interventions of obstetricians had "never been conclusively tested for the relative risk and benefit." Senator Edward M. Kennedy added "the development of obstetrical technology far outstrips our capacity to assess its appropriate value. As a result common practice is established before appropriate practices can be defined."

Some doctors are troubled that routine practices have not been evaluated scientifically. The oxytocin challenge test (OCT) is one such intervention, used primarily when a woman's pregnancy is more than two weeks past her due date. The OCT is also called the contraction stress test. The woman is given just enough oxytocin to stimulate several hard contractions while the fetal heart rate is monitored in response to the contractions. The theory is that, if the fetal heart rate is abnormal, labor must be induced immediately. G. Eric Knox, M.D., of the University of Alabama Medical Center, said in a discussion evaluating the use of the OCT in prolonged pregnancies:

> I also concur with Dr. Kirschbaum that the OCT itself has never been validated in the way that he suggests appropriate (prospective, randomized trial with non-intervention control group). Be that as it may, what has happened is that enthusiasm for this test [OCT], like many other previously touted forms of fetal assessment [HPL, estriols, etc.], becomes so widespread that when investigators go to a Human Use Committee and ask if they may compare an OCT versus non-intervention or expectant management, they are told, "No, by denying this patient this test you would be performing an unethical study." I would suggest, and I assume Dr. Kirschbaum would agree, that through this type of reasoning we are perhaps doing an unethical thing by introducing therapies into our practice prior to having them well validated by appropriate, controlled studies.

We don't want to just *tell* you that what obstetricians do is unscientific. We will show you.

SEVEN

THE OBSTETRICIAN'S
BLACK BAG OF INTERVENTIONS

Jenny and Dick talked eagerly about their first baby due in a week. "It seems like we've waited so long for this," Jenny said. "We were married two years when we decided to have a baby, then it seemed to take forever to get pregnant!" she added, blushing now. "We've finished our Lamaze course," Dick broke in with a sparkle in his eyes. "I know we can use everything we learned." Jenny seemed to be reminding Dick when she said quietly, "Our teacher emphasized that this is not natural childbirth, and I shouldn't be a martyr. She said just enjoy it, and do whatever is best for the safe delivery of the baby."

As the days went by, and the due date came and went, Jenny became discouraged; it seemed so difficult to move around now. One week after her due date, she awakened slowly, aware that what woke her was a heaviness, a tensing in her lower abdomen that had come and gone several times before she was fully awake. Was this it? She glanced at the clock and saw that it was almost time to get up anyway, so she sat up and started timing her contractions. Disappointed, she noticed there wasn't much of a pattern—first ten minutes, then eight minutes, then twelve minutes. By now Dick was waking up, and he asked what she was doing. When he found out she was timing contractions, he jumped up and scurried around nervously getting ready. Jenny told him she didn't think it was labor. But within an hour the contractions had settled into a fairly regular pattern of every eight minutes, and she decided to call her doctor. He told her to come in since he was already at the hospital (it was seven A.M.). It sounded to him like she was probably in labor. Now they both really got excited. This was the big day! By the time they got to the hospital, it was eight o'clock. Jenny missed Dick, who had gone to sign her in, but she was busy undressing to get into bed. She was disappointed to find out from the nurse's examination that she was only two centimeters dilated. The contractions were already hard to handle, especially without Dick there.

Before the years of high-technology births, mothers-to-be were often sent back home if they came to the hospital in very early labor like Jenny. But sending a mother home once she comes to the hospital—even in very early labor—is now almost unheard of.

MOTHER PUT TO BED TO LABOR

In most countries women in labor are encouraged to walk around rather than go to bed, but there is a belief system in the United States that it is safer for the woman to be in bed. Several times in one year, Denver General Hospital did not have enough beds for all women in labor, so women in early labor *had* to stay upright, either sitting or walking the hospital halls. A misinformed nurse observing these women told a *Denver Post* reporter, "That's dangerous!" In fact, it is *not* dangerous; it is beneficial to the laboring woman and the fetus.

There is no research showing any benefit in putting the laboring woman to bed. On the contrary, there is research that shows a danger to the fetus when a mother labors on her back, and benefits to a side-lying, upright, or walking position in labor. A world authority on the supine (or flat-on-the-back) labor and delivery position is Roberto Caldeyro-Barcia, M.D., director of the Latin American Center for Perinatology and Human Development of the World Health Organization (WHO) in Montevideo, Uruguay. He and later researchers in the late seventies, using randomized controlled trials, discovered that the supine position is the *worst* one for labor and delivery. It has the disadvantage of "adversely affecting pain and comfort, uterine activity and maintenance of normal blood pressure," says Frederic Ettner, M.D., in *21st Century Obstetrics Now!* A drop in the mother's blood pressure affects the circulation of blood within the uterus, resulting in poor oxygen supply for the unborn baby. Dr. Caldeyro-Barcia states, "Except for being hanged by the feet, the supine position is the worst conceivable position for labor and delivery."

Raising the woman to a semisitting position in bed, some-times called "the Lamaze position," for labor and delivery has the same problems as the supine position, says certified nurse-midwife Katherine Camacho Carr in her 1980 review of the medical and cross-cultural literature on a woman's position in labor and birth.

Standing, strolling, sitting, kneeling, or on hands and knees are the way for a woman to labor upright. When the upright position is used, labor is much shorter than in the on-the-back position. The upright position, with the assistance of gravity, increases the strength of contractions and dilates the cervix faster. Women report less pain in the upright position. There is also less need to use drugs to speed up labor, or relieve pain, and babies are in better condition at birth. Finally, women *like* being upright. According to Caldeyro-Barcia, 95 percent of women given a choice choose to be upright. It's also important to point out that there is no research showing that the on-your-back or the semisitting position for labor gives as good results as the upright positions.

Carr, who presented her review of labor and birth positions to a 1980 conference on "Benefits and Hazards of Hospital Newborn Care," referred to Joyce Roberts', Ph.D. research at the University of Illinois in 1980, showing the side-lying position was one of more uterine efficiency than was the sitting position. In terms of efficiency of contractions and shortening of labor, Carr's review concludes there is an order from best to worst for labor position:

1. Walking or standing
2. Side-lying
3. Sitting
4. Lying down or lying on the back in a propped posi-tion (Lamaze position)

By now Dick was back with Jenny, trying to get her back in control, helping her with her slow breathing, encouraging her to relax. At this point the nurse came in with some equipment and asked Dick to leave. Jenny felt miserable and embarrassed as she submitted to the prep and enema and the procedure to put an IV opening in the back of her left hand "just in case," the nurse said. Jenny realized that her contractions were not regular at all now, sometimes very mild, sometimes a little uncomfortable. Jenny was still at two centimeters dilation.

IV

In most other industrialized countries, a normal laboring woman is allowed to eat and drink lightly. In the United States, as a substitute for this light eating, an IV or intravenous pathway is inserted into the woman's arm. Fluids may be given through the IV to sustain the woman as she fasts throughout a long labor. And the IV allows a quick means of giving general anesthesia, analgesia, and fluids for emergency surgical intervention. The woman is required to fast "just in case" of an emergency. If a woman receives general anesthesia, she is unconscious. If she is not watched carefully, she may vomit and inhale the fluids—and may die. The responsibility for observation rests with the anesthetist, who can quickly turn a woman's head if she vomits and avoid any peril. The most common use of the IV, however, is to give Pitocin, either for induction or labor or to speed up labor.

There is no research that shows that an IV needs to be used before there is an emergency, or that having an IV in place in a normal laboring woman has made a difference in an emergency. Hospital ob nurses and birth attendants know how to start an IV quickly when needed.

There are risks to an IV. The woman may develop an infection at the site of the IV. Also, the "nothing by mouth" rule for a laboring woman according to a medical textbook can lead to abnormal blood chemistry ("metabolic acidosis"). This condition in the mother results in less oxygen for her unborn baby.

More U.S. hospital staffs are recognizing the benefits of encouraging a normal woman to drink and eat lightly during labor, according to Dixie Elsberry, C.N.M., M.S.N., Director of Midwifery Services, North Central Bronx Hospital. This hospital's policy is longstanding in allowing self-regulation of nourishment during a normal labor, Elsberry told us. In a demonstration review of this policy in 1989, Elsberry reported that those women who nourished themselves at home during labor were likely to come to the hospital in more active labor than women who did not take nourishment. Women who do self-regulate their nourishment know what, or if, they need to eat and drink during labor, she told us.

PREP

The prep is the shaving of the perineal or pubic area. Over half of American women giving birth routinely have their perineal or pubic area shaved as part of being admitted to the hospital. The medical reason given us is that it reduces infection. Research in the 1960s, using randomized controlled trials involving 7,600 women giving birth, showed that the infection rate was lower among those who were *not* shaved.

ENEMAS

Enemas are still a routine part of hospital admissions for over half of laboring women. There is no research proving any medical benefits of an enema. Many mothers experience a natural bowel cleansing in labor. They may have several bowel movements over a period of minutes or hours as the baby moves down in the pelvis. Some birth attendants believe this cleansing gives the baby more room in the mother's pelvis. If a mother does not have this natural diarrhea, she may feel more comfortable having an enema. Also a fear of passing feces with pushing contractions may inhibit some women who have not had an enema. These possible benefits suggest the choice of an enema should be left up to the laboring woman.

Jenny had now been at the hospital two hours, and her contractions were becoming weak and irregular. The doctor examined her for the first time and found she was still at two centimeters dilation. He said he was going to break the amniotic sac "to get things moving." Jenny didn't feel anything, just a little wetness between her legs. However, within minutes, her contractions became strong again, and she needed Dick to help her with her breathing. Dick, feeling anxious now that he was doing the real thing and not just practicing, worked with Jenny, reminding her to take her cleansing breath at the beginning and end of the contractions.

AMNIOTOMY

Amniotomy is the deliberate breaking of the bag of waters surrounding the baby. The nurse or doctor uses a blunt, sterile instrument to puncture the amniotic sac. Amniotomy is so common in laboring women in hospitals that few nurses and doctors have ever seen a laboring woman with a bag of waters intact during late labor or delivery. Trying to change the practice of routine amniotomy can be difficult.

In a 1979 discussion of fetal monitoring in the *American Journal of Obstetrics and Gynecology,* Robert Munsick, M.D., professor of ob/gyn at Indiana University School of Medicine, notes that early amniotomy becomes a "routine reflex; how else can the scalp electrode be placed?" He told how difficult it was to get his ob/gyn residents in his hospital in Indianapolis to stop amniotomy. "Attempts by me through entreaty, counseling, and even cajolery failed to influence this practice." What finally worked was to post a "Wanted" notice in the residents' lounge: "Wanted—Delivered Alive—$50.00 Reward!—A fetus delivered in a caul." Within ten days of posting the notice, four infants were delivered in a caul (with amniotic sac intact).

Amniotomy is done to speed up labor, to induce labor (usually accompanied by Pitocin), and to get the bag of waters out of the way to apply the electrode to the fetal scalp, necessary when using an internal fetal monitor.

There is a speedup of labor when the bag of waters is ruptured early in labor. Researchers M. Martell, M.D., et al. found in 1976 that early amniotomy reduced labor by about an hour. In 1974 Dr. Caldeyro-Barcia found that early rupture of membranes speeded labor by "a little more than half an hour." The question is, Is it worth it? Is the amount of time saved worth the loss of protection normally given by the amniotic fluid? Before rupture, the bag of waters provides a cushion of even pressure from contractions, and protection from excessive molding of the head as the baby moves through the mother's pelvis. After rupture, the pressures on the baby's head during contraction are direct and uneven. Also, the umbilical cord can be compressed, sometimes denying the baby necessary oxygen. "I didn't know, when I was an intern, about the literature showing that the amniotic fluid protects the head," a family practitioner told us. "To me it was just something that was in the way, and the sooner you ruptured the membranes, the better off you were."

When the bag of waters is not ruptured artificially, 95 percent of women who start labor spontaneously at full term, and have uncomplicated, unmedicated labors, will have the bag of waters intact until very late in labor or even during delivery. This provides a significant measure of protection to the baby and to the baby's lifeline, the umbilical cord. Most women who have their bag of waters rupture naturally—even in early labor—can have normal labor and deliveries. However, whenever possible, it seems reasonable to allow the extra margin of safety the intact bag of waters provides. There is a direct benefit to the mother, too, since the longer her bag of waters is intact, the lower her risk of infection is. "Avoiding amniotomy would probably reduce many of the abnormal factors seen so often in labors, including severe drops in fetal pH, cord compression, infections, and increased numbers of cesarean sections," says certified nurse-midwife Katherine Camacho Carr, reviewing obstetric practices that protect the unborn baby during labor and birth in the journal *Birth*.

Within a few minutes of the amniotomy, two nurses came in pushing a large machine, the electronic fetal monitor. They had Jenny spread her legs again so they could screw the electrode to the baby's scalp. Dick was fascinated by the machine, by the colors and sounds—the winking and blinking of the lights. He felt they certainly were receiving the best in care. The only problem Jenny noticed was that whenever the nurse came into the room, she went straight to the fetal monitor as if Jenny were no longer there. The nurse didn't ask anymore how Jenny felt.

ELECTRONIC FETAL MONITORING

Fetal monitoring is keeping track of the baby's heartbeat as a means of measuring fetal distress and possible need for intervention. Traditionally, this has been done by the nurse listening to the baby's heartbeat with a stethoscope (auscultation). In the seventies a substitute for auscultation came into use. Originally intended for high-risk laboring women, electronic fetal monitoring (EFM) is now used almost universally in the United States.

There are two kinds of EFM, external and internal. *External* electronic monitoring is indirect monitoring that picks up the fetal heart rate by the use of ultrasound waves. The external monitor is considered much less accurate than the internal monitor, having unreliable readings form 43 percent to 65 percent of the time, reports Madeleine Shearer, editor of *Birth*.

The *internal* fetal monitor measures the fetal heart rate directly by an electrode inserted in the baby's scalp, and measures the mother's uterine contractions by a catheter placed just inside the uterus. Electronic fetal monitoring is high technology with beeps and readouts that seduce you into believing you're getting useful information. For some onlookers, the machine is mesmerizing. "It is almost like watching television to stand in a labor room and watch this monitor," says Shearer. "The paper comes out and lies in folds in the drawer of the cabinet upon which the machine is set. A lighted green window up on the left of the monitor has an oscilloscope display of the fetal heart pattern. Then right next to that is a digital display in red, the numbers constantly flickering with each beat of the heart. I stand and watch and think to myself, 'How could I possibly question this advanced technological breakthrough in obstetrics?' Just the added information alone must be worth the effort."

Many, if not most, obstetricians wholeheartedly believe in electronic fetal monitors. They do not believe there are enough nurses in hospitals to give the one-to-one care necessary for the nurse to regularly monitor the baby's heartbeat with a stethoscope. That a machine can substitute for a nurse is a widespread misunderstanding; *someone* must monitor the machine. Editor L. J. Stonstegard, R.N., commented in 1981 in the *Perinatal Press*, "None of the studies perceived that the monitor allowed the professional care provider to perform other functions due to decreased time requirements for patient care. Rather they noted that *more* attention might be necessitated." In 1982 researcher Judith Lumley, Ph.D., of Queen Victoria Medical Centre, Melbourne, Australia, described as "sobering" that the United States, "the richest country in the world [is] unable to provide women giving birth with the necessary one-to-one patient care."

Doctors see the electronic fetal monitor as useful, proven, and therefore essential for assessing fetal well-being. They cite studies done with thousands of births that show that where fetal monitors are used, the perinatal death rate goes down. They conclude that the decrease in the perinatal death rate is due to the use of the fetal monitor. However, these studies only compare years of use of the fetal monitor with years when the fetal monitor was not used. When comparisons are made involving different time periods, the limitation is that you can't pick out any one factor, such as the fetal monitor, to explain the decrease in the death rate. That conclusion could be made scientifically only if randomized controlled trials (RCTs) are done.

Nine prospective, controlled trials have been carried out over a decade comparing electronic fetal monitoring and nurse fetal monitoring. Careful analysis of the results show *no benefits* for machine over nurse. All studies showed that EFM increased the risk of cesarean birth, sometimes dramatically, over the group of women whose labors were monitored by nurses, *while there was no better outcome for the baby*.

Commenting on his own coauthorized study of 34,995 women in Dallas, Kenneth Leveno, M.D., said in 1986, "With electronic monitoring, we were identifying more abnormal heart rates that led to more cesarean section, and the result was that the babies' outcome was no different." The problem was the fetal monitors "do not precisely identify the baby in distress all the time. Most children with abnormal fetal heart rates are really in good condition."

In their summary of the monitoring trials reported in *Lancet* in 1987, authors A. Prentice and T. Lind agreed with this assessment. They noted van den Berg et al. reported that 71–95 percent of babies diagnosed as distressed during labor did not have that diagnosis confirmed at birth. The good condition of the babies at birth means that the original reading of fetal distress ("positive reading") was a "false positive." The fetuses were diagnosed as distressed when they were not. Most of those babies in such good condition at birth were born by cesarean when they could have been born vaginally.

Fetal scalp sampling is encouraged by some obstetricians to verify a monitor's readout of fetal distress. This involves taking a sample of blood from the unborn baby's scalp. If the sample is normal, the obstetrician can have confidence the baby is not distressed. But researchers have shown the same problems with fetal scalp sampling as with EFM: sometimes there is indication of a distressed fetus when the baby is normal. Writing in the *New England Journal of Medicine,* Emanuel Friedman, M.D., Sc.D., concluded, "The promise of such major technological advances as continuous electronic monitoring of the fetal heart rate and fetal-scalp blood sampling has not been fulfilled."

Although the studies showed no benefit for the high-risk women who had EFM, the researchers believe that, because there is a *possible* (but unproven) benefit, high-risk women should consider having EFM. The *Lancet* authors noted, "However, interpretation of.the wealth of information is still difficult and many mothers will have operative deliveries for 'distressed' babies who show no such distress at birth." Researchers agree that, because there are no benefits and documented dangers, low-risk women should not have EFM, but should instead have a nurse regularly monitor the baby's heart rate. In 1979 the National Institute of Health Consensus Development Conference had come to this same conclusion, recommending that the nurse should monitor the fetal heart rate every fifteen minutes during the active phase of labor, and every five minutes in the second stage of birth.

The widespread use of EFM in the United States is the best example of the unscientific nature of American obstetrics. Auscultation will be discouraged because doctors and hospitals have decided to use and promote EFM, and they have the power, according to Dr. Lumley. In her 1982 article, "The Irresistible Rise of Electronic Fetal Monitoring," she quotes another writer describing the stages of medical innovation: "The success of an innovation has little to do with its intrinsic worth (whether it is measurably effective as determined by controlled experimentation) but is dependent upon the power of the interests that sponsor and maintain it, despite the absence or inadequacy of empirical support."

The risks of *external* monitoring to the baby involve the unknown effects of the use of ultrasound. The risks to the mother include intervention in a normal labor because of the unreliability of the reading or because of a "false positive" reading. She is put to bed and told to lie quietly when freedom of movement is important to a normal laboring woman. If you feel you cannot avoid the external monitor, lie on your side during use and *ask* if you can have the monitor removed after a normal reading is established in fifteen or twenty minutes.

The risks to the baby of the *internal* monitor include the loss of protection of the bag of waters because of amniotomy, as well as injuries from misplacing the scalp electrode, infections, and (rarely) death due directly to infection from the scalp electrode. The mother has a risk of greater infection rates, possibly from early amniotomy (required for the internal monitor) or increased internal examinations. She, too, loses her freedom of movement, feeling tethered to the bed. In addition are the problems of starting her on the road to active medical management of labor and delivery, and an increased likelihood of having a cesarean section.

"Fetal distress" (often a false positive reading) is not the only likely cause for a cesarean in women who use internal fetal monitors. "Failure to progress" in labor was the most common reason for a cesarean when EFM is used ("fetal distress" is second) according to Havercamp et al. in 1979, and Minkoff and Schwarz in 1980. "Monitors may play a key role in *causing* the increased cesarean rate for failure to progress," say Howard Minkoff, M.D., and Richard H. Schwarz, M.D., of the Downstate Medical Center, Brooklyn, New York. The researchers suggest that "the stress that monitoring might create for patients" is responsible for failure to progress in labor.

Thirty to 40 percent of women react negatively to the use of the EFM. Dr. Munsick presented a possible explanation of how the mother's psychological reactions may result in cesarean section for failure to progress.

> We begin by restraining a woman early in her labor. We allow her to see the FM's chattering stylus and its winks; often we even torture her unnecessarily with hours of its staccato sounds at 150 beeps per minute and we watch the monitor and not her. She dare not interrupt our silent vigil. Anxiety gives way to fright and anger . . . [leading to] abnormal contractions and these in turn cause arrest of labor. . . . And we then apply the modern-day obstetric panacea—cesarean section.

The two diagnoses of failure to progress and fetal distress are very important in the increasing rate of cesareans (see next chapter). Because of this, and because of the strong recommendations against the use of EFM in low-risk women, you need to find out if your chosen birthplace can give you the recommended nurse fetal monitoring. This demands a high degree of one-to-one nurse-patient contact for laboring women in hospitals, and many hospitals do not have adequate staff to do that. If your hospital is understaffed, consider hiring a private-duty nurse (a monitrice) to give you the nursing care you need.

At noon, when the nurse came in to check the fetal monitor, she also gave Jenny another exam and remarked, "You certainly are not cranked up yet; you're just three centimeters." Those had to be about the most discouraging words Jenny had ever heard. When the doctor suggested that a "little" Pitocin would make Jenny's labor more normal, Jenny readily agreed. The nurse pulled in a stand with a bottle on a six-foot pole and quickly got the "Pit" going since the IV was already in place. Jenny felt an immediate change in the contractions. They seemed much closer and more intense. Dick redoubled his efforts to help her stay in control, massaging her arms and legs, and lightly stroking her tummy. Soon the contractions were three minutes apart and sixty seconds long, and getting harder to cope with. Jenny switched to accelerated breathing. The nurse came in about every fifteen minutes now, and several times made an adjustment in the IV that increased the Pitocin drops flowing into Jenny's hand.

INDUCTION AND AUGMENTATION OF LABOR

Induction of labor means to start labor artificially. Augmentation of labor means to speed up a labor that has started naturally. "I have seen hundreds of deliveries screwed up because of unnecessary intervention," said one nurse interviewed by writer Judith Glassman. "In many hospitals 60 percent of labors are chemically induced or stimulated even though Pitocin often causes overly strong contractions, as well as blood pressure problems in both mother and child. It's just easier for the doctor to administer Pitocin than to supply emotional support."

In the medical management of labor and delivery, the usual way to artificially begin labor is to break the bag of waters and start the intravenous administration of Pitocin. The staff of the U.S. General Accounting Office estimates that 12 percent of all labors in the United States are artificially begun. Rates varied by region, however, with a high of 16.4 percent in the Northeast. However, some doctors believe that rates of induction would be much lower if it were done only when the risk of continuing the pregnancy was greater than the risk of inducing labor and delivery. The conditions where continuing the pregnancy presents a threat to life or well-being of mother and baby include severe blood incompatibility between mother and fetus, some diabetics, severe preeclampsia, severe high blood pressure, kidney disease, and an overdue pregnancy (postmaturity) where there has been *proven* a danger to the fetus. If induction of labor were carried out only when these conditions were present, Dr. Caldeyro-Barcia estimates that, at most, 3 percent of births would be induced. If that is so, it means that three-fourths of the inductions in the United States today are putting the mother and baby at risk for a less than sound medical reason. Authors Iain Chalmers and Martin Richards writing in *The Benefits and Hazards of the New Obstetrics,* concluded that "It has not been possible to demonstrate any striking advantage or disadvantage of a widened use of the induction of labor. The truth of the matter is that we are ignorant about the circumstances in which the benefits of induction outweigh the disadvantages and are likely to remain so using the research techniques employed so far."

Intervening to speed up a labor begun naturally is much more common than induction. Estimates of augmentation range from 20 to 40 percent of all labors that start spontaneously. "We used to have women laboring twenty-four, forty-eight, and even seventy-two hours!" an obstetrician told us. "We won't allow that anymore. I don't think augmentation is overused." Speeding up the labor goes along with the belief that the states of normal labor must fit within a carefully defined standard of time. "Shortening the phases of normal labor when there is no sign of fetal distress has not been shown to improve infant outcome," says Doris Haire, D.M.S., maternal advocate and president, American Foundation of Maternal and Child Health.

Pitocin is a synthetic version of the hormone oxytocin, which is produced in the body of the laboring woman and is one factor in the progress of her labor. Pitocin is usually (but not always) highly effective in beginning or speeding up labor, as many of you reading this book can testify. If Pitocin must be used, administration through an IV is preferred, because it offers the best means to control the dosage over a period of time.

However, even the most careful administration of Pitocin simply does not duplicate naturally occurring labor. This is because the progress of labor is under the dual control of the baby and the mother. The complex chemical and hormonal interrelationship of the mother and baby in starting and continuing labor is still not clearly understood. But we do know that it is impossible to reproduce normal labor. Mothers given Pitocin often describe the contractions as being longer and stronger, and with a shorter period between contractions, than those they experienced in unaugmented labor.

During both normal and induced or augmented labor the blood supply to the uterus (and therefore the oxygen supply to the baby) is temporarily reduced. With normal contractions, however, there is time between contractions to allow the baby's blood to be well oxygenated, to enable him to "hold his breath," so to speak, during the next contraction. In induced or stimulated labor, there are two ways the baby's oxygen supply can be shortchanged. The time between contractions is shorter; there is less time to oxygenate his blood between contractions. The contractions are longer; the fetus goes for a longer period of time before he receives a full supply of oxygen. For the unborn baby, it can be like being pushed into a swimming pool before he had a chance to catch his breath, and then having someone push him down deeper, just when he had bobbed to the surface for much-needed air. This possibility of an inadequate oxygen supply for the baby is one reason that all induced or augmented labors are considered at risk for developing complications.

Research shows the most significant risks of either induction or augmentation of labor to be:

- Higher rate of complicated labors and deliveries
- More use of analgesia or anesthesia because of the intensity of the contractions
- Fetal distress
- Higher rate of jaundice in the newborn
- Greater chance of delivering a premature baby (induction only; why all induced labors are "high risk")
- Postpartum hemorrhage (induction only; there has been no research to determine if hemorrhage is associated with augmentation of labor)
- Higher rate of ruptured uterus and placental separation, which may lead to the death of the mother or baby

While there is consensus that the risks of Pitocin are worthwhile when continuing the pregnancy would be life threatening, there is no evidence of benefits outweighing risks in the vast majority of inductions and augmentations being done. "The timing of spontaneous delivery is controlled by complex mechanisms which are still incompletely understood . . . and which have as their end point the delivery [of the baby when] survival of the newborn is most likely," said an editor of *Lancet*.

"The data on induction, oxytocin, and cesarean section all point to the same conclusion: Intervention is resulting in iatrogenic [physician-caused] pathology in women and their babies who might well have had spontaneous vaginal deliveries if they had been left alone," said Richard W. Beard, a British medical doctor, criticizing the widened use of induction in his country.

The first randomized control trial of Pitocin versus the upright position was finally done in 1980 at the Los Angeles County/University of Southern California Medical Center. This RCT studied the effectiveness of Pitocin versus the upright position in getting stalled labors going again. Women whose labors had slowed were randomly assigned to one of two groups. In the first, women were given the usual routine of Pitocin. In the second group, women were not given Pitocin; instead, they stayed out of bed, either walking, standing, or sitting. The study showed stimulation of labor was more effective by using the upright position than by using Pitocin.

Jenny, scared, began to complain about the contractions. They were more overwhelming than painful. The tremendous sensations she felt in her lower body were unlike anything she had ever felt before. It seemed to take too much effort to stay in control, to work with her body; otherwise there was pain. "I wish there was more time in between. It seems like only a few seconds from the time one is over until another one starts. They hurt." At this point the nurse returned to check Jenny and said that things seemed to be on track now, she had dilated a centimeter in the last hour and was now four centimeters dilated. Jenny's contractions were now every two minutes and she thought "I think I need the anesthesia now, I can't take this if it's going to get worse than this." She told Dick she needed something, and he rang for the nurse. The nurse said, "I'll let the doctor know." A half hour later the doctor arrived to give Jenny an epidural injection remarking, "If I were having a baby, I'd want an epidural as soon as I could." He added,

*however, that four centimeters was about the earliest he felt he
could give an epidural. Within fifteen minutes, Jenny became
talkative and could hardly feel the pain. She felt good about
being able to talk coherently to her husband now without
grimacing with discomfort.*

ANALGESIA AND ANESTHESIA

Analgesia are drugs used in labor to relieve pain. Anesthesia are drugs administered in labor and delivery to block or
obliterate sensation. Most mothers given analgesia or anesthesia believe them safe and assume they are given to relieve pain
and discomfort. According to *Williams Obstetrics*, a textbook
used by obstetrical residents in their training, "Vast experience
has shown that obstetric analgesia and anesthesia, when
judiciously employed, are in general beneficial rather than
detrimental to both baby and mother." The obstetrician's belief
system requires the use of analgesia and anesthesia because it
is thought to result in "more careful, gentler, and frequently
easier deliveries" and in "healthier mothers and more living
babies," according to the textbook. Recognizing the risks of
drug use, the writer of the text goes on: "The search continues
for drugs that singly or in combination produce effective
analgesia, amnesia, and sedation during labor but at the same
time are completely safe for the mother and the fetus." The
purpose of any drug, whether analgesia or anesthesia, then, is
not just for pain relief but also to produce memory loss of
labor, to quiet the mother, to make deliveries easier, and to
ensure healthier mothers and more living babies.

Analgesia and anesthesia use in the United States is very
widespread. National data of use are incomplete, but comprehensive reports from many hospitals indicate that almost all
(80–95 percent of birthing women, depending on the hospital)
receive analgesia, anesthesia, or both. The analgesia (drugs
given for pain relief) rate seems to range from about 40 to 70
percent. The anesthesia (drugs given to block sensation) rate is
estimated at around 65 percent. It's unusual to find a hospital
with better rates than these.

Almost all birth attendants agree that in complicated deliveries, whether vaginal or cesarean, analgesia and anesthesia are
beneficial because they sedate or anesthetize a woman so that
essential intervention can be carried out. The disagreement

comes in deciding what is a complicated delivery and whether the birth attendant may, by intervening, be *causing* complications. In hospital settings the complication rate, intervention rate, and drug-use rate are much higher than in alternative settings. The excellent outcomes for mother and baby in alternative settings show us that complications—and the need for intervention—can be avoided in most births. There is no research that proves that for these uncomplicated deliveries, analgesia and anesthesia use "permit more careful, gentler and frequently easier deliveries resulting in healthier mothers and more living babies" as the medical textbook indicates. There is evidence that, especially for those normal mothers and their babies, the risks may outweigh the only proven benefit, which is pain relief for the mother.

Analgesia and anesthesia:

1. May slow labor by changing the strength and frequency of contractions so they are less effective, requiring the use of Pitocin.
2. Almost always cause some drop in the mother's blood pressure, and may cause a serious drop, with life-threatening consequences to her or her baby.
3. Dull the experience for he mother, reduce or eliminate the physical pleasure of birth, and, immediately after birth, may make her less responsive to her baby.
4. Anesthesia may slow the second stage of labor by relaxing the vaginal walls, and often interferes with the mother's ability to bear down, requiring a forceps delivery.
5. Anesthesia prevents the mother from feeling how hard she is pushing the baby against her perineum and, because she does not have the "protective reflex" of feeling the birth, the birth may be too fast to gradually stretch the perineum, resulting in perineal tears and damage.
6. With anesthesia the mother risks headaches from misplaced injections or other neurological damage that may be temporary or, rarely, permanent.
7. Cause short-term neurological and behavioral abnormalities in the baby, such as breathing and sucking difficulties, and may cause a dulling of the baby's ability to respond to the mother in the attachment process.

8. May cause long-term neurological and behavioral disorders in the baby.

The results of extensive research on the effects of analgesia and anesthesia on the newborn are frightening. Yvonne Brackbill, Ph.D., and her associates have done the most comprehensive research on the short- and long-term effects on infants whose mothers were given drugs during labor and delivery. Esther Conway and Dr. Brackbill, working through the University of Denver, published their results in 1970, showing that anesthesia and analgesia impaired the muscular, visual, and neural development of the baby two to five days postpartum. At that time, Conway and Brackbill suggested that it was possible that anesthetics and analgesics caused permanent damage to the infant.

Nine years later, Dr. Brackbill, research professor of psychology and obstetrics and gynecology at the University of Florida, reported on the lasting behavior effects of obstetric medication on children to two different government bodies, a Senate subcommittee in 1978 and a committee of the Food and Drug Administration in 1979. For her reports, Dr. Brackbill reviewed forty-one studies on obstetric medication and infant/child behavior. All but two of the studies found significant drug effect. Dr. Brackbill reported four key findings from the studies. First, obstetric drugs affect the child's behavior negatively (they interfere with normal function). Second, the behavioral effects are dose related; that is, the stronger the drug and the larger the dose, the greater the behavioral effect. Third, Dr. Brackbill reports, "At all ages, the effects are more clearly visible when the tasks are difficult, that is, when they require the child to exert itself to make an effort to cope with problems." And fourth, the behavioral effects of obstetrical medications persist for years.

For her 1979 report to the FDA, Dr. Brackbill presented additional evidence of obstetric drug damage. Working with Sarah Broman, Ph.D., a psychologist at the National Institute of Health, Dr. Brackbill had analyzed data from a study of 53,000 women who gave birth at twelve different teaching hospitals from 1959 through 1966. Broman and Brackbill studied the data on the 3,500 women in the project who were the *healthiest* and who had the *most uncomplicated* pregnancies, labors, and deliveries, trying to rule out the possibility that any results showing damage to the babies would be due to complicated pregnancies or deliveries. In this select, healthy group, Drs. Brackbill and Broman found that obstetrical medications affect the children's behavior at least through seven years of age.

Among the older children whose mothers had received drugs during labor and delivery, there were lower reading and spelling scores, and lower scores on a visual-motor test. Dramatizing the results of their analysis, Dr. Brackbill concludes, "On the whole, I estimate that 95 percent of births in the United States hospitals nowadays are medicated. This means 3,500,000 medicated births out of 3,700,000 total births per year. If the average I.Q. loss per medicated birth is four points, this means 14,060,000 I.Q. points lost to new U.S. citizens every year. Cumulatively, that figure should put the problem of obstetric medication at the head of the class of national health priorities."

Doctors are concerned, however, that if women have full information on the risks of brain damage to their unborn babies when drugs and anesthesia are used, they will be frightened away from using them when needed. This issue came up in Dr. Brackbill's presentation to the committee of the FDA. Another doctor questioned that a mother might refuse a needed cesarean section because of the risks of anesthesia. Dr. Brackbill's reply was, "I see evidence everywhere I turn that women are capable of making risk-benefit decisions." The American Academy of Pediatrics Committee on Drugs agrees, and has recommended that doctors "use the smallest possible amount of medications when it is needed, and to discuss the benefits and side effects with the mother, preferably in advance of the birth."

A related issue in the use of analgesia and anesthesia is the lack of research on the safety of the drugs used. Toxicologist-pediatrician Mark Thoman, M.D., says, "Every drug is a controlled poison." Many of us believe that the Food and Drug Administration would not allow drugs that are unsafe to be used in obstetrics. In a study of this issue, Doris Haire, D.M.S., reports that the dictionary definition of safe ("free from harm or injury") is not the definition used by the FDA; in fact, they have no definition of what "safe" is. In a letter to her, the director of the FDA advised her that the FDA does not guarantee the safety of any drug, even those drugs that the FDA approves as "safe." Furthermore, the FDA does not require the drug given to a woman during labor or delivery to be proven safe for the unborn baby. Says Dr. Haire, "There is no doubt in my mind, and in the minds of many other individuals working with brain-injured children, that a large proportion of brain-injured and learning disabled children are the result of obstetric drugs administered to women to relieve discomfort or pain, or to induce or stimulate their labor. Most women are unaware that obstetric drugs diminish the supply of oxygen to the unborn baby's brain and can result in brain damage."

The American Academy of Pediatrics discourages the use of drugs for the laboring woman and states that no drug has been found safe for the baby *in utero*.

In the next hour and a half, Jenny and Dick chatted. They even became a little bored. Jenny felt hungry, but knew she couldn't eat. Her sense of smell seemed very sharp; everything reminded her of food. She hadn't eaten since last night's dinner, and it was almost twenty-four hours since then. Jenny felt nothing from the top of her tummy down, but she could, strangely, feel the baby moving around. At 3:30 she became aware that the epidural was wearing off. About that time the nurse came in for a check and told her she was six centimeters dilated and doing fine, but she helped her turn on her side because her blood pressure was "a little low."

Jenny wasn't so sure that she was doing fine. She was afraid of feeling the overwhelming contractions again. She asked Dick what she should do. He suggested they start timing the contractions again, and get back with the breathing. By 4:30 she was eight centimeters dilated and feeling unable to handle the contractions again. She rang for the nurse to come back. "Please, I need something now!" She felt she didn't do very well the next half hour waiting for the doctor, losing her breathing rhythm, even though Dick was now breathing along with her with each contraction. Nothing seemed to be working. At 5:00 the doctor arrived, found she was at nine centimeters dilation, and gave her a second injection of epidural anesthesia. As the sensations of labor began to disappear (much to her relief), she overheard her doctor talking to the nurse outside her door. "If I could have talked her into waiting another half hour or so for the first one, I probably wouldn't have had to repeat it. By 5:30 Jenny was feeling nothing and became very excited when the nurse coming in to check her told her she was nearly fully dilated and almost ready to push.

A few minutes later the doctor returned to check her and

confirmed she could now push. Dick and the nurse helped Jenny round her back and grab her knees. "Push as long as you can!" the nurse encouraged. After about twenty to thirty minutes the stretcher was wheeled in for the move to the delivery room.

MOTHER'S DELIVERY POSITION

The usual position for an American woman giving birth in a delivery room in on her back, with her legs in stirrups. This is known as the lithotomy position. More than three-fourths of obstetricians consider the lithotomy position best for delivery, according to a *McCall's* survey. "Maybe the position is undignified for the mother," one doctor wrote, "but it's convenient for me." And that's the only good thing about it. The position is for the convenience of the delivering doctor. There are no benefits and several serious drawbacks for the mother and baby.

In *The Cultural Warping of Childbirth*, Doris Haire, D.M.S., summarized the literature indicating the problems in the lithotomy or on-the-back position for delivery.

1. It adversely affects the mother's blood pressure and the blood supply to her heart and lungs.
2. It decreases the normal intensity of contractions.
3. It makes it difficult for the mother to push the baby out and, therefore, increases the need for forceps. (You feel as though and you are, in fact, pushing the baby *uphill*.)
4. It makes it difficult for her to expel the placenta, which increases the need for procedures such as pulling on the cord, which put her at risk of hemorrhage.
5. Because the mother's legs are pulled wider apart than is normal for an easy delivery, and the baby's head presses against the back of the perineum, there is an increased need for an episiotomy to prevent tearing.

Many mothers find delivery not only safer but far easier curled on their side, or in a semisitting position with the soles of their feet on the bed, with a comfortable, relaxed spread of their legs. However, there are five upright positions that use gravity to assist the woman in delivery. They are: sitting, squatting, on hands and knees, kneeling, and fully supported standing.

Jenny liked the idea of moving to the delivery room. Now she knew her baby was almost here. As the nurse and Dick helped her slide onto the delivery table, she felt another contraction coming, a tightening of her tummy with no other sensation. "I need to push!" she exclaimed. But she had to wait while her legs were positioned in the stirrups, and the sterile draping carefully arranged around her legs and stomach. Dick placed himself at her head. The nurse put a pillow under Jenny's shoulders. For another twenty minutes, Dick and the nurse encouraged her to push fully with each contraction. Finally the doctor told her he was going to help her with forceps and "a little cut." She'd probably feel some pressure in her back, he mentioned. As he worked positioning the forceps, he said, "This one is staying in one spot, so push hard. It's pretty tight . . . okay, now we're moving, just lie back and let me do the rest." An eight-pound girl slid into the world at 6:18 P.M. The nurse took the baby from the doctor, who cut the cord immediately. The nurse brought the baby around to Jenny and Dick for a brief look. Jenny and Dick were thrilled to see their new daughter. Both had seen the delivery in the overhead mirror with feelings of awe from watching the miracle of birth. The nurse took the baby over to check and clean up. Within a few minutes the nurse brought the baby to Dick and asked if he'd like to take his new daughter to the nursery "while the doctor finished up here." The doctor explained that Jenny had torn, even with the episiotomy, since the baby was in there "awfully tight," and he'd had to go a little higher with the forceps than usual.

EPISIOTOMY

Episiotomy is the cutting of the perineum to enlarge the birth opening. This practice is so widespread that there is hardly an American woman today who has given birth vaginally who has not had an episiotomy. The current estimate is that 62 percent of women giving birth receive an episiotomy. This compares to an 8 percent episiotomy rate in the Netherlands and a 3 percent rate in Sweden—information that leads one to believe that it is not women's perineums that are different from country to country, but medical fad.

Doctors give three reasons for doing an episiotomy. In *Williams Obstetrics* the reasons are stated as fact. First, an episiotomy substitutes a straight incision for a tear, and that is better for healing than a laceration would be. Second, an episiotomy "spares the baby's head the necessity of serving as a battering ram against perineal obstruction. If prolonged, the pounding of the infant's head against the perineum could cause brain injury." And third, an episiotomy reduces the likelihood of deep tears, called third-degree or fourth-degree (through the rectum) lacerations. An underlying belief of many physicians, touched on in the textbook, is that an episiotomy prevents excessive stretching, which would lead to a relaxed perineum and reduced sexual pleasure for the woman's male partner.

There is no research to support any of these beliefs. Dr. Lewis Mehl's research comparing two large groups of women who delivered either at home or in hospital gives interesting information that suggests that an episiotomy doesn't prevent severe laceration. In the home-birth group, only 10 percent had episiotomies, and yet fewer than 2 percent had either third-degree, fourth-degree, or cervical tears. In the hospital group, 87 percent of the women had episiotomies. Nevertheless, just over 14 percent of the women had third-degree, fourth-degree, or cervical lacerations. The in-hospital women had seven times more severe lacerations, though they had nine times as many episiotomies as the home-birth women.

A review of the literature on episiotomy was reported in 1989 by James M. Thorp, Jr., M.D., and Watson Bowes, Jr., M.D. The review described and summarized twenty-five studies of how often third- and fourth-degree tears happened. In nearly 50,000 women who had episiotomies, 6.5 percent had third- or fourth-degree tears. In nearly 39,000 women who did not have episiotomies, 1.4 percent had similar tears. Women with episiotomies had almost five times as many severe tears as women without episiotomies. Thorp and Bowes concluded that routine episiotomy is not supported by the evidence, and "may well increase the incidence of third- and fourth-degree lacerations."

The high rate of episiotomies and the many severe lacerations in hospital deliveries occur because (1) obstetricians simply are not trained to ease out the baby's head any other way than to enlarge the opening with an episiotomy, (2) the lithotomy position is nearly universal for hospital delivery, and (3) large numbers of deliveries have forceps used.

If your birth attendant is not familiar with, or unwilling to try, a delivery without an episiotomy, you can increase your chance of avoiding an episiotomy and tears by:

1. Choosing an upright or side-lying position for delivery.
2. Avoiding anesthesia.
3. Pushing only when you feel the need, for five to six seconds at a time.
4. Stopping pushing for one or two contractions when you feel a burning sensation.
5. Asking your doctor to use a gentle massage with warmed olive oil to stretch the perineum during the pushing stage.
6. Preparing your perineum with the Kegel exercise and massage.
7. Asking your doctor to avoid forceps if at all possible.

INSTRUMENT DELIVERY

Forceps, in use since the 1500s, are a metal device placed around the baby's head to lead it through the birth canal. A newer device, the vacuum extractor, uses a plastic cup on the baby's head and a suction tube. Both devices apply traction to the baby's head to shorten delivery. The textbook *Williams Obstetrics* describes "elective low forceps" as forceps used when "the obstetrician elects to interfere knowing that it is not absolutely necessary for spontaneous delivery may normally be expected within approximately fifteen minutes. The vast majority of forceps operations performed in this country today are elective low forceps. One reason is that all methods of analgesia interfere to a certain extent with the mother's voluntary expulsive efforts."

The elective use of low forceps is sometimes called preventive use of forceps (meaning "to make delivery easier") and is widely used in the United States. Instrument delivery is used in 20–30 percent of all deliveries, according to estimates, going as high as 50 percent in some American hospitals. This contrasts with obstetrical care in Europe where, until recently, many centers had instrument delivery rates of lower than 5 percent. "The incidence of forceps delivery remains low in the Netherlands where childbirth is still considered a physiological process and is much more a matter of social and emotional support than of surgery and pharmacology," according to W.M.O. Moore writing in *Benefits and Hazards of the New Obstetrics*.

There is no research to support the elective use of forceps. Forceps are being used without a scientific basis, in normal deliveries, when there is no need to hurry the delivery. The risks to the infant are of hemorrhage within the head, and damage to nerves serving the face and arms. For the mother, episiotomies almost always accompany the use of forceps. In spite of this, severe lacerations of the mother's perineum are more frequent when forceps and episiotomies are used.

SUMMARY: INTERVENTIONS OF THE OBSTETRICIAN

Obstetricians are not scientific in their practice. None of the ob's interventions has been evaluated and proven helpful, beneficial, or better than avoiding the interventions for the 80–95 percent of women who could have normal labors and deliveries—and most of the interventions have substantial risks. What they do "depends on training and how they make a living, not on the result of randomized control trials," said Thomas Chalmers, president of Mt. Sinai Medical Center of the City University of New York, speaking about all doctors when quoted in *USA Today*.

The only scientific means of evaluating the interventions used by the obstetrician is by randomized controlled trials. A few studies have been done for three of the ob's interventions. For two of these, shaving of the perineum and the use of the fetal monitor, randomized controlled trials have shown no benefits in normal labors, and in fact, show some risks to the mother and, in the case of the fetal monitor, risks to the baby, too. The third intervention tested was Pitocin to stimulate labor. The upright position—walking, standing, or sitting—was *more effective* in the randomized controlled trial than was the Pitocin in stimulating labor.

Most obs' interventions, then, are experimental—that is, we don't know if using them is more beneficial than not using them—because randomized controlled trials to prove their benefits have not been done. Obstetricians *think* they are beneficial because of their experience in using them. There are, however, known risks, and when the doctor says the interventions are "safe," he means he *feels* safe using them. You, however, may not agree that an unproven intervention is "safe." It's your decision.

There is some research that does indicate which of the ob's interventions are the most dangerous to your baby. Amniotomy, induction or speeding up labor by drugs, the use of the on-the-back position for delivery, and anesthesia and analgesia were identified by several speakers as among the most common causes of infant brain damage and mental retardation at a conference in New York City in 1975 sponsored by the American Foundation for Maternal and Child Health.

At the 1977 American Public Health Association annual meeting, Lewis Mehl, M.D., reported his computer-assisted research on what determines the condition of the baby at birth. The four obstetric interventions identified most closely with poor outcome for the baby were Pitocin for induction or stimulation of labor, analgesia, forceps, and amniotomy. Testifying before a 1978 Senate Health Subcommittee Hearing on obstetric interventions, Dr. Haire said she believed "that at least a large percentage of learning disabled and handicapped children result from obstetric practices which interfere with normal biochemical checks and balances provided by nature to assure the normal progression of labor and a good maternal and infant outcome."

It has been as scary for us to write about the unproven interventions of the obstetrician as it is for you to read it. We are afraid for the risks being taken with the lives and health of women and their babies, when those risks are unjustified in normal births; and we can hear women who are reading this book say, "Why are you telling me this? It's only making me frightened of what might happen."

The active management of normal labors and deliveries is new in the history of childbirth. As recently as the early to middle 1970s several of the obstetrician's interventions were used only in complicated cases of labor and delivery, where the health and welfare of the woman or her baby clearly justified them. Now the technology is being used on most women in labor whether the labor is normal or not. *It will probably be used on you if you don't negotiate to prevent its use.*

Usually when complications happen in childbirth, the birth will still result in a live mother and a live baby. Advances in obstetrical technique are saving more babies from complicated births. Perinatology (the care of the unborn and the newborn) has resulted in the greatest saving of babies in trouble. If your baby is two pounds or more, it is more likely than ever that your baby will live, regardless of what kind of childbirth you have. If the obstetrician's interventions were reserved for the 5–20 percent of births where they can be justified, we could be pleased about the advances made to ensure a healthy baby in a complicated birth. However, the technology is also being used in the other, normal deliveries; yet the risks to the health and welfare of the mother and baby seem very great for the unproven benefits.

These interventions may not only be unsafe, they are also changing the experience of childbirth for women and babies, with far-ranging results. What have we lost? The mother becomes a nonparticipant in the birth of the baby and is denied both the joy and pleasure that is possible. And because of problems resulting from the interventions—problems either in mother or infant requiring intensive treatment after birth—the infant is separated from the mother. What we are losing here is the experience of childbirth at its best: an exuberant experience of enormous courage, effort, and incredible pleasure. We are losing the kind of childbirth experience that empowers us, that makes us feel better about ourselves as women, that helps us grow and develop as mothers, that is important in the attachment process with our babies. More than that, the active management of labor and delivery is leading to an epidemic of cesarean births at costs that we are just beginning to tally.

EIGHT

THE CESAREAN EPIDEMIC

The most common cause of cesareans today is not fetal distress or maternal distress, but obstetrician distress.

—DR. GERALD STOBER,
NEW YORK CITY OBSTETRICIAN

Typically, a laboring woman does not see her doctor in the hours before birth. Then he strides in, takes charge, and accomplishes an efficient, quick delivery. But she has been on his mind from the time the hospital nurse notified him of her arrival. He has been on call for her, all the while seeing other patients in his office or offices. In his mind, the danger is mostly to the baby. He has never lost a mother, but no matter how hard he tries, he has had a "poor outcome" for a baby several times in his career. The constant anxiety in his mind is, Am I going to get a healthy baby? The uncertainties of labor's progress result in more anxiety than almost any obstetrician can handle. He usually gets in there and does something.

BELIEF, TRAINING, AND MONEY ARE BEHIND THE CESAREAN EPIDEMIC

When physicians are asked why cesareans have increased, the most frequent reason they give is the threat of a malpractice suit. Helen Marieskind, Dr.P.H., a Seattle public-health specialist who has interviewed physicians and evaluated cesareans for the federal government, was the first to report this belief. In the interviews, physicians called cesareans "defensive medicine" and said that, even if a baby was "less than perfect," if a cesarean had been performed, they were covered.

Acknowledging this widespread belief, Lynn Silver, M.D., M.P.H., and Sidney Wolfe, M.D., of the Public Citizens Health Research Group reported that doctors and the public "commonly perceived that the threat of malpractice is a major cause of the increasing c-section rate." In their report, *Unnecessary Cesarean Sections: How to Cure a National Epidemic*, Silver and Wolfe reviewed the relationship between state cesarean rates and malpractice premium rates. The authors report, "Variations in malpractice premiums were unable to explain the enormous variations between hospitals and physicians in the use of this surgery. In fact, there is no empiric evidence demonstrating that the performance of unnecessary cesarean sections lessens the legal risk for an obstetrician."

"Cesarean sections mean better babies" is another important belief causing the dramatic rise in cesareans.

- "You get pregnant to have a healthy baby, not a vaginal delivery."
- "We are looking for a neurologically and psychologically sound human being."
- "Now, in an advanced country, we expect a baby to survive."

The above comments were made by medical experts interviewed by Silvia Feldman, Ph.D. Until the 1960s, the obstetrician's emphasis was on saving the mother, since maternal death rates had been so high. When maternal mortality rates dropped dramatically, the emphasis shifted to the baby.

Women now find themselves faced with the ultimate intervention—a cesarean—because the doctor believes cesareans result in fewer damaged or dead babies. For years obstetricians linked the falling perinatal mortality rates with the increasing cesarean rates (see chapter 6). That belief was shown false with the publication of a study by O'Driscoll and Foley in 1983. The authors reported on 108,987 infants born in National Maternity Hospital, Dublin, from 1965 to 1980. The perinatal mortality rate plummeted in Dublin just as it was doing in the United States, but the cesarean section rate remained below 5 percent in Dublin. Throughout Europe, cesarean rates remain far below U.S. rates with as good or better perinatal mortality.

The evidence is growing that cesareans do not produce "better babies" and may be resulting in more damaged babies. For example, Roberta Haynes de Regt, M.D., et al., reported in 1986 on 65,647 deliveries in Brooklyn over a five-year period, comparing cesarean rates and outcomes for clinic patients versus private patients. The clinic patients had higher risk factors, and their babies had lower birth weights. Yet their babies did better than the private patients' babies. Private patients with a significantly higher rate of cesareans had a significantly greater number of babies with poor outcomes: birth injuries or low APGAR scores (a measure of condition at birth). Silver and Wolfe summarize, "Surgery is more likely to make the infant or his mother ill, rather than perfect and whole. The myth of the perfect cesarean baby should be laid to rest."

Despite the evidence, the widespread belief that a cesarean is better for the baby persists among obstetricians and the public. It is often given to a mother in labor as a persuasive reason to undergo a cesarean. And certainly, told that something might happen to her baby if she goes ahead with a vaginal delivery, a woman is unwilling to take that risk. But the public needs to know that we cannot always expect a baby to be whole or to survive. "Most fetal death and damage is unpreventable, in that it is related to events or factors before delivery, over which physicians have no control," wrote Emanuel Friedman, M.D., Sc.D., in the *New England Journal of Medicine*. "It is unrealistic, therefore, to expect every delivery to result in a living, healthy, unaffected child."

"Infants were stillborn not because of delayed diagnosis or delivery, but because the severity of fetal distress was so great that it precluded saving the babies," said Leveno and Cunningham, commenting on their study of selective and universal electronic fetal monitoring in 34,995 pregnancies in Dallas. "This may be our most important result, since the expectations of patients, obstetricians, and more recently, attorneys are such that all fetal deaths in labor units are considered preventable. They are not."

An obstetrician's training contributes to his anxiety about the dangers of childbirth and to his urge to resort to a cesarean delivery. "I believe the present high-risk childbirth model is creating more anxiety than obstetric personnel can handle, and the increasing cesarean rate is in part a manifestation of this anxiety," says Philip Sumner, M.D., coauthor of *Birthing Rooms*. Many doctors recognize the problem that obstetrical training emphasizes high-risk care. Doctors get little or no training in normal obstetrics, and are, therefore, poorly prepared to handle normal labors, according to Dr. Marieskind in her cesarean evaluation study. Residents receive little or no training in normal birth, in monitoring the fetal heart rate by stethoscope, in vaginal breech deliveries, or in vaginal births after a cesarean, for example. By contrast, they receive extensive training in the use of technology in labor and delivery: in the use of electronic fetal monitoring, ultrasound, scalp sampling, anesthesia, forceps, and surgical deliveries. Obstetricians are more likely to perform cesareans when they are trained in the high-risk model of obstetrics.

In addition to the obstetrician's belief and training, there is a financial and time-management incentive behind the increasing cesarean rates. Physicians are paid more for a cesarean delivery than for a vaginal delivery. Silver and Wolfe refer to studies showing that "patients with the best-paying insurance plans have the highest c-section rate. While physicians may or may not be deliberately or consciously performing c-sections for financial reasons, these findings, which have been replicated in studies in the U.S. and other countries, clearly show that financial factors probably are associated with a physician's decision to perform a c-section."

Changing the incentive can lower cesarean rates. Silver and Wolfe report that "one health maintenance organization, Total Health Care, Kansas, was able to rapidly lower its cesarean rate from 28.7 percent to 13.5 percent in one year simply by changing to the same reimbursement whether the woman had a cesarean or a normal delivery."

"Time is a *dear* commodity," said Richard Porreco, M.D., director of AMI/Saint Luke's Perinatal Program in Denver, speaking at the *Birth* journal conference in 1989. He went on to explain how time management spurs cesareans: "With out-patient and in-patient surgery and several offices in which to see patients, the doctor has little time for expectant management of labor. The influence of time is seductive. The doctor doesn't think about time determining whether he does a c-section, but it does."

Obstetrician Joseph Nouhan, M.D., Saint Louis, agrees that time management affects the way a doctor practices. He prefers low-intervention obstetrics, giving a copy of this book to each pregnant woman coming to him, saying, "This is my philosophy of childbirth; read it and tell me what you want." He observes, "My practice is run the way I like, but it takes time to be with women in labor and help them have a natural birth. I see how the other obs work and it's easier for them. Usually they don't go to the hospital during a woman's labor, but call in an order for the anesthesiologist to give an epidural. Epidurals slow labor, and even if the woman is pushing, they know they will have time to make the delivery."

Evidence of unnecessary cesareans for convenience comes from several different reports, the first from Susan Doering, Ph.D., a research scientist at Johns Hopkins University. She found that 80 percent of a small sample of emergency cesareans were performed during the day rather than randomly around the clock. She also reported on unpublished research of L. K. Gibbons, Ph.D., showing that 58 percent of cesareans on first-time mothers, supposedly emergency situations, were done during the day, and only 42 percent were done at night. Similar results were found in a third study, a survey of five New York City hospitals by personnel with the state's Maternal and Child Health office. In women having their first babies, 62 percent of emergency cesarean deliveries were performed during the working day, and only 38 percent were performed at night.

Beliefs, training, and economic incentives are major issues in the cesarean epidemic. Many other elements affect the cesarean rate, and we will explore those factors.

CESAREAN RATES DIFFER AMONG DOCTORS AND HOSPITALS

Whether you have a cesarean depends much more on the hospital you choose—and the doctors who practice there—than on you. Among the ten hospitals with the most deliveries covered in the Baltimore COMA Survey, cesarean rates ranged from 12 percent to 32 percent. Our M.O.M. Survey data showed that, among the eleven physicians in the survey (who delivered most of the babies), the cesarean rate ranged from 5 percent to 23 percent. This wide variation among hospitals and doctors has now been confirmed by a nationwide study.

Silver and Wolfe's 1989 report on unnecessary cesareans (see earlier in this chapter) brought together for the first time current available national data on cesarean section rates. Throughout the country cesarean rates showed extraordinary variation among hospitals, with no correlation to high-risk deliveries. The rates ranged from 53 percent of all deliveries at Hialeah Hospital, Dade County, Florida to zero.

Few hospitals have low rates. Out of 2,388 hospitals listed in the report, only 284 had a cesarean rate of 15 percent or less. In the whole state of New York, only five hospitals have low rates: Saint Joseph (Chemung), Moses-Ludington (Essex), Bronx Municipal, North Central Bronx, and The Hospital (Delaware). Yet Tennessee with far fewer hospitals and people, has twenty-one such hospitals. Tennessee residents can not assume all hospitals there have low rates of cesarean sections. Twenty-three Tennessee hospitals have cesarean rates above the national average. New York and Tennessee are used here as examples. Your state is likely to have the same wide variations.

Silver and Wolfe list 106 hospitals in sixteen states on "the cutting edge," those hospitals with cesarean rates of 35 percent or more, including twenty-two California hospitals, eighteen Florida Hospitals, eight New York hospitals and five New Jersey hospitals. One-third of the hospitals on this list had rates of 40 percent or more. Seven of the highest "cutting edge" hospitals are in Florida, contributing to Florida's position as the state with the highest cesarean rate, 27.9 percent. (Washington, D.C., is higher with 30.3 percent).

Dramatic variations occur within cities. For example, in Saint Louis, Saint Louis Regional Medical Center with over 2,000 births had a 10 percent cesarean rate. Saint Johns and Saint Joseph hospitals with 7,600 births between them, had a cesarean rate three times higher, at 31 percent each. Whether you have a cesarean or not is very likely to depend on your choice of place of birth.

Hospitals do not perform cesareans, doctors do. Silver and Wolfe reported on all doctors in the state of Maryland delivering more than twenty babies a year in 1987. The differences are startling. Variations among doctors were greater than among hospitals. Rates for individual doctors varied from no cesareans to 57 percent. Of the 484 physicians studied, nearly half had personal cesarean rates of 30 percent or more. Forty-three doctors had rates of 40 percent or more. Only twelve doctors (one out of forty) had personal rates at or below 10 percent, "although many Maryland physicians practice low-risk obstetrics," report Silver and Wolfe.

Within each Maryland hospital rates among doctors often vary hugely. Frederick Memorial Hospital staff had the greatest differences from 0 percent to 42 percent cesarean sections. Three of the doctors there, with rates of zero to 1 percent, stand in dramatic contrast to the rest of the staff. More typically, most hospitals had a few doctors with low cesarean rates, most doctors with high rates in the 20s and 30s percent, and one or two doctors with a cesarean rate of forty percent or more. Maryland hospitals overall showed a very slight decrease in cesareans from 1987 to 1988.

Maryland is different from many states only by the fact that it is one of the states with the highest cesarean rates and was chosen by Silver and Wolfe to be the example of variation of cesarean rates among doctors. You are likely to find similar variation among doctors in your city. For example, childbirth educator Paulina Perez, R.N., A.C.C.E., reports that doctors in her city of Houston have cesarean rates of 15 percent to over 50 percent.

"The data in this report make it crystal clear that much more than the size of a woman's pelvis or the health of her baby, the factor which is most likely to decide how she delivers her baby is the practice style of her obstetrician," report Silver and Wolfe. "Differences in c-section rates can only be accounted for by different policies that physicians use to manage their patients."

Depending on the doctor you choose your chance of a cesarean can vary from nearly nonexistent to one chance in two. "While hospitals have tremendous variability in their overall rates, in many hospitals this variation can be accounted for by a few physicians who dramatically abuse cesarean surgery," conclude the authors.

How do you find a hospital and doctor with low cesarean rates? You can get a copy of Silver and Wolfe's report (see Appendix) to identify rates for individual hospitals. Maryland residents can use the report to identify their doctor's cesarean rate by asking him which physician code number in the report was his. Massachusetts became the first state to pass a Cesarean disclosure law. It was initiated by the consumer group, Cesarean Support, Education and Concern, Inc. Every hospital there is required to give women its cesarean rate and rates of other common maternity practices.

In 1989 a new Standard Birth Certificate in all states enabled state officials to have detailed information on cesarean rates and other maternity practices by hospital and physician. Some state governmental agencies are not waiting for legislation and are publishing the data for consumers. Call your local health department—and your state legislator—and ask that the information be made public if it hasn't already.

Finally, simply ask hospital administrators and doctors what their cesarean rates are. "When I began suggesting that my students ask their obstetricians about their cesarean section rates, I supposed that physicians with high rates would hedge, or at least be embarrassed," wrote childbirth educator, Henci Goer, A.C.C.E. "I couldn't have been more wrong. Doctors seem proud to tell patients that their cesarean rate is 20 percent or more."

THE EPIDEMIC

An epidemic is an outbreak of anything that spreads or increases rapidly. We certainly have an epidemic of cesareans by that definition. The cesarean birth rate was 3 percent in the decade before 1970 when doctors looked at a cesarean as a last resort, a life-saving measure for the woman or her baby. Increasing just over 1 percent a year, cesareans rose from 5.5 percent of all births in 1970 to 24.4 percent of all births by 1987, report Paul Placek, Ph.D., and Selma Taffel, B.B.A., of the National Center for Health Statistics. One-fourth of all births today are by cesarean delivery. Placek and Taffel project that if current trends continue, 40 percent of U.S. births will be by cesarean in the year 2000.

A cesarean rate of 24.4 percent of all births is so high that health-care providers separate cesareans into two groups: those that are primary or first-time cesareans, and those that are repeat operations—operations for another birth after a previous cesarean. More than one-third of all cesareans are repeats, and just under two-thirds are primary cesareans. That means over 8 percent of all births today are repeat cesareans, and about 16 percent of all births are first-time cesareans. Before 1970, when doctors were extremely cautious in doing a first-time cesarean, the primary rate was a small 1.5 percent of all births. If you are having your first baby, or you have never had a cesarean and are having another baby, your chances of having a cesarean delivery today are eleven times greater than before 1970. That's an alarming change in the way babies are delivered and represents a fundamental and widespread change in medical practice.

Taffel reports that nearly 930,000 cesareans a year are now being performed, the most common major surgery in the United States (650,000 hysterectomies a year is the second most common major surgery, also done by ob/gyns). The cesarean epidemic has not gone unnoticed by the popular press, by government officials, or by doctors themselves. In the 1980s Canada and the United States each had a national consensus conference to review the world literature and to discuss and come to agreement on clear and strong recommendations to reduce cesareans. These recommendations by the U.S. National Institutes of Health (NIH) task force and the Canadian National Consensus Conference were published in major journals for obstetricians. The cesarean rates continued to soar, going up by 50 percent in the eighties. Most obstetricians failed to use the guidelines.

"The majority of American physicians, hospitals and third-party payors have continued to stick their heads in the sand and ignore over 10 years worth of overwhelming evidence that American women are being subjected to an onslaught of unnecessary and dangerous surgery," conclude Silver and Wolfe in their national report on unnecessary cesareans.

What is an appropriate cesarean rate? You decide. Edward Quilligan, M.D., dean of the School of Medicine, University of California, Irvine, reviewed the literature and suggested an 8 percent national rate. European rates range from under 5 percent to 12 percent. Richard Porreco, M.D., reports a 6 percent cesarean rate for the clinic he directs at AMI/Saint Luke's, Denver. Obstetrics department head Norbert Gleicher, M.D., coauthored the report of a successful program that lowered the cesarean rate to 11.5 percent for all deliveries, private and clinic, at Mount Sinai Hospital, Chicago. Using worldwide data, Silver and Wolfe estimated a target rate of 12 percent.

These rates are all far below almost all hospital and doctor rates and the national rate in the United States. Using the target rate of 12 percent, Silver and Wolfe estimate at least half, or nearly five hundred thousand of the cesareans in the United States annually, are unnecessary. Using our estimate of an additional two thousand dollars for a cesarean delivery over a vaginal delivery, these unnecessary cesareans cost $1 billion each year. What price can we put on the human cost in injury, illness, and death to women and babies for these unnecessary cesareans?

EPIDEMIC WORSE FOR
FIRST BIRTHS, OLDER WOMEN

We need to make a distinction between women laboring for the first time (called primiparas) and women who have already had babies (called multiparas).

Obstetrician William Cook, M.D., describes his view of the difference:

> The fact that a first childbirth is usually so different from subsequent births as to be almost unrelated is of such prime importance that it should be emphasized by every childbirth instructor and author (but isn't) . . . the effect of much childbirth education is to blur the distinction between the often long labor and difficult delivery of the first child and the shorter and easier labor and delivery of subsequent births.

The cesarean birth rate is much higher in primiparas than in multiparas who have never had a cesarean, three to eight times higher, according to a Massachusetts Department of Public Health study. The risk of cesarean birth has increased for everyone, but the risk is much greater than it used to be for a first-time mother. The typically longer labor of a primipara is an important factor in the cesarean epidemic. (See the section "Abnormal Labor" later in this chapter.)

The most common age for a woman to have a baby is in her twenties. However, a shift in the timing of births has resulted in many more women having babies in their thirties than in the past, according to the National Center for Health Statistics. More than one-fourth of all births are to women over thirty years old. Steady increases in first births to women in their thirties and forties is another trend reported by the center. The risk of a cesarean delivery goes up as the age of the mother increases from the teens to age forty or more. A woman in her early twenties has one chance in four of having a cesarean; a woman thirty-five years old or older has one chance in three.

Phyllis Mansfield, Ph.D., a specialist on age and childbirth, reviewed the scientific literature and found little reason for obstetricians to continue in their belief that older women, especially older women having first babies, are at high risk. She found "the vast majority of the 109 studies on age and childbirth so flawed as to be totally useless." The only clear risk of older women is for a Down's syndrome baby, a genetic deviation linked with mental retardation.

The higher cesarean rate of older women is not related to any evidence that women age thirty-five or older or their babies benefit from a cesarean rather than a vaginal birth. "Premium baby" is a term obstetricians have coined for any baby especially desired by the mother—particularly the older, first-time mother. The need to "guarantee the product" (so to speak) results in increased cesareans for these premium babies. Look for a birth attendant who will see you as the healthy, normal pregnant woman you are.

WHY THE EPIDEMIC?

A doctor is legally required to give a specific medical reason for performing a cesarean. "The fear of a malpractice suit," "a premium baby," "first birth," or "I don't know how to do a vaginal breech birth," are not reasons obstetricians write on medical records. Until the 1970s the most likely medical indications for cesarean delivery were different from what they are today. The primary cesarean, viewed as an emergency lifesaving event for mother or baby, was done for such medical complications as life-threatening maternal bleeding (hemorrhage), placenta blocking the birth canal (placenta previa), or baby's head too large to pass through the pelvis (severe cephalopelvic disproportion, or CPD). There were other, quite rare, reasons, too—including a repeat cesarean, always done, but still unusual, because there were so few women with previous cesareans.

Four reasons account for over 80 percent of cesareans today:

- Repeat cesarean birth (for a mother who had a previous cesarean birth)
- Abnormal labor
- Fetal distress
- Breech position of baby

REPEAT CESAREAN BIRTHS

"Once a cesarean, always a cesarean," has been a strong belief in American obstetrical care since the early 1900s. The practice of requiring repeat cesareans was started to avoid the risk of uterine rupture at the scar site, a life-threatening situation.

Even today, any uterine scar may rupture (a more serious, sudden bursting of the scar) or separate before or during labor. However, a change in the kind of incision done in cesareans has resulted in a greatly reduced possibility of separation or rupture, and a greatly reduced threat to the lives of the mother and baby. The "classical" cesarean operation was performed through a long vertical incision from the navel to the pubic hair, and then a similar vertical incision in the uterus. However, today's preferred method for cesarean delivery is a low horizontal incision in the uterus, after first cutting a similar low skin incision. Over 90 percent of cesarean deliveries are now done this way. The skin incision is called a "bikini cut," implying that it won't be visible when you wear next summer's bikini. This widely accepted, newer technique has greatly reduced the risk of separation or rupture of the uterus in subsequent pregnancies or labors—to less than 1 percent.

Even then, more than 90 percent of the problems consist of a partial separation of the old scar with no dangerous results to mother or baby. A rupture of a low horizontal cesarean scar is exceedingly rare and less serious than a rupture of a classical uterine scar. "Mortality fears for mother and infant due to rupture of the uterus in trial of labor are unjustified by present statistical data," said obstetrician Luella Klein, M.D., then president of the American College of Obstetricians and Gynecologists (ACOG). "As far as is known, no mother has died due to trial of labor in recent years regardless of scar type."

Most countries do not have a policy of repeat cesareans. Trials of labor and successful vaginal deliveries following cesareans are common. Over three decades many studies in the United States with tens of thousands of women in different medical centers have shown that most repeat cesareans are unnecessary. Both national consensus commissions documented that vaginal birth after a previous cesarean (VBAC) is as safe for the baby and safer for the mother. ACOG's review of the literature showed maternal mortality is at least twice as high for repeat cesareans as for VBACs. ACOG set out guidelines to encourage vaginal delivery after a cesarean.

Most practicing obstetricians are simply not listening. Nearly 90 percent of United States women who have cesareans and give birth again have repeat cesareans. Repeat cesareans, more than one-third of all cesareans, are the most obvious reason the U.S. cesarean rate climbs each year.

ABNORMAL LABOR

The diagnosis of abnormal labor accounts for 28 percent of cesareans. *Dystocia* (pronounced dis-toe-sha) is the medical term for abnormal labor. Dystocia means there is difficulty in the progress of the labor ("failure to progress"), for any of three reasons: weak contractions ("uterine inertia"); a poor position of the fetus; or an abnormal-size pelvis that prevents the baby descending or passing through the mother's birth canal (cephalopelvic disproportion, or CPD).

Drs. Banta and Thacker, in their literature review on fetal monitoring for the U.S. Department of Health, Education and Welfare, reported that true CPD occurs rarely (in 2 percent of first-time labors), yet is a common reason given for cesareans. Richard Hausknecht, M.D., went even further in the NIH task force report, noting the "indiscriminate overuse of the waste-basket term, 'dystocia.'" The task force found that when the diagnosis of dystocia or failure to progress is made, cesareans did not improve infant outcome compared to vaginal birth.

> There is no magic number of hours beyond which labor should not continue.
>
> —EMANUAL A. FRIEDMAN, M.D.,
> DEVELOPER OF "FRIEDMAN CURVES"

Doctors use the "Friedman curves" to decide whether a labor is abnormal. Friedman analyzed the progress of labor, averaged the time for many normal labors, and drew graphs to show the average labor. He describes two stages of labor, latent and active. The latent phase is early labor, the period of time when the cervix becomes effaced (thinned out) but dilates slowly, up to three to four centimeters. A normal latent phase, according to Friedman, can last up to twenty hours in a first-time mother, and up to fourteen hours in a woman who has already had a baby, but averages nine hours. The active phase of labor (sometimes called "true labor"), when the cervix dilates faster and steadily, is from four centimeters to ten centimeters of dilation. The average time for the active phase is four to six hours.

Doctors misuse the Friedman normal labor curves, according to Friedman himself. At the "Crisis in Obstetrics—Management of Labor" conference, reports Diony Young, "He asserted that the Friedman labor curve 'is being abused more than it is being used appropriately' and that to intervene with a cesarean for prolonged labor is 'unthinkable.' "

"We've forgotten that most women deliver in time," said Edward H. Hon, M.D., at the same conference. "If you allow twenty-four hours to elapse before intervening, you wouldn't have the high cesarean rate." Doctors misuse the Friedman curves when they equate slow progress with abnormal progress. They tend to forget that the graphs are based on averaging many labors of widely varying lengths. Most obstetricians view a normal labor (to full dilation of the cervix) as lasting no more than a total of twelve to fourteen hours for early and active labor. Yet twelve to fourteen hours is the length of the *average* first labor, according to the Friedman curves. Many perfectly normal labors will last longer than that, some much longer.

"People should recognize that because America thinks of itself as a can-do society, doctors emphasize the risk of doing nothing and tend to minimize the risk of doing something," said Lynn Payer, author of *Medicine and Culture* to writer Joanne Silberner. "Try asking your doctors, 'What do I risk if I don't do anything at all?' Sometimes you'll be surprised, because if they are honest, they may say that you don't risk much. Sometimes they will try to scare you, and this is the point where you should get a second opinion."

Very prolonged labor (over twenty-four hours) is associated with increased perinatal mortality. That is, according to the research, in very long labors there is a small increased risk that the infant will not survive. However, according to Drs. Hellman and Pritchard, authors of *Williams Obstetrics*, the textbook used to train obstetricians, we don't know if the increased perinatal mortality is the result of the longer labor itself, or if it is because of the complications from the interventions that the doctors use to speed up or end labor.

Researchers suspect anesthesia as a cause of many cesareans for dystocia. Friedman found that the use of analgesics or regional anesthesia (such as epidural, caudal, or spinal anesthesia) given before the mother has gone into active labor often results in a prolonged latent (early) phase of labor. At the 1989 *Birth* conference obstetrician James Thorp, M.D., described an association between epidural anesthesia in first labors and an increased risk of cesarean for dystocia. The studies at the University of Houston medical school showed two to three times more cesareans for dystocia in first labors in the epidural group than in the group of women without anesthesia. If the epidural was given at or before five centimeters of dilation to the women with slower labors, they had a six times greater risk of cesarean section for dystocia than women with slow labors but no anesthesia.

Oxytocin to speed slowed labors helped to reduce the cesarean rate in the Mount Sinai Hospital experiment. Where oxytocin use has been successful in slowed labor, it is used only when labor is clearly established. Hellman and Pritchard warn that "one of the most common mistakes in obstetrics is to try to stimulate labor in patients who have not been in labor at all." They direct doctors to consider oxytocin only when the woman is in active labor.

Oxytocin, primarily for first-time labors, is also considered an important part of Dublin National Maternity Hospital's very low cesarean rate. Other factors include sending a woman home who is in latent labor and giving continuous one-to-one labor support by a midwife. Some observers believe the labor support is as important as the oxytocin. In randomized controlled studies, Marshall Klaus reports the laboring women who had continuous caregivers (doulas) had their labors shortened by half. The cesarean section rate was also halved with little oxytocin use.

Water is being discovered as an assist to slowed and painful labors. French obstetrician Michel Odent reported in *Lancet* on the use of a warm water pool for women experiencing painful contractions and labor not progressing at five centimeters dilation. "In most cases, the cervix becomes fully dilated within 1 to 2 hours of immersion in the pool, especially if the lights are dimmed," wrote Odent. In the one hundred births under water reported, there were no complications and no infections.

In the first one hundred water births at the Family Birthing Center near Los Angeles, obstetrician Michael Rosenthal, M.D., also reports no complications and no infections. "About half the women choose to get in the water at some time during the labor process, and half of those stay there and deliver in the water," said Dr. Rosenthal in the video *Water Baby: Experiences of Water Birth,* by Karil Daniels.

Odent believes the water helps women to let go and become instinctive in giving birth. "When labor stalls, you must do what your intuition tells you feels right," say Beverly Savage and Diana Simkin, in *Preparation for Birth*. "This may mean removing the monitor and going for a walk, having a snack, taking a shower, calling a friend, yelling out or having a good cry. Surprisingly, loss of control can help, because tears produce a tremendous release of tension, which will allow labor to proceed."

The second stage of labor is the pushing stage, the time from full dilation until the woman pushes her baby out. Epidural anesthesia can increase cesarean section for dystocia in the second stage as well, reported Thorp at the *Birth* conference. An epidural interferes with the woman's ability to push and also, by relaxing a woman's pelvic floor, prevents the natural progress of the fetus through the birth canal. Anytime epidurals are given, instrumental delivery is 2.5 times more frequent than without the epidural, report H. M. Kaminski, et al. The instrumental delivery rate might be even higher, but because of fears of malpractice suits, "the obstetrician is less likely to intervene with forceps, and therefore, an increased incidence of cesarean for dystocia could result," said Thorp.

Most obstetricians allow one or at most two hours for the pushing stage, believing that longer than that is dangerous for the baby. They seem unaware of a 1976 study of the pushing stage of 4,403 first-time mothers by Wayne Cohen, M.D. The Harvard Medical School study shows "no adverse influence of a long second stage on perinatal or neonatal mortality in nulliparous [first-time mothers]. The elective termination of labor simply because an arbitrary period of time has elapsed in the second stage is clearly not warranted."

"Cesarean section for dystocia in nulliparas represents the single most important factor in the cesarean epidemic," reports Thorp. Because most doctors do repeat cesareans, the large number of women given cesareans for dystocia usually will have a cesarean for their next birth, magnifying the effect of the first cesarean.

What to Do for "Abnormal Labor"

Especially if this is your first baby, think about staying home from the hospital as long as possible. Hospital staff tend to measure the length of your labor from the time you arrive at the hospital. Because first labors tend to be longer and often harder for the woman to handle (she's never experienced this before, and her cervix is opening for the first time), staff distress goes up. You are likely to avoid the diagnosis of abnormal labor if you stay home until you are *sure* you are in active labor and that you really don't want to stay home any longer.

By staying home in early labor, you can drink, eat, rest, or sleep (all important in a long labor) when you want to, without feeling any pressure to have your labor fit the hospital's standard of how fast you should be dilating. Consider having a doula with you (see chapter 11) to help you and your partner relax with a long early labor at home. Or have a trained labor-support person with you who can examine you, tell you where you are in your labor, and help you.

"What is wrong with a woman waiting until it is time for her to deliver, coming into the hospital, staying two to eight hours and taking her baby home?" said Paul Wexler, M.D., chairman of the Department of Obstetrics and Gynecology of Rose Medical Center, Denver.

The NIH task force noted that "failure to progress may, in fact, be false labor or prodromal labor or otherwise not abnormal." False labor is the "practice" contractions of the last few weeks (for many first-time mothers) or the last few months (for many subsequent pregnancies). Prodromal labor is very early labor or, some would say, the contractions that signal that labor may come soon (hours or a few days away).

- If you are not in true labor (four centimeters or more), go home (or stay home), eat, drink, sleep, and wait.
- Your long labor may be perfectly normal for you.

If you are in active labor, four centimeters or more, and have been diagnosed as failing to progress, Diony Young of the International Childbirth Education Association recommends trying the following nonmedical alternatives:

- Asking for more time.
- Trying position changes, particularly upright ones; use one position for a while, then try another—maybe what you need is variety.
- Walking.
- A warm shower or bath.
- Loving encouragement (tell your helpers you need their encouragement in words and touch).
- Change in environment (ask if you can leave the hospital for a walk in the park—or at least try the early-labor lounge or lobby).

- Privacy with one's partner (shoo everyone else out, leave a guard at the door, and you and your mate can cuddle, kiss, massage, or whatever you need—maybe talk!).
- Breast and nipple stimulation. Remember, breast and nipple stimulation can make the uterus contract and can work for those women who have enjoyed it as part of lovemaking and either are uninhibited in a hospital setting or can arrange for the privacy they need—or use a breast pump.
- Removal of persons who cause stress (be honest).

To avoid failure to progress in the second stage of labor, use one of the efficient delivery positions discussed in chapter 12. If you have no choice but to use the delivery table, you can help your second stage in several ways, most of which need to be agreed on ahead of time.

- Have the delivery table tilted down at a slight angle; you won't feel you are pushing uphill as much.
- Avoid stirrups. They can quickly be swung into place if needed. Your legs should be relaxed and spread apart so you are comfortable. This position allows you to relax your perineum, so your pushes are more effective. It also protects your perineum from tears and episiotomy, because there is no tension holding back the birth.
- If you must use stirrups, have the nurse adjust them for you in an upright, supported sitting position, so you are not forced to lie flat because the stirrups are fixed for that position.
- With each pushing contraction, have your helpers lift you to an upright position; round your back, hold onto your knees, but don't pull on them (causes perineum tension); relax your perineum, and push, using your abdominal muscles.
- Have a stack of pillows behind your head and shoulders so you can relax between contractions without lying flat.

FETAL DISTRESS

The diagnosis of fetal distress accounts for 10 percent of all cesareans. Fetal distress is most often defined by variations in the fetal heart rate which are considered abnormal. The difficulty is in telling whether the fetus is simply normally distressed or is in true distress needing intervention.

Researchers in Sweden, Great Britain, and the United States have identified what is happening in normal birth to cause unnecessary cesareans for fetal distress. Most infants diagnosed as distressed during labor are in excellent condition at birth after a cesarean. The process of labor does stress an infant, resulting in a release of stress hormones (catecholamines, pronounced "cat-a-cola-means") that are crucial for the protection and good health of the fetus.

Catecholamines cause vital processes in the fetus which help it survive and adapt at birth, according to researchers Hugo Lagercrantz and Theodore Slotkin. The effects of the catecholamines on a fetus, which include a *slowing* of the heart rate, protect it from less oxygen during contractions. (In adults catecholamines *increase* the heart rate, part of the "fight or flight" response.) The slowed heart rate may be diagnosed as fetal distress needing a cesarean, when it is a sign of the fetus adapting beautifully to the stress of labor.

The stress hormones do other good things. The lungs are stimulated to change in several ways, including absorbing amniotic fluids so the baby can breathe at birth. Blood flow increases to the heart and brain, protecting these vital organs. The fetus is put into a highly alert state that researchers believe may help in mother and infant attachment at birth.

The fetus has several means for increasing catecholamines. One of the best is the compression of the fetal head during the pushing stage of labor, conclude Lagercrantz and Slotkin. They say this may be the reason infants born by cesarean after labor have a much higher rate of breathing difficulties (and lower measured catecholamine levels) than babies born vaginally. Repeat cesareans where the fetus experiences no labor also show breathing problems and the lowest levels of catecholamines.

The electronic fetal monitor (EFM) is almost universally used to measure the fetal heart rate. In chapter 7 we discussed the problems of the EFM in showing fetal distress and increasing the risk of cesarean birth without any better outcome for the baby.

Obstetrician, researcher, and professor Edward H. Hon, M.D., is the inventor of EFM. "Most women in labor are much better off at home than in the hospital with the electronic

fetal monitor," he said at the "Crisis in Obstetrics—
Management Labor" conference, reported by Diony Young.
He believes that "most obstetricians don't understand the
monitor. They're dropping the knife with each drop in the fetal
heart rate. The cesarean section is considered as a rescue
mission of the baby by the white Knight, but actually you've
assaulted the mother."

In their comprehensive review of the literature, the NIH
task force summarized the most common suggestions for
reversing fetal distress without resorting to surgery:

- Give the mother oxygen.
- Change the mother's position.
- Give intravenous fluids (hydration).
- Turn oxytocin off if it is being used.

A simple means of preventing the overdiagnosis of fetal
distress is to use a nurse to regularly monitor the baby's heart
rate. In addition, the widespread use of oxytocin needs careful
evaluation. Pitocin can intensify natural contractions, reducing
the oxygen supply to the baby and triggering fetal distress.
Because this is so well-known, women receiving Pitocin are
usually placed in the high-risk category. So another way to
prevent a diagnosis of fetal distress would be to avoid the use
of Pitocin in the first place. Try other means of stimulating
labor, such as having the mother walk.

BREECH PRESENTATION

Ten percent of cesarean delivery rates are due to the
decision to deliver almost all breech presentations by cesarean.
Most babies are born head first. In a breech birth the baby's
bottom comes first, called a frank or complete breech presentation, or rarely, the baby's feet come first, called a footling
breech presentation. Breech presentation happens in 3–4 percent of deliveries. The labor lasts no longer than the average
headfirst presentation. Breech position is nine times more
common earlier in pregnancy than at term, which means that
most breech babies naturally rotate to a head-down position
before the end of pregnancy.

Perinatal mortality and complication rates are higher in
breech presentations than in headfirst presentations. There are
often other problems, such as prematurity and placenta previa

along with the breech presentation. However, even when problems such as these are not present at breech deliveries, the outcome for the baby in a breech presentation may not always be as good as for headfirst presentation. Because of this, there has been a shift to cesarean delivery of most breech births. Some obstetricians will not deliver any breech presentations vaginally (and some of them have not had any training in vaginal breech deliveries either).

The trend toward cesarean delivery of breech presentation is a major area of controversy among obstetricians, however. The reason for the controversy is that cesarean birth increased from 12 percent of all breech presentations in 1970 to 86 percent in 1988. In spite of the greatly increased use of cesarean delivery, there is no evidence of a better outcome for the baby: there was no overall decrease in mortality for breech presentations during that period, and no evidence of better health in breech newborns.

Studies from different medical centers and hospitals report successful vaginal deliveries with term and premature breech presentations, now adding up to thousands of births. In United States medical centers at least 50 percent of breech presentations are now delivered vaginally. At National Maternity Hospital in Dublin, where the cesarean rate has remained very low, nearly 80 percent of breech presentations are delivered vaginally. Several older, experienced obs told us, "So, what's new? I've always delivered most breech babies vaginally." Obstetricians Michel Odent and Leo Sorger use the supported squat position for breech presentation because of gravity's assist, more pelvic room for the fetus, and faster delivery.

The consensus is no longer that a cesarean is assumed simply because of fetal position. The new consensus is represented in the Canadian commission's report that "a cesarean section should not be performed for breech presentation unless it can be shown to be justified." Obstetricians can use the recommendations, widely publicized in their journals, for vaginal delivery of breech fetuses.

Another solution to reducing cesareans for breech is to get the baby in a headfirst position. "External version" is a term used to describe gentle manipulation by the doctor of the mother's abdomen during the last month of pregnancy to turn the baby from a breech to a headfirst position. Increasingly successful efforts in external version mean "we may be able to reduce the incidence of breech delivery to approximately 1 percent to 1.5 percent," according to obstetrician Edward Quilligan, M.D., with the University of Southern California School of Medicine.

No medical procedure such as external version is without risks. Two nonmedical exercises to turn breech presentation are the tilt position and the knee-chest position. The tilt position was originated by obstetrics professor (now retired) Juliet De Sa Souza, M.D., at Grant Medical College, Bombay, India.

If, by the beginning of the eighth month of pregnancy, the baby is still in a breech position, the mother lies in the tilt position for ten minutes, twice a day. With an empty stomach, lying on her back on the floor, knees bent so that her feet are flat on the floor, the mother puts three good-sized pillows under her bottom. De Sa Souza reported in 1977 that 89 percent of 744 babies in breech presentations turned to a headfirst position with this exercise, most within two to three weeks. Once the baby has turned from a breech to a head-down position, discontinue the tilt exercise.

The knee-chest position is assumed by kneeling and leaning forward until your head rests on your folded arms (your head will be lower than your bottom). You'll find that you have to spread your knees to accommodate your late-pregnancy abdomen. Starting at the thirty-seventh week of pregnancy, assume this position for fifteen minutes three times a day, the first time before arising in the morning and preferably with a full bladder. The slight weight of the full bladder is thought to encourage the fetus to turn. Do the exercise for seven days. Both of these exercises have yet to be tested in randomized controlled trials with sufficient numbers to know whether they are really helpful or whether fetuses turned because they often do anyway.

OTHER REASONS FOR THE INCREASE

A wide variety of reasons account for the remaining 17 percent of all cesareans: increased "elective" (by choice, not emergency) cesareans for mothers at high risk (for example, for some mothers with serious kidney disease); increased elective cesareans for babies at high risk (for example, multiple birth, or cesareans when *active* genital herpes in the mother is confirmed); or cesareans for prolonged pregnancy or premature rupture of membranes. Many of these are widely accepted as necessary, but others have no evidence of better outcome. For example, twins may be delivered by cesarean, or the first is delivered vaginally and the second by cesarean, with no evidence of better outcome for the babies.

PREMATURE RUPTURE OF MEMBRANES

PROM, as it is called, does not refer to the old high school dance. The letters stand for premature rupture of membranes, meaning that the mother's bag of waters has broken before labor begins. It is one of the most common complications in pregnancy and can result in a c-section, often unnecessarily. You can lessen the chance you will have PROM.

The routine weekly pelvic examination usually done in the month before your due date is "associated with a significantly higher incidence of PROM," according to obstetrician J. P. Lenihan, M.D., reporting in *Obstetrics and Gynecology*. A pelvic examination is when the doctor puts his gloved fingers in your vagina to examine your cervix, the opening to your uterus. Lenihan recommends no pelvic examinations during the last three months of pregnancy unless there is a valid medical reason for examining the cervix. Discuss this recommendation with your birth attendant to lessen your risk of PROM.

There is strong controversy among obstetricians over what to do when the membranes rupture before labor. Some argue for immediate delivery to reduce the risk of infection in the mother and the baby. Others say that because PROM is often associated with a pregnancy not yet at term, that is with prematurity, nothing should be done. These two approaches are termed "aggressive" and "conservative." The aggressive approach means delivery within twenty-four hours of ruptured membranes by induction or cesarean if necessary. The conservative approach means waiting with close attention for either spontaneous labor or signs of infection. Several studies now show that the conservative approach results in less breathing distress in newborns, because of less prematurity.

More and more, obstetricians are coming around to believe that it is better for the baby to take the conservative approach with PROM, if delivery is going to mean a premature baby. Most, however, still believe that if PROM happens in a term pregnancy, and spontaneous labor does not begin within a few hours, they must induce labor or do a cesarean to make sure the baby is born within twenty-four hours.

Research shows that here, too, most doctors are being too aggressive. The study of D. I. Conway, et al. confirms results of previous studies showing most women will start labor spontaneously within twenty-four hours after PROM at term, reported editor Madeleine Shearer in the *Birth* journal. The women with spontaneous labors had significantly fewer cesareans and other interventions than women induced early for PROM. At least 90 percent of women with PROM near term begin labor within twenty-four hours and deliver within forty-eight hours if doctors will simply wait that long.

One study giving strong support for using the conservative approach whenever PROM happens, whether at term or not, was reported by Kenneth A. Kappy, M.D., et al., in the *American Journal of Obstetrics and Gynecology*. Most of the women who were not yet at term with PROM went more than twenty-four hours before labor started. Nearly 20 percent continued their pregnancies more than seven days before labor began, and the longest period of time between PROM and labor was fifty-eight days.

Most of the women whose pregnancy was at term with PROM went into labor before twenty-four hours. However, several women had their pregnancies continue up to a week or more before labor began; in one case for fourteen days. Infection rates (the fear of doctors when they diagnose PROM) were very low. A critical difference in management was that no pelvic exams were done. The key reason doctors give for the aggressive approach—infection—is often the iatrogenic (doctor-caused) result of pelvic examinations after membranes have ruptured.

The placenta continues to manufacture amniotic fluid and sometimes the tear in the membranes seals over. The study by Kappy et al. shows that it is safe to allow a pregnancy to go on for days or weeks after PROM, whether the woman is at the end of her pregnancy or not. If PROM happens to you, talk to your doctor about these studies. Try to negotiate for those precious twenty-four hours to start labor on your own. If you get the extra time, are nearing the end of the twenty-four hours, and haven't started labor, try natural labor induction: nipple stimulation or castor oil (see "Prolonged Pregnancy" in this chapter). Most of the following common-sense measures suggest how to avoid getting an infection:

- Allow *no* pelvic examinations.
- Avoid intercourse.
- Avoid sitting in water, take showers instead.
- Stay home until labor starts, rather than go to the hospital.
- Avoid contacts outside the family (alien germs).
- Watch for signs of infection, such as an elevated temperature and pain or tenderness in the abdomen.
- Drink plenty of fluids.
- Keep in touch with your doctor.
- Wait for spontaneous labor to begin.
- If you have active genital herpes and PROM, you will need a cesarean within six hours to avoid the possibility of infecting your baby.

CESAREAN DELIVERY FOR ACTIVE GENITAL HERPES IN THE MOTHER

Genital herpes is a viral venereal disease. The Center for Disease Control in Atlanta estimates that 25 million men and women have genital herpes, with as many as five hundred thousand new cases each year. Genital herpes is an incurable disease that becomes latent (without symptoms) but can reappear in the infected person. Usually, the first infection, called primary genital herpes, is the most uncomfortable and lasts about three weeks. Recurrences are usually milder and last nine or ten days.

If a baby contracts herpes from the mother at the time of delivery, it is a very serious disease for the baby. The risk of death or chance of the infant becoming abnormal as a result of the disease is very high. Researchers believe that only mothers with active lesions in their genital area at the time of delivery are at risk of passing the virus on to their babies. Even then, the risk of the baby contracting the disease is low if the active lesions are from a repeating infection. The risk is very high if the lesions are from a primary infection of the mother.

An automatic cesarean for every woman with herpes is *not* necessary. "Thousands of babies are born every day to women with genital herpes," said Lawrence Corey, M.D., of the University of Washington School of Medicine, Seattle. "Vaginal deliveries are usually possible, and the babies are perfectly normal. Even abdominal delivery is not foolproof. Neonatal herpes infections have occurred after abdominal delivery."

Charles Prober, M.D., et al. at Stanford University School of Medicine studied the risk of infection in babies exposed to the active virus during delivery to women who had histories of repeating herpes infections. None of the infants got herpes. The researchers believe the risk of a baby acquiring an infection from a mother with a repeating infection at delivery is low. The mother passes resistance to the disease (antibodies) to the fetus, and repeating infections are milder than primary infections.

However, because of the seriousness of the disease in infants, the researchers recommend cesarean section if a woman with recurrent herpes has visible lesions when she goes into labor. If the woman has no symptoms, they do not recommend a cesarean because the chance of passing on the virus to the baby is very low. They concluded that the baby of a woman having her first herpes attack at the time of delivery had a very high risk of contracting herpes and should be delivered by cesarean.

A special risk to the baby of a woman with a history of herpes in her or her mate is the use of the internal fetal monitor. Edward Kaye, M.D., and Elizabeth Dooling, M.D., of Boston City Hospital reported on neonatal herpes associated with fetal scalp electrodes. In the cases reported, the mothers had no signs of active herpes, but their babies contracted herpes at the site of the insertion of the electrode. Because of this reported risk, a woman with a history of or suspicion of past genital herpes in her or her mate should strongly consider refusing the use of the internal fetal monitor. "We have shown that neonatal herpes simplex virus must be considered an added risk of fetal monitoring," say the authors, who question the use of internal fetal monitoring in low-risk labors because of the added danger.

PROLONGED PREGNANCY

When nine months pregnant, some of us feel as if our pregnancy is prolonged. When we go much past the "due date" everyone asks, "Haven't you had your baby *yet?*" Think about adding a week to the due date you tell everyone.

The due date is estimated by counting 280 days forward

from the first day of your last period. Forty weeks is the average "term" pregnancy, and later than forty-two weeks is considered prolonged. The problem with this average due date, of course, is that you may not be average. Your menstrual cycle may not be average (twenty-eight days). Or maybe it is normal for you to have a forty-three week pregnancy for *this baby*.

In 1965 an obstetrician wrote, "There is less than a 50 percent chance that labor will ensue within a week of the estimated date (early or late). I emphasize the word 'estimate.' Relax and be patient. Enjoy your pregnancy secure in the knowledge that your baby will be born when it has completed its normal growth and development in the uterus." Although you may get the impression from your obstetrician that he is sure of your due date, and he must induce you at forty-one weeks or forty-two weeks or whatever, nothing has changed. Due dates are still estimates, and women still start labor when they are ready.

True prolonged pregnancy (no mistake in dates) has an increased risk of perinatal mortality (death of the fetus before or during birth). Perinatal mortality is low at term and beyond, but it is higher at forty-two weeks (three fetal deaths per thousand births) and at forty-three weeks (four per thousand) than at forty weeks (2.3 per thousand), report Mary Halperin, M.D., and Murray Enkin, M.D., in *ICEA Review*. Though this increased risk is widely known, no one really knows what should be done about it.

"All studies since 1978 on the management of postterm pregnancy have found no benefit, or increased risks, with routine termination of pregnancy at 42 weeks of gestation," report Madeleine Shearer, R.P.T., and Milton Estes, M.D., in the *Birth* journal. Routine induction leads to delivery of some premature infants because of mistaken due dates. Almost all reports agreed that about 50 percent of pregnancies called prolonged are not past term but reflect mistaken due dates. The use of sonograms (ultrasound) in estimating due dates was "remarkably misleading," wrote the authors. It led to "marked escalation in other tests, interventions in labor, and cesarean sections." The authors found it "disturbing that women's own due date calculations seemed to carry less weight than did sonograms in managing these pregnancies."

Even with some certainty that a pregnancy is prolonged, current tests for fetal well-being are not a great help in determining which pregnancy needs to be ended with induction or cesarean. The authors reviewed the literature for all current tests and found only fetal movement counting (FMC) of benefit. FMC is having the mother count the number of fetal movements in a certain time period. S. Neldam carried out a randomized controlled trial with 3,600 women. Half the women were told to count fetal movements for one hour three times a week from the thirtieth week of pregnancy to delivery. Other tests were used to confirm distress if the women reported reduced fetal movements. These women had significantly fewer fetal deaths than the women who were not told to use FMC.

The nonstress test (NST) and contraction stress test (CST) are both commonly used today in pregnancies past forty to forty-two weeks. Both use the external fetal monitor. The NST simply notes the fetal heart response when the mother indicates the fetus has moved. The CST measures the fetal heart response to a challenge of induced contractions, either with oxytocin or nipple stimulation. Shearer and Estes report Grant and Mohide's analysis of four randomized controlled trials of these two tests. In all the trials all women received NSTs and CSTs, but only half of the women had the test results revealed to their doctors. Grant and Mohide found that "in each of the four trials, there were [significantly] *more* deaths in the group for which clinicians had access to the test results ('revealed') than in the 'concealed' group." Having the information from the tests resulted in worse outcomes for the babies.

You may find yourself with a true prolonged pregnancy and a doctor pressuring you to accept induction. If you don't want to change doctors, and you are ready to give into the pressure, try natural induction first. In order from most fun to least fun:

- Sexual intercourse with orgasm
- Nipple stimulation by you, your mate, a baby, or a breast pump
- Castor oil

None of these work if your body is not ready for labor, but they are much less risky than oxytocin induction. Castor oil irritates the intestines, causing diarrhea and stimulating contractions. Midwife Anne Frye of Informed Homebirth suggests: "Take two ounces castor oil, two ounces orange juice and two ounces hard liquor. Take a hot shower. One hour later, take the same formula (sans liquor) and a high enema. One hour later take the same formula (castor oil and orange juice) and another hot shower. The idea is the liquor loosens up any psychological reservations the mother may have to labor beginning. I've seen labor start after the first dose!" Drink a lot of water so you don't get dehydrated from the diarrhea.

CESAREAN SURGERY

"A cesarean section has become less a matter of last resort and truly simply another method of delivery," said Basil Maloney, M.D., discussing breech delivery at a West Coast ob/gyn meeting in 1979. What most physicians don't know, and might even be shocked to discover, is that most women don't take cesareans quite as casually as they do. The aftereffects and recovery from a cesarean birth, for some women, are about as close to hell as they choose to get. For others, it can be less dramatic, but still traumatic.

The surgery itself, however, *is* an easy, quick, and usually safe procedure. Because cutting into the abdominal wall is involved, all cesareans are major surgery. In preparation for surgery, a catheter is put into a woman's bladder, the abdomen and perineum are shaved, and an IV is inserted in the back of her hand. The IV and catheter remain in place for about twenty-four hours after the surgery. Regional anesthesia (a spinal or epidural), which allows the mother to be awake but without feeling below her waist, is administered. In an emergency situation, a general anesthesia (gas) can be used. The advantage to gas is that it takes effect immediately, in preference to the fifteen to twenty minutes taken by regional anesthesia. A drape is placed at about chest level, to keep the woman from observing the surgery. Then the abdomen is sterilized with a cold anesthetic solution.

The first incision is made in the abdomen, usually a four- to six-inch "bikini cut" just above the pubic hair line. The bladder is separated from the uterus and pushed down out of the way before another horizontal incision is made in the lowest part of the uterus. The baby is lifted out of the uterus within ten minutes from the beginning of surgery. The afterbirth is removed, the uterus is sutured, the bladder is stitched back into place, and the abdominal incision is closed. The total surgery takes about an hour, with most of the time spent in sewing up the incisions.

HOW SAFE IS "SAFE"?

Well, why not have a cesarean? With the cesarean section rate so high, your chances of having one are pretty good, one in four in fact. Why fight the system? It's an easy, simple, safe operation for the doctor to perform, and if he says, "I think you need a cesarean," isn't it easier to just go along? Yes, it is. And if you do have a cesarean, the chances are excellent that you will survive, and so will your baby.

CESAREAN RISKS TO BABY

Although cesareans are safe today, they are certainly not as safe as vaginal deliveries, either for the mother or the baby. A baby is always considered at high risk for complications when born by cesarean section. Madeleine Shearer, editor of *Birth*, reviewed the literature and summarized the four most frequent complications of cesarean to the infant, in order of their frequency:

- Jaundice
- Fewer quiet alert periods after birth
- Respiratory distress
- Drug effects

Jaundice

Jaundice is an overdiagnosed, overtreated problem in more than half of all newborns and is a recognized risk of cesarean delivery. Why is not known. Newborn jaundice sometimes requires treatment of the infant under bilirubin lights. Having a blindfold placed over his or her eyes for nearly twenty-four hours a day for several days can be uncomfortable, frustrating, and perhaps even terrifying for the infant. Certainly, the treatment interferes with early contact between mother and her baby.

Fewer Quiet Alert Periods

Infants born by cesarean section have fewer quiet alert periods after birth, the time when the infant is most likely to respond to its mother. Mothers and babies need all the help they can get in the early time they are getting acquainted with each other. A cesarean-born baby has fewer of these ideal times, when he is neither sleeping nor crying, but awake and taking in his surroundings—most importantly, his mother.

Respiratory Distress

Breathing difficulty or respiratory distress is the most feared of the frequent complications of a cesarean baby. "Babies delivered by cesarean section are at a considerable disadvantage during the first few days of life," reported British researchers John Brice and Colin Walker, studying respiratory distress. Breathing difficulty may be temporary or may be the much more serious respiratory distress syndrome (RDS). This disease varies from mild to severe, and often requires mechanical assistance for the baby to breathe.

Studying how doctors cause RDS, R. L. Goldberg, M.D., et al. observed that a major factor in RDS was a misjudgment of the actual length of pregnancy and a too-early ending of the pregnancy by induction or cesarean. "The ill-advised timing [by doctors] of cesarean sections is threatening to become the leading cause of respiratory distress, or hyaline membrane disease in infants," said Lewis Gluck, M.D., University of California Medical Center, San Diego.

However, several studies found an increased risk of RDS from the cesarean section, not only from poor timing. At all gestational ages, more babies had RDS when delivered by cesarean than vaginally, reported M. Douglas Jones, Jr., M.D., et al. studying 16,485 birth records at University Hospital, Denver. Researchers at the University of Washington, Seattle, identified two important factors in RDS and their relation to cesarean surgery. Labor (preventing RDS) and lung fluids (causing RDS) were found by E. White et al. to be significant factors linking cesareans and RDS.

These findings fit with the research on catecholamines (see "Fetal Distress," this chapter). Naturally produced by the infant in reaction to the stress of labor and delivery, catecholamines help the fetus by clearing the lungs of amniotic fluid so the baby can breathe at birth. Babies born by cesarean section do not have the high levels of catecholamines of vaginally born infants.

Drug Effects

Drug effects on the cesarean infant can be noticeable and are the fourth most common complication. The infant may appear to be drugged, or slowed down, because of drugs or anesthesia given the mother during labor and delivery. The baby may also have an elevated blood pressure from drugs given to the mother to correct her *low* blood pressure as a complication of the anesthesia.

Additional Complications

In addition to these four common complications the medical literature shows babies born from *planned repeat* cesareans (cesareans done before labor begins) are at risk from two additional complications. They are more likely than babies born vaginally to have abnormal neurological responses, and more likely to have these abnormal neurological responses still present when the babies are a year old. Abnormal neurological responses are a rare complication in repeat cesareans performed after labor starts.

CESAREAN RISKS FOR MOTHER

There is no medical question that a vaginal delivery is safer for the mother almost all the time. Regional anesthesia, availability of blood transfusions, a horizontal uterine incision, and antibiotics have made cesareans safer for mothers than ever before. Yet the maternal death rate after a cesarean is *still* higher than it is for a vaginal delivery. There is some controversy about how great the difference is. Maternal mortality for vaginal deliveries is placed at less than one death for every 10,000 live births. Obstetricians generally quote maternal mortality for cesareans four to six times higher than for vaginal births.

Some studies suggest that the maternal death rate after cesareans is even higher. Women who deliver babies by cesarean section face a risk of death twenty-six times greater than those who deliver vaginally, according to John Evrand, M.D., and Edwin Gold, M.D., Brown University researchers. Their study covering an eleven-year period in Rhode Island found much lower maternal mortalities with a vaginal birth and higher cesarean maternal mortalities.

Cesarean maternal mortalities were also higher than commonly reported according to a study by George Rubin, M.D., et al. of the Center for Disease Control, Altanta. If a cesarean mother dies after she leaves the hospital (from a pulmonary embolism, for example) her death is not likely to be recorded as a "maternal mortality." Comparing death certificates of women with birth certificates of babies born up to sixty days before a woman's death, the authors found a maternal death rate of 9.7 per 100,000 live births (or 1 per 10,000) for vaginal deliveries, but a rate of 105 maternal deaths per 100,000 live cesarean deliveries (or slightly more than 10 per 10,000). The cesarean mothers were more than ten times likely to die than the mothers who gave birth vaginally. The authors consider these mortality figures low because they limited their search to sixty days before the women's deaths and they excluded maternal deaths associated with stillbirth.

In both these studies, half of the maternal deaths after a cesarean were directly caused by the operation, from pulmonary embolism (a blood clot migrating from the surgical incision to the lungs) or from complications of the anesthesia. About the same time other researchers were also finding that half of the maternal deaths associated with cesarean section are directly caused by the operation itself. Death from pulmonary embolism and complications of anesthesia are "an inevitable risk of any pelvic operative procedure," say authors Iain Chalmers and Martin Richards, writing in *Benefits and Hazards of the New Obstetrics*. In a study of cesarean section deaths in England and Wales, these authors found that half the maternal deaths following a cesarean section were caused by these two complications. "Earlier studies have underestimated the risks of cesarean sections," concludes Rubin. "Physicians should carefully assess the risks whenever they are considering performing cesarean sections."

The true cesarean maternal death rate, or the odds of a mother dying after a cesarean delivery, are about one per thousand. Certainly this relatively high rate, compared to vaginal delivery, should be a strong reason for caution when the question of cesarean comes up.

Other reasons for caution are the complications, the physical problems, that cesarean mothers have: severe pain from the operation itself, pain from the intestinal gas resulting from shock to the intestines, and possible future cesareans. Hospital stays are longer, costs are much higher, and the physical recovery from the surgery and birth takes much longer than the recovery from a vaginal birth. The woman who has a cesarean may also find she no longer has maternity insurance coverage for her next birth. Industry-wide, the usual policy is to terminate maternity coverage after a cesarean delivery for a woman with an individualized insurance policy or a group policy that has a small number of employees (ten or less).

Almost half of cesarean mothers have serious complications from the surgery, some complications more easily treated than others. The three most frequent of the serious complications are infection, hemorrhage, and internal problems from scarring or injury to other organs, according to editor Madeleine Shearer's review of the literature. Women who are internally monitored during labor, and then have a cesarean, have more uterine infections than cesarean mothers not internally monitored. Overall, the cesarean uterine infection rate is fourteen to forty-five times higher than uterine infections following vaginal deliveries. The cesarean mother is at greater risk than the vaginal mother of developing other infections too, for example, in her bladder and in her abdomen.

NEED FOR CAUTION

If you are advised to have a cesarean, you must be ready to ask, "Is this really necessary?" It's probable that this crucial question must be asked by your husband or your doula to protect you, because you are likely to have been laboring for hours, to be tiring, to be vulnerable and open to any suggestions around you.

Most doctors will not like your questioning their decision. Because there is no evidence that cesareans improve infant outcome when the diagnosis of abnormal labor is made, you and your doctor will have to relearn toleration of a long labor. You may have to remind your doctor to try other measures to reverse fetal distress, such as those recommended by the NIH task force. Knowing that a vaginal birth is possible in place of a repeat cesarean or for a breech presentation, you have to doctor-shop during your pregnancy to get what you want. Finding Dr. Right is still your best bet for a vaginal birth.

THE EMOTIONAL PAIN OF A CESAREAN

Almost all cesarean mothers survive the surgery, and their wounds eventually heal. However, the emotional pain can be much harder to heal, and this is an area physicians pay little, if any, attention to. Whatever the reason for the cesarean, it tends to promote a poor self-image for the newly delivered mother: "My body screwed up," is the common complaint. If a woman has had a vaginal birth before this cesarean delivery, the feelings about herself may not be as poor. But most women need to try to understand what happened, why *they* couldn't give birth vaginally. Yet many women complain that their doctors leave them with little or no lasting understanding of all the medical concerns leading up to the cesarean.

Another emotional problem can occur with maternal-infant attachment, which may be difficult because of the inevitable separation during the first hours or day following delivery, when the mother is in so much pain. Some mothers who have been given a regional anesthesia for the surgery and no drugs to knock them out have found they can take advantage of the first hour in the recovery room before the anesthesia wears off. They are not yet feeling the pain of the incision and can respond to their babies. But maternal-infant attachment can be affected by the surgery. "We are finding that mothers are upset with their babies because they had to have surgery," said nurse Debbie Pile, interviewed for a television documentary on cesareans. Nurse Pile says the mothers feel toward the baby that "it's your fault I had to have the cesarean. I was relaxing and breathing and it was you who developed fetal distress."

All new mothers are vulnerable and need loving care from those around them so that they can learn to love their babies. Cesarean mothers need more loving nurturing and for a longer period of time after birth. Many decide they just won't go through it again and make sure of that by having themselves sterilized. Postpartum sterilization is far more common for cesarean mothers at all ages, according to the U.S. Public Health Service.

The physical pain and emotional trauma of the cesarean experience has been much overlooked by doctors. Our next chapter gives one mother's story.

• NINE •

HAVING A CESAREAN
IS HAVING A BABY

SANDY'S STORY OF TWO CESAREAN BIRTHS

With my first baby, I was in labor for nineteen hours before my doctor decided a cesarean was indicated. I was very, very upset, and my husband was very frightened. All the rules of the game had been changed on me. I had totally lost control. I had never had surgery, and I was angry and frightened at the thought of it. The abruptness of it all shocked me, and then, of course, there is always the underlying threat that maybe things will not come out well. It was very traumatic.

The anesthesiologist on call preferred to give gas, and my doctor recommended I go along with his specialty. They put me out and then it was over. When I finally woke up—after five hours of fading in and out—everything ached. I was intensely sore where they had cut. I wasn't inclined to move, to hold my baby, or to breastfeed her—which broke my heart and disappointed my husband greatly! My body just hurt too much.

The physical pain was one thing, but the emotional and psychological pain was, I think, worse. Sometime before I finally woke up, they had shaken me awake, and told me three times that I had a girl. I felt very empty, very empty, very detached from the whole experience. They said, "Hey, take a look at this," and I thought "big deal." I did feel my husband's presence in the room when I would wake up for a minute before falling back to sleep. I would see him sitting in the chair holding the baby, and there was a great deal of comfort in that. When I finally unfogged enough to talk to my husband and my sister, who is an obstetrical nurse, I felt good that they were there and that they were taking care of the baby; at least the baby was in the hands of the people that I loved.

One of the things that upset me most in my first cesarean was that neither physician, neither my family practice doctor nor my ob, asked me anything about how I felt about the cesarean. There was no emotional support or concern from either of them. There I was feeling, okay, now here you are, you have this pain in your belly. You have this baby you feel detached from. You have what was supposed to have been a wonderful experience all turned upside down.

You do need someone to talk to after a cesarean, regardless of whether it's a traumatic one or not. My sister was there for me, and we talked continuously for hours. She also got after me to start walking really soon. It was very painful to get up and walk around. It almost didn't hurt too much if you lay still and didn't move, but moving—changing your position in bed, or trying to get up—was enormously painful. I didn't want to do that. But she told me that the sooner you start walking, the sooner you start passing gas, which means that the intestines have begun working again, and you are beginning to recover. That was the magic word!

I had wanted to nurse my baby as soon after birth as possible. Well, that was a joke. I knew that nursing helps the uterus to contract, but I was so fearful of any additional pain, I wasn't going to let that baby anywhere near me. My sister knew my fears and told me that, because this was my first baby, I probably would not feel the uterus contracting, especially because there was so much pain down there anyway. She very gently kept urging me to nurse, and with her help I did it. She helped me get the baby on the breast, and I discovered that there was no additional pain . . . just a wonderful joy.

After that, I felt emotionally very good for the rest of my three-day hospital stay, because I had my sister, my husband, and my baby all rooming-in with me. My sister acted as my advocate after the surgery, and it was wonderful for both me and my husband to have her around. Together, she and my husband made me feel good about everything—about the baby and the experience—and I felt optimistic about the future. So, all in all, I would describe my first cesarean as a positive experience, because I felt so cared for during my hospital stay (by my family), and later, when I went home. I felt emotionally high for months afterward.

After my second cesarean I was extremely depressed. As high as I was with my first, I was that depressed with my second. We had a trial of labor, sort of as an experiment, because a vaginal birth after a cesarean had only been done three or four times at my hospital. I was four centimeters dilated when they decided to do a cesarean. I thought they were pretty quick to jump in as soon as they saw that the labor wasn't going fast.

I realize now that I was very apprehensive about another cesarean, and I would have been willing to labor forever to avoid surgery. I should have talked out my fears long before the labor. My worst fear was the overwhelming remembrance of the pain. That, and remembering the recovery, remembering just how complicated the whole thing is, emotionally and physically.

I had decided beforehand to have an epidural if a cesarean were needed, so that I could stay conscious and have my husband with me. He had to wait outside while I was given the epidural, and I felt alone and frightened. I had to curl up into the fetal position, which was difficult for me because of my big belly. The better fetal position you get into, the better chance the anesthesiologist has of hitting the epidural space. My back was numbed, but he had to poke around several times. I was afraid, thinking, "What are they doing behind me?"

Later, as I lay on the table holding my husband's hand, I barely knew he was there. I kept thinking, "They are going to cut me up again, dammit." I felt that the anesthesiologist was moving too fast. Everything was moving too fast, and no one cared how I felt. People were bustling about in the delivery room, and I was feeling very helpless. My second chance at a vaginal delivery was shot. Once again I had lost all control over the situation. Why the hell was this happening to me again?

Once the surgery started, it happened within minutes. They were taking the baby out, but I didn't know it. I was still thinking, "When are you going to start?" I was holding my husband's hand, just looking at him, trying to block everything else out, frightened to death. My sister, who was with me again, all of a sudden said to me. "It's a girl," and I didn't know that they were cutting me open yet.

They showed the baby to me just briefly. I started crying and shaking a little bit, and they said later, "Oh, Sandy was so touched, it was such a euphoric experience because she was crying." I was crying because I thought, "God, it's another girl, and I have to go through this one more time to have a boy, and I can't do it. I can't do it again." My sister went down with the baby to the nursery. They called back over the intercom to say that she weighed ten pounds. That's the one positive, happy feeling that I will have from the whole experience—the utter astonishment I felt at having such a large baby.

I was so cold in the delivery room and shaking with chills. I shook more and more until I was out of control—apparently because I had hemorrhaged so badly, and my body was compensating for the loss of fluids. That really frustrated me. The anesthesiologist gave me something, and I went out. It was all over. Once again, I didn't have a chance to be with my baby after the delivery.

The pain after my second cesarean was more intense, because my emotions were so negative, I believe. It was also made worse by my getting a spinal headache. The anesthesiologist was not able to get into the epidural space well enough; and the epidural had turned into a spinal. It was complicated by a tightening of all the muscles in my back, which was more painful to me than the headache. Two days later they ended the headache and muscle spasms when they did a "blood patch"— injecting some blood from my arm into the epidural space. Because of the headache, though, I hadn't been able to get up and move around to help my recovery. Also I didn't have the same kind of support in the hospital as I did the first time. At the last minute the person I had lined up to care for my two-year-old couldn't come, and my sister went home to take care of her.

Emotionally I was a mess. My baby was in the nursery more than she was with me—no rooming-in this time. I was feeling very negative that I had had another painful experience, and I didn't have anyone in the hospital to help me. When I got home, my sister did not have the physical energy she had the first time to sit and talk with me, to empathize. She was too busy keeping up with the two-year-old, the cooking, and the rest. My husband was involved with his work, so he wasn't available very much. So I felt alone, and it was very stressful for me. After three months my belly was still hurting every day, all the time, because every time I lifted my two-year-old, I pulled on my incision.

I finally figured out that the physical part would have been barely noticeable *if* I had felt good emotionally. But I was mad at everything. I was mostly mad at my husband. Yet there was no way he could have been what I wanted him to be. I wanted him to make it all go away, and he couldn't. I was mad that I had no energy, and every little stress became impossible to cope with. I was mad at my physicians, and it wasn't until weeks later, at the urging of a friend, that I actually even acknowledged that. I was mad as hell at the anesthesiologist for knocking me out after the delivery, and for screwing up my recovery with a spinal headache. I was even mad about having hemorrhoids.

I am still angry about the whole experience, and I still haven't talked to anybody about it. My poor husband is afraid to bring it up; he's just trying to keep his head above water to keep me from biting it off all the time. He can't begin to understand my anger, and I'm just now beginning to accept that he never will, and it's not his fault. I've alternated from thinking I am going to get a stress-related disease, because I'm not coping well, to my marriage is going to break up because I've turned into such an unhappy shrew. What alternatives!

After my first cesarean I felt I was physically recovered after three weeks, although it was three months before I felt that all the fog was out of my head. But I was feeling very high, and very well loved, and very excited about the first baby. This second time I didn't have the gas, which I am grateful for, but I have an awful lot of anger bottled up. There were even times when I have felt suicidal in the last four months. After three months I began feeling better because I went home for Christmas and let other people take care of the baby, and I just slept and relaxed, so I broke the fatigue and self-pity cycle. Once or twice since then, I have regressed and have felt like I was going back to the old depressed mode. It's now four months postpartum. I announced to my husband a week ago that my incision didn't hurt anymore. But, then, after spending a whole day painting my daughter's bedroom, it began hurting again, and it's been hurting ever since. Nothing to run to the doctor about, but just enough pain to annoy me.

Finally, after four months, I am feeling more in control of my life again—but I'm working at it damned hard. The phrase that I often use when I think about the difference in the cesareans is that the first time I was surrounded by "a love bath," that is, love, concern, and security coming from my mother and my mother-in-law (who were both there to help when I came home from the hospital); my sister, who took care of my emotional needs and taught me how to care for my new baby; and my husband, who was just thrilled with the new baby. I felt good about myself and about my baby. After the second cesarean, there was no love bath. It just didn't happen.

For some reason I just felt all alone and negative—about myself, the experience, and especially about my future.

Some people would say, "Just give me a cesarean and forget the pain of labor." Well, I don't think there is a comparison between the pain of a cesarean and the pain of labor. Labor is a transitory pain. It's over when it's over. Labor pain is a physical thing. With a cesarean, however, there are so many other factors involved besides the physical: the emotional pain of apprehension and fear, the resentment and the anger, and the feeling of having lost all control—first over your body in pregnancy and in surgery, but also over your life. That's why—unless there is enormous support to make it a positive experience—the pain of a cesarean is really so much worse. When labor is over, the pain is over. When the cesarean is over, I don't think the pain is ever over—unless it was nipped in the bud by some very energetic, loving people.

Sandy is every cesarean mother. She is also a real person, though her name has been changed to protect her privacy. The fear, the disappointment, the anger, and the grief are almost universal feelings of cesarean mothers—albeit to different degrees. Support groups have sprung up across the country just for women who have had cesareans, so every cesarean mother can have the chance to express her intense feelings about her baby's birth, and to feel the support and understanding of other women who have had the same experience.

Where do these incredibly deep and intense feelings come from? Almost all women know how babies grow and how they are born. Nearly every woman grows up believing that some day she will become pregnant and give birth. A woman's monthly menstrual cycle is a regular reminder of her fertility and how her body is made to bear children. A woman's very image of herself, carried with her for years, is shattered when she must have a cesarean delivery. "I felt like a terrible failure," said one mother, Jane Richardson. "It was like training for the Olympics, then falling down the stairs. I had practiced so hard. I did nine months for this delivery. I know other women who feel guilty too, and they say 'if only I had breathed better and tried harder.' I felt disappointed, cheated, deprived, ugly, and angry."

The feeling of failing is intensified in women who prepare for childbirth. They are prepared to be in control, to participate in the delivery of their child, to experience the joy of giving birth vaginally. Suddenly all that is taken away. They lose the support of their husband when they need him the most, and they lose the moment of becoming acquainted with their newborn baby after birth, a time they have looked forward to as the culmination of their pregnancy. Cesarean mothers have suffered a loss, a loss of the birth experience they had prepared for, a loss of intimate contact of the mother, father, and newborn, and a loss of the very image of themselves as able to give birth vaginally. Grief is the normal human response to loss. Knowing that a cesarean was done for the sake of their baby is a great comfort to cesarean mothers, but it does not make up for the sense of loss and need to understand "Why me?" Cesarean mothers need a long time to heal emotionally.

In spite of what they have been through—the major surgery, the physical pain, the grieving—cesarean mothers cope. They learn to mother their babies. They heal and often go on to have another baby, even though it often means another cesarean. Cesarean mothers nurture, touch, and breastfeed their babies just the same as mothers who give birth vaginally. However, cesarean mothers need more comfort, more understanding, more help after their babies are born. They also could use a lot more respect for their incredible courage in immediately putting their baby's needs first, and readily giving up the kind of birth experience for which they have waited so long.

> Every birth is a perfect experience in its own way. It takes profound courage for a laboring woman to confront complications and to willingly open her already open self even further to include unfamiliar people and procedures into her experience. Monks spend lifetimes in soggy caves trying to achieve this state of humility that women are able to experience through giving birth, being then vessels through which the ultimate creative impulse is served and manifest. There is truth to be gotten and beauty to be seen in all births. Who is to say if one set of circumstances is more perfect than another, and who is to say that the mother whose child is taken from her at birth did not "bond" with the child?
>
> —KATE BOTLOS,
> ASSISTANT EDITOR, *MOTHERING*

"Grapefruit are sectioned but women give birth," is a phrase cesarean mothers have come up with to remind doctors that cesarean mothers, too, need family-centered births. By using the information we've assembled, you the reader can greatly reduce your chances of having a cesarean. But mothers sometimes really do need cesareans. You may have done all you can to reduce your risk of cesarean, and then find yourself in labor with the necessity to have an abdominal delivery.

Because the possibility is there for all women, you need to know what you can do to make your baby's cesarean delivery as good an experience for you, your husband, and your baby as it can be.

WHAT CESAREAN MOTHERS WANT FOR THEIR DELIVERIES

Women who have had cesareans are very sure about what is important to them. Cesarean mothers across the country strongly agree that they want to be awake. They want their mates with them, and they want as much visual and physical contact with their baby as possible. In other words, like all women, cesarean women want a family-centered birth—plus lots of the extra help that they need, because of their surgery, in holding and caring for their newborn. In surveys cesarean mothers' opinions were stronger and more unanimous than those women who had vaginal deliveries. Because of what they have been through, they are much more sure about the importance of the father's presence and about having contact with their babies. Cesarean mothers want hospitals and doctors who will give them the following options:

- To be awake, if possible
- To have the father with them during and after surgery
- To see the baby immediately after it is born
- To hold the baby when surgery is completed
- To be encouraged to hold and care for the baby if it must be in a special nursery
- To care for the "well" baby in their room whenever they want

Every mother needs to have her care individualized. Because almost all cesarean mothers want these options, doctors need to support their patients in getting them. Hospitals also need to change their policies so that family-centered maternity care is as strongly supported for cesarean mothers as for mothers who deliver vaginally. The care a cesarean mother receives needs even more sensitivity to her preferences, however. For example, while almost all cesarean mothers have a lot of pain following surgery, they will vary greatly in what they are willing to try to do—walk the first day, nurse their babies, have rooming-in, or have visitors.

Most cesarean mothers want to be awake. Although any kind of anesthesia has its risks, the National Institute of Health's task force recommended that women have the option of receiving regional anesthesia when they have a cesarean.

Women want to have their partners with them during and after surgery. A woman's fear and anxiety when a cesarean is recommended is high enough without having her key support person denied her. Fathers also are reassured by staying with their mates. Many hospitals are easing their policies to allow fathers to be present for a scheduled or repeat cesarean. It's unusual, however, to find a hospital that will allow fathers to stay in an emergency—a sudden cesarean that is decided on during labor. It's unlikely though, in most emergency cesareans, that the need for the cesarean is so urgent that a staff member cannot take the time to include the father in the preparations, allowing him to change his clothes into a scrub suit and stand by his mate. Emergency cesareans allow plenty of time for careful preparation, explanation, and some choices on the part of the parents if the baby is not in acute fetal distress. Having the fathers with them is so important to cesarean mothers, it should be the exception, not the rule, when fathers are asked to wait outside during an emergency cesarean.

If your partner is with you, he will not be able to see the surgery, just as you will not. The cesarean mother lies on her back on the delivery table. A drape is raised above her midsection, so she cannot see beyond that point. She does not see her baby born through the abdominal incision, and neither does the father seated next to her head. If the doctor keeps up a running commentary on what he's doing, however, the parents can participate in the excitement of the few minutes before the baby is born. Then the baby should be carried around the drape for them to see. If the baby is not in breathing distress, there is no reason why the father cannot carry his newborn to the nursery for an examination while the doctor closes the incisions on the mother. If the father does accompany his infant to the nursery, the new mother may prefer to have a familiar person stay with her. The doula, perhaps.

Cesarean mothers want to see the baby immediately after birth and to hold their baby when surgery is completed. Women who have had cesareans are keenly aware of what a difference it can make in their feelings toward the baby if they are given the chance to view the baby immediately after it is born, and, then, when surgery is completed, to hold and get acquainted with their baby in the recovery area before the anesthesia has worn off. For many women it may be the only chance they have to get acquainted with their babies for another twenty-four to forty-eight hours because of the pain following surgery.

Women want both parents to be encouraged to hold and care for the baby if it must be in a special-care nursery. Klaus and Kennell's research strongly supports this preference, because many women who are separated from their babies have much more difficulty developing a normal mother-baby relationship.

Women want to care for their "well" baby in their room whenever they wish. The pace of each mother's recovery will vary, but after the first day or so she will have the strength and inclination to begin to care for her baby. If the father and doula take over the care of the baby for the first day, the mother can, as Sandy did, gain great comfort from knowing her baby is being watched over and cared for by those she loves. Having the father and doula stay with the mother for much of her hospital stay gives her the extra care and assistance she needs.

QUESTIONS FOR YOUR DOCTOR: WILL HE OR WON'T HE?

To get what you want for a cesarean birth you must negotiate in advance, during your pregnancy. If you have had a cesarean and *may* be having another cesarean, you are more likely to have strong preferences to negotiate for during your pregnancy. If you have not had a cesarean, your chance of having one today is high enough that if you want it to be as family centered as possible, you must negotiate for this ahead of time. Although most of you are not anticipating a cesarean delivery, we are suggesting that you negotiate for what you want in a cesarean birth, just in case. Negotiation is your tool for getting what you want. (Review chapter 5.) Decide what you *may* want (you can change your mind later) and get that insurance policy in writing, just as you did for the other options you want for your vaginal delivery.

Many hospitals have eased their policies to make cesarean birth more family centered. Allowing fathers to attend cesarean deliveries that have not been anticipated, however, is unusual. Looking back, surveyed mothers felt most strongly about having the fathers there. If the hospital and doctor you have chosen already allow fathers to be present for cesareans that are planned, the next step is to persuade them to permit your partner to be with you should you need an emergency cesarean. To do this you need to find out the position each hospital anesthesiologist takes on letting fathers into the surgery, since he can veto your doctor—and often does.

The anesthesiologist is *the boss* in the operating room. He decides whether your partner and doula can be there; he decides on the anesthesia for surgery; and he decides the drugs routinely given "pre- and post-op" (before and after surgery). Your doctor knows which anesthesiologist may be flexible and go along with your preferences. He can often handle the negotiations for you. But if your doctor can't "put it in writing," you may want to negotiate in person by scheduling an appointment for you and your partner with the anesthesiologist. A personal interview may be the only way to convince the anesthesiologist that you want *him* to be on call for you, so you can avoid pre- and post-op sedation (until the anesthesia wears off), and so you can have the regional anesthesia.

Depending on how important cesarean delivery options are to you, if you cannot negotiate for what you want, remember you can change doctors during your pregnancy. You'll feel discouraged if you have to start your search over again for the hospital and Dr. Right. And you'll have to overcome the natural feelings of dependency in pregnancy. But having your baby *your* way is the reason you are going to all this trouble, remember?

If your cesarean-born baby must be in a special-care nursery after birth, you will need to negotiate with the pediatrician so you and your partner can have as much contact with the baby as possible.

VAGINAL BIRTH AFTER CESAREAN (VBAC)

"The best way to reduce the number of cesareans is to be sure the *first* one is necessary," says Gerald Stober, M.D., New York City obstetrician. But for the 900,000 or more women who are given cesareans every year in the United States, that advice comes too late. Many of these women are looking to the future, not the past, and want to have a vaginal delivery for their next baby. If you are one of these women, scientific evidence strongly supports your having a vaginal birth after a cesarean.

Experts now agree that routine repeat cesareans are not acceptable because vaginal delivery is safer for a woman and her newborn. These experts have been convinced by the huge numbers of vaginal births after cesareans that have now been reported in the medical literature. If a woman has had one previous cesarean with a low horizontal uterine incision, a vaginal birth is recommended, assuming no current specific medical reason for a cesarean.

Reports are accumulating of vaginal births for women with two, three and four previous cesareans. Women with two or MORE previous cesareans "should not be discouraged from attempting a vaginal delivery," according to the guidelines issued by ACOG. In an attempt to affect the cesarean rate, ACOG endorsed VBAC (pronounced vee-back). ACOG's guidelines for VBAC are very similar to those for any other vaginal birth: The hospital should have the capability to begin performing a cesarean within 30 minutes of the decision to do one. A doctor should be readily available (on call) to evaluate the labor and for the surgery.

So far, most obstetricians have been ignoring recommendations for VBAC. Nine out of ten women with a previous cesarean have a routine repeat cesarean. More and more obstetricians are willing, even eager, to try a VBAC, but you have to look for them (a family practitioner backed by an obstetrician can also give you a VBAC). Christiana Syed wrote to La Leche League International to tell them of her efforts resulting in a VBAC.

> For a few weeks after Eric's birth, it was easiest and most comfortable for me to believe that my cesarean

[first birth] was necessary. But then I started to question, and to read, and then through friends in my La Leche League group, to get in touch with people who helped me come to terms with my cesarean and myself. I've always thought it terrible that in this culture we have to do so much work during pregnancy—soul-searching, reading, talking, careful thinking, searching for the right health-care provider and birthplace, making birth plans, and confronting doctors. All this to assure the birth experience that ought to be every mother and child's uncontested right! Now, however, I am very glad to have done this work, and I urge other women to do the same. Only by doing so can we be certain, whatever the outcome of our births, that we have done the best for ourselves and our babies, and only by doing so can we hope for a future in which no woman will have her self-trust, her strength, and her faith in her own body and her mothering undermined by dangerous and unnecessary interventions.

HOW TO INCREASE YOUR CHANCES OF A VAGINAL BIRTH AFTER CESAREAN

Your choice of birth attendant can make a difference in whether or not you have that vaginal delivery. Just as cesarean section rates vary among doctors and hospitals, so, too, do the rates of vaginal delivery following cesarean. Success rates of 50–90 percent vaginal delivery after previous cesarean are reported in the medical literature. So ask what your doctor's success rate is.

You can be misled by a doctor who says he is in favor of VBAC. One doctor we know has been allowing labor trials for almost all of his patients who had previous cesareans, but only 30 percent of them deliver vaginally. His low rate of success seems to come from his belief (as told to another physician) that he can tell during the first hour of labor whether a woman can deliver vaginally after a previous cesarean.

The two most common reasons for a repeat cesarean after a trial of labor are "Failure to Progress" and "Fetal Distress." Review these sections in chapter 8 for suggestions to prevent or resolve these problems. Staying home until you are well established in labor is a tactic used by many women who have VBACs.

"Women wanting a VBAC should go to the hospital when

a normally laboring woman would," Richard Porreco, M.D., director of Maternal Fetal Medicine at AMI/Saint Luke's Hospital in Denver, told us. He considers the attending doctor's attitude a key factor in whether a woman will have a VBAC: "Success is related to the doctor's enthusiasm for VBAC. You can't treat her like a time bomb." Over seven years and one thousand VBACs later, Porreco remains convinced that unless a new reason for a cesarean is present, a trial of labor is "the best and safest form of obstetric management." One hundred percent of his clinic patients with previous cesareans start labor, and 90 percent have VBACs. To insure a high success rate, "Pitocin and regional anesthesia ought to be used for the same indications as for any other laboring women."

Porreco finds "increasing enthusiasm around the country for [women to have VBACs with] vertical and classical scars." He reminds couples "that in the unlikely event" of scar separation during birth, there is not enough data to assure couples that the fetus will be saved.

Childbirth education and support groups are particularly important to women wanting VBACs. "The uterus works the same whether it has a scar on it or not," wrote childbirth educator, Elizabeth Conner Shearer, M.Ed., M.P.H., commenting on the similarity of educating VBAC women and others. "Effective preparation for childbirth helps women accept the pain of birth, to appreciate it as a sign of how strong and well their bodies work, quite different from the pain that signals injury or illness." The special difference for VBAC parents, Shearer said, is "to know, trust, and rely on their bodies to give birth . . . when their bodies did *not* 'work right' the first time." She says parents need to understand the reason for the previous cesarean to be realistic about their chances for a vaginal birth after cesarean.

Shearer was a member of the NIH task force on cesarean birth. She makes special note of "how unscientific 'CPD' and 'failure to progress' are as diagnoses. All 'CPD' means is that *the baby did not get out in the time the doctor thought s/he should*" (Shearer's italics).

The Cesarean Prevention Movement (CPM) offers support groups and help all over the United States. A small group of dedicated women founded CPM in 1982. They recognized the need for an organization to give practical help to women in the face of the cesarean epidemic. The national CPM office receives up to two hundred calls and letters a week from women wishing to avoid a cesarean or to have a VBAC, according to Esther Zorn, president of CPM. Not only pregnant women call. "We've had mothers of pregnant daughters call us for information to help their daughters avoid a cesarean," Zorn told us.

C/Sec, Inc., was the first cesarean support group for parents. Writing in the C/Sec, Inc., newsletter, Zorn noted, "The medical profession is finding it difficult, if not impossible, in some areas of the country, to listen to their own medical reports . . . and make steps to correct medical practices which are leading to unnecessary major surgery on pregnant women. . . . It will take time for women to understand and then act on their understanding that birthing is their responsibility, not to be handed over 'carte blanche' to an 'expert' who has learned about birth from a textbook and as an onlooker."

Finally, there is some evidence that your belief in your own ability to give birth naturally is important to a vaginal birth after a previous cesarean (it's important in any vaginal birth). "As you consider your decision to have a VBAC, you will probably have to deal with some fears," writes Marianne Brorup Weston, et al., in "Vaginal Birth After Cesarean." "The unknown is always scary and you may find yourself afraid of pain, of a long labor, of possible complications, of trying something new and unusual, of failure, of another cesarean. . . . The list goes on and on."

"Two thing are most important for a woman about to have a VBAC," said Nancy Wainer Cohen, a VBAC counselor, in the video, *Once a Cesarean: Vaginal Birth after Cesarean.* "One is absolute confidence in herself and her ability to give birth to this baby, a feeling that her body is designed to give birth to this baby, that she is going to be fine, that the process is safe. The second is to have wonderful support people around her, people who believe in her and who believe in the process of birth, who are patient, kind, loving and knowledgeable, and who are not going to pressure her or very subtly make it more difficult for her to have this baby."

Cohen coined the term VBAC. Following a cesarean delivery with her first child, she had two vaginal births (the last one at home). She has counseled hundreds of women in VBAC. Among the more than 90 percent who had VBACs are women who had more than one previous cesarean, women who had breech presentations, women with vertical and classical uterine scars, women who delivered babies weighing over ten pounds when they had cesareans for CPD with five-pound babies, and three women who had twins through VBAC. Cohen explained to us why she thought these women were so likely to have a VBAC: "They are free to have the same labor as anyone else. They have no IVs, no electronic fetal monitor. They walk in labor. They eat or drink as they desire. They have confidence in their body, and they have loving support during labor. They have no time limit on their labors." Cohen added that some of the women had very long labors of up to forty hours, some at home before going to the hospital for the birth, and some in the hospital.

"I am finding it common to see VBAC mothers experience what I have termed 'emotional dystocia' at some point during labor," wrote childbirth educator and monitrice, Polly Perez in *Childbirth Alternatives Quarterly*. "To get past this point requires infinite patience on the part of the caregiver as well as the ability to work with the mother toward resolution of the emotional block. . . . Much time has been spent in labor discussing fears and anxieties that she was not able to confront until that time. I am awed by the strength of these women to complete not only the physically but emotionally demanding tasks of labor and birth."

Having a VBAC is unusual in most places in the United States. Just as it took time for family-centered maternity care to become widely accepted, it will take time for most doctors to feel comfortable with VBAC. Having VBAC is a pioneer effort in most places. "I am convinced that the best preparation for birth involves choosing caregivers who understand the emotional as well as the physical components of birth, the grieving and healing prior to labor, and the importance of trusting in one's body and baby," wrote Perez. You'll need persistence and determination to find a willing birth attendant. Just as important for you, you'll need to have people around you who are loving, caring, and supportive of your labor.

What if you end up needing another cesarean? Counselors who help women prepare for a VBAC say that every woman is glad she made the effort, for she had the labor, she knew it was the best time for her baby to be born, and she would never look back and wonder what might have been. She had done her best.

• TEN •

UNDERSTANDING YOUR FEELINGS:
IT'S NOT ALL HORMONES

> As a first-time mother I still find myself, more than half
> a year later, remembering my (our) birth experience. I
> think I am finally coming to an understanding of the
> many feelings I had then and accepting the miserable
> ones as well as the elation.

—A MOTHER QUOTED BY LEAH YARROW IN *PARENTS* MAGAZINE

Few of us are prepared for childbirth's impact on our feelings.
We open ourselves up—physically and emotionally—to a
degree not thought possible. And if it's our first baby, ready or
not, we're thrust into the new role of motherhood. We now see
the world with different eyes, while coping with up and down
emotions. These feelings are normal.

You've looked forward to caring for your baby, but now
that the baby's here, you worry. Maybe you really weren't
prepared enough, you say to yourself. Bone-weary collapse
seems just around the corner. As most of the sixty-four
thousand readers who responded to a *Parents* magazine survey
said, the biggest surprise about parenthood is the fatigue.
Fatigue alone can produce a kaleidoscope of feelings, mostly
negative.

Women's intense feelings after childbirth are certainly not
new. "As long ago as the 4th century B.C., the medical writer
Hippocrates was theorizing about the biological basis of this
strange sorrow and/or madness that could invade the mind of
the new mother," reported Maggie Scarf in her book on
women's depression, *Unfinished Business*.

Some of the new mother's emotions bother both herself and
those closest to her. She's just not herself, and no one knows

why. She experiences mood swings, more than the usual amount of tears, irritability, and constant energy lows. These symptoms are usually labeled "postpartum depression." On the other hand, when the new mother thrills at feeding and holding her baby, and when her tears are tears of joy, these actions are labeled "maternal." But the truth is that, to some degree, all of these feelings are normal, not just the so-called positive ones. No one, including a new mother, is ecstatically happy all the time. Nor is her mate. A 1986 study showed that husbands have an emotionally unique time after the birth, too. They experience nervousness, worry, anxiety, as well as enthusiasm and happiness.

Some combination of all of these feelings is normal, but the actual number of how many women experience the continuum from having a bad day to the baby blues or all the way to postpartum depression is unknown. Estimates in this country and Europe are that about 50 percent of women experience the bad day/baby blues, and 10 percent have true postpartum depression (loss of sexual and other interests, irritability, undue fatigue, inability to cope).

But when a woman does experience postpartum depression, are hormones the culprits? If they are part of the reason, they're certainly not all of it. Maybe it has something to do with being in the hospital. British research shows that postpartum blues are less likely in women who return home forty-eight hours after giving birth. To exonerate female hormones even more, in many other cultures and in home births in this country, women reportedly seldom experience postpartum depression.

At The Farm, a once thriving agricultural community in Tennessee, head midwife Ina May Gaskin found that of the thousands of births that have taken place there, only .03 percent of those mothers experienced depression. However, a home birth by itself is not a guarantee of avoiding depression. If the new mother is isolated, which she wouldn't be at The Farm, for instance, that loneliness and lack of support might result in depression.

MISSING PIECES

A combination of birth experiences labeled the "missing pieces" can cause your emotional seesaw to continue on the downside longer than is comfortable. You don't have to undergo all these experiences to feel the impact of postpartum depression. Many women feel the effect with only a few. The missing pieces are unfulfilled expectations, unrealistic expectations about pain and self-control, invasion of your privacy, distractions, memory loss, unwanted interventions, and separation from your baby.

UNFULFILLED EXPECTATIONS

There are reasons why today's new mother may be especially perplexed and sometimes profoundly confused by her feelings. Women, especially younger women, and those in the educated middle class have come to expect the best.

You're harder to please. Simply having a live baby is not enough anymore. You want the best experience, too. If you can control conception with the Pill, you expect to be in control of your birth and enjoy its pleasure, too. Maggie Scarf points out, "You're told now you can do it all, have it all; and when you end up not having it all or not doing it all well, you feel guilty—and depressed." And perhaps shortchanged.

Because there's more information available on birth now, the process is not so mysterious anymore. Nearly all of you go to childbirth-education classes. You know to eat well and avoid drugs. As far as you know, you're doing everything you can to have a good and safe birth. Why, then, doesn't childbirth always result in what you wanted? Because birth isn't that predictable and neat a package.

Then *Parents* magazine writer Leah Yarrow said that the letters they received after their poll of sixty-four thousand readers "suggest that women spend considerable time struggling to come to terms with the disparity between the expectations they had of their labors and births and their actual experiences." This is especially true with women who have unexpected cesareans.

The truth is that the act of giving birth plunges you into the hands of a force much bigger than your ability to control it or fully anticipate it.

PAIN

Many new mothers are stunned by the pain they felt. No one said it would hurt so much, or if someone did, you didn't think it would happen to you. Pain in childbirth is not new to women, of course. When your mother or your aunts, perhaps, told you a horror story about birth, you knew those were pre-Lamaze times your relatives were talking about. After all, you had much more information available to you now than they had.

Many of us have been told that if we did it right—breathed and relaxed correctly—we'd feel a contraction, not pain. For some laboring women, that's true. For most others, it's not. In the *Parents* magazine survey, most of the mothers found childbirth to be painful, and one-third said childbirth was "the most painful experience" they had ever had. Only one-third of the mothers reported that "medication took all the pain away." Research in 1987 confirms the same low rating of satisfaction with pain relief from drug use. Not only does pain persist, some women become passive spectators because of the drugs and the lack of exertion. Psychologist Niles Newton, Ph.D., says this may lead a new mother to feel that the medical profession—not she—produced the child.

Sociologist and birth researcher Ann Oakley says, "The deliberate misrepresentation of the pain of childbirth adds to the risk of postpartum depression, since it makes realistic anticipation impossible." She continues, "A woman who has been misled about 'painless childbirth' has been found to be more likely to panic and request drugs when those sensations turn out to hurt. . . . Furthermore, a man who withstood hours of severe pain, refusing anesthetic to benefit another, would be a hero, but a woman who experiences pain is made to feel inadequate." Her pain becomes a "mark of failure."

Yes, the latter part of the first stage of labor is painful. But contrary to what many doctors believe, the second stage—the pushing part—often is not. For the baby's safety, most women don't receive anesthesia until they are quite near the pushing stage. Consequently, they never know that the most painful part is nearly behind them with the exhilaration of pushing just ahead.

Labor can be painful, exhausting, and still euphoric. We know. It's happened to both of us and to many other women. In 1982 British researchers confirmed that women who give birth without anesthesia suffer more pain than anesthetized women do, but they also experience greater pleasure. The laboring woman is aware of the pain, but the physical high from endorphins comes too. Pain can also be moderated with the appropriate people support.

LOSS OF CONTROL

Prepared childbirth classes lead you to believe that you will be making your own decisions about how delivery will be handled. My own experience was quite the opposite. The staff treated me as a "body," not a person. They administered anesthesia for delivery without asking me if I wanted it, but simply because that was the usual routine.

Maintaining control means many things to a laboring woman—the control of pain, the control of her actions, and the control of emotion. Researcher R. Rubin found "loss of control in any form may result in loss of self-esteem and bring on a feeling of shame and humiliation."

Then there's the staff view. Doctors believe pain relief is of first importance, when in reality, women's worst birth memories are of the interventions used. As for who guides the course of your stay in the hospital, routine usually prevails. And emotion—nurses and doctors often become anxious if a laboring woman expresses deep feeling. According to Barbara Katz Rothman in her book, *In Labor: Women and Power in the Birthplace*, childbirth educators go along with the idea that a woman needs to control her emotions:

> According to the rules of the game, if the laboring woman chooses to deal with her pain by crying or calling out, she has entirely forfeited her right to make decisions. Much is made in childbirth-preparation circles of the woman's being in control during labor, but all that is meant by that is control over her expressions of pain. A woman who maintains a fixed, if somewhat glazed, cheerful expression and continues a regular pattern of breathing is said to be "in control," as she is carted from one room to another and literally strapped flat on her back with her legs in the air.

LACK OF PRIVACY

Psychologist Newton believes that people, being territorial animals, are more relaxed in the home. However, birth in our society usually takes place in a hospital. What is it that women don't get in hospitals that is part of their biological need? Privacy, for one thing. It's difficult to provide true privacy for any hospital patient. You are handled by strangers (the nurses on duty, a doctor on call for your own, perhaps medical students, interns, residents, nursing students).

Thousands of hospitals are taking a step in the right direction by offering a more homelike appearance with wall-papered and curtained birth rooms. But having your baby in one of these birth rooms is no guarantee that you'll feel at home. "It is not the way the room looks that matters," sociologist Rothman states. "What matters are the attitudes of the attendants—the beliefs, values, and ideas they hold about women, babies, and birth."

DISTRACTIONS

A woman in labor craves peaceful surroundings, yet many laboring women have described how disturbing overheard conversations and laughter from the hall can be (or being asked questions by the staff when you're in the middle of a contraction). Because of the physical and emotional intensity of giving birth, laboring women's senses soar. According to Elizabeth Loftus, a psychologist at the University of Washington at Seattle, in her book *Memory,* hearing memory is apparently stronger in humans than touch, sight, or smell memory. Twenty and thirty years after the event, many a woman still remembers the conversations staff members had (as if she, the woman in labor, was merely an object) while she was in the labor room or on the delivery table.

MEMORY LOSS DURING BIRTH

It's normal to talk about your births. You'll want to replay the experience again and again. In fact, you need to. So much so, that if you can't remember everything, you're often troubled and anxious.

Dyanne D. Affonso, professor of nursing at the University of Arizona, coined the term "missing pieces" to describe postpartum feelings after interviewing 150 women in Hawaii and Arizona. She found "that more than three fourths of the women interviewed indicated that they could not remember, or were distressed by vague ideas of, some period or periods during their labors or deliveries." Women described finding themselves thinking often about what they could not remember. Researcher Karen Stolte in 1986 found that in the decade since Affonso's work was first published, women still had "missing pieces," but fewer women reported them. One aspect remained the same though. Women still want to talk about their births.

One of the reasons for the memory loss Affonso gives is the use of "high-risk equipment like the [fetal] monitor." Use of this equipment "may result in a laboring woman not hearing what is said to her, or if she heard it, she may forget it later." Her anxiety about the use of this equipment creates a crisis in her mind. Upset and distressed, she literally can't hear what's said to her.

Women who receive little feedback from doctors or nurses about their progress—where they are in labor, how fast they're dilating, and the condition of the baby—also have a sense of not understanding or remembering what happened, whether their labors were long or short, states Affonso. During their hospital stay women who couldn't remember found themselves asking the same question over and over to one person, or even asking "the same question to different persons such as the nurse, doctor, husband, or even the cleaning lady."

Drugs used for a vaginal birth have their effect on memory loss, too. And about cesareans, Affonso said, "especially women who encounter an unexpected cesarean section are vulnerable to forgetting certain important areas of their child-birth experience." According to the *Parents* survey, women who have cesareans (half of whom were not awake at their child's birth) experience the most shock of any new mother when they compare their experience to their expectations.

UNWANTED INTERVENTIONS

Ann Oakley found that "having the blues during postpartum hospital stay was associated with epidural block, dissatisfaction with the second stage of labor and instrumental [forceps] delivery." She also found that "becoming depressed at some point in the five months following birth was also preceded by obstetric intervention and feelings of dissatisfaction about the birth per se." She associates this dissatisfaction with the mothers' sense of loss of control in labor and the management of the birth itself.

Routine hospital procedures often trigger a sense of low self-esteem. In her book *Birthing Normally: A Personal Approach to Childbirth*, Gayle Peterson points to draping, shaving of the pubic hair, enemas, and routine episiotomies as unrecognized attempts to hide the fact that birth is sexual. They also serve to make women feel demeaned.

SEPARATION FROM YOUR BABY

> When the mother is really the first human being to have contact with the baby and that contact is continuing within several hours, she is the expert for her baby, and feels it, and develops a tremendous amount of confidence, even skills; fathers too, and others. They all feel very close to the baby, very responsible for the baby. There is no third party interfering with this."
>
> —MIDWIFE, QUOTED IN *IN LABOR: WOMEN AND POWER IN THE BIRTHPLACE*

Most of you want to be with your baby after the birth. That's clear. But according to the *Parents* survey, less than half of women have their babies with them as long as twenty minutes after birth. Author Yarrow states: "In our cross-tabulations we discovered that the amount of time mothers were allowed to bond with their babies after birth may have a significant impact on their assessment of the birth experience. Mothers who stayed with their babies for less than ten minutes were much more likely to say their birth experience was negative or a mixture than were those who bonded for a longer time."

Rooming-in mothers developed maternal feelings significantly sooner and felt more confident and competent in caring for their newborns than did mothers having limited contact with their babies, according to 1977 research reported by Niles Newton. Further it was shown that mothers who felt confident about themselves consequently gave more affection and evaluated their own children in more positive terms, thereby increasing the self-esteem of their children.

In spite of all the pluses rooming-in offers, American

hospitals don't provide as much rooming-in as you might suppose. In the *Parents* survey, "a little more than half (56%) did have some form of rooming-in, but only a small percent (6%) of all mothers had their babies with them all the time."

THE NEED FOR A SUPPORT SYSTEM

The missing pieces of your birth can be prevented or diminished by family and friends because they can let you know how special you are, a necessary ingredient to help you avoid depression. You probably will have your mate with you during your labor and the birth, so you will have the presence of someone who cares for you. What more could you need or want? Another woman, that's who. As wonderful as it is to have your mate with you, we believe most of you will benefit from an additional support person.

From the beginning of time, the traditional companions for a laboring woman and the new mother have been, and continue to be, women. In a study of 186 cultures reported in 1982 in "Birth, Interaction, and Attachment," pediatrician-anthropologist Betsy Lozoff, M.D., was able to "find only two cultures in which a man actually did something to help deliver the baby."

Traditionally, women have helped other women give birth. Isolated families where new mothers have only their mate for support are not the best environment for women. It's too easy for the new mother's needs and emotions—and her partner's—to be overlooked. A strong support system is helpful for all women to prevent postpartum depression. It's essential for women who are single or having their first baby, those who have had a cesarean or whose baby died, or those who have a poor relationship with their mates.

PEACEMAKING, APOLOGIES, AND MISPLACED COMPASSION— HOW THEY MIGHT GET IN YOUR WAY

Your behavioral style may get in the way of your pleasure in your birth and your baby. If it's important for you to please other people and always play the *peacemaker,* if you want to avoid criticism at all costs, speaking out about your childbirth preferences may not be the thing for you to do. The price you pay for silence, however, is anger and/or depression—now or later.

You may speak out daily on your job or in your home, but react differently in your dealings with the authority of doctors and hospitals. "Oh, what will they think of me?" you wonder. This attitude stops you from getting what you want. We often feel responsible for everyone's comfort and well-being, including that of the hospital staff. As women, we should learn to count to ten before taking the blame or backing off from a request we've made. And if that doesn't work, count to twenty.

How do you know when you're in your *apologizing* (or "I won't make trouble") mode? You'll know if you've said some of the following statements to yourself:

- It's very important to me that I don't have an electronic fetal monitor; I'm probably not right, though. After all, the doctor must know more than I do about this.
- My doctor doesn't agree with me that I should stay out of bed and walk around during labor; I must be wrong, so I'll do what he wants me to do.
- I couldn't convince the nurses to bring me my baby— they probably know better than I do. And I hate to be obnoxious by insisting.

And then there's *compassion.* Many women try to "out good" everyone else by always being fair and understanding (especially of men). There's nothing wrong with compassion and fairness; they are noble attributes. But they can stand in the way of getting what you know is best for you and your baby. For example, one mother told us that she didn't use the hospital's alternative birth room, even though she wanted to, because the doctor said delivering a baby on that double bed might hurt his back. Another mother spent a miserable night anxiously listening to the cries from the nursery, fearing her baby was crying for her. She was in tears and her breasts were full, yet she feared disturbing the nursing staff by asking for her baby.

Many people adopt a passive, nonassertive attitude for coping with difficult situations. Even though that's not always the best response in our daily life, in pregnancy it is a *perfectly normal* response. For you, as a laboring woman, the most important reason for avoiding hassles in the hospital, for avoiding disagreements of any kind, is your physical and emotional vulnerability. That's true no matter how assertive a person you are ordinarily. Enlist the help of your partner or doula (see next chapter) to fend for you.

Sometimes, it's true, you may feel that yielding is simply the most rational way to cope with some situations. And it certainly can be. We only encourage you to first understand your choice of options, and their individual importance to you, then choose your own actions.

COPING WITH YOUR ANGER FROM A PAST BIRTH

I would have liked to have been allowed to find my own best position for comfort in labor and delivery. I found it excruciating to lie flat on my back—yet it was insisted that I do so (because of fetal monitor). I tolerated labor very well in a standing, bent-over position, but I was forced to lie in bed—which I hated. Also, to be moved from a bed to the delivery room was further agony—I really didn't want to be disturbed at such a crucial point. It was only through the help of my husband that I managed. Then they kept me from my baby. I still get angry when I think about it.

So what do you do if you've already had a birth (or a gynecological) experience that's left you feeling angry? You find ways to cope with that anger and, even better, use that energy in a positive direction.

Give yourself permission to be angry. Having a baby is one of a woman's most important life experiences. If your baby's birth wasn't what you wanted, you have a right to be angry. You can't go back and do that birth over, but you can understand what you're angry about.

Write down all the things about your birth experience that made you unhappy. This may help you answer, "At whom am I angry?" Maybe you're angry at everyone. The nurse, for ordering you to lie down when you felt more comfortable sitting up. Your mate, because he didn't speak up enough to protect you or left when you needed him. The hospital, because you weren't allowed to use the birth room—someone else got there first. Your friends, because they didn't tell you what to expect. Your doctor . . . ah, your doctor. Most of us don't allow ourselves to be angry at our doctor. Whatever happened, someone besides him was responsible: the nurse, the hospital, your mother, or your husband. After all, the doctor "gave you" a healthy baby. But the fact is, most of what happens to a woman in a hospital is the responsibility of the doctor.

What about being angry at yourself? Are you beating yourself over the head with: "If I had only . . . arranged ahead of time . . . demanded my baby . . . stood my ground . . . held out a little longer before accepting drugs . . . ?"

Make a list and identify what you're angry about, and at whom. Now look at the list again. Is it enough for you to place blame? If it satisfies you, okay. However, most of us find it doesn't relieve us of our anger. Besides, placing blame just isn't so simple. If you blame your doctor for your treatment, remember he's only doing what he was trained to do. You could blame the nurse—except you know she's only doing what the hospital expects of her. So who are you going to blame? Your partner? You have to live with that person. Besides, he probably did his best. Like you, the experience was far different from his expectations. He may be angry as well. Yourself? You have to live with yourself, too. Now that you know you're disappointed, perhaps feel betrayed, angry, or enraged, what are you going to *do* about it?

Make a decision about what you'll do next. What are your choices? Among them are:

- *Do nothing*. One option that we all choose sometime or another is to do nothing. You can leave that anger buried deep within you. We've been asked why we would recommend doing nothing. Is it as productive as other suggestions? Maybe not. But we believe every woman has her own timetable for working through her feelings. And some of you will need to put that anger on a shelf in the back of your head for a while before taking it down, dusting it off, and deciding what to do next.

- *Take action*. Anger creates energy that you can funnel not only into helping to change doctors' and hospitals' attitudes, but into changing your actions in the future for your health care. One New York mother, infuriated by what she felt was an unnecessary cesarean when she was ten centimeters dilated, and who also felt insulted by what her doctor said to her, refused to pay the doctor or the hospital. Both the hospital and doctor had advertised that people didn't have to pay if they weren't satisfied, and she didn't, though her Blue Cross coverage would have paid.

Some women I've talked to weren't upset about their sections. I was upset from Day One. I cried a lot, felt like I failed, felt selfish. I got pregnant again and channeled all my anger into doing whatever we could to have a VBAC. And finally, in the seventh month, relaxed and waited for the birth. It was worth every tear to get there.

—WISCONSIN MOTHER

• *Talk about it.* Whether your birth expectations were met or not, whether you reacted with anger or not, whether you have "missing pieces" from the birth or not, you have a need, common to all women, to talk about your baby's birth. In doing the M.O.M. Survey, we were struck by the depth of feeling—often rage—of many women who answered our questions. And *Parents'* Leah Yarrow stated: "The need to examine and explain the birth experience was dramatically evidenced in the torrential response to our recent birth experience poll."

Get a friend who will listen to you, someone who will comfort you when you cry. For if you are grieving, you are grieving over a real loss. Boulder Hospice nurse Marcia Lattanzi says, "You don't recover from grief, you manage it." And the more important the loss, the more profound the experience will be.

Women who had children long ago produce vivid accounts of their own birth experiences for us, as if they are still working on understanding them. And maybe they are. One mother, who gave birth to twin daughters thirty years ago, still wonders what the twin looked like who was born dead and then immediately taken away. Another wonders what her labor was really like with her oldest son, now in his twenties. She was drugged as soon as she arrived at the hospital and was left alone to labor. There was no one to ask about what happened. But you're not likely to be left alone in labor today. In fact, we encourage you to have at least two people with you.

One cesarean mother who had been asleep at her daughter's birth told us that when her baby was one day old, she asked the nurse who had been with her during her labor, and who also accompanied her to the operating room, to tell her, in detail, just what happened. That mother taped the conversation she had with the nurse and treasures it because it fills in some of the missing pieces of her memory.

Talking it out is cathartic, but it's more than that. Women have a need to preoccupy themselves with all the details of pregnancy, birth, the hospital stay, and those first few weeks at home. They talk of the pain and the pleasure, all the while putting the pieces of the experience together. Having a baby, especially the first time, changes your life dramatically. You're suddenly an equal with your own mother, and a sister to every other woman who has borne children. You're affected profoundly, and you yearn to understand.

- *Write letters*. Even if it's been several years since your child's birth, you can still write a letter to your doctor or the hospital, telling them what you liked about their care, and what you didn't like. Hospitals pay attention to these letters, and will pay special heed if you also send a carbon copy to the chairman of the hospital's board of trustees. This board is responsible for getting patient/consumer input. You'd be helping the board to do its job by giving them your opinions.

  If your complaint is about your doctor, write a letter, being as clear and specific as you can, to the local medical society. Do this especially if you had anything done to you against your wishes. Ask for a copy of the letter they send to the doctor. Your public librarian can tell you what medical society covers the geographic area of your doctor's office (it may not be the same as where you live). If you don't receive satisfaction locally, you can appeal to the state level, the state attorney general's office, the state medical licensing agency, or the grievance committee of your state's medical society.

- *Tell doctors and hospitals directly*. When the M.O.M. Survey brought out angry comments from women about their past maternity care, every obstetrician we talked to told us (and we believe them) that they didn't think women were unsatisfied with their care because their patients hardly ever expressed these complaints to them. Doctors are not likely to change if they believe women are satisfied with their medical care. We know it's probably a lot easier for all of us to tell other women what we think, and we know that confrontation makes many people ill at ease. It's certainly not always easy to say, "Doctor, when I was in labor and called for you, I was disappointed and angry that you weren't on call. A doctor I didn't even know delivered my baby. I expected you to be there." However, it's still most effective to tell your complaints to your doctor.

To complain, follow the same steps as in negotiating. Plan ahead what you want to say, practice in advance, remain logical and self-controlled. Take a friend to help you stay calm.

- *Become hospital changemakers yourselves.* That's what we did. Why and how we worked with our community hospital to make maternity care changes that women wanted is described in the Appendix, "How to Be a Changemaker."
- *Do things differently in the future.* If you're angry about your previous birth experiences, the most important step for you to take is to resolve to do things differently in the future. What happened then, happened, and it's over now. Do what you can and move on.

But you don't have to be angry to want to do things differently the next time. Take what you learned from your experience and, step by step, develop a new relationship with health professionals.

• ELEVEN •

YOUR SUPPORTERS—YOUR MATE, DOULA, CHILDBIRTH EDUCATOR, AND MONITRICE

I relied heavily on the constancy of my husband, allowing his strength to sustain me through despair, tears, exhaustion, and hints of epidurals and analgesia.

—NONA L. MCNATT, R.N., C.N.M.,
QUOTED IN *OBSTETRICS AND GYNECOLOGY*

Your supporters are your best guarantee for avoiding unnecessary interventions in the hospital, for getting the options you want, and for receiving the pleasure you deserve.

Although American childbirth practices have changed dramatically in the last thirty years, too many women still give birth emotionally and physically alone. They have no mate, no family, no friends in the birth room, just doctors and nurses who are usually too busy to have much time to give to a laboring woman. Yet through the ages women have intuitively known that a laboring woman needs a lot of emotional and physical support.

In this chapter we'll discuss the role of four different supporters for you. The first is your mate. He is not the choice, however, for the one in four United States women today who are single when they give birth, nor are men the partners of the growing number of lesbians who give birth. The next supporter is the childbirth educator. The other two are innovative in hospital births in our culture—the doula and the monitrice. *Doula* is a word (popularized by anthropologist Dana Raphael, Ph.D., in her book *The Tender Gift*) describing a woman who nurtures and cares for a mother in labor and birth, as well as for her and her baby later—a woman who "mothers" the mother. *Monitrice* is the 1960s Lamaze word for a labor coach, but in our use, the monitrice is a nurse hired to give one-to-one care to you in the hospital.

YOUR MATE

> Pam and Gerry stared at each other during her labor continuously—each strengthening the other. He kissed her face often and she thanked him with both looks and words for understanding her need. When she finally got to the pushing stage she was most comfortable standing up. Gerry held her up for hours, letting Pam's body be as limp as possible. Immediately after both of their babies were born, the voices in the delivery room hushed as we watched Gerry and Pam. Each was lovingly cradling one of their twin daughters and gazing into the eyes of that infant.
>
> —DOULA

When the Lamaze method of prepared childbirth was developed in France, a woman trained to be a labor coach stayed with the mother. When this childbirth education method crossed the Atlantic to the United States, the husband took over the role of that woman. We believe your mate's presence is crucial and not to be duplicated by any other person. He is most important to the mother as her lover and the father of her baby.

During the last twenty years, more and more fathers-to-be entered labor and delivery rooms. For most women, their mate is the most important support person for them. The husband's presence and participation is necessary for the woman to have a "peak" experience in childbirth, according to psychologist Deborah Tanzer, Ph.D. Tanzer's research found evidence that joy and ecstasy in childbirth are directly related to the mate's presence. This peak experience is also possible for cesarean mothers whose mates stay with them through the birth.

In our M.O.M. Survey, 99 percent of the women reported they wanted to have their husbands with them in both labor and delivery. Robert Bradley, M.D., who made popular the husband-coached childbirth concept, said, "I include the father because there is simply no substitute for him. People watching husband-coached childbirth often say that they feel like intruders in a room where a man and woman are making love." This emotion shared with the husband replaces those heartfelt, sincere displays of affection that many a woman used to give to her obstetrician when he caught the baby . . . and the father was nowhere in sight.

Fathers are not only there now, but many hold their newborns in a Leboyer warm-water bath within minutes of the birth; and occasionally a father catches his own baby in a hospital setting.

It's clear that the more that's done to keep birth in the hands of the new mother and father, the better they each feel about themselves and each other. This intimacy, says Lucy R. Waletzky, M.D., a Washington, D.C., psychiatrist, can reduce the stress many new fathers feel. She states that the most common negative reaction of a new father is jealousy. Among Waletzky's suggestions to men for more enjoyment of their fathering, she includes: attend prenatal birth classes; stay with your wife when she's in the hospital for the labor and birth; and then stay with your baby and your wife as much as you can after the birth.

Historically, a man has not been the person who gives the major support to the laboring woman. And not every father wants to be present for his child's birth or throughout labor. That's his choice. Having your mate there is not the only way to have a baby. Some mates feel guilty because they don't want to be there. If he's not interested, plan to have at least one doula with you. What's important is that you receive the physical and emotional support that you need.

When the mate is there, his role in childbirth has become more than that of a lover. Most of the time, this person is also labor coach and doula. He or she helps the laboring woman to cope successfully with contractions, and comforts her with word and touch. The mate attempts to keep track of the hospital options the couple wants.

But if the husband's presence were enough, 82 percent of the women in the Baltimore COMA Survey wouldn't have been dissatisfied with their birth experiences. The huge increase in medical intervention in childbirth leads us to question whether the mate alone can adequately meet all the needs of a laboring woman in hospitals today.

THE DOULA

As a Lamaze teacher, I'm often asked to go to the hospital and stay with a woman and her husband during labor. It's exhausting work, but so worthwhile. I love to go when I can. I do more than coach the woman in labor. I also explain to the couple the things the staff has told them, but which are still unclear to the couple. I try to ask questions that the mother wants to ask but it obviously too preoccupied to mention. I comfort the father, who often wonders if he's doing the right thing. Usually I find that the nurses are glad to have me there, especially if they're understaffed.

No childbirth class can totally prepare a couple for what happens in the hospital. I don't just mean the labor. It's more than that. It's being in a strange place. It's expecting that you'll get what you want just because you talked to your doctor about it before. It's just not that simple. I'm the go-between for the couple and the staff. I try to clarify any confusion, especially when the staff suggests interventions the couple said they didn't want. But most of all I do what I can to create the best environment for the woman and her husband. I know it's one of the most important days in their lives.

—DOULA

In all but one of 150 nonindustrialized cultures studied by anthropologists, a family member or friend, usually a woman, is present during the labor and birth. Studies by researchers John Kennell, M.D., Marshall Klaus, M.D., Steven Robertson, Ph.D., and Juan Urrutia, M.D., give evidence that having a caring, attentive woman present during childbirth is healthier, not only for you, but for your baby as well. This research, conducted in a Guatemalan hospital, showed that one group of laboring women who had doulas with them had fewer complications and healthier babies. These mothers were also more affectionate with their newborns than another group of women who were alone. The women with the healthiest outcome were continuously attended to by these untrained women, who simply held their hands, rubbed their backs, and talked to them throughout labor. With doulas present, the average labor time was cut in half. The researchers say these results suggest anxiety may slow or stop labor and may cause fetal distress—prime reasons for medical interventions.

The laboring mothers in this study did not have their husbands present, so the question is raised: Couldn't the father take the place of the doula? Yes and no. In fact, even greater benefits may be expected when the father *and* a woman friend remain with the mother throughout the labor and birth. We think the father plays a unique role, and that no woman can substitute for what he does. But we also believe there is a special role for a doula, which the father can't fully duplicate.

The Guatemalan research shows clearly that having a doula can prevent problems in the laboring woman. Women without doulas had three times as many complications, such as cesarean birth, stillbirth, forceps, and slowed labor requiring the use of Pitocin. We believe that in a hospital birth today, having a good and safe birth requires a doula not only as comforter, but as both buffer and advocate with doctors and nurses for the laboring woman and her husband.

Ideally, a doula is someone who is related to the mother or already knows and cares for her. She doesn't have to be a childbirth education teacher, though thousands of these compassionate women have been doulas for their students, nor does she have to have special training. "Doula" (see Appendix for more information about birth assistants and mother-helpers.) Hopefully, she's a mother herself, wants to help other women, and will be accepting of the laboring mother's wishes. Don't overlook prospective grandmothers (though all are not appropriate.) These women are generally very supportive to both the laboring mother and the father, and their support helps to strengthen the bond of the newly extended family. And, of course, grandparents are often invaluable once the baby's born.

Some women may want more than one doula. In fact, it is common to find several women in attendance in out-of-hospital birth centers or at home births. When you have your baby, you, too, may want to invite several women; but check with your hospital in advance (going to the hospital administrator if you need to), since many hospitals have a limit on how many people can be with you in the labor room. You may have to negotiate to have more.

You may be wondering if laboring women ever have brothers or prospective grandfathers present. Some certainly do. One mother who gave birth in a birth center told us euphorically how her brother held her while her husband caught the baby as it was being born, others have told us of other helping male relatives.

- *She nurtures the mother*. The doula rubs the mother's back, holds her hand, and, as much as possible, keeps in soothing body touch with her. Since the father is doing this, too, isn't that enough? Some of the time it is, sometimes it isn't.

  The doula also offers the "female" connection, a same-sex empathy much like the identification men have with other men in a time of crisis—like soldiers on a battlefield. The doula probably has had a baby herself, so she has the link of experience. She understands the physical, emotional, and spiritual processes of childbirth. Some mothers who have given birth with doulas present tell of receiving an energy from these women, often described as a healing strength. Giving birth draws women together, while not precluding the simultaneously special relationship the laboring woman has with her husband. Often doulas describe reliving their own birth experiences—a feminine link through the ages.

  It seems right to be with other women. Another woman present at the birth often can help the mother discard inhibiting social concerns, such as worrying about making too much noise, or complaining too much, or not pleasing others. A doula can help the mother know that she—and she alone—is the center of this birth. Her needs and the needs of her baby, are the only ones that matter just now.

- *She calms the father*. Though the father's unique role makes him the key to the mother's joy and rapture, he can also benefit from the doula's presence. Fathers, especially first-time dads, can be unsure of what's expected from them during the birth process. As labor becomes progressively more intense, the woman becomes consumed by her body's contractions, and all attempts at casual conversation are gone. Some fathers may worry that all is not well. It is at this point, especially, that the doula can encourage and reassure the father—telling him that what he's doing (talking softly to the mother, kissing her face, wiping her brow, whatever) are all comforting and crucial. Also, though the father is not physically giving birth, he's still investing enormous energy. The doula's helpful presence and her kind and encouraging words can help to reduce the father's anxiety.

- *She serves as a buffer.* Some nurses understand the laboring mother's need for encouraging glances and comments, but they can also be severely limited in how much time they have for each patient. Others, though well-intentioned, deflate mothers and may delay the progress of the labor by comments like, "Gosh, your contractions aren't as strong as they should be," or "Get hold of yourself—quiet down," or "If you don't hurry up, they'll probably give you a c-section." The mother doesn't need any negative statements during labor. In contrast to this, the doula continually reminds mom of how well she's doing.

The doula can also calm the staff. During the course of one labor a doula reported that the nurse would look visibly upset when she'd come into the room and find out that the electronic fetal monitor was malfunctioning because of the position of the belt on the mother's abdomen. Knowing that the mother now thought she had done something wrong or that her baby was in trouble, this doula intervened and cleared up an accelerating misunderstanding. "The machine malfunctioning again, isn't it?" said the doula to the nurse. "The baby's just fine. It's the machine that has the problem." When the nurse readily agreed, the mother visibly relaxed.

Just having another person present during the labor, in addition to the father, reduces the chance of negative comments from the staff, since we're all generally on our best behavior when there's an audience.

One mother reported that she wanted to get up and move around during labor, even though she had an IV hookup and fetal-monitor attachments. The doula's reminder to the nursing staff, along with her readiness to help the staff work out the problems of the patient moving while attached to machine cables, led to a satisfactory solution that allowed the mother to walk around. If someone hadn't taken the role of the diplomat, the go-between, it's unlikely that mother would have moved from her bed.

The doula's there to see that hospital routine does not overshadow the parents' needs. The presence of the father and the doula can form a protective bubble around the laboring woman.

▪ *She serves as advocate*. Active labor is not the time for a pregnant woman to be assertive. She has more important things to do than to have to remind nurses and doctors of what birth options had been agreed to. The mother needs to focus her mind solely on her body sensations. She can hardly do otherwise. So it might fall onto the dad's shoulders to renegotiate options. But this is a dissipation of his energies as well. Having a doula there to handle these matters allows the father to concentrate solely on his wife and her needs during labor.

As labor progresses, you may feel yourself getting "bogged down" in middle labor (four to seven centimeters), or when approaching the pushing stage. Quite normally you'll wish you were somewhere else. Or you'd give anything if the birth could happen "right now." You may even reach the point where you don't care whether you have anesthesia or not, a cesarean birth or not. That's normal.

If labor seems to slow, a lot of people (especially nurses and doctors) get nervous unnecessarily. That's when the doula can step in and gently remind everyone that the baby is fine. She can also monitor to see that the mother's preferences—from no routine IVs to a sitting-up position for birth (which may require a special prop behind her in the bed or on the delivery room table)—are honored. When the doula calmly reminds those present of what the mother wants, she helps everyone—parents and staff alike.

This part of the doula's role may make the parents uneasy before they even get to the hospital. What if the doctors and nurses become angry with the mother because this person is interfering? And what if parents in the future won't get what they want because they and the doula are too demanding now? One mother expressed the fear that if she were too exacting about her baby's cesarean birth, the hospital would change its policy of allowing fathers to be present at cesarean births.

It's not the doula's intent to tell the staff how to perform their jobs; it's her purpose to remind everyone of what the mother wants. Nurses and doctors, of course, want to do their jobs well. They, too, want a healthy, satisfied patient. Although parents may have an initial fear of reprisal, women who have played the part of the interface between staff and parents have not usually been criticized. It does occasionally happen in a tense moment. Nurses and doctors are human, remember? But we have never heard of hospitals eliminating options they once offered because of the presence of a doula.

You may be convinced that you want a doula with you and your husband when you're in labor, but are reluctant to ask a friend to come with you. It seems like a lot to ask of someone. But women we've talked to who have played the role of the doula consider it a privilege, a rare opportunity.

Once you've selected a doula (or two), before you go into labor, review with her what's important to you for your birth. Describe what agreements you have with your doctor or the hospital. Be as specific as you can about what you want her to do. You may not be comfortable with a doula providing all the functions we describe in this chapter. Fine. Tell her what *you* want her to do for you.

• *She helps after the baby's born.* While you've been pregnant, you've probably gotten a lot of attention, especially if this is your first baby. After birth, who is there to turn to? Your baby's needs take from you. That's your infant's right. A mother needs mothering herself to love and care for her infant. A doula is priceless after the birth. We know from the surveys that such friends are important breastfeeding supporters, and they are essential for mothering after you go home, too. She may, or may not, be the same person who was your doula during your labor and birth. Find someone whose attitude mirrors that of the midwife who told us that her most important role with a woman is to help her through her transition to motherhood—to give her encouragement and confidence as she learns to be a mother. On The Farm in Tennessee new or inexperienced mothers were housed with women who had already had several children so that the new mother could learn from the experienced mother.

Psychiatrist Lucy Waletzky encourages father, too, to find a support system for themselves after the baby's born. She says, "Perhaps it would help to have someone mother the father." Mothers have friends and family to call, plus volunteer organizations like La Leche League. Men can talk to their own fathers, their friends, or men they work with who have children.

Since many hospitals are accustomed to having only the father stay with the mother during the labor and birth, as well as be a constant visitor once the baby's born, you will probably have to make special arrangements in advance for the doula. Check with the hospital and your doctor. If you have one doctor for the birth and another for your baby, check with both. If possible, arrange to have your doula come at any time while you're in the hospital. The hospital visiting hours may not suit your needs or your doula's schedule.

No one cares for you as much as your family and friends. Inviting them to help you is a plus for them, too. It's an invitation to share in some precious moments in your life and the life of your baby and for some mothers, can be a form of insurance that the doula will care for your child. Klaus and Kennell report in *Parent-Infant Bonding* that Raven Lang, lay midwife, "noted that the observers of the labor and birth became more attached to the infant than other friends of the family who did not witness the birth."

What can you do if you live a thousand miles from your nearest relative and none of your friends have babies? Make new friends. Find someone else who has a new baby—she'll speak your language. What about your neighbors, a co-worker, someone from your childbirth education class or La Leche League? Create your own circle of supporters.

THE CHILDBIRTH EDUCATOR

Childbirth education in the United States began in the forties, largely influenced by British obstetrician Grantly Dick-Read and his book, *Childbirth without Fear: The Principles and Practice of Natural Childbirth*. During the 1950s and 1960s Dick-Read was followed by Robert Bradley, M.D., and his husband-coached childbirth; ASPO (American Society of Psychoprophylaxis in Obstetrics), a teacher-certification group responsible for the widespread use of the Lamaze method; and ICEA (International Childbirth Education Association), an umbrella organization of childbirth educators and consumers. Now, in the 1990s, there are many more classes. (See "Your List of Helpers," in the Appendix, page 329.)

Childbirth educators offer instructions on relaxation and breathing during labor, physical exercises, and a description of the course of labor. A tour of a local hospital ob unit is included, and most instructors give information on analgesia and anesthesia, breastfeeding, and changes in sexuality. Most of the classes are taught at the end of pregnancy for six to eight sessions, but instructors also have one or two prenatal classes in the first trimester.

In addition there are classes that specialize, such as those for women who are having cesareans, those planning VBACs (vaginal birth after cesarean), and for women who want home births. The typical childbirth educator also keeps herself informed about ultrasound, which nearly every United States woman uses at least once and the full array of genetic testing.

Today, American women in general expect childbirth to be painful and an event that requires drug use for pain relief. On the other hand, women who attend classes often anticipate that the childbirth educator will "fix" that. But attending classes is no guarantee for most women that they will have a painless, fast, and easy labor.

Millions of women are more informed today because of the work of childbirth educators; nevertheless, childbirth educators are often criticized for failing to deliver more. Repeatedly women say, "My birth experience didn't match what she said it would be." Or "She led me to believe that I would get what I wanted." Or "Why didn't she teach me how to cope with the pain better?" Maybe the mother didn't hear what the childbirth educator said. Or maybe you never experienced as much exertion as labor requires. Or maybe you're expecting more than she can give you.

> Our childbirth educator asked if there was anything we'd have liked to know that we didn't find out from her. I told her that I didn't think she had stressed enough that the contractions could get almost unbearable at times. "That's funny," she said, "I really try to emphasize that in my classes, and people all seem unable to take in what I'm telling them." I think she was right about that. I didn't think it would happen to me.
>
> —NEW JERSEY MOTHER

Many childbirth educators say they walk a fine line between giving consumers information and getting along with doctors. For instance, one childbirth educator said she encouraged couples to use the birth room in a local hospital because they were more likely to get the options they wanted there. The doctor this educator worked for, however, wouldn't use that room because he was more comfortable in the delivery room. The childbirth educator finally quit telling couples about the birth room.

Independent childbirth educators, those who are not in the direct employ of hospitals or doctors, rely on referrals for new customers. Some couples choose a class because of a suggestion from a friend, but most couples choose a childbirth educator because of a referral from their doctor. So even some self-employed childbirth educators try not to go out of their way to anger local doctors by volunteering negative information about the use of fetal monitors, for example, when educators know that the local hospitals use these monitors routinely.

In years past, Lamaze instructors taught women distraction and conditioned responses (like special breathing techniques) to use during labor. Bradley instructors, on the other hand, encouraged women to breathe normally and tune into their bodies. Childbirth educator and author Penny Simkin, R.P.T., told us that many Lamaze instructors changed their classes because of the influence of British childbirth educator Sheila Kitzinger. Today, most Lamaze instructors encourage women to have a greater awareness of their bodies during labor. And like many Bradley instructors and others, they take an eclectic approach—they teach their students techniques from many sources, including yoga breathing and visualization.

Shop for a childbirth educator as you would for a physician or hospital. Childbirth educators vary enormously in what they offer, in their beliefs, and in their experience. Take the issue of pain which is the most important for most women. If you want to cope with pain drug-free, you need to be taught *how* to do that, not just that it is safer for the baby if you do. Some instructors spend time describing nondrug methods of coping with pain. Others spend a whole class and more describing analgesia and anesthesia—with the admonition, "Don't be a martyr."

Interview childbirth educators on the phone. Ask your friends. If possible, look at each teacher's class kit (the handouts couples get). How consumer oriented is the material?

Childbirth educators cannot guarantee that you'll have your version of a "good experience." The person to ensure that is you, by virtue of information you gather, your choice of both birth attendant and location, and whether you have enough support during your labor and birth.

THE MONITRICE (YOUR PERSONAL OB NURSE)

Although the hospital you plan to use may be fully staffed with nurses, most of you will be having your baby at a hospital that's not. Eight out of ten American hospitals do not have enough nurses for routine care. And the shortage may be on the ob floor.

I do not consider myself a complainer—but believe me, when you need something, have a question, or are in pain, and ring for a nurse, you don't expect to wait for two hours before they answer your call. Many a time I had to call two or three times.

There are hospitals that advertise birth rooms and a birth center, but laboring mothers are routinely turned away because nurses aren't available to work. Although mothers are promised the use of these rooms by both physician and hospital, the mothers are sent instead to the traditional ob unit. If this happens to you, you may find that one nurse will be responsible for as many as six to eight women in labor.

What can you do to avoid paying the consequences of a nursing shortage when you're in labor? Choose a nurse-midwife as your birth attendant for a hospital birth. Traditionally they stay with a woman throughout all of the labor, so there is no need to have a nurse with you, too. If hiring a nurse-midwife is not an option for you, hire a private-duty nurse, a monitrice, to be with you. Hiring a nurse to provide primary, or one-to-one, nursing care for you is uncommon for hospital births but not new.

To overcome resistance to their efforts to institute the birth room program at Manchester Community Hospital in Manchester, Connecticut, in 1969, Philip Sumner, M.D., and his colleagues had to supply their own nurses for the first birth room used. "What at first seemed to be a hardship turned out to be the greatest single asset of our program," says Dr. Sumner, "since it enabled us to introduce the concept of the monitrice. One-to-one, uninterrupted support by the highly motivated and sympathetic monitrice has helped ensure the success of our program."

Fourteen maternity nurses trained in the Lamaze method of prepared childbirth were on call on a rotating basis for patients of Dr. Sumner and his partners. They were hired privately by the patients, came to the hospital when the woman arrived in labor, and stayed with her through labor, delivery, and recovery. The monitrice monitored the fetal heart rate with a fetoscope, continuously if necessary, so that electronic fetal monitoring was used for normal births only when the monitrice felt she would like the additional data it might provide. Other U.S. physicians have since used monitrices, too, particularly if insurance paid their fee.

Do you definitely need a private-duty nurse in addition to your mate and your doula? Will your care suffer if you don't? Yes and no. It won't if your birth attendant is a midwife. What if you're in a hospital that routinely uses electronic fetal monitors on all patients, and you want to be an exception to the rule? When you discuss this preference with your physician, your argument will be much more persuasive if you tell him that you're willing to hire a private-duty nurse who will monitor your baby's heart tones by fetoscope, though insurance probably will not cover the cost. Having a nurse of your own do that—whether your hospital is short of staff or not—makes this option more manageable for your physician. Your willingness to hire a nurse also shows how important this preference is to you. (Check with the nurse you're hiring to find out if she's been trained to use a fetoscope for fetal heart tones.)

To find a monitrice, call hospital ob units and ask if they

have on-call ob nurses. If they do, contact one of them. She will already have gone through the hospital orientation and have hospital privileges. If an ob nurse tells you they don't use on-call nurses (and/or they have enough nurses on staff already), unless they provide one-to-one care, go further. Call the director of nursing or the hospital administrator. Undoubtedly, there's a procedure for hiring private-duty nurses at your hospital, because most likely your hospital already has private-duty nurses available for the medical-surgical patients.

Ask your childbirth educator. Since most childbirth educators are also nurses, some of them will have hospital privileges and, in addition, may be working at your hospital part-time. Or ask your doctor if he knows of nurses who work part-time on the ob floor.

Nurses don't agree on what the ideal number of obstetrical patients per nurse is. But research shows that the ideal ratio for you, the consumer, is one-to-one nursing care. Unquestionably, both you and your baby will be healthier. Primary or one-to-one nursing care is standard in out-of-hospital birth centers, and midwives stay with mothers during all of the labor and birth at home. If you plan to have your baby in a traditional hospital unit, you can't expect the hospital to provide one-to-one care. You'll have to provide that yourself by hiring a monitrice.

All women benefit by having their mate, doula, and monitrice present. But if you are expecting your first baby, these supporters are especially helpful to you. First-time mothers are likelier to have interventions of all kinds than women who have already had a baby. Labor and birth will be an entirely new and untried experience to you, and you will need all the help and reassurance you can get.

• TWELVE •

HOW TO HAVE A NORMAL VAGINAL BIRTH

(and Avoid an Unnecessary Cesarean)

In her seventh month of pregnancy Kathy finalized her birth plan with Dr. Right. By then she had discovered there were a lot of things that seemed very important to her, such as checking into the hospital as late as possible, hiring her own nurse to be with her at all times (a monitrice), and having other women there with her (as well as her husband).

When Kathy told her doctor she wanted to stay home as long as possible in labor, and to call him when she felt like coming to the hospital, he agreed. But his sudden laughter showed that he felt she wouldn't last very long at home. Hiring the nurse was okay with him, too, since there was a shortage of ob nurses at the hospital. To avoid having a fetal monitor, he said, the private-duty nurse, or monitrice, would have to check the fetal heart tones. Getting him to agree to these things was easier than she had expected. However, getting him to agree to the presence in labor of her mother-in-law, Maria, and her friend, Julie, was more difficult. He suggested the monitrice and her husband were enough. He couldn't understand why she wanted other women to be there, but finally he agreed to that point as well.

When Kathy was negotiating with Dr. Right, she noticed that he paid more attention to what she said when she talked about what was safe for her baby. When she told him what she wanted, he listened, but not as carefully as when she said she wanted to avoid interventions unless absolutely necessary because they might not be safe for her baby.

Kathy listened and agreed when her doctor said that her birth-plan preferences might have to be overridden in an emergency situation. Kathy typed up two copies of her birth plan. Both she and Dr. Right initialed them. Then he took one copy for her hospital chart, and she kept the other with her.

Kathy had been a light smoker when she became pregnant. Cigarettes had not tasted good to her during the nausea of early pregnancy, so she quit smoking. She had been an occasional drinker but she found, as her pregnancy proceeded, that alcoholic drinks didn't seem to taste good anymore, either, so she cut back on this too.

The unborn baby is the loser when a woman smokes or drinks during her pregnancy. Studies done in various medical centers have linked smoking with an increase in the risk of sudden infant death syndrome (SIDS), miscarriage, premature birth, premature separation of the placenta from the uterine wall (placental abruptions), placenta abnormality low in uterus (placenta previa), premature rupture of membranes (PROM), fetal distress during labor, and low birth weight. Heavy smokers tend to gain less weight during pregnancy than nonsmokers, and this is one reason for their baby's lower birth weight. However, studies indicate that smoking directly affects the unborn baby, reducing the amount of oxygen that reaches the baby and causing growth retardation.

Pregnancy and alcohol don't mix either. Doctors have long known that a heavy daily use of alcohol is connected with a set of birth defects in the baby known as fetal alcohol syndrome. As researchers began to take a closer look at the effects of alcohol use in pregnancy, they discovered that they simply could not find a safe level of use. So strong is the evidence that the March of Dimes, the National Council on Alcoholism, and the U.S. Surgeon General recommend, "If you are pregnant, don't drink alcohol."

The same guide for intervention in birth can be applied to any drug use in pregnancy: avoid use unless the benefits outweigh the risks. For example, a pregnant woman may need to continue medication for epilepsy to prevent seizures.

Earlier in her pregnancy Kathy had taken a relaxation class. As her pregnancy progressed, she tried to practice relaxation half an hour before bedtime. The evenings when she practiced were followed by a better night's sleep than those evenings when she skipped practicing. Now well into her eighth month, she noticed that sometimes her stomach became firm to the touch and she became conscious of the heaviness of her abdomen. After a few days she realized that these sensations were the uterine contractions of late pregnancy. She was thrilled at her discovery. She decided that whenever she experienced these very mild contractions, she would practice her relaxation—as a sort of conditioning to respond with relaxation whenever she felt a contraction. Her days seemed very full because she needed to move more slowly, and she tired very easily. Some days she could hardly make it through her teaching job, often going directly to bed when she got home from work.

Early in her pregnancy her doctor had referred her to his nurse to discuss a good diet. Gaining weight rather than trying to hold the line was emphasized. So Kathy was astonished to find that some women in her childbirth education class had recently begun dieting because they had "gained enough weight," according to them.

Current research is very clear in showing that having a healthy baby of normal birth weight is linked to the woman's prepregnancy weight, and to whether or not she has gained enough during pregnancy. Even women who are twenty pounds or more over their normal weight when they became pregnant need to gain weight. "It is never appropriate for a pregnant woman regardless of her size, to lose weight or avoid gaining," wrote Carol Pietz, M.S., R.D., L.D., a specialist in maternal/infant nutrition.

In a national study of weight gain and outcome of pregnancy, Selma Taffel, B.B.A., a statistician with the National Center for Health Statistics, reported that a significant number of women do not gain enough. A majority of women either are given no advice or are given a weight gain limit that is too low. Both these groups were likely to gain too little weight, putting their babies at higher risk of low birth weight or fetal death. Women gaining less than twenty-two pounds were at the highest risk. The more weight women gain, the better the birth weight of their babies and the better the outcome. The best fetal outcome came with a weight gain of 26 to 35 pounds, only slightly better than gaining more than 35 pounds. These figures are much higher than many doctors and women themselves are using. Editor Madeleine Shearer reported that a survey showed 25–80 percent of women in childbirth education classes were dieting to hold the line at their seven-month weight gain.

The end of pregnancy is not only the time when the baby has a huge growth spurt, doubling his weight from four to eight pounds, but it is also a time of rapid growth of his brain cells. "Even mild degrees of maternal undernutrition in the last few weeks can interfere with the normal growth and development of the normal fetal brain," says Dr. John Dobbing, British research professor, quoted by Gail Brewer in *What Every Pregnant Woman Should Know, The Truth about Diets and Drugs in Pregnancy*. Written in consultation with Tom Brewer, M.D., an ob/gyn, this book advises women:

- Don't worry so much about weight gain; eat according to your appetite.
- Make good nutrition your primary concern.
- Don't restrict salt intake.
- Be very careful about drugs, especially diuretics, which are dangerous to women and their unborn babies.

The Brewers' advice resulted from Dr. Brewer's research on toxemia, a metabolic disease of pregnancy. For years, doctors prescribed weight control and salt restriction, together with diuretics (water pills) to prevent toxemia. The Brewers explain, however, that these prescriptions contribute to low birth weight and brain-damaged babies, and may actually trigger toxemia by promoting malnutrition in the pregnant woman.

In normal pregnancy the woman's circulating blood volume expands by more than 40 percent to take care of the nutritional needs of the woman and her growing baby. The expanded blood volume is determined and maintained by adequate salt intake. If you have ever tasted your own blood, you know it is very salty. The crucial need for salt is the reason that salt should *not* be restricted in pregnant women, the Brewers say.

Given the American passion for being skinny, it's not easy for a woman pregnant for the first time to watch her body contours change, to see her waistline go, her stomach begin to protrude, and her body put on fat where she never had it before. So it's important for you to realize that you'll gain the right amount of weight for you if you eat when you are hungry, taking in nutritious foods and avoiding empty calories. Women underweight before pregnancy will need to make special efforts to eat enough to gain more than normal-weight women.

It's hard to cut out cakes, pies, cookies, candy, and fried foods, which have a lot of calories and few nutrients; but it's also important to get all the nutrients you and your baby need each day by concentrating on milk products, fruits, vegetables, whole-grain cereals, breads, fish, poultry, and lean meat. However, you need not be a meat eater to get the high-protein nutrition essential in a healthy pregnancy if you carefully combine grains and vegetables to form the complete proteins your body needs. *Diet for a Small Planet* gives an excellent explanation of ways to combine foods to get complete proteins, without eating meat.

Kathy had arranged to stop working in her eighth month of pregnancy. By then her baby's movements reminded her of its presence many times a day. She began to turn away from outside interests and to turn inward. She decided not to fight it, but to go with her feelings. At least once a day, but especially when she was changing clothes and could see her nude body, she would put her hands on her stomach and talk to her baby. The uterine contractions of late pregnancy—which some experience and some don't—came a little more often. Wherever she was, she used them as an opportunity to practice her relaxation, letting calmness flow through her body.

Kathy had tried to take a walk every day during her pregnancy. Now that she was no longer working, she had more time for walking. Every day she looked forward to getting out to walk a mile or two.

Pregnant women need regular exercise to stay fit.

> Walking, swimming, and bicycling are enjoyable activities that not only provide excellent general exercise but bring you into the fresh air and sunshine. Done regularly, they combine many of the desirable features of prenatal exercise planning: to strengthen muscles, build up endurance, improve circulation and respiration, adapt to increasing weight and changing balance.

> —ELIZABETH NOBLE, R.P.T., *ESSENTIAL EXERCISES FOR THE CHILDBEARING YEARS*

Women who have been inactive prior to becoming pregnant need to ease slowly into exercise. Strenuous exercise that leaves a pregnant woman gasping and exhausted, either right after exercising or later, is not good, for her or her baby. Easy does it. Exercise, done regularly, in a way that causes you to breathe deeper and faster, helps you to be physically fit and better able to cope with physical and mental stress.

Another benefit of regular exercise while pregnant may be

an increased secretion of endorphins in labor. Endorphins, the "well-being" hormones we mentioned earlier, are linked to your pleasure in the birth process. Daniel B. Carr, M.D., et al., reporting in the *New England Journal of Medicine,* demonstrated an increased endorphin response in women exercising regularly. Exercise increases the blood levels of endorphins, and conditioning enhances the effect. Women who exercise regularly have higher levels of endorphins when they are exercising than women who exercise irregularly. Although we know of no such research on pregnant women, it may be that by conditioning in pregnancy, a woman may increase her endorphin levels when she is in labor and her uterus is working strenuously.

Even if it's late in your pregnancy, you still have time to do one exercise more important to you for your health than any other. The pelvic floor (made up of the pubococcygeous or Kegel muscle) supports your expanding uterus, which holds your baby. Exercising your Kegel muscle makes your perineum stronger, yet more "stretchy," more resilient, in the pushing stage of labor. Relaxing the pelvic floor while pushing with the abdominal muscles eases your baby's way out and helps prevent tears and episiotomies.

You exercise this muscle by contracting or tightening and then releasing. To find the Kegel muscle, try stopping your flow of urine. The muscle that tightens at that moment is your Kegel muscle.

Elizabeth Noble, R.P.T., describes the Kegel exercise:

> *Remember:* Quality is more important than quantity. Slowly contract the muscles as you would in making a hard fist, not just closing your fingers but clenching to bring in every muscle fiber. About 5 in a series, holding each contraction for about 5 seconds. . . . Always end with a contraction. . . . Fifty a day, at least, during pregnancy and postpartum. Fifty a day, at least, *for the rest of your life.*

Kathy especially enjoyed her contacts with other pregnant women and nursing mothers in her childbirth preparation class and in La Leche League meetings. There was a common bond of excitement, anticipation, and fear that these women instantly understood. Women who already had their babies talked about how helpful friends had been before, during, and after birth. Kathy realized a few weeks before her baby was

*born that having other women with her during her birth was
not just a preference, it was a really strong need. She was glad
her husband's mother, Maria, who had four children, would be
there because she was experienced in giving birth, was a
loving, calm person, and was the grandmother-to-be. She was
also a supportive friend to her daughter-in-law Kathy. She was
especially glad that her friend Julie, who had a three-year-old
son, had agreed to be there. Kathy wanted Julie to handle any
questions or problems there might be with the hospital staff, so
that Kathy and Tim could concentrate on the labor.*

As we discussed in chapter 11, a laboring woman needs to
have another woman or women with her. In many other
cultures the grandmother-to-be, midwife, or another exper-
ienced-in-birth woman is always present with a laboring
woman. Most of the time their reassuring message is unspoken
but understood: "You will give birth; you can stand the pain;
you can find your own way to labor; I have done it, and I am
here to let you know you can do it too. Your body is made to
give birth, and all will be well." Women learn about giving
birth and breastfeeding from other women. They instinctively
trust other women.

*When Kathy's due date came and went, she was not too
depressed because half the women in her childbirth class still
had not delivered. By the forty-second week of her pregnancy,
however, she was tired of lugging around thirty-five extra
pounds. She felt very discouraged to learn at her routine
prenatal visit that the baby's head was not yet engaged in her
pelvis. Her friend Julie had arranged to call her every day so
that Kathy would know where she would be and could reach
her. This time when she called, Kathy wept and said, "I'm so
tired of being pregnant." Julie said all the right things. She
even correctly anticipated Kathy's unspoken thought that
maybe—just maybe—she'd accept induction just to get the
pregnancy over. Kathy felt better after talking with Julie. She
returned to her acceptance of the truism that the baby would
come when it was ready, and not a moment sooner. But it felt
good just to know that someone else could empathize with her
impatience.*

*For those last five days all Kathy thought of was the baby.
It seemed to her that her brain had turned to mush, and that
she must be the most uninteresting conversation partner. All*

she wanted to talk about was the baby. Concentrating on anything else seemed impossible. One morning in the grocery store where she always shopped, she became very frustrated when she couldn't find half the things on her list. She just felt weird. When she got home from the grocery store, she had some gentle contractions, not any different from before, and automatically relaxed through each one. When she had four contractions in an hour, however, a feeling came to her that maybe this was the real thing. She called her husband, Tim, and asked if he could take off work for the rest of the day. "Are you in labor?" he asked. "I don't know, but I need you," said Kathy.

Almost all women know when they are in true labor that will soon lead to the birth of their baby. The problem comes from thinking and worrying about being in labor when you are not. Everyone, women and their birth attendants, has "difficulty in accurately timing the onset of labor," said Gordon C. Gunn, M.D., of the Department of Obstetrics and Gynecology, University of California, Los Angeles and Torrance. "This problem is especially true in primigravidas where regular uterine contractions may not result in cervical dilation and where cervical effacement [thinning of the cervix] usually precedes the onset of true labor." True labor consists of regular uterine contractions resulting in a progressive opening of the cervix. Early labor, when the cervix gradually thins, can precede true labor by many hours or days. If you are near term and are having regular contractions, you may be in early labor. The contractions could go on for several days, perhaps alternating hours of regular contractions with periods of rest (when you should!).

What's the rush to get to the hospital? If you are in the 1 percent of women who have a very rapid labor and birth (an hour or two), you may end up among the tiny number of women who have a baby in the car on the way. In her review of all available data, Doris Haire, D.M.S., reported at a La Leche League International conference in Chicago that infants born in cars have the lowest infant mortality of any group. Everyone else may be anxious, but mothers and babies do fine. "Nature unaided will usually conduct a successful delivery," said Gregory White, M.D., home-birth attendant to over one thousand women during thirty years of practice, and author of

Emergency Childbirth. "Childbirth is not nearly so dangerous as a wild ride in an automobile."

Dr. White says to stop the car for the birth. "The mother, sitting in a slumped down position in the back seat, can deliver the baby over the edge of the seat into the hands of the attendant; or she may lie across the seat. As soon as the baby has been born and is breathing freely, it may be placed between the mother's legs and the trip to the hospital continued; it is not necessary to deal with the cord or wait for the afterbirth."

Stay home until you feel sure you are in well-established labor and will deliver soon. If you are feeling very uncertain, consider having a vaginal examination to establish dilation. If it is during a weekday, you can go to your doctor's office. Call his secretary first, of course, to alert him you are coming. Set this up ahead of time with him, so you can be taken right in for a quick check, rather than a possible long wait in the waiting room. If it is outside office hours, go to the hospital emergency room for a dilation check. If you are not at least four to five centimeters dilated, you will not have checked into the hospital, and you can return home without upsetting hospital routine.

For nine hours, from ten in the morning until seven in the evening, the contractions continued, never too close together, never really regular, but always there. As each one came, Kathy stopped what she was doing and allowed a wave of relaxation to pass over her body, at the same time breathing slowly and deeply. She wasn't interested in regular meals, but did become hungry during the day and had a small snack three or four times. Between six and seven o'clock in the evening the contractions were so light she was hardly aware of them. She felt very sleepy because she had missed her nap that day, so she decided to go to sleep. Because he felt he might be up later for the real thing, Tim got into bed with her, put his arms around her, and the two of them fell asleep.

Two hours later Kathy woke up because she felt she had to have a bowel movement. A half hour later she had another bowel movement, and a half hour later another one. The contractions had come back, about every twenty minutes now, and seemed stronger than she had ever felt before. Suddenly Tim laughed and said, "You know what, I think the baby's moving down and you have labor diarrhea." Kathy wasn't at all sure of anything at this point, except that she knew that she felt a little hungry again and wanted to take a shower. So first she snacked, and then she stood under a warm shower. She found that the water not only helped her to relax during the contraction, but the sensuous feeling of the water on her skin seemed to help her tune into her body better. She decided she wanted Maria and Julie to come. After Tim called them, it seemed only minutes before they arrived. Kathy was surprised at how relieved she felt just to have them there.

Supported and cared for in a safe, quiet place, a woman can turn inward and listen to what her emotions tell her to do in labor and birth. Such a philosophy of care was used by Michel Odent, M.D., and the six midwives with him in practice in Pithiviers, France. "What we try to do at Pithiviers is to rehabilitate the instinctive brain, the emotional brain, the brain which is close to the body, in a world that generally just knows and takes into account the other brain, the rational brain," said Dr. Odent at a 1982 conference, "Birth, Interaction and Attachment" moderated by Marshall Klaus, M.D., and John Kennell, M.D. "Michel Odent has put together clinically much of what is known from recent research to be of value in human childbirth," said Klaus and Kennell.

Odent, author of *Birth Reborn*, directed the obstetric unit at Centre Hospitalier in Pithiviers. In a 1983 interview, he told us that his unit is in a public hospital giving all maternity care for the local population, without selection, including immigrants and women with complications (for example, previous cesarean delivery). Induction, amniotomy, oxytocin to speed labor, and analgesia or anesthesia (unless for cesareans) are not used. Episiotomies are rare. The cesarean rate is 6 percent.

The emphasis is on providing a millieu, a setting for the woman "to forget what is cultural and to reach a level of consciousness in which she listens to the instinctive, emotional brain, to find for herself positions for labor and birth," said Odent in the journal *Birth*.

The change in level of consciousness, the regression of a woman to the more primitive, feeling level of awareness results in a safer, smoother, faster, and less painful labor and birth in the thousands of women who have given birth at Pithiviers. The average primipara labors five hours from two centimeters to ten centimeters dilation, less than half the average labor reported for American primiparas. Yet a short labor is not a goal of the birth attendants. When we asked Odent how long he's willing to wait for a birth, he said, "As long as it takes. We have no clocks anywhere in the birth rooms."

During pregnancy, couples can attend weekly group meetings (with the midwives), which emphasize the excitement, happiness, and normal nature of childbirth. Group singing is included to enhance familiarity with the midwives and to reduce women's inhibitions. Odent described five needs during labor affecting the woman's ability to tune into her emotional, instinctive brain.

The human factor. The midwife acts as a substitute for the laboring woman's mother, expressing love and support and giving skin-to-skin contact in preference to talking, which is kept simple and to a minimum.

The setting. The birth room, where the woman labors and gives birth, is like a living room with a large comfortable platform with soft cushions. To avoid the suggestion of the "right" place to labor or give birth, there is no bed. There is a wooden birthing chair.

Reduced sensory stimulation. Absence of noise, talking as little as possible, reduced lighting even to the point of semidarkness, help the laboring woman tune out the world and turn inward.

Warm water in labor. "The efficiency of water during the first stage is mysterious," said Odent. "We observe many times that a good bath in warm water with semidarkness is the best way to reach a high level of relaxation." Some women prefer to shower. Some immerse in the small pool in the unit. Women are encouraged to use the pool if their labor has stalled at five centimeters. "It is common that within an hour the woman is fully dilated," Odent told us. Sometimes the women have felt so comfortable they have stayed in the pool and given birth there, very quickly. "Our purpose is never to have a baby born under water," said Odent. "But it is important to know that it happens. The baby will not breathe until it contacts air—like a dolphin."

Positions for labor and birth. There is no confrontation at Pithiviers, no telling a woman what she must do or not do. Women search for the position of most comfort. Many women kneel, bending forward during a contraction. Odent has observed that this particular posture often helps a woman forget what is cultural, turn inward, and regress from logic to feeling. (It also helps the rotation of the baby's head in the pelvis, as in a posterior presentation of the baby.) But there are no "best" postures. Some few women deliver in the birthing chair, some lying on the platform. The most common position sought out for births is a "standing-squat": the woman's knees are bent as if she were seated, but spread apart. Her full weight is supported by someone standing behind her, holding her. "When the mother is at risk, or the baby is at risk, as in twin or breech deliveries, for example, the standing-squat position for delivery is imperative," says Odent.

After delivery, the mother, usually in a sitting position, is active (rather than prone and passive), and ready to hold and caress her baby. The naked mother and baby, comfortable in a birth room warmed for them, have easy touching access to each other. Cradled against the mother's breast in a natural nursing position, most newborns find the mother's nipple and begin nursing with no effort on the mother's part.

From his experience at Pithiviers, Odent believes the optimum level of consciousness in birth is reached in a safe, quiet, and supportive environment, and is accompanied by optimum secretion of oxytocin by the mother, and, very likely, a secretion of endorphins that protect both mother and infant against pain. "It is easy to understand that any drug given to the woman in labor can disturb the system of endorphins," says Odent. "More generally speaking, one cannot study protection against pain without studying at the same time the capacity to have pleasure and a sense of well-being."

Kathy found she was most comfortable if she changed positions often or slowly walked. With each contraction she would automatically relax and breathe deeply. In between contractions she felt nothing at all. Though she was concentrating on the present moment, she suddenly realized she was really getting very good at what she was doing. The long labor gave her a chance many, many times to use her relaxation with each contraction. About two o'clock in the morning she found that she was no longer comfortable relaxing and breathing through a contraction. She had to stop and lean against a chair, or the wall, or Tim, for the contraction to stay manageable. She felt somewhat irritable at one point when Tim laughed nervously in response to her abrupt command to stop walking. She said, "If you think it's so funny, why don't you try this for five minutes?" Then they both laughed, and Kathy said, "You know what, I want to go to the hospital."

Tim called the doctor's answering service to let them know they were coming in, and also called the nurse they had hired to be with Kathy. Maria, Julie, Kathy, and Tim all went in one car for the fifteen-minute drive. Kathy did not feel comfortable sitting in the car. When one contraction came during the trip, she asked Tim to pull over and stop because she couldn't relax as they bumped over the road. After she arrived at the hospital, Kathy realized that she was most comfortable if she just kept walking, so she walked in a little circle in the labor room. She undressed, making a trail of clothes behind her. The hospital admitting nurse examined Kathy and told her she was five centimeters dilated. She was disappointed, until her cheering section reminded her that "you're halfway there." The monitrice arrived half an hour after Kathy and began the procedure she would carry out every fifteen minutes during labor. She listened for the baby's heart tones for thirty seconds immediately after a contraction. She pronounced the baby doing "just fine." She drew a little flower on Kathy's stomach in the place that was easiest to hear the baby's heart tones.

Kathy was finding the contractions more difficult to handle and felt there must be something she should do. Then she remembered what another friend had told her. "You don't have to do anything, just relax and let your uterus open up your cervix." She thought of this often, and it helped her to let go and allow her body to work. She even tried visualizing the uterus and cervix working together with each contraction.

Contractions are the means by which a woman's body labors and gives birth. In her book *Preparation for Childbirth*, Donna Ewy, Ed.D., explains contractions:

> Probably one of the greatest fears a woman has concerning childbirth is how can a baby pass through such an obviously small opening without excruciating pain. The whole function of "labor" is to allow the contractions of the uterus to open the cervix (the lower part of the uterus to about 4 inches, the diameter of the baby's head. After the cervix has opened the baby passes through the birth canal. The tissues of the vagina are extremely elastic, and once the cervix opens, the baby passes through with relative ease.

The woman's response is different for the two stages of labor, the first, the opening of the cervix, and the second, when the baby passes through the birth canal.

Relaxation is the first and most important response of the mother to first-stage labor. You don't have to *do* anything. Contractions are involuntary. Let the body work. In her book, *Exercises for True Natural Childbirth,* Rhondda Hartman says: "The only help you can give the uterus with its work in the first stage is to "let it be." To do this requires great concentration on relaxing . . . just remember any part of your body in tension is going to add tension to the uterine contraction. It also detracts from the uterus's efficiency. Stay out of the way and let the uterus do its work."

Controlled breathing is another helpful technique in labor. The primary purpose of controlled breathing is as a distraction, however, and if carried out over a long labor can be very tiring. The easiest and least tiring breathing to accompany relaxation is the effacement breathing, or relaxed-chest breathing, of the Lamaze method; or the abdominal breathing of the Bradley method.

A woman's response to second-stage labor is very different from the first stage. Rhondda Hartman describes it like this: "Second stage is a time for strenuous activity and total involvement with the work going on inside you. Rather than trying to keep out of the way of the working uterus, as in first stage, now you will make your strong pushes coincide with the effort of the uterus, so second stage will be as efficient as possible."

The nature of the contractions change, the time between them is longer. Contractions are still involuntary, but a woman can now effectively use her abdominal muscles to assist the contractions in pushing her baby out.

Kathy continued her slow walking with Tim right beside her, his arm around her upper back, partially supporting her. When a contraction came, she leaned her full weight against him to relax. When the contraction was over, she complained of the pain and suggested that she must not be doing very well. Her childbirth education class had given her the impression that if she relaxed and breathed correctly, she wouldn't have any pain. Her monitrice explained that even though she was relaxing and breathing very well, the intensity of the contractions was stretching her cervix open. That's something some women simply feel to be more painful than do others. But

Kathy was reassured that they would all help her get through it.

As they discussed the intensity of the experience, Kathy's mother-in-law, Maria, said that, of her four births, three had been without drugs or anesthesia. She had a mixture of experiences with those three, she said: with one labor and delivery there was no pain at all; with another, there was a kind of searing pain at the peak of contractions; the last birth, a five-hour labor, hurt most of the time. Sometimes she felt as if she just couldn't stand the pain anymore, but the people she had with her got her through. They were going to do that for Kathy too.

Maria mentioned one thing that had helped her was to yawn and stretch between contractions. It seemed to help get rid of extra tension. Kathy tried it, and it did seem to help her relax fully between contractions. As the morning rolled in, more suggestions were offered. If what was suggested felt right to her, she would try it. More often than not, everything she tried worked for a while. But then the pain would build again during a contraction, and she would feel overwhelmed. She tried several different positions seeking comfort, turning inward, moaning.

Tim could see she was getting very tired and very hot, and he suggested they take a shower together. Kathy was so involved with her contractions that she couldn't think of things to do and the idea of a shower right then sounded like a clever idea. (Tim had brought his bathing suit to the hospital just in case Kathy wanted to shower during labor.) It was slow going because, although Kathy had a good three minutes between contractions, she walked slowly. Before she got from bed to shower, she had two more contractions. While she waited them out, she stood with her arms draped around Tim, who supported her weight.

The shower cooled, refreshed, and relaxed Kathy, and once more she felt she was going to make it. In fact, there were moments when Kathy could almost laugh at herself. As the labor went on, she felt not only her body but her mind was opening up. She felt free to express whatever it was she was feeling—early in labor, her pleasure and excitement that the baby was almost there, and now, later in labor, her pain and despair at ever getting through it. She felt that those around her gave her permission to do whatever it was she needed to do, and that was probably the best help of all.

When things frequently got tense, Julie's job seemed to be to remind everyone that the baby was just fine. The monitrice was continuing her regular monitoring, and the baby's heart rate was strong. Tim drew strength from his mother and from Julie, both of whom praised him for the way he was helping Kathy. Sometimes he was uncertain that he was being helpful, because of Kathy's irritability. But Julie and Maria reassured him by saying things like, "Oh, I know that feels good to Kathy." They could see that Kathy was responding to his touch. Tim opened up, too, as the labor went on, and felt free to kiss, touch, and hold Kathy, to express his love and support for her. Tim noticed that sometimes when they were kissing, Kathy's mouth was tense and she was feeling a lot of pain. He suggested she might be tightening up her bottom. They discovered that smooching a lot helped to keep her mouth and her bottom much more relaxed. There seemed to be a connection between the two.

About seven o'clock in the morning, after five hours in the hospital, and about twenty hours since labor had started, Kathy was flushed and sweaty. It didn't seem possible that the contractions could hurt more, but they did. She felt confused because now she felt she had no time to recover between contractions. The monitrice told Kathy she had all the signs of being in transition, and she was going to alert Kathy's doctor. When he arrived, he agreed Kathy was in transition, and there was no need for a vaginal check. He did suggest that they might move labor along now if they broke the bag of waters. Julie reminded him how strongly Kathy felt about not artificially breaking the bag of waters. He said yes, he had remembered that, and it was fine.

Kathy was in transition for two hours. It was the worst time for her. Her pain, discomfort, and confusion were at their height, and she needed the quiet assistance from those around her.

The intensity of pain experienced in childbirth is often unexpected by prepared women, who assume that if they just relax and breathe well enough, there will be no pain. It is difficult to predict ahead of time which women will have pain and how intense it will be. The childbirth literature suggests that about 5 percent of women have painless labors and births. So clearly, most women do have pain in labor and delivery.

In our culture, pain is considered abnormal, either due to

disease or injury, and a symptom to be avoided or medicated. Obstetricians see the relief of pain as an obligation. It goes against their training to see a woman suffering in labor, and many feel the woman is a martyr, a little crazy, or both, to refuse analgesia or anesthesia. Mothers who have had painful labors and deliveries without drugs, but with caring and supportive birth attendants, family, and friends there, usually see it differently. They describe the pain as a catalyst that pushed them deeper within themselves, almost a guide to lead them to discover a physical and mental capacity they had not previously known. This change of consciousness is described by Michel Odent. It does not involve a control of pain but a surrender to it that leads to the woman's own body producing pain-tolerating hormones, endorphins, which also cause the after-birth high. Many of these mothers remark on the tremendous euphoria immediately following birth. They have found that the exquisite pain of labor in a loving, supportive, peaceful environment is followed by the most exquisite pleasure after birth.

Kathy had not felt hungry all night and had only felt the need for drinking water and apple juice. However, during the transition, she was aware that she was tremendously thirsty and, over a two-hour period, drank about six full glasses of water. About every hour, the monitrice reminded Kathy to get to the bathroom and try to urinate, "so a full bladder won't be in the way of the baby."

The last two hours of labor were truly the hardest work that Kathy had ever done in her life. She frequently felt overwhelmed and at one point during a contraction started to pant the words, "Help, help, help, help." Julie picked up on the word and repeated it with her over and over, then put her hands on Kathy's shoulders, looked into her eyes, and said, "Now breathe with me, Kathy." And slowly Kathy got back into the rhythm of breathing and relaxing with the contraction. Julie's eyes never wavered from Kathy's during the contractions of those last hours, and to Kathy it was a lifeline.

Author Donna Ewy, Ed.D., includes many comforting techniques in her book *Guide to Family Centered Childbirth*. She summarizes them by saying, "Three key methods that will help you get her back in control are eye contact, firm voice, and a secure touch."

A nurse discusses the power of eye contact with a laboring woman:

> One of the many useful ideas discussed in *Spiritual Midwifery* is the technique of "catching eyes" with the woman during those parts of her labor when she feels like she is disintegrating or losing her perspective. The transference of power and feeling between two people whose gaze is fixed on each other and who are breathing in rhythm during a very intense moment in their lives is so charged with energy that it makes one stand back in awe. The power is tremendous. The problem is that, as a culture, we are not comfortable with prolonged eye contact. It is something that people need to be taught. However, in my experience in the hospital, it has been worth the effort to try. When a woman suddenly looks lost or desperate, I say, "Open your eyes and *look* at me, I'll breathe with you." If she'll do it, if she will allow herself to trust you enough to maintain eye contact, you can get her through almost any kind of a contraction just by the power of being there and experiencing it with her on a level that is difficult to appreciate unless you have been there yourself.

> —PEGGY VINCENT, R.N.,
> *BIRTH*, SUMMER 1977

Tim was sitting next to Kathy, massaging her thighs where she seemed to be feeling a lot of tension, lightly stroking her face, kissing her between contractions, and telling her she was "almost there" and doing great. Gradually, over the space of about three contractions, Kathy started grunting at the end of each one. The monitrice felt she was probably fully dilated, did a vaginal check, and found that Kathy was indeed ten centimeters dilated.

The contractions seemed to change. There was much more time in between, and Kathy felt like pushing with each one. The monitrice notified Kathy's doctor, who was waiting in the doctor's lounge. He checked Kathy and confirmed that the baby's head was well engaged, that she was fully dilated, and that she could go ahead and push. Kathy felt as if she wanted to stand and lean against Tim. He stood behind her, supported her under her arms, and held her full weight during each contraction as she pushed whenever she felt like it. Marie remarked that it was a good thing that her son had been a football player, and the laughter broke some of the tension.

Kathy spent the next hour and a half pushing in different positions. She stood, hanging onto Tim. She squatted, supported and balanced by Tim and Julie. She lay on her side. Near the end, she sat on the bed with Tim behind her, supporting her, the top of the bed tilted up, pillows supporting Tim's back.

Historically, the most common position for birth in various cultures has been some form of the upright position. For first-time deliveries, which normally have a longer second stage, the upright position (standing, sitting, or squatting) and changing positions shorten second-stage labor. Contractions are stronger and more regular, and the woman seems to be able to relax more completely between contractions. Women seem able to push more effectively because of the assist from gravity in the upright position.

Late in pregnancy try out several positions for birth, so you are familiar with how they feel.

- Sit on the toilet, upright, with back support, hands on your knees to simulate a birth chair. Better yet, try out the one your local hospital may have.
- Lie on your side curled up. (Good if the birth is going very fast.)
- Kneel on the floor, then lean forward, on all fours, or with your upper body leaning on the couch. (Good for back pain.)
- Stand, bend and spread your knees as if to sit in a chair, and have your partner hold you under your arms from behind, supporting your full weight.
- Squat. (The pelvic opening is increased 20–30 percent.)
- Sit with your back supported and your legs comfortably spread apart, knees flexed.
- To get a feel for the "uphill" lithotomy position we hope you can avoid: Lie on your back on the floor with your bottom close to the couch. Bend your legs so your calves rest on the seat of the couch.

In each position, practice your Kegel exercise, so you are familiar with the feeling of releasing your pelvic floor in a delivery position.

* * *

"Okay," said the doctor, "now here's what I want you to do. When a contraction begins, take two deep breaths, in and out. Take a third breath and slowly release it as you push for just as long as you want. You will be making some kind of a sound as you push. Relax your bottom while you are pushing. Whenever you need another breath, inhale slowly and then slowly release your breath as you push. When a contraction is over, take a deep breath and relax."

Julie, who was standing next to Kathy and who had her hand on Kathy's arm, felt her tense when the doctor was telling her what to do. "Hey, you don't have to remember those instructions, Kathy," said Julie, "because your doctor is going to talk you through each contraction until it's old hat for you. You don't have to worry about anything—you just have to keep your bottom relaxed." Julie could feel Kathy's arm relax. With each contraction the doctor gave his instructions. Soon Kathy picked up her own natural pushing rhythm. It felt good to make "uhhhhhh," grunting sounds, letting out her breath while she was pushing for about five or six seconds with each breath. Her doctor told her to bear down only when she felt the need to push, without trying to hold her breath or prolong a push. He told her that by pushing this way she was getting lots of oxygen to her baby. For several of the contractions the monitrice placed her hand on Kathy's perineum. It helped two ways. The monitrice could feel when Kathy's perineum was tense or when it was relaxed, and she could tell Kathy. It also helped Kathy because by having a firm hand on her perineum, she could visualize better where she needed to relax.

Kathy pushed whenever she felt the urge; then, suddenly, the bag of waters burst. Kathy felt a warm jet of water between her legs. She was astonished at how much water it seemed her body was putting out. Soon a few centimeters of her baby's head could be seen at the vaginal opening. The monitrice, who sensed that Kathy was tiring, took Kathy's hand and guided it down to touch her baby's head. "You see, Kathy, there is your baby's head; it's almost here." Touching the top of the baby's head with the baby still inside her thrilled Kathy. She felt renewed energy. Slowly the head stretched the perineum until it bulged so large it looked ready to burst. But the slow stretching was doing its job. It looked as if the doctor could avoid doing an episiotomy. Kathy felt better when she was pushing. When, suddenly, the doctor told her to stop pushing so he could ease the baby's head out, the sensation of *stretching and pain was tremendous. As the head emerged, Kathy screamed in pain. She felt that she might rip up the front, but there was no tearing. There was another short wait before Kathy felt the next pushing contraction. When it came, Kathy's baby was born with one push. Immediately the doctor gave the baby to Kathy to hold. Her eight-pound, one-ounce baby boy was born just before ten in the morning, twenty-four hours after she started early labor the previous morning.*

Kathy was laughing and crying at the same time and all sensations of pain were gone. She felt only enormous pleasure. About ten minutes later the doctor clamped the cord on the baby's side, but allowed the cord on the mother's side to bleed freely into a bowl. During her pregnancy Kathy had taken a medical article to him showing that when the cord was left unclamped on the mother's side, it shortens the third stage of labor (the delivery of the placenta) and blood loss is greatly reduced. There was close to a half cup of blood in the bowl when Kathy felt a mild contraction, then felt the soft placenta fill her vagina. She pushed and expelled it easily.

Kathy loved the feeling of her wet, warm newborn lying against her breast, the two of them covered with a blanket. Tim put his hand under the blanket on his son's back. Kathy's love for her husband and baby seemed to expand moment by moment until she felt her love radiating out to include the whole world. The words that kept passing through her mind were "miracle—it's a miracle."

SUMMARY: HOW TO HAVE A NORMAL VAGINAL BIRTH AND AVOID AN UNNECESSARY CESAREAN

PREGNANCY

1. Choose a place of birth where there is the least intervention, or a hospital with very flexible routines.
2. Choose a midwife, a doctor with a midwife philosophy, or a doctor with whom you can negotiate for your preferences.
3. Decide what is important for your birth, write up a birth plan, and ask your doctor to sign it.
4. *Gain* weight, using nutritious foods and liquids.

5. Do not smoke or use alcohol.
6. Avoid any drug use unless the benefits outweigh the risks. Avoid aspirin, which has been found to cause bleeding in mothers and babies even when taken days before birth.
7. Learn deep relaxation, slow deep breathing, and other breathing techniques that you may use in labor.

LABOR

1. If you have premature rupture of membranes, stay home and wait for labor (it may be days), unless you have active genital herpes.
2. If you are near term (within three weeks of due date), stay home in labor until you feel you must go to the hospital. Return home if you are not at least four to five centimeters dilated. (Particularly important for first labors, which tend to be longer.)
3. Eat and drink as you desire. Sleep when you can.
4. Urinate frequently.
5. Avoid efforts to intervene in a normal labor.
6. Hire a monitrice for labor support and to monitor your labor and your baby's heart rate, especially if that is the only way you can avoid a fetal monitor.
7. Walk, stay upright or in a side-lying position, unless your labor is going very fast and you are more comfortable in another position. Try different positions to find the ones of most comfort to you. Change positions.
8. Alternate resting and walking for a long labor.
9. Have at least one woman you know and like with you—your doula—in addition to your husband.
10. Use warm water, a soaking bath or a shower, to help you relax and open up if your labor stalls at five centimeters or so.

DELIVERY

1. Use almost any position but on your back with your legs in stirrups. Upright positions allow gravity to help—especially important for first-time mothers whose deliveries tend to take longer.

2. To avoid depriving your baby of oxygen and to allow time for the perineum to stretch slowly (and avoid an episiotomy) use exhale-pushing, also known as gentle or physiological pushing:

- Push only when you feel the need.
- Release your breath very slowly when you push.
- Push no more than five to six seconds at a time. Take another breath when you still feel the need to push.
- Take a deep breath when each contraction is over.

THIRTEEN

YOUR HELP ON THE INSIDE— THE NURSE

> Before the baby was born, I read many books and talked with my friends. All the time I was focusing on the birth process itself. Then, there I was, in the hospital. I was dealing with hospital bureaucracy, and I'd never been in a hospital before. I was flabbergasted. I was on my back, and all my defenses were down. I found out that nurses can be either condescending or helpful. Nurses make *all* the difference. The nurses really count. They're the ones on the line. They're there all the time.
>
> —NEW YORK MOTHER

If you're like most pregnant women, you're narrowing your focus. You're thinking of your changing body and how different your life will be in a few months. While you may have carefully scrutinized your physician and the options available at your hospital, you're not likely to have given much thought to the nurses who will be almost your entire contact in the hospital. Perhaps no one has told you that how you're treated during your stay depends mostly on the nurses, the people with whom you'll spend more than 95 percent of your in-hospital time. So that you'll have more understanding of, and perhaps more control over your hospital stay, we'll describe what you can expect from nurses, why they do what they do, and how you can get what you want from them.

NURSES' TRAINING

Nurses, 98 percent of whom are female, are the largest group of health professionals in the world. The typical nurse is a hard-working woman who wants to help others. All nurses, regardless of education, pass the same state exam after graduating from an approved program. Programs vary in length, cost, and intensity. Of the three training programs, the one producing two-thirds of all hospital staff nurses is the three-year hospital school. Associate degree and university-based programs make up the other third.

Although all of these graduates are trained to work in hospitals, the emphasis in the programs varies. Nurses who receive their training in hospital schools are the most likely to care for you. The training of these nurses emphasizes good bedside care—which is to your advantage. But they are also trained to meet the needs of the hospital, and consequently the physician, first—which may be to your disadvantage. That's why many of the hospital-school graduates may not be con-sumer oriented as the collegiate nurses are.

How does that affect your hospital care? Be reasonable with your expectations. Don't expect the nurses to automatically ask you what you want. They will, however, want to cooperate with you if you are clear and persistent about the options you want, just as you have been with your physician.

The changes over the years in nurses' education have brought mixed blessings to the consumer. On the one hand, nurses teach better and listen more. They don't just tell patients what to do. On the other hand, Florence Nightingale might not recognize her sisters today. Although nurses are still the "hands-on" practioners of the health-care profession, they, too, have been caught up in technology. Most nursing schools, for example, don't teach nurses how to listen for fetal heart tones with a fetoscope. They are taught to use a fetal monitor instead. Knowledge of new medications and emer-gency procedures takes precedence over knowing how to help the normal laboring woman with breathing techniques or with relaxation.

THE DEMAND FOR (AND SHORTAGE OF) NURSES— AND HOW THAT AFFECTS THE CARE YOU RECEIVE

A nurse can get a job wherever she goes. Indeed, many hospitals actively recruit her. Nearly all health-care institutions report available positions and often severe shortages. And the demand for nurses is expected to increase past the year 2000 while the glut of physicians grows.

In 1989 the typical nurse earned about $25,000 a year, though some positions pay more. Although this salary is a big improvement over the past, it's still only one-sixth of what the typical obstetrician makes in a year after he pays for overhead and his malpractice premium ($149,104).

Although a nurse can always get a hospital job, when she does, she often assumes enormous responsibilities. And while working rotating shifts and holidays—times when hospital floors are traditionally understaffed—she may also be expected to assume housekeeping tasks. In addition, "defensive" medicine has increased the amount of time a nurse spends with charting and other paperwork, while the nursing shortage means this same nurse has more women to care for. A common complaint for many nurses is that they can't spend enough time with patients and give quality care. This directly affects you, the consumer.

WHAT MOMS SAY THEY WANT FROM NURSES

Nurses were consistently gracious, overextending and involved in my care and excitement over childbirth. The best way to describe it is that I felt loved and "mothered" by the nursing staff! Much appreciation and thanks.

I would like to comment on one nurse in particular—I don't know her name. She tried in every way possible to make my stay as uncomfortable as she could—even after my daughter was born. She came into my room and gave me this long lecture on how bad and childish I had acted during my labor. It was extremely painful for me, and I did the best I knew how to keep in control while in labor. When the pain got really bad, she came in and said to me, "You're not having any pain yet. You just wait. It'll get much worse"—instead of a word of encouragement. And on the day I was discharged, she gave the information to me for postpartum care and then said to me, "Now this is your responsibility for eighteen years and don't forget it!" I am glad now to have a chance to let someone know what I went through during my stay, and hope no other woman will have to put up with this woman's bitterness.

* * *

These two mothers had their babies in the same hospital at about the same time. Your care, too, can vary that much in the same institution. We've read hundreds of comments from mothers regarding the nursing staff and find that most comments, however, fall somewhere between the two quotes above. The care most mothers receive is neither perfect, nor perfectly horrible.

DURING THE LABOR AND BIRTH

The theme throughout all the comments from mothers is that they want help, not hindrance; respect, not tolerance. They crave information.

My labor nurse only seemed to know how to offer me drugs when I was uncomfortable. I know she wanted to help me, but it wasn't the right kind of help. I wanted her to encourage me and show me what to do with my breathing.

And when mothers got that support, they were indeed grateful.

Without the labor nurse at Community Hospital in Boulder I would have folded. My comfort was her main concern. That labor nurse was super!

BREASTFEEDING

In the three surveys, as well as in most of the comments we've received since then from mothers, the emphasis for infant feeding is on bottle-feeding, not breastfeeding. That may be because no special help is usually needed for bottlefeeding mothers. Nurses are trained well to show you how to hold both your baby and the bottle, as well as when and how to burp your infant.

In both the Boulder and the Wenatchee surveys, mothers rated nurses, physicians, childbirth instructors, La Leche League leaders, husbands, and family for help in breastfeeding. Who was helpful? Nurses help more than doctors, but nurses were not as uniformly helpful as were LLL leaders and childbirth educators. Husbands and friends fared well in giving breastfeeding support, too.

Incidentally, the higher the breastfeeding rate in your town, the better the help from the nurses and doctors will probably be. The staff, like anyone else, does best what it usually does on a regular basis.

I was told by the nurse not to nurse before my milk came in because the colostrum was "useless"; told not to let him breastfeed for more than five minutes every three hours or I would get engorged; told if I nursed while lying down I might suffocate the baby and told never to sleep with my baby; told it was very odd not to send my baby to the nursery at all and that perhaps I was "too attached" to my infant.

Only a minority of women found nurses' advice with breastfeeding as shockingly inaccurate as the above. But when they did, they often reacted angrily. New mothers expect nurses to be as competent with their infant feeding advice as they are with blood-pressure checks or the use of drugs. Is this a reasonable expectation? Yes. The nursing mother is no longer an occasional patient. She's the majority.

However, the nurses who are on duty when you're in the hospital may not have had access to current information in breastfeeding, or they may have no personal experience with breastfeeding their own children. And then there's resistance to change. In 1982 Lawreance Gartner, M.D., of the Pritzker School of Medicine at the University of Chicago stated: "I agree that both hospital practices and the support available for the majority of mothers who are breastfeeding are quite inadequate. A lot of bad advice is handed out about breastfeeding, even within good hospitals. . . . You do, in fact, have to go through a formal retraining of groups of nurses, some of whom in fact are resentful about the mother who wants to breastfeed.

BREASTFEEDING COUNSELORS

Paula J. Adams Hillard, M.D., an obstetrician herself, wrote of her own childbirth experience in *The Female Patient:* "The person who meant the most to me was a breastfeeding counselor; I now feel that every postpartum floor in the hospital should have someone available to encourage women to breast-feed their babies. Even though I had relatively few problems with breastfeeding, it meant a great deal to have my questions answered and to be able to read the excellent material I was provided."

Regardless of how helpful the surveyed mothers found the nurses to be with breastfeeding, almost unanimously they thought the hospital should hire a person especially trained to help breastfeeding mothers. It's more than information these mothers want. They want support from someone who understands that breastfeeding is a complex giving and receiving between mother and baby. It's a feminine art, not simply a method of feeding. The importance of breastfeeding help continues. A 1987 British study showed that new mothers' greatest source of dissatisfaction was inadequate help with breastfeeding.

During my hospital stay, all the nurses and nurses' aides seemed to have their own fixed ideas about the care of my baby. I was trying to nurse, and all they seemed to care about was getting Bridgette to drink the glucose solution they provided.

The best breastfeeding counselor is a woman personally experienced with nursing her own child or children and who thinks breastfeeding, in general, can work for nearly any woman who wants to nurse. She does not perceive breastfeeding as a problem, and does not think it is messy or inappropriate in our culture. This breastfeeding counselor knows that no one knows the baby better than its own mother and, most importantly, makes no value judgments about the new mother's lifestyle, whether she's married or single, employed away from home or at home all day. She conveys the pleasure of breastfeeding and helps the mother feel good about her choice.

If you have a doula who fits the description of breastfeeding counselor, you need not look further. But if you don't, contact La Leche League, your childbirth educator or the lactation consultants listed on page 330. (Some breastfeeding counselors are hired by hospitals, but an ongoing service like this is rare.)

Many childbirth educators and most midwives, nearly all of whom have been breastfeeding mothers, also help their own clients with nursing.

AND *PLEASE!* NO CRITICISM

> One time when the nurse came into the room, I said to her: "Isn't it incredible how patient Kathy is with this labor? She has this machine hooked up to her, she is in a strange environment, and she's really tired. You are not letting her eat or drink. And she puts up with all of it, is so patient, and she allows her body to labor." The nurse said, "Yes, she's doing so well. We are proud of her, but we wish she'd hurry up her piddly labor. We'd hate to have to do a cesarean just because she's so slow."

—DOULA

That negative comment strikes fear in mothers. It certainly doesn't enhance a laboring mother's belief in herself. And she won't forget that comment either—not if she's like other women we've spoken to. Nor will her labor go faster because of the threat. It may only serve to convince mom that she's a failure. She can't even get a baby born on time.

But wait a minute! Whose time are we talking about? Why did the nurse say that? Perhaps because nurses are incorrectly taught in school that normal labors should progress one centimeter an hour. Or perhaps, as we've been told by nurses, that particular nurse is just having a bad day. Frankly, we think birth is too important for our caregivers to have bad days, difficult as that may be to control.

Being criticized about your "noisy" behavior during labor or being taken to task because your baby "only" gained half an ounce after a feeding is *never* helpful. If there's a better way for you to do something, there's also a helpful, encouraging way to tell you.

You wouldn't want your mate in the throes of lovemaking to whisper in your ear: "Darling, you're wonderful, but *gee* you're so slow (or noisy or quiet)." Comparisons that suggest you're somehow not up to standard are just as inappropriate when you are giving birth or nursing a baby.

As a laboring woman and new mother, you'll thrive on praise and support. Insulate yourself with the affectionate bubble of family and friends. Have your husband and doula with you. Protect yourself from demeaning comments by nurses, unintentional as they may be. Although all of you will not be subjected to these remarks, many of you will. Anticipating them in advance may deflect their sting.

HOW NURSES SEE THEIR ROLE ON THE MATERNITY FLOOR

LABOR AND DELIVERY

Maternity floors can be a tranquil oasis in a hospital filled with the sick and dying. Birth, after all, is not an illness. It's a celebration. But there's the other side of the picture, too. "Most people don't recognize that the maternity floor is also an extremely stressful and high-tension area," said one ob nurse. Even though it may not happen often, a nurse never knows who the next emergency patient will be. Just like the doctors she works with, her eye is trained to look for problems.

The emphasis in nurses' training is on what to do when nature can't seem to manage by itself. Nurses are taught how to put an IV in your arm, and, at a doctor's direction, how to measure the appropriate amount of Pitocin to get your labor started or speeded, and when to give you drugs for pain relief.

For some nurses, childbirth is nothing new. They've seen hundreds before. And when they report to the nursing station that they have "five in early labor," you may be seen as just part of their job on that particular shift. It's very exhausting for nurses to get emotionally involved with each birth. Many nurses learn early to keep themselves at arm's length. In addition, patients are not a nurse's only responsibility. There's paperwork to be done, and above all, she must do whatever the physicians tell her. The nurse's role is not an easy one. She has enormous responsibility, but often little authority.

Other nurses, though, still see each birth as sacred, not routine. Each birth for them is new and exciting. They get involved with the couple during labor and enthusiastically make personalized arrangements for the parents whenever possible. They don't talk loudly and laugh in the halls with other nurses. And they keep their voices hushed in a room with a laboring woman. They avoid examining her during a contraction, because they know that can be painful. And they tell her what to expect next in her labor. They believe the mother's needs are paramount.

Maybe you'll be fortunate enough to have one of these enthusiastic, helpful nurses. Are there very many? Not enough. Not because nurses don't want to give you the best of care—they do. But there may not be enough staff on the floor to permit your nurse to spend much time with you. Or her training or lack of experience with what you want gets in the way.

THE VIEW FROM THE NURSERY

> You know in England they don't use the nursery in the hospitals anymore; they just store things in them. They know the baby belongs with the parents and not in the nursery. Ultimately we'll get around to that here [in the United States].
>
> —JOHN MOYER, M.D.

Although hospital planners still usually include large nurseries in the blueprints for new ob units in the United States, the concept of nurseries—a place to keep babies away from their mothers—is under fire. We humans are the only species that routinely separates mothers and babies. Forty years ago, when nearly all mothers were totally unconscious by the time they gave birth in hospitals, it might have been logical to appoint someone else (the nursery nurse) to be the infant's caregiver. Although hospital nurseries may become the health-system dinosaur of the future, if you're pregnant now, you'll probably still have to cope with nurseries during your hospital stay.

Sandra Gardner, pediatric nurse practitioner, addressed her health-care colleagues in *Keeping Abreast, Journal of Human Nurturing*. But the message she sends is for the consumer, too. It's a good description of the view from many hospital nurseries:

> Terri Martin delivered her first infant by c-section three days ago. She has eagerly been breastfeeding her infant for the last two days. This morning she spiked a temperature of 101 degrees. While her physician was making rounds he . . . found no signs of infection. The physician wrote orders for the nursery nurses that

the "Baby may come to the mother's room to be breastfed; breastfeeding is not to be discontinued. . . ."

As the nurse enters the [mother's] room she states,
"Well, I just want you to know that I do not approve of
bringing this baby out to breastfeed. You realize that you
have a temperature, and you don't care any more than
that about your baby's health." The nurse reaches into
the crib and produces a surgical mask. Handing it to the
mother she states, "You *will* wear this while this baby is
in this room." The mother replies, "The doctor told me
that he could not find any reason for my elevated
temperature and most likely it was because my milk was
coming in. He did not say anything about wearing a
mask while I breastfeed the baby." The nurse says, "I
don't care what the doctor said or didn't say; it's not *his*
nursery, it's *my* nursery. As long as I'm in there you *will*
wear this mask while this baby is in this room."

"Far fetched?!"

"Unlikely?!"

"It couldn't happen here!"

"Not us!"

. . . This "real life" incident and many others
happened in community and teaching hospitals in this
country.

You, too, may find yourself wondering, "Whose baby is
it—the hospital's or mine?" And that's true whether you're
breastfeeding or bottle-feeding. Nurses who choose to work in
the nursery lavish love on their small charges. That's the good
news. Gardner describes the bad news: "Neonatal nurses may,
in fact, treat their small patients as their own children and
irrationally block, deny, and compete with the biological
mother for time with the new baby."

For many nurses the definition of a "good" patient is a
woman who is quiet, uncomplaining, and totally passive.
Why? Because passive mothers make the nurse's job easier.
Gardner quotes nurses who say, "The families don't stay in the
hospital very long, and it would be chaotic to try to meet
everyone's needs. The hospital order must be maintained and
as soon as they go home, they can do what they want to do."

* * *

I suppose that in order to be a good nurse, there has to be some part of your brain that says, "I love routine." Because every time I have ever been in the hospital, the smallest bit of change in routine seems to be a threat to the nurses.

Are all nursery nurses threatened by mothers who want to break the routine? No, of course not. But enough are that if you're forewarned, you're forearmed. You can turn that nurse's devotion to your baby into a benefit for both you and your baby.

Or maybe you'll be fortunate enough to have nursery nurses like the ones recently described to us:

> I stayed in the hospital two days. The nurses were so helpful. They brought Brenda every two hours, and made sure I knew how to get her started at the breast. They told me to let the baby nurse as long as she wanted. They told me Brenda didn't need water; she just needed me. Over and over they told me how well the baby and I did together. I'm so thankful to those nurses.
>
> —COLORADO MOTHER

Following is a letter Sandy Gardner quoted from a mother who also was grateful to the nursery nurses:

> When I was in the hospital, I developed a fever [101 degrees]. They thought it was from my breast engorgement, but they would not take any chances. They kept the baby away from me for two days. They wouldn't even let me in the nursery area. When he came back, he would not take the breast. They told me to use a nipple shield halfway through, then try. He screamed like someone was killing him. So in the hospital, I just used the shields, and I was going to break him when I got home. On the second night home, he screamed all night. As you probably know, a baby has to work *very hard* to get any milk out of the shield. So, I put him on the bottle. I cried for two days straight. I wanted to breastfeed *so* bad.
>
> But one thing for sure I know that he got excellent care in the nursery.

This mother's experience was full of disappointment and frustration. How can you avoid that yourself? Don't take potluck with the nurses who will be helping you with your new baby in the hospital, but you'll need to tell your nurse what's helpful. And you'll get much-needed assistance in that area from both your mate and/or your doula—the people who care the most for you.

The mother above, while frustrated and sad, was also grateful to the nursing staff for taking care of her baby. All new mothers are generally grateful to both doctors and nurses, no matter how they were treated. After all, regardless of what happened in the hospital, most mothers get their desired baby. But there's another reason, too. We do want to trust the people who have so much control over our lives—even if it is for only a few days. They are crucial days. And we want to believe that they did what was best for us.

HOW TO GET YOUR NURSE TO BE A HELP, NOT A HINDRANCE

Some of the nurses were really mean, but I was dependent on them. Had there been an emergency, I wanted them to be on my side. I was afraid that if I was a difficult patient, the nurses might take forty-five minutes to answer the bell—just when I needed them the most.

THE ROLE FEAR PLAYS—GETTING PAST IT

You're flat on your back and feeling helpless. You know doctors and nurses don't like "troublesome" patients. (Translated, "troublesome" refers to patients who make requests outside the routine.) And, yes, hospitals *are* intimidating.

Your best guarantee of getting what you want, of not having to cope with unpleasant personnel, of having your stay be the best it can be, is to have your mate and/or doula with you all the time. All of us, including nurses, are on better behavior when there are witnesses present. A deliberately long delay in answering a bell is impossible if you have someone with you who can go out to the nurses' station and get a nurse in person.

Nothing terrible will happen simply because you are persistent. You have everything to gain by letting your wishes be known. You are dealing with people who want to be helpful. But understanding that it's possible for some nurses to be unpleasant, you can protect yourself with your family and friends. And if you should run across a truly nasty nurse, tell the head nurse or your doctor. One of them can arrange to have other nurses care for you.

GETTING WHAT YOU WANT

Communicate your preferences clearly, frequently, and repeatedly to get what you want. If you don't, no one will read your mind—not doctors, not nurses. Be specific. Most misunderstandings occur when the nurse is confused about what you want. You've had an opportunity to develop a relationship with your doctor over many months. You'll have only minutes, or maybe hours, with any one nurse.

There is a nursing hierarchy that's usually not clear to patients because the nurses all wear uniforms; therefore, they all look alike. LPNs (licensed practical nurses) and nurses' aides are paid less and have fewer months/years of training than RNs (hospital-school nurses) and BSNs (college-trained nurses). The range of duties for LPNs and aides is more limited, and they are always under the supervision of an RN or BSN. A glance at the name tag of any nurse will tell you what category she is in and who's the boss. If you're not sure who to talk to about a request you have, ask for the head nurse.

We've heard many comments from mothers who didn't get what they wanted in the hospital. But you can, if you're prepared to do the following:

1. *Negotiate in advance* with your doctor for any option that is important to you.

When the nurse says to you, "We never do that here," or "It's against hospital policy," or "I've been working here for ten years, and I know Dr. X won't allow that"—or any other statement that doesn't get you what you want—tell her, "*Dr. X said I can* (walk around during labor, keep both my mate and friend with me, have my other children visit me, etc.)" or "*Dr. X said I don't have to accept* (an enema, drugs during labor, or sugar water for my baby, etc.)."

Plan on someone saying it for you more than once, however. Shifts change, nurses sometimes rotate patients. If your mate and doula are there, you won't have to do the talking.

2. *What to do if you didn't negotiate in advance.* What if something you never anticipated happens and there was no

prior negotiation with either your doctor or the hospital? Don't panic. Be clear and specific.

Example: With your first two births you were not "prepped" in the labor room. So it didn't occur to you to talk to your current doctor about that. But you're no sooner in your hospital room with this baby than the nurse comes in with her shaving kit. You could say, "I know you're just doing what you're supposed to do, but I don't get prepped during my labors. If you have any questions about that, please talk to Dr. X."

Now, if it's that simple, why would most mothers in that situation submit to the procedure? Because they are caught by surprise, and feeling so vulnerable, they perceive that the nurse really seems to be the boss in charge. The mother feels helpless. If you are all alone, the struggle to disagree with the nurse might seem overwhelming. Don't be alone.

Reasonableness and persistence are the key. You don't have to submit to any procedure that you don't want. You are entitled to a full explanation of everything the staff wants to do to you. You are not obligated to participate in *their* routine.

THE MOST TROUBLESOME AREAS OF CONFLICT BETWEEN NURSES AND NEW MOTHERS

ROOMING-IN

Even though you may have arranged in advance with your baby's doctor to have your baby with you as much as you wanted, this option is often the most difficult to obtain *smoothly*.

Part of the problem is in the definition of "rooming-in." For many mothers, either breastfeeding or bottle-feeding, it means keeping your baby with you as much as you want—up to twenty-four hours a day. But that's not the common hospital definition for rooming-in. At one place, it means the babies come out during the day. At another place, it means the babies can be with the mothers all day and once at night (except, of course, during visiting hours). It's not often that hospitals intend for you to have your baby all the time.

If your experience is like that of many other mothers, you will have to remind at least one nurse on every shift that you've made different arrangements for your baby. When a nurse comes to take your baby to the nursery after the birth or after the feeding, you can explain to her that you've made arrangement for the baby always to stay with you, unless you decide differently. You'll probably have to tell every nurse you see that you're keeping your baby with you. You may have to get a private room to arrange for rooming-in, and you may have to forego visitors. Each hospital's rules differ in that regard, too.

FEEDING YOUR BABY ON DEMAND

Another common arrangement that mothers make that often doesn't go smoothly is "demand feeding." With "demand feeding," your baby mostly stays in the nursery, but comes to you when she or he wakes up. But sometimes this doesn't happen—nurses forget or they get too busy.

When you want your baby and she's not available, the worst thing you can do is nothing. Hospitals are busy places, and it's easy for the staff to be occupied with other duties or simply to forget that you want your baby more than other postpartum mothers.

What can you do? We know many mothers who walked down to the nursery and got their babies every two hours or so. If you're not up to walking there, have your mate or your doula go down to the nursery and get your baby for you. That's acceptable in nearly all hospitals. If it's not possible for you or anyone else to go to the nursery in person, just keep asking for your baby. Persist.

BREASTFEEDING

Though help for breastfeeding mothers is better than it was thirty years ago in hospitals, there are still many mothers who have experiences like the following:

> When I was in the hospital, the nursery nurses told me it was hospital policy that all babies, even my breastfed son, get two bottles of formula for a PKU test. They also told me that my baby, like all the others, gets sugar water between feedings because new mothers like me can't produce enough milk. When my breasts got engorged on the third day, the nurses showed me how to use a nipple shield so that the baby could suck more easily. Now that my baby is a week old, I'm wondering what's the matter with my milk. My baby doesn't

seemed satisfied and fusses at my breast even though I
know he's hungry.

—COLORADO MOTHER

Although the nurses who cared for this mother wanted to be
helpful, their standard routine for breastfeeding mothers guarantees that many, if not most, new mothers will find that
breastfeeding is not going well a week after the birth.

What went wrong? The number-one interference with
successful breastfeeding in the hospital is not getting your baby
as much as you want or need. Next on the "no-no" list are:
formula in the nursery, sugar water or "Baby Coca-Cola" as
some nurses label it (or even plain water), and nipple shields.

A test for PKU (phenylketonuria), a rare genetic disease,
can be performed on a completely breastfed baby just as well
when the mother's milk comes in. Many surveyed breastfeeding mothers didn't want their babies getting bottles of any kind
in the hospital—but especially bottles of formula. Some babies
become allergic to cow's milk (one of the most common
allergens) with even the briefest contact with formula in their
early days. Others get confused with trying to suck from two
different nipples—the mother's and a rubber substitute.

And still other babies who drink anything from a bottle in
the hospital may become too tired to vigorously nurse at the
breast. There's another reason to avoid bottles in the hospital,
too. The delicate balance between supply and demand of breast
milk can only be maintained when the baby nurses frequently
at his or her mother's breast. The more the baby nurses, the
more milk the mother produces. This frequent feeding is also
the key to managing newborn jaundice, which is discussed in
the next chapter.

There are two kinds of shields associated with breastfeeding. One is helpful—the breast shield. The other (with rare
exception) is not—the nipple shield. The nipple shield, which
is worn over the mother's nipple while the baby sucks, draws
the nipple out so that the baby can grasp it. Theoretically, it
might seem helpful. In practice, it's not. The breast shield is
worn inside the mother's bra during the last months of pregnancy or in the early weeks after birth to draw out an inverted
nipple. If you have true inverted nipples, buy breast shields
(*not* nipple shields) and wear them before the baby is born.

Nurses often recommend the use of the nipple shield to
relieve temporary engorgement when your breast feels hard.

However, there are better solutions to that problem than wearing a nipple shield. Very frequent nursing will prevent or later alleviate engorgement. Or hand expression just before nursing relieves pressure and softens the nipple area so the baby can latch on.

With the inappropriate use of rubber nipples, a nipple shield, and supplements of either formula and/or water that this Denver mother experienced, it's not unlikely that by day seven when she's home with her baby she's wondering what went wrong. Can this mother's problem be solved? Sure, with good help and support. But without help, like many mothers in that situation, she will wean earlier than she wants and probably always believe her body just didn't work right.

What can you do to avoid formula for your baby in the hospital? Arrange in advance with your baby's doctor that your baby's chart indicate that she or he's not to get formula for any reason. Discuss with him that you want your baby's PKU test given after your milk comes in.

Remind the nurses that your baby doesn't get formula. Many mothers tell us that nurses automatically bring in bottles of sugar water periodically during the day. You don't have to give those bottles to your baby, especially if you've discussed that, too, with your baby's doctor. "No sugar water" can be put on the infant's chart, also. (Or pin a note to your baby's shirt if he goes back to the nursery—"No bottles, please.") (What about extra water if your baby has jaundice? See chapter 14.)

A rule of thumb to use when you are in any hospital situation is: *Don't plan on getting everything you want without effort on your part.* That's especially true with breastfeeding. You, your mate, or your doula will have to remind nearly every nurse you see—on every shift—that your breastfed baby doesn't get bottles. Or that you want your baby now. Get help from those who care for you during your hospital stay, and that alone will improve the care that the nurses give you with rooming-in, demand feeding, and breastfeeding.

Despite our criticism of some nurses, there are ob nurses who are not only extraordinarily helpful to mothers, but courageous as well. An increasing number of nurses refuse to give medications to mothers when they believe these drugs will be harmful. And many bend the rules as much as they can to accommodate patients' preferences. There are others who spend endless hours trying to change hospital policies from the inside to meet the needs of consumers. Nurses do make all the difference in your hospital stay. Work with them, so that you can have a good and safe birth and hospital stay for you and your baby.

▪ FOURTEEN ▪

YOUR BABY DOCTOR

> We pediatricians know that 75 percent of our patients
> get better without us. That knowledge keeps us hum-
> ble.
>
> CHARLES TAYLOR, M.D.,
> PEDIATRICIAN IN PRIVATE PRACTICE
> FOR MORE THAN TWENTY-FIVE YEARS

Just as other doctors do, the pediatrician-to-be spends most of
his residency learning how to treat sickness, especially rare
diseases in children. The emphasis in most pediatric training
programs is certainly not on normal processes, although the
bulk of any pediatrician's private practice is taken up with
earaches, diaper rash, sore throats, colds—and anxious mothers. But pediatricians know that children usually get well no
matter what the doctor does or doesn't do.

SPECIAL INFLUENCES ON A
PEDIATRICIAN'S PRACTICE

At last eight out of ten American women choose an
obstetrician for their pregnancy and birth, but not nearly that
many women choose a specialist, a pediatrician, for their child.
A pediatrician's income depends on a regular influx of new
patients. Even though an increasing number of his patients are
adolescents, the largest share of a pediatrician's caseload is still
younger children. Pediatricians care for more children in the
birth-to-two-year range than do family doctors. As children get
older, family doctors take a bigger share of the market. A
pediatrician's income is doomed without newborns.

Not only are pediatricians competing against family practitioners and nonphysician specialists (like pediatric nurse practitioners and physician assistants), pediatricians more than ever compete against each other because there is a surplus of them.

DEPENDENCE ON OBSTETRICIANS FOR NEW PATIENTS

New mothers usually base their choice of a baby doctor on either their friends' suggestions or their obstetrician's recommendation. A pediatrician, who doesn't have the advantage of an already-established relationship with you or your family, depends on having a "good word" put in by obstetricians. Most are well aware that they can't "rock the boat" with obstetricians if they expect to get referrals.

For instance, pediatricians know not to fuss at hospital meetings about the effects routine obstetrical interventions may have on babies. (Pediatricians are usually present at scheduled cesareans, but they generally do not consider it appropriate to suggest that the obstetrician wait until the mother's labor starts first—thereby reducing the chance of prematurity for the baby, a primary concern for pediatricians.) In the medical pecking order, obstetricians are near the top in income (because they're surgeons), and pediatricians are usually at the bottom (because they use the least technology). Obstetricians don't have to listen to pediatricians.

When pregnant patients ask about a baby doctor, some obstetricians may refer them to the new pediatricians in town. That gives the new doctor a chance to build up his practice. But the newcomer will usually get the referrals only if he shares similar philosophies with the obstetricians and, in some cases, knows his place. Pediatricians are keenly aware of the need to get along with obstetricians. Economic reprisals are real. Peer pressure is intense among doctors, and the urgency to conform to whatever the local medical norms are is relentless.

FORMULA COMPANIES

Formula companies pursue pediatricians and family practice doctors as earnestly as drug companies pursue all physicians. These manufacturers sponsor seminars and medical research, and help underwrite pediatric journals through advertising. Formula companies pay for some worthwhile projects that would never happen without their financial support. But medicine today has—at best—a tainted marriage with these companies. Much of a physician's information on formula comes directly from the manufacturers. There's seldom an objective, third-party source of information. Even many mothers get breastfeeding information from formula companies in free pamphlets.

Short-term breastfeeding is good for these companies. Formula sales have gone up as breastfeeding rates have increased, paradoxical as that might sound. The reason, according to one formula company representative, is that women who breastfeed are likelier to wean to a formula during the first year of the baby's life, rather than to regular milk. (Most nursing babies are weaned to a bottle by the age of three months.)

If you plan to breastfeed at all, the influence of the formula companies can be insidious. Most mothers take home one of the ubiquitous new-mother hospital packs, which always contain some sample formula. A Canadian study shows that mothers who do take these packs home wean to a bottle and start solids in a matter of a few weeks—much earlier than mothers who don't take the free samples home.

And if you plan to bottle-feed your baby, the influence of the formula companies can be misleading. Naturally, each company promotes its own product as the best one, but, as one former salesman for a leading formula company said to us, "There's not a dime's bit of difference between Similac and Enfamil." Infant formula is an enormously profitable, $700 million plus business annually. The supporters of breastfeeding—consumers, and even the American Academy of Pediatrics—don't have the money to provide the information blitz that's standard in big-business marketing.

Obviously, there's a place for formula companies and their products. There will always be baby bottles and parents who need them. But you as the parent, with adequate information, can make your own decision about what and when to feed the baby. The more you make your own decisions for your baby, the more self-confident you'll feel as a parent. (For a comprehensive explanation of how to choose a formula for your baby, see *The Joy of Twins* by Pamela Patrick Novotny, Crown Publishing, 1988.)

HOW TO FIND DR. RIGHT FOR YOUR BABY

The Dr. Right who cares for your baby serves you best when he observes the child's health and development, and equally important, reinforces your ability as a parent to make decisions about your own child. Taking your baby to a doctor who intimidates you will only delay your self-confidence, use of your own common sense, and your growing maturity as a parent. Your doctor's flexibility and willingness to listen to you are as important as his knowledge.

Review chapter 5 in which we describe the steps for finding the right doctor for your pregnancy and birth. Here, we'll describe those unique parts of the search process for finding Dr. Right for your baby. Just as in looking for your doctor, check with the nurses who work on hospital ob floors, childbirth educators, and La Leche League leaders. Nurses can tell you which doctors are likeliest to have patients who room-in with their babies or who are helpful and enthusiastic about breastfeeding (if you choose to breastfeed). Nurses know which doctors are willing to arrange for your other children to visit even if it's not hospital policy, or which doctors will examine your baby in your room with you present instead of doing daily exams only in the nursery.

THE PRENATAL INTERVIEW

We suggest you interview doctors for your baby's care before your baby's birth—even though most parents don't. Take your partner or a friend with you. You are likely to "hear" better. If you currently have a family practitioner caring for you, you'll be able to ask him the appropriate questions about your baby's care as you see him through your pregnancy.

There are many mothers and fathers who meet their baby's doctor for the first time after he's already examined their baby in the hospital. Some mothers find they don't like this doctor once they meet him, but are extraordinarily reluctant to change doctors once they've gone that far. ("At this point," they say to themselves, "what difference does it really make?") Somehow, it all seems so final and official. (It's quite similar to, but not as intense as, the feeling that many women have once they've allowed a doctor to examine their bodies.) Yes, of course, you can switch doctors at this point. But it's easier to interview them in advance of the birth and decide then.

THE FIRST QUESTIONS

Your own list of questions will depend on the particular options you want in the hospital after the baby's born, and your philosophy of child rearing. What's really important to you? If you think babies should be raised on a schedule—whether it's feeding, weaning, or bedtime—then you should look for a doctor who agrees with you. If, on the other hand, you prefer fewer rules or feel confident you don't need or want frequent consultation with a physician, you can find that out, too, in advance. Many of the following questions can be answered by phone.

1. *How much are your hospital charges and fees for office visits?* In most places, pediatricians charge a similar fee. Family practitioners and other health-care providers may charge somewhat less. However, that varies from town to town.

2. *Do you charge for phone calls?* Many pediatricians spend six hours or more during their work week on the phone with parents, according to Edward J. Saltzman, M.D., speaking for the Academy of Pediatrics. Most physicians do not charge for these phone calls, but some do. Typically, most parents of first-born children call frequently.

3. *Do you return the call of every parent who calls?* Some pediatricians make every "callback." Some have trained personnel, usually nurses or nurse practitioners, return the calls. Some parents find that these trained personnel are very helpful. Occasionally, the person who handles your phone call may not share the same attitude about the issue in question as you or your doctor does.

   For instance, in one city many breastfeeding mothers chose one doctor in particular because she not only had breastfed her own children, but was most helpful with any problems the mothers had with nursing. However, the people who answered some of her office phone calls were not as knowledgeable and supportive of breastfeeding as the doctor was. In another instance, one mother chose her doctor because his philosophy of mothering was similar to hers. However, the nurse who took some of his calls had a different attitude. What the mother and doctor called "meeting the baby's needs" the office nurse labeled "spoiling."

If you find that the person who's handling your phone call is not on your wavelength, you can request that the doctor call you back instead. That's your privilege.

4. *What is the scheduled length of your appointments?* The closer his appointments are (ten to fifteen minutes apart, rather than twenty or thirty, for instance), the more likely it is you'll do some waiting, as well as be rushed through your appointment when you do see him. Most doctors allow more time for complete physicals, and therefore charge more for them than they do for routine office visits.

5. *How often do you want to see the baby in the first year? Why?* Pediatricians more than family practitioners will schedule several "well-child" visits for your child. Pediatricians believe this to be a form of preventive care and an opportunity for parent education. Feel free to discuss in advance with your doctor the purpose of these "well-child" visits, so that you can decide in consultation with your doctor what's appropriate for *your* child's care. We all need encouragement as mothers, but you decide if it's always worth an office-visit fee to find out how much your baby weighs and the fact that your doctor thinks your baby is doing well.

6. *Do you have a "sick-child" waiting room?* Some doctors try to avoid mixing the well children and the sick children in the same reception area. Young children are very susceptible to contagious diseases.

7. *If you share a practice, will I always see you?* Not likely, unless your doctor has no partners and never takes a day off. If you are scheduling an exam well in advance, it's easy to ask for a day that your doctor will be in the office. However, if you have a sick child and are calling up on short notice, you'll get whomever is in the office or on call. The same is true of night and weekend emergencies. As a matter of fact, your doctor and his partners may share their "on-call" times with another group of doctors. Just as

with obstetricians, what this means for you is that you may have a doctor you've never seen before caring for your child in an emergency. If it's important to you, arrange to meet all the doctors who might cover for your baby's doctor in an emergency, or when you're in the hospital.

8. *Do you have evening or Saturday hours?* Although nine-to-five office hours are still the rule for many doctors' offices, there is a growing number who are accommodating working moms and dads. And now there are off-hour pediatric centers that deliver immediate care at night and on the weekends in some cities.

HOW YOUR DOCTOR CAN (UNWITTINGLY) SABOTAGE YOU AND YOUR BABY . . . AND WHAT YOU CAN DO ABOUT IT

In the last chapter we described three areas in which mothers and nurses sometimes clash: rooming-in, feeding your baby—when your baby wants to eat regardless of the clock (demand feeding)—and breastfeeding.

You may have areas of conflict with your baby's doctor, too. True, you will spend most of your time in the hospital with nurses. But the doctor who cares for your baby has the power to make "good care" better and "bad care" worse. Understanding that, you'll have a much better chance of your baby doctor giving you the help you need in the hospital with bonding (including rooming-in and delayed newborn eyedrops), breastfeeding, and the care for newborn jaundice.

BONDING

In the not-so-long-ago past, as new mothers, we were told that our infants couldn't see for days, couldn't smile for weeks. Now there's an explosion of information that describes almost endless sensory abilities of newborns. Much of the best-known research supporting the need for parents and infants to be together soon and often from birth comes from pediatric researchers, Marshall Klaus, M.D., and John Kennell, M.D.

Child abuse stimulated their early studies. They found that

welcoming mothers into the nurseries and encouraging frequent contact between mothers and newborns reduced the incidence of battering. But as many now know, early, frequent contact benefits all babies, all parents, not just those at risk of child abuse.

In 1982, William A. Cook, M.D., obstetrician and author, had this to say about bonding: "I may be wrong, but the significance of the 'maternal sensitive period' and bonding, if it exists at all in the human seems to me over-emphasized. It is an interesting idea and I have nothing against its exploration. But it is only an idea, a postulate, an unproven formulation, and should not be accepted uncritically or taken to be revealed doctrine as it has been."

Many doctors still view bonding as a consumer fad. Some doctors not only don't read their own pediatric research, they don't really believe it. What they learned in their medical training is the last word.

Eager to get on the bandwagon of new trends and keep their maternity beds full, though, many hospitals advertise "bonding time" and "bonding rooms." Since many hospital personnel think there's a time limit to bonding, both doctors and nurses may think they've satisfied you and your newborn's needs by giving you your hour. Klaus and Kennell and others never meant to imply that the bonding process was one of glue, a magic sixty minutes at birth.

The idea that gazing into your baby's eyes while holding him lovingly for the first hour will create an attachment for life—at least through those first hard eighteen years—is misleading. That moment is an exhilarating experience for parents and should be encouraged for that reason alone. But attachment doesn't work like that. Love relationships are much more complicated. The issue really is getting acquainted with your baby, and she or he with you, as easily, as early, as continuously as possible. That takes time—lots of it. And hospitals don't always make that easy.

ROOMING-IN

I want my baby with me at all times. If, however, there is some terrible reason that this could not happen, I would want my baby on request. The set schedule of seeing the baby is the worst possible idea!

* * *

I was not pleased with the rooming-in. My baby was taken to the nursery several different times for checkups, and I had to complain loudly in order to have her returned to me. It does not take three to four hours for a physical or for a heel stick!

Don't expect doctors and nurses to share your view of bonding or rooming-in. If having your baby with you as much as you want—which is a primary preference of mothers—is important to you, too, then you'll have to negotiate with both your baby doctor and the hospital. Be specific. Describe what you want. Your conversation might be something like this:

YOU: *I want to have my baby with me as much as I choose.*

THEY: Yes, you can do that. We believe in rooming-in.

Now don't stop here. We've learned from talking with many mothers that you need to ask more. For instance:

YOU: *Can I keep my baby during visiting hours? Can I keep my baby at night?*

THEY: You can have your baby whenever you want, except during visiting hours (three hours in the afternoon and another three hours in the evening); at night (nearly all mothers find out they don't want their babies at night; besides it's not safe for the baby to be with you when you are asleep); and for an hour in the morning when the pediatricians come in to check the babies in the nursery.

From that answer, it's clear that they expect your baby to be someplace other than with you for two-thirds of any given day. If you know that you'll want your baby with you about eight hours a day, then this hospital has what you want. If, however, you want the option of having your baby with you more than that, you have several alternatives:

1. *Talk to both your baby doctor and the hospital in advance.* Ask if you can arrange for a private room. Often patients who get a private room can keep their babies with them during visiting hours. Since the hospital staff may then want you to forgo having visitors yourself (except your mate), you may need to negotiate to have grandparents and/or a doula present, as well as the baby.

You can also tell them that although their experience at the hospital is that most mothers don't want their babies at night, you do. Many satisfied mothers can tell you that the more they roomed-in with their babies, the more self-confident they were when they took the baby home. Rooming-in doesn't necessarily increase your fatigue. Rather, it increases your knowledge of your baby and, therefore, your self-assurance. And if you're nursing, rooming-in almost guarantees a good milk supply because you'll be feeding your baby whenever he or she's hungry.

Many pediatricians are happy to examine your baby in your room with you, but they are seldom asked to do so. If you cannot arrange to have your baby checked in your room, you can go to the nursery while your baby is examined there. Or, if you can't go yourself, your husband or doula can be with the baby in the nursery at all times.

2. *If you cannot negotiate an acceptable compromise on rooming-in, look for another hospital (or a birth center).*

But what if you're part of an insurance plan that binds you to one hospital, and that hospital won't agree to your plan? If it's important to you, make an appointment with the hospital administrator and plead your case for an exception for you. You'll get further than you would if you wanted to change the rules for everyone. See "How to be a Changemaker," in the Appendix for more information.

Let's say you've found a hospital that offers the rooming-in arrangement you want. Once you've arranged with your baby's doctor to write on your chart that you are rooming-in, the doctor has not done everything he can for you.

If the arrangement doesn't work out the way you want (the nurses don't want to bring the baby at night, or you are receiving criticism from the staff because you want the baby with you all the time), *the next move is yours.* You can let your doctor know that you are not satisfied with the arrangement, and he can talk to the nursing staff. He is in charge of your hospital care. He is the last word on the floor.

He can even remove a nurse from your care, but that's probably not necessary. Or he can remind the staff of your special arrangements. Theoretically, every patient's care is unique, though we know that in practice most patient care is routine. Only you, or someone acting in your behalf (your partner and/or your doula), can get personalized care for you.

Doing your part when you don't get what you want means speaking up, taking action. If you've arranged to have your baby whenever you want, but the nurses come to get your infant anyway, don't give your baby to the nurse. You have as much power as you choose to have. Tell the nurse if she has any questions about it to discuss it with your doctor (or the head nurse).

You'll only spend a few days in the hospital. But your doctor has to work with the nurses every day. For that reason, he won't be enthusiastic about complaining to the staff—especially if you haven't explained your preferences to the staff yourself. But he will speak up, and you'll make it easier for him if you've already done your part.

NEWBORN EYEDROPS

One of the consequences of a pregnant mother having a sexually transmitted disease (STD), like chlamydia, gonorrhea, or syphilis, is that she may pass it onto her infant who may develop newborn eye infections and other problems. (Newborn infections from maternal herpes or genital warts are handled differently.) That's why eyedrops of erythromycin, tetracycline, or silver nitrate have been put into all newborns' eyes within minutes after births for years.

Back in the not-so-long-ago past, no one much objected to this procedure because everyone erroneously "knew" babies couldn't see anyway. But much more is known now about a newborn's capabilities. And many question a procedure designed to help a minority while inflicting an unnecessary interference of irritation and vision blurring on 100 percent of all babies.

Researcher Perry Butterfield in 1983 said:

> Infants with silver nitrate in their eyes do not follow an object or scan around the room. They also are fussier and rarely have their eyes open within the first three or four hours. Infants who have not had silver nitrate or other eye prophylaxis are quiet and alert after birth, able to scan the room and follow faces and objects. And their parents, especially fathers, are more affectionate and involved with their babies.

However, STDs are second only to the common cold now in the number of infections, and many women have more than one STD at a time.

WHAT ARE YOUR ALTERNATIVES?

1. *Let's not assume all mothers have an STD.* You can sign a waiver asking for no treatment to the eyes of

your newborn. You may feel more secure in doing that if you ask your health-care provider during your pregnancy to give you tests for a possible STD infection. Each STD is diagnosed with a different test, and none are 100 percent accurate, however, so you may want to get more than one, especially if your results are positive. False-positive (that is, you're told you have a disease when you don't) rates are as high as 20–30 percent.

2. *Postpone the treatment*. If there's no getting around your state law that your baby *must* have the eyedrops within the first twenty-four hours, then negotiate to delay the drops until later in the first day of the baby's life, when the infant is sleeping, rather than give them in the midst of a waking period, which the first hour often is.

3. *Request one of the antiobiotics, erythromycin or tetracycline, and avoid silver nitrate*. Though erythromycin is used more now than it once was, it's not used universally. These antiobiotic ointments cause fewer eye infections than silver nitrate and are effective as a first line of defense against infant infections caused by chlamydia, which is far more common than gonorrhea. Researchers disagree over whether silver nitrate is equally as effective. However, none of the eyedrops are used by themselves. If any infants show signs of STD infection, they are treated with other drugs, too.

Whom do you negotiate with for a different-than-routine arrangement for these eyedrops? Since the authority for that decision may vary from place to place, talk to both your doctor and your baby's doctor.

BREASTFEEDING

Medical support for breastfeeding has come a long way. When our older children were born in the 1960s, the image of the breastfeeding mother was more bovine than madonnalike. (You can breastfeed, of course, my dear, but you'll lose your shape, perhaps your husband's affection, and eventually all your milk.)

Now more doctors than ever favor breastmilk. But your baby doctor's help with nursing your infant is more than just his writing "breastfeeding" on your baby's hospital chart. Your pediatrician will not only check your baby every day, but he'll come in and talk with you, too. Much of his advice focuses on infant feeding.

For all the lip service given, many doctors' enthusiasm for breastfeeding still exceeds the amount of helpful advice they offer. Your doctor's "how to" knowledge might be lacking if:

- Accurate breastfeeding information was not part of his training, and is not now a current interest.
- He has not learned what is helpful by observing his patients or his own breastfeeding wife.
- She is a woman, but has not breastfed a baby herself.

HOW TO FIND A DOCTOR WHO IS HELPFUL

How do you know when your doctor's help is "helpful"? Inform yourself in advance. Read the excellent information available for consumers today. Many mothers have successfully breastfed without their doctor's support by learning from other nursing mothers. But why set up obstacles for yourself if you don't have to? Find a doctor who's not only enthusiastic about breastfeeding, but knowledgeable and supportive, too.

When you interview prospective doctors for your baby's care, go beyond asking them if they approve of breastfeeding. Ask if he'll be discussing breastfeeding with you every day that you're in the hospital. According to Warren M. Kleinberg, M.P.H., reporting in the *American Journal of Public Health*, mothers who receive well-informed counseling each day in the hospital have fewer breastfeeding problems later than the mothers who receive breastfeeding counseling only on the day they are discharged.

Ask what percentage of his patients are breastfed at birth. Then ask how many are still breastfeeding at three months or six months. If the number is almost nil (the number will be less than the number breastfeeding at birth), it suggests that he probably isn't very knowledgeable about breastfeeding problems.

How does he handle breastfeeding problems? Ask if he thinks babies should always be weaned if the mother gets a breast infection or sore nipples, or the baby has diarrhea or what growth charts call "slow weight gain?" These are all common problems that can be better managed without weaning the baby from the breast if you get the right information.

YOU CAN BREASTFEED AND WORK

Many of you will be returning to work when your infant is a few months old. Can you still breastfeed? Of course. But you'll benefit from information unique to your situation. Thousands of working mothers have found ways to manage both outside jobs and nursing babies.

The doctor you choose probably doesn't know how to help you with the unique management of this style of breastfeeding. Not many health professionals do. What you do need from him is his support for your decision to breastfeed. Many mothers who work feel guilty about the separation, whether bottle-feeding or breastfeeding. The last thing a working mother needs is a doctor who is negatively evaluating her ability as a parent.

If you plan to return to work, mention that to any doctor you interview. You'll know soon enough what his attitude is. He still may not have the information to help you, but perhaps may be able to give you the names of mothers in his practice who have successfully breastfed and worked.

Where do you get help if you plan to be a working and nursing mother? Ask your childbirth educator. These women often know mothers who combine working and nursing. Call La Leche League. (Few of these LLL volunteers however have any personal experience with working and nursing.) If you find that the LLL person you're talking to is not helpful, ask her for the name of a mother who has worked and nursed, or call a lactation consultant. Mothers who've breastfeed and work, like other pioneers, are often quite enthusiastic and willing to share tips with other women. And, whether bottle-feeding or breast-feeding, surround yourself with people who are supportive of your decision to be a working mother.

NEWBORN JAUNDICE AND BILIRUBIN LIGHTS

My baby was two days old when she turned yellow on her face. I'd had a beautiful birth, held her immediately, and felt tied to her closely. I was still riding a wave of excitement over her arrival when the pediatrician came in to tell me there was a problem. It had to do with the jaundice which could in some way go to her brain and make her mentally retarded. I was terrified, and quickly agreed to the treatment with the lights in the nursery. I didn't understand whether or not she was in grave danger at the time, and the next 24 hours were difficult for me and my husband. I was given her for feedings every four hours and carefully looked to see if the jaundice was less noticeable, but she was as yellow as ever. She didn't nurse well as she received water in the nursery frequently to wash out the jaundice. The doctor came in that evening to tell me she needed further treatment. I left the hospital, as we couldn't afford to run up a hospital bill for me. I visited to nurse several times a day but it was difficult with another child at home, and I was very tired. Luckily she was better in 30 hours and came home.

—NEW MOTHER QUOTED IN *BIRTH*

The media have frequently broadcast and printed complaints about today's childbirth practices. Obs are criticized from coast to coast, but pediatricians usually are patted on the back. Just as obstetricians have, though, they've made their mistakes, too, often because of inadequate testing of new procedures and products.

PHisoHex, a special soap with the ingredient hexachlorophene, was used in thousands of hospitals before being banned. The number of birth defects in babies born to hospital workers who washed up with PHisoHex was much higher than in the population at large.

Visual impairment in premature babies, called retrolental fibroplasia (RLF) was epidemic in the 1940s and early 1950s. According to William A. Silverman, M.D., in his 1980 book, *Retrolental Fibroplasia: A Modern Parable,* fifty different causes were suggested before researchers found through randomized controlled trials that RLF was caused by hospital staff giving these premature babies what turned out to be too much oxygen. RLF was iatrogenic (doctor-caused)—unintentional, but tragic.

A postscript to RLF: Pediatrician Jerold F. Lucey, M.D., editor-in-chief of *Pediatrics,* stated at the 1982 American Academy of Pediatrics meeting in Honolulu that "excessive oxygen therapy for small, premature infants is not the only major cause of RLF." A second RLF epidemic is occurring, but lack of research impedes progress. "Oxygen can certainly cause RLF," Dr. Lucey said, "but after twenty-five years of knowing this, we are still unable to give effective recommendations for oxygen usage." So the research continues.

Dr. Silverman thinks RLF is more than a tragic mistake—it's a parable, a sign of our times. Careful testing is not always done. In his book, he lists twenty-six therapies used on babies. Only 19 percent of the innovations lead to sounder practice. The newest pediatric treatment on the list is "phototherapy for hyperbilirubinemia." Dr. Silverman placed a ? by this treatment.

Most of the public haven't discovered this new pediatric scandal—the misuse of bilirubin lights for the jaundice of full-term, healthy newborn babies. Jaundice is the most common newborn complication. At least half of all full-term babies and eight out of ten prematures develop some form of this condition.

And it sometimes runs in families. Newborns with prior siblings who had jaundice are three times more likely to have jaundice than other infants, 1988 research shows. This is true whether infants were breastfed or bottle-fed.

Jaundice is a yellowing of the baby's skin and the whites of eyes. It's caused by excess bilirubin in the blood system. Bilirubin is described as "an orange-yellow pigment, a normal product of the breakdown of hemoglobin contained in red blood cells." Most newborn jaundice is a normal reflection of the baby's adjustment to life outside his mother's body, and some believe it serves a useful purpose.

The current medical concern about jaundice in the newborn is twofold: it's possible—though it actually happens rarely, and then only to infants who show signs of other illness—that if the level of bilirubin in the blood goes high enough, a condition called kernicterus develops, which can cause brain damage. The second concern, which is at the root of the proliferation of newborns being put under bilirubin lights, is that a certain level of jaundice (and pediatricians don't agree on what this level is) may cause neurological damage in the child.

THREE KINDS OF JAUNDICE

The most severe and rarest newborn jaundice is caused by Rh or ABO blood incompatibility. This jaundice is visible at birth or within the first twenty-four hours.

Another rare jaundice is caused by a substance in breast

milk that makes the baby moderately jaundiced for several weeks. This jaundice doesn't develop until the baby is several days to a week old or more. At most, one in two hundred babies might be affected. No brain damage has ever been reported from a case of breast-milk jaundice, although many mothers of affected children have been told to wean either temporarily or permanently.

The most common newborn jaundice is physiologic jaundice, a normal condition. It first appears when the baby is two or three days old. It's the sometimes casual and cavalier treatment of this jaundice in otherwise healthy, full-term babies with phototherapy (bilirubin lights) that is unnecessarily exposing infants to phototherapy's side effects and increasing the number of babies being separated from their parents soon after birth. *Our criticism is not aimed at the appropriate use of the bilirubin lights for the 10 percent of jaundiced babies who are premature or sick full-term infants.*

BILIRUBIN LIGHTS

Bilirubin lights, or phototherapy, combine bright blue (or green) and white fluorescent lights. When exposed to these strong lights, bilirubin in the baby's body decomposes. Though current treatment is phototherapy, tests reported in 1988 show that a drug that blocks the formation of bilirubin may be given to infants in the future. Certainly babies have benefited from phototherapy, but just as with most other medical interventions, the use of bilirubin lights was designed for a few and ends up being used on many.

In many hospitals, half of all babies, including the full-term healthy babies, are kept blindfolded and separated from their mothers for most of the day for two or three days at a time while undergoing phototherapy. Although phototherapy has been used for more than twenty-five years, it is still not clear which babies should be put under the lights, how long they should be there, what wattage the lights should be, how effective the process is, and how extensive the side effects are—especially long term.

How can doctors and hospitals allow the management of normal newborn jaundice to be so unclear, you ask? Easy. Available research is not conclusive. Besides, each doctor believes his evaluation and method of treatment—whatever it is—is right. Hospitals aren't in the business of policing medical procedures. The hospital's job is to keep the beds full, and the use of phototherapy contributes to this. Not only do the babies stay an extra two or three days, but often the mothers do, too. This adds thousands of insurance-paid dollars to the hospital revenue. Though hospitals do not coerce you or your doctor to use phototherapy, they are rewarded by your use of this therapy.

J. H. Drew, and other researchers, have shown that some of the very common short-term effects of the use of bilirubin lights are irritability and restlessness, intestinal irritation, lactose intolerance, feeding problems, riboflavin deficiency, water loss, diarrhea, short-term growth retardation, and skin rashes. W. T. Speck, et al., stated that phototherapy "may alter intercellular DNA of human cells and may be a carcinogenic hazard." In 1981 Cathy Hammerman, M.D., and others, reporting in *Pediatrics,* added to the list of cautions when they stated: "Since monochromatic blue light in particular has been associated with staff discomfort and vertigo, it is theoretically important not to deliver excessive doses of irradiance." Jerold Lucey, M.D., reflected the opinion of many physicians when he stated in *Medical World News* that the long-term effects of phototherapy still are unknown.

Being blindfolded and deprived of touching, except for a few hours of feeding, for two or three days keeps infants from experiencing normal sensations. Oded Preis, M.D., et al., reported in the *Journal of Pediatrics* that those babies who were not blindfolded, but whose eyes were protected from the lights by a screen, "had behavior patterns more like normal healthy newborn infants, as compared to those with conventional eye pad coverage, who tended to have more frequent periods of restlessness and irritability."

Touching is the most natural thing in the world. Hands hold, feed, and bathe the newborn. Arms rock him or her. His mother's body comforts her. Babies who are kept under the bilirubin lights sometimes spend twenty hours out of every twenty-four just lying there, uncomforted by touch, sight, and the sounds of mother's voice and heartbeat.

Because babies lose water from their bodies when they're under the lights, nurses are instructed to give them extra water. According to researchers Edward F. Bell, M.D., and others, some babies get so hot during phototherapy that they develop a fever. Giving water for dehydration is different, though, from the erroneous belief of most doctors and nurses that giving babies extra water helps "flush out" the bilirubin. Pediatric researcher and expert on neonatal jaundice Lawrence Gartner, M.D., and Kathleen Auerbach, Ph.D., both at the University of Chicago, stated in 1986 that the feeding of water does not reduce the bilirubin levels. It does, however, interfere with breastfeeding. In some hospitals babies are not removed from the bilirubin lights at all, so that the breastfeeding mother is forced to temporarily (or permanently) wean. Unless a mother is highly motivated, it's often difficult for her to keep nursing.

Certainly no parent or physician wants to have a brain-damaged child, especially when it can be prevented. So doctors sometimes put a child under the bilirubin lights "just in case." But when to use the lights varies from hospital to hospital, doctor to doctor.

In the past, a significant number of infants demonstrated neurological damage when their bilirubin levels exceeded 30. (These were otherwise sick babies showing several signs of disease.) Many doctors, consequently, were taught that, in order for bilirubin levels to remain in a safe range, intervention should occur if the level exceeded 20.*

The "danger" number has dropped drastically, so that today babies with levels as low as 9 are sometimes considered at risk. The worry is that if lower levels don't cause kernicterus, they may still negatively affect future intellectual performance. In fact, studies by several researchers, including Gerald Odell, and Rosalyn A. Rubin, show *no* relationship between bilirubin levels up to 23 and IQ scores at five years. David Stewart, Ph.D., editor of *The Five Standards for Safe Childbearing*, asks the question: "Does this mean that the rates of mental retardation and infant death were higher in the past because of the lack of treatment for normal, physiologic jaundice? There are no data to indicate that this is so."

In some United States hospitals, full-term, healthy babies with bilirubin levels of 9 and 10—more often 12 and 13—are considered in danger, though historically 20 used to be considered the "danger" level. In Great Britain, reports Marshall Klaus, M.D., "bilirubin lights tend to be used at a higher level of bilirubin, around 16–17." In 1982 La Leche League International stated: "Some authorities set a limit of 25 in

---

*The serum bilirubin level is measured in milligrams of bilirubin per 100 milliliters of blood. This ratio is then expressed as a percentage. A bilirubin level of 20 can also be expressed as "20 mg. percent."

babies with non-Rh jaundice." Information on just what constitutes a dangerous level is sketchy at best.

Pediatricians who have been in practice for many years tend to pay more attention to the physical signs of the baby—for instance, is the baby lethargic or not sucking well? Some newer pediatricians pay more attention to the number—the bilirubin level in the blood. "If your baby's bilirubin level reaches 12 [or 10 or 13], we'll have to put the infant under the lights," is a common statement made to parents.

Dr. Gartner stated at a 1982 medical meeting:

> If you start babies' phototherapy when the bilirubin level is at 10 to 13 (sometimes 15), which is where most people will start phototherapy . . . you will find the great majority of these babies, in fact, have already started on the decline of the bilirubin at the time that you started the phototherapy. . . . Ninety to ninety-five percent of those babies really didn't need phototherapy and were about to turn the corner anyway.

Researcher H.M. Lewis, and others in *Lancet II*. August 1982, found that jaundice may persist twenty-four to forty-eight hours longer if infants are not given phototherapy at these lower levels (13–14), but the level of jaundice itself won't increase and in 1986, researcher R. Paludetto found that full-term jaundiced infants with bilirubin levels as high as 14.3, who were not treated with phototherapy, were no different from other infants the same age who did not have jaundice. They all conclude that the risks of phototherapy outweigh the benefits at these levels.

IATROGENIC (DOCTOR-CAUSED) REASONS FOR PHOTOTHERAPY

1. *Drugs, especially Pitocin.* Studies show that the use of Pitocin, in particular, but perhaps also epidurals and other drugs (like sulfanamids, Valium, some tranquilizers, morphine, and vitamin K) increase jaundice in many newborns. According to P. C. Buchan, reporting in the *British Medical Journal,* there are indications that the higher the level of Pitocin in your body, and the longer it's been there, the higher the jaundice level will be in your baby.

   There are other researchers who think the problem

may not necessarily be Pitocin's chemical effect. If Pitocin is used at all, it can be an indication that the baby would have been born later and is premature, suggests P. Boylan, M.B., writing in the *British Medical Journal*. Researchers Chew and Swann include amniotomy, the breaking of the bag of waters (a routine procedure used with Pitocin), for the same reason.

2. *Increased cesareans*. One of the most frequent complications of cesareans is jaundice in the baby. Now that one in four births is a cesarean, there are more jaundiced babies. It's not clear why this is so. Perhaps jaundice is a common complication of cesareans because of drugs used on the mother. Also, delayed breastfeeding, a factor in jaundice, almost always occurs after a cesarean birth.

3. *Use of vacuum extractor*. This is a metal or plastic cup that uses suction to "vacuum" the baby's head. It's believed to be less traumatic to the baby's head than forceps, and is not commonly used in the United States. However, babies who are born with the help of vacuum extractors are more likely to have jaundice and to be treated with phototherapy, according to 1986 European research.

4. *Fear of malpractice lawsuits*. "Many physicians have been forced to think of their patients as potential lawsuits rather than real people with medical problems," reported the *Journal of Insurance*. According to Donald Blim, M.D., past president of the American Academy of Pediatrics, "Less than one percent of suits filed in a recent year involved pediatricians at all." But when it does happen, the likeliest area to be targeted with malpractice suits is the newborn period. Blim continues: "We would predict that the most likely situation for possible pediatric vulnerability has to do with pediatric procedures performed at, or very nearly following, birth. For this reason we often have noted pediatricians being named as co-defendants in suits along with obstetricians, anesthesiologists, hospitals, and others who have participated in the birth experience."

Lawsuits for newborn jaundice do occur. Dr. Gartner stated: "Unfortunately, and perhaps I'm colored by this, I see a fair number of lawsuits that I am asked to comment on, where a suit has been brought specifically because the bilirubin has gone up and the baby has kernicterus and these do occur. It's hard to find them in the literature, but they are certainly in the law courts. And they are very real."

"If you are going to err," another pediatrician told us, "err on the side of intervention."

5. *Convenience—phototherapy is handy.* As one pediatrician said two decades ago, "Now that every hospital is getting the bilirubin lights, for sure we pediatricians are going to diagnose more jaundice." And they have. Babies don't have to be sent to a high-risk center for phototherapy. It's as near as the nursery. In fact, in some hospitals even nurses can order blood tests for bilirubin counts without a physician's okay.

When a nurse tells a pediatrician that the bilirubin level is 10 or 12, he may feel he has to do something about it. Not too long ago many of those babies wouldn't have had blood tests at all. The doctor would have made an evaluation of the baby by examining him or her. If the baby wasn't lethargic, if it nursed well and seemed normal, though jaundiced, the doctor would not have been likely to intervene.

Just as X-ray machines and ultrasound equipment are used more when doctors have them, phototherapy use increases with availability. Prior to the bilirubin lights, babies were placed by a sunny window at home for a few hours or the ultimate treatment for very sick infants was a blood exchange.

6. *Fear of criticism.* If you're a doctor, using technology means you're up-to-date. Some pediatricians we spoke with told us they felt newborn jaundice was being overtreated. But even so, they sometimes put babies under the bilirubin lights just to avoid criticism from their peers. The pressure to be "scientific," to use the available technology, is great.

HOW TO AVOID UNNECESSARY PHOTOTHERAPY FOR YOUR BABY

1. *Avoid drugs.* Avoid going to the hospital too soon; wait until labor is well established. If Pitocin is

suggested to you because your labor slows, consider the nonmedical techniques described in chapter 8.

2. *If you breastfeed, do it early and often.* An important key to preventing or controlling jaundice is to move the bilirubin out of the baby's body via meconium, the black bowel movement of a newborn. The most effective way to do that is to breastfeed early and often (every two hours or so), especially in the first three days without any supplements. Colostrum, which is produced by the mother's body until the "true" milk comes in, has a laxative effect and promotes the passage of meconium.

   Room-in, if possible. If not, arrange for demand feeding. Protect yourself by finding a breastfeeding counselor, especially if this is your first baby. Go home early if you can, where feeding a baby frequently is easier, because there are no hospital routines to interfere. Nursing infrequently may actually increase your baby's jaundice, Dr. Gartner says, by causing "starvation jaundice." Your baby needs you and your milk. "Supplementation with water or glucose water will worsen the problem," Gartner continues, "or at least won't alleviate the jaundice."

3. *Ask your doctor why your baby needs phototherapy.* Let him know you know there is controversy about when to use phototherapy. Ask him to explain why a normal condition that affects most babies is not normal in your full-term, healthy baby. Ask him to describe the guidelines he uses and why. Ask him to tell you what symptoms your baby exhibits in addition to a certain bilirubin number. Ask him what the risks of treatment are. Ask that the hospital do another blood test (if they haven't already), just to make sure the number is accurate. Blood tests for bilirubin are often inaccurate. Several years ago in Indiana, sixty-seven labs measured bilirubin in samples that averaged a true value of 18. Lab results varied from 10.9 to 24. And if none of this satisfies you, you can always ask for a second opinion. Ask another doctor in your town. If you don't know whom to call for a second opinion, call La Leche League or NAPSAC and ask for referrals.

WHAT TO DO IF YOUR BABY
DOES NEED PHOTOTHERAPY

1. *If possible, stay with your baby even if your infant needs to be under the lights.* Ask if the hospital has portable bilirubin lights that can be placed over *both* you and your baby (though you may find the lights just as uncomfortable as your baby does). Or have the portable bilirubin light unit placed in your hospital room, so that you can at least be with your baby. You will quite naturally be concerned about your baby if the infant needs phototherapy—you will be reassured if you are able to see him or her.

   If your baby is treated with phototherapy, there is a valid concern about your baby having adequate liquids. Denver pediatrician Marianne Neifert, M.D., at the University of Colorado Health Sciences Center, suggests you can express your milk and give that to the baby for extra liquids in addition to nursing her or him frequently. (A breastfeeding counselor will be helpful in showing you how to express your milk.)

2. *Discuss home phototherapy for your baby with your doctor.* Babies treated for jaundice in the hospital receive seven times as much phototherapy as babies treated at home, though the outcome of the babies was similar in 1987 research reported in the *British Medical Journal*. Portable bilirubin light units are available at rental agencies. Other doctors, like pediatrician Jay Gordon, M.D., in Los Angeles, have sent home hundreds of jaundiced babies with instructions for sun phototherapy with good results.

   Dr. Gordon suggest that you place your naked baby in a direct sunbath for five to ten minutes at a time, two or three times a day. (Use common sense. "July and August in California would be too hot," he adds.) At other times keep the baby in front of the window in indirect light. Leave on all the lights in the house, since any light will help. Dr. Gordon has the parents bring the baby into his office at least once a day during home therapy and asks the parents to call him immediately if there's a change in the quality of the breastfeeding—if the baby slows down or doesn't nurse as vigorously. If the parents are not comfortable with home phototherapy, or if the baby is not doing well and does need to be hospitalized, he suggests that the mother and baby go to a hospital where the mother can stay twenty-four hours a day, and breastfeeding never has to be stopped. It's been Gordon's experience that the vast majority of babies don't need to be hospitalized for phototherapy treatment.

What about vitamin E for a jaundiced baby? Steven J. Gross, M.D., in his Duke University study found that jaundiced premature babies had reduced bilirubin levels when they received fifty milligrams of vitamin E each day for the first three days of life. Premature babies are much more susceptible to the consequences of bilirubin than full-term healthy babies. (He did not study full-term infants.) Some lay midwives have told us that they recommend that mothers give their babies vitamin E once on the first day. Dr. Gordon suggests to mothers that they pierce a capsule of vitamin E (two hundred or three hundred units), spread it on their nipples and let the baby nurse it off gradually.

Though the hospital staff may tell parents that their baby is in no danger because he's under the lights, most parents are terrified. They often feel a sense of failure or guilt. So instead of feeling warm, loving feelings about their wonderful baby, they may be anxious and worried. Many parents whose infant has been under the bilirubin lights carry lingering doubts for years that there's something permanently wrong with their child.

If your doctor suggests phototherapy for your infant, let him know how important it is to you that your baby stay with you. Since treating newborn jaundice with bilirubin lights might be an everyday occurrence for him, he may not see the situation as the crisis you do. Discussing your baby's situation in detail may also relieve some of your doctor's anxiety about a malpractice suit.

You've got time to talk about this with your doctor if your baby has physiologic (normal) jaundice or even the rare breastmilk jaundice. (We're not talking here about jaundice caused by blood incompatibility or a premature or sick full-term baby.) With physiologic jaundice, it's not a we-must-do-something-in-the-next-hour emergency, although being in a hospital often makes it seem so.

CIRCUMCISION
A MATTER OF PREFERENCE

Circumcision is the removal of the foreskin of the penis, and for some people like the Jews and Moslems, among others, it's a religious ritual. In the last three generations in the United States, however, the circumcision of newborn boys in the hospital has been cultural (like father, like son), and has been performed by obstetricians or pediatricians.

Most infant boys (60 percent) in this country are circumcised (though nearly all were in the 1960s), while the rate in England and Scandinavia is less than 1 percent. And as an indication of its disfavor these days, circumcision is not paid for by many insurance companies. Medical and surgical complications from circumcision do occur, and the operation is a painful one if the infant is not given an anesthetic—which is usually the case.

The primary medical reason given for this procedure was that a circumcised penis was supposedly cleaner. However, research shows that poor hygiene, not an intact foreskin, causes rare infections. It was also believed, erroneously, that circumcision would reduce the risk for cancer of the penis, which is rare, and cancer of the cervix in female partners. Another myth has been that circumcision improves sex (it doesn't).

In a "maybe" turnaround from their 1975 statement, the Academy of Pediatrics (AAP) in 1989 said there may be a health advantage to circumcision after all. In a study of two hundred thousand males in army hospitals, uncircumcised males were ten times more likely to have urinary tract infections, which are rare among males. However, many critics, as well as the AAP itself, say there are problems with the study and consider the findings only tentative. And whether or not uncircumcised males are more likely, or less likely, to contract sexually transmitted diseases remains controversial.

WHAT ARE YOUR ALTERNATIVES?

1. *Decide for yourself.* In spite of the new research, the AAP has stated "there is no absolute medical indication for circumcision." There are, of course, religious and cultural reasons that may be important to you.

2. *If you decide not to have your son circumcised, don't sign the release that allows your physician to perform this operation.* This procedure is not required by law. The decision is up to you.

3. *If you decide to have your son circumcised, request that he be given a local anesthestic to block the pain,* though that humaneness is not common yet. But then be aware there are always potential side effects from anesthesia. For years, many people have believed that babies couldn't feel the pain because of an underdeveloped nervous system, in spite of the infant screams. Many mothers didn't know how upset their sons became because the circumcision was performed in the nursery, and the mothers couldn't hear.

A San Francisco pediatrician told us that "only a minority of people want the right to make decisions about their child. Many parents don't think they're capable. They forget to depend on themselves." But no one knows or cares about your child more than you do. Do your part . . . so that the care for your child is the best it can be.

Your baby doctor wants to do a good job for you and your child. He wants you to feel good as a parent. He knows any baby has a better chance with self-confident parents. Choose a pediatrician who shares your philosophy, whom you feel comfortable with, and with whom you can build a partnership for the better health of your child.

▪ EPILOGUE ▪

"I feel overwhelmed." "So much to think about!" "I think I'll leave everything up to the doctor." When you reach this point in the book, you might feel a little panic.

We knew some of our information could be scary, and it wasn't until we were well along in writing that we realized how much information has been kept from pregnant women. Maternity care is the most important consumer service we buy. If we are not informed, we don't know what good care is, much less how to get it.

"Okay, so you've informed me; but do I really have to do all those things you say to get what I want? It seems like so much trouble." Yes, it's work. But how many times in your life do you give birth? Isn't it worth the effort to get a good and safe birth?

By working for what you want you are contributing to better maternity care for all women. Thousands of women will read this book. Some will take one step. ("I will get a woman friend to be with my husband and me during my labor and birth.") Others will draw up a detailed birth plan and persist to get many options. Others will decide there are really only two or three things important to them, talk with their doctor, and get his agreement. Add up all these individual changes, and you have a widespread demand for better maternity care. Yet all you need to do is take one step for yourself.

"What happens if I do all that you suggest and my beautiful birth plan goes awry?" Your satisfaction with the birth will not be based on whether the birth goes according to the plan. It will be based on whether the family is kept together, whether you receive pleasure from the birth, and whether you feel good about yourself afterwards. If you have carefully chosen Dr. Right and the place of birth, and have set up a support system (your partner, one or more doulas, and a nurse for one-to-one care), your satisfaction with the birth is likely to be very high whatever happens. Why? Because the environment and supporters will ensure that even though the birth is different from what you planned, you can open yourself to whatever the experience brings. Dealing with the unexpected, with your supporters' help, you will find an inner strength, a capacity for courage and coping, you did not know was within you.

• APPENDIX A •

HOW TO BE A CHANGEMAKER

So far, this book has focused on helping you get what you want for you and your baby. Appendix A is a guide to help you create improved maternity options in your hospital for all women. Of course, these same steps apply to changing other bureaucracies, too.

Our local hospital administrators never asked for our input. From day one, we offered our opinions totally unsolicited. It's an understatement to say that we were not very popular with them. In spite of our pariah status, we were very successful. When the local hospital announced plans for a new ob unit several years ago, we set out to persuade the hospital administrators to offer women the maternity options they want. All of our original goals were met. The hospital added to its blueprints an in-hospital birth center; facilities for labor and delivery in the same room in the traditional unit; mostly private postpartum rooms; and more.

If you're thinking, "What changes can I make? What makes me an effective changemaker?" remember, as a childbirth consumer, no one knows better. And you can't get fired. Doctors and nurses who want to make changes always face a threat of peer pressure, even dismissal. But as a consumer (who is buying medical service), we're convinced that you, too, can be successful in making changes.

The strategies that worked for us didn't come to us neatly prepackaged. We learned a lot from trial and error. Other tactics were learned from watching hospital administrators, doctors, and board directors, or from talking with successful business people.

If you believe that hospital administrators and doctors are all-powerful, all-knowing, all-doing—don't read on. But if you're not sure, take what is helpful to you from our formula for success. If we did it, so can you. We built our confidence and knowledge one step at a time. We didn't always know how we were going to accomplish the next step. We just knew we'd do it. You may not need to use each and every strategy, or you may discover new ones. Use what works.

We've divided the strategies into two sections that are equally important: what worked for us, and what strategies were used against us.

WHAT WORKED FOR US

1. *Choose your partners well.* Look for optimists; avoid naysayers. As Henry Ford said, "If you think you can or you can't, you're always right."

   Look for risk takers. Avoid those people who always say, "Yes, but . . ." Beware potential partners who think they have to ask permission from those in authority. Getting approval is unimportant and works against success. Some people will always disapprove of you, no matter what you do—especially when you're questioning the status quo.

   Keep the action group very small, or energy dissipates when trying to achieve harmony. Rule by consensus is usually a guarantee you'll have only a discussion group. It's better to have a strong leader or two to implement the goals of the group. If you give your group a name, make it positive sounding—not negative. Be *for* something, not against.

2. *Do your homework.*

 • *Set concrete, measurable goals and deadlines.* Don't just say, "Someday we want Hospital X to have more family-centered maternity care." Do say, "Within eighteen months (or twelve, or twenty-four) we want Hospital X to provide a birth room where families can stay together during the birth process, any mother can room-in as much as she wishes, and siblings can visit both the mother and the new baby on the ob floor."

   Having established your goal and deadline, then you can make your timetable. Sometimes events outside your control determine your deadline. We had to finish and publish the M.O.M. Survey within nine months because that's when the hospital was going to have the first set of blueprints for the new ob unit available, and we wanted the impact of the survey to come before the blueprints were literally set in concrete.

We established our goals when we saw the M.O.M. Survey results. Because the results from all three surveys (Boulder, Wenatchee, Baltimore) are the same, you are safe in assuming that these goals represent women in your area, too. Or do your own survey. Also, be sure to find out what other hospitals are offering.

▪ *Go to experts for help.* Once we decided our goal was to give the hospital input from consumers, we realized the best method was a survey. We consulted with a local university sociology professor, who counseled us on the appropriate way to do the survey and to train the telephone surveyors.

When asking experts for help, remember that you don't always have to do what they suggest. Use your own common sense, too. One of the doctors we asked to review our survey results before they were published was aghast that not only did one in five women want a home birth, but that we actually intended to print that information. Yes, we did want his input. But we didn't agree with him on deleting the data on home-birth preferences.

▪ *Know what's in it for the hospital to change.* Your success in changemaking will come as a result of a partnership with the hospital. When hospitals change their policies to offer the maternity care women prefer, hospitals benefit, too.

—It gets the government off the hospital's back. Federal policymakers want hospital care to be more consumer oriented.

—It will get women off the hospital's back, too. Fewer complaints from consumers.

—But most of all, these changes make money for the hospital. Administrators need healthy financial statements. Offering women what they want means more mothers use the facilities. And families who come to hospitals to have babies tend to return when they need hospitalization again.

If your town has more than one hospital with a maternity unit, you're in luck. Since the hospitals compete with each other for the same patients, they'll be especially interested when you tell them women will use the hospital that offers these options.

—The hospital's prestige will increase. Hospitals like to make money *and* be progressive. You'll give them that chance.

3. *Decide it's your battle.* You've done your homework. You've thought through your goals, established a timetable, selected your partners, found your experts, and come to understand what's in it for the hospital to change. You're probably riding the high from your initial enthusiasm and zeal, but somewhere along in the process you'll have to decide that it is indeed *your* battle—or that it's not.

Do you have the persistence to stay in for several years? Is this issue of maternity change paramount with you? If you feel you have only two or three months to devote to this project, you're not likely to accomplish your goals—unless your partners pick up the slack.

Persistence is the key. If you persist, you can find a way to succeed. But none of us can fight every battle that beckons. If you decide that this project *is* your battle, form a network of supporters. Feel free to call us.

4. *Go with what is,* not what you wish were true. It's counterproductive to insist otherwise. Let's say you've got your heart set on an out-of-hospital birth center. But your state's health department laws prevent such an establishment. You could work through the legislature to change the laws, but maybe you want more immediate results. So then you go to your local hospital and suggest they construct a birth center in the hospital down the hall from the traditional ob department. However, don't expect to find any building funds budgeted for your project.

When hospitals say they can't do what you want, ask what they *can* do. Remind them of the need for the facility. Back your requests up with some statistics. If the hospital is unwilling to make a long-term commitment, discuss a short-term pilot project. Compromise is inevitable. It's a necessary part of changemaking.

5. *Go to the top*. In most hospitals (privately-held hospitals are an exception), the top is the board of directors. When we first published our survey, we were ignored. But we didn't allow that to go on for long (three weeks), and you can't be ignored, either, if you go to the top.

To make sure that our hospital's board of directors knew about us, we sent a letter to the chairman. We also sent copies to the homes of all of the other members. The letter described briefly what women wanted, based on our survey, and what specific changes the hospital would need to make to provide those options. The list of changes the hospital would have to make was what we called our "fat minimum." (That's more than we absolutely had to have, but allowed space for compromise.) The list of changes was also concrete and clear. Telling hospital administrators that women want "family-centered maternity care" is too vague. Telling them women want their other children to visit them in their hospital rooms, for instance, is specific.

You'll increase your chance of getting what you want by offering solutions, not just problems. That thoroughness separates you from those who "just want to complain."

Although hospital boards of directors are supposed to represent the community, they seldom hear directly from the public. These boards are predominantly male and are often composed of bankers, businessmen, and university administrators. You cannot expect them to know much about childbirth if you don't educate them.

6. *Work on all levels, cover all flanks*. We kept contact with all levels—other consumers, childbirth educators, hospital administrators, doctors, nurses, the board of directors, even a government agency (the Health Systems Agencies) that would eventually review the hospital plan to renovate and expand the maternity unit. We encouraged and helped organize

public meetings with panel discussions on maternity options.

We didn't keep secrets. We sent copies of our letters to all, to let everyone know what we were doing. You cannot be ignored if you're obviously and persistently visible—by phone, mail, or in person.

7. *Use the power of groups.* Well-known Canadian obstetrician Murray Enkin, M.D., once said that "one couple is weird, two are a committee, and one thousand are a movement." Swell your ranks, broaden your support by forming alliances with others. In union there is strength."

At about the same time we began our M.O.M. project, a new group, the Boulder Perinatal Council, began to meet at the hospital. This group was established as an information exchange, not as an action group. But because it did exist, we asked for and received support from many of the member agencies for our project.

The hospital increasingly recognized this group as the "official" consumer voice. Having this group support accelerated our progress. If you're not already part of such a group, contact other organizations with perinatal interests and form your own. The local director for the March of Dimes, Becky Messina, was the key organizer for the Boulder Perinatal Council.

But don't just look for support from other health organizations. The hospital received support letters for changing maternity options—at our urging— from women's political groups, the YWCA, and other organizations that don't focus exclusively on health.

8. *Look for insiders.* When Woodward and Bernstein exposed the Watergate scandal, one of their sources was an unidentified White House insider labeled "Deep Throat." Do you know of a doctor or nurse who's on the staff who may be a "closet" supporter of your goals? He or she is likely to be a doctor who is more progressive than the others, or a nurse who wants the hospital to make its policies more consumer oriented. Do you know a member of the

board of directors who will let you know what discussion, if any, is made of your project at board meetings? Will this board member put the topic of maternity options on the board-meeting agenda? Do you have a relative, neighbor, friend, or member of your social group who has inside knowledge? For example, among our "bridges" was Roberta's husband, who, as a doctor, was a member of the hospital's staff and privy to many medical meetings.

These "bridges" can keep you apprised of the temperature inside the institution. Remember, you don't need their agreement with your project, just some interest.

9. *Use outside connections*. Outsiders can be influential. Sometimes there is nothing like a name. If they don't influence the hospital policymakers themselves directly, these outsiders can certainly make you—the changemaker—feel better.

In the early months after we published the survey, we got a lot of negative feedback. We heard complaints about our survey methods or criticism that we were butting into other people's business. Then along came a letter from internationally known pediatric researcher Marshall Klaus, M.D. (we had sent him a copy of our survey results), telling us: "You've done an excellent survey." It certainly reassured us that we were on the right track.

At about the same time we asked fifteen or twenty medical professionals, both state and nationally known figures, for letters of support for our M.O.M. project in our attempt to get more funding for additional projects. We didn't get the funding, but we got the letters. Those letters increased our confidence. Don't overlook politicians and other public officials. They are potential sources of strong support for you.

10. *Use publicity*. Get attention. No matter how much the other side wants to ignore you, getting publicity forces them to recognize you. It keeps the pressure on and prevents the hospital from sweeping your project under the rug. In a magazine interview, John Kenneth Galbraith commented that women at Harvard made inroads in getting equal treatment only

when they presented a "mood of menace." This mood, he said, "must be strong enough so that it can induce a certain measure of alarm. That alarm is mostly achieved by uninhibited public criticism, which is something the people resisting women don't want to hear." We gave a copy of our survey to a newspaper reporter and invited an interview. The resulting article was the first of nearly one hundred nationwide about the M.O.M. Survey and maternity care in Boulder.

You, too, can make maternity care in your town a public issue. Following are steps that worked for us:

• *Keep media journalists informed about your project.* The most likely person to contact at a newspaper is the one who covers the women's page. The best contact person at radio and TV stations is the public-affairs director. At cable TV companies, it's the local access director. Reporters are always looking for news, but that doesn't mean that they'll necessarily be interested in supporting your pet project. It's up to you to find the appropriate person and let her or him know that maternity care in your community is not just a local, isolated issue, but a national issue. Meet her or him in person. Give that person background information to read. A media release, hand delivered, is helpful for newspapers, radio, or TV. It should describe what women want locally and what changes the hospital would have to make.

Most reporters do not have the luxury of a lot of time to research issues. By giving them background material, whether it's newspaper clippings or surveys like ours, you're expanding their available information. But that doesn't mean they necessarily will write the story the way you want, or that they'll do a story at all.

If a reporter does write anything on your project, thank that person afterward. Reporters seldom get anything but negative feedback. Get others to write or phone, too. Although women reporters may have a lot of empathy for your project, especially if they're mothers themselves, we found there are male reporters who are very interested in this issue also.

▪ *Encourage letters to the editor.* The letters to the editor mirror current concerns of the community. They are an ideal place for you and your allies to go public. But it's often tough to get people to actually write the letters and send them in. Make it as easy for them as possible, though, because these published letters can create a bandwagon effect.

It's very discouraging to send in a letter to the newspaper and then discover it's not printed. It's a fact of life that newspapers don't publish all the letters they receive. Call or go in and talk with the publisher (that's going to the top) and/or the person responsible for that section of the newspaper. Tell that person of your project and ask if he or she will run all letters that come in on that issue. That person may agree. If so, you're that much ahead.

Give potential letter writers ideas for letters (or even rough drafts). Know the rules for letters to the editor. Do they have to be typed double-spaced? Do they have to include an address? Does it help if the letters are hand delivered? (It often does, especially if you bring a baby with you.) Give your letter writers all the information you can.

▪ *Consider petitions.* Getting petition signatures is a form of publicity, as well as a means to rally public support. It's a concrete way to acquaint the population with your specific requests. Petitions with dozens (hopefully hundreds) of signatures not only make a strong statement to a hospital, but they may also interest the media even more to cover the story of maternity care in your town.

11. *Act like an equal at meetings.* Eighty percent of the message you convey is in your body language, even when you're speaking. You may be uneasy, but you want to appear calm.

▪ *Dress like you mean business.* No jeans or casual clothes when you're in three-piece-suit territory. That's going with what is. You want them to listen to you, not judge you "unlistenable" because of what you're wearing. You'll feel more successful and powerful if you look as though you belong there. Even if you feel anxious and insecure, you can become what you pretend to be by dressing for the part. At least one of you should wear a "color of authority" if you have it—navy blue, gray, or beige.

Yes, you can dress like you mean business with a baby in tow. As a matter of fact, having a baby along can be to your advantage. It's a definite visual reminder of the issue at hand, and we found that administrators and doctors were disarmed with a baby present. That's a disadvantage for them that can work for you. Roberta's infant daughter, Amanda, accompanied us for about a year after she was born. Roberta was sometimes distracted caring for Amanda, but Diana took up the slack. Besides, distractions gave us time to think.

Be on time for meetings. You don't want to apologize for being late. You don't want to apologize for anything.

- *Be prepared.* Know exactly what you want to accomplish. If you've done your homework, you'll feel more competent, tactful, and dignified. When we had meetings with hospital administrators, we knew what our "fat minimum" was before we went into the meeting. We expressed it to ourselves this way: "Today we'll find out their timetable for approval of the blueprints." Or, "Today we'll find out what the next step is in changing the policy on allowing siblings to visit their moms."

If you decide your goal in advance for any particular meeting, it's easier for you to say, as the time draws near for the end of the meeting, "We've covered many items in our discussion today, but I promised the others I wouldn't leave until I found out X."

- *Keep your cool.* You can often set the tone of any meeting by your own behavior. Avoid showing anger during the meeting. Ventilate that anger before the meeting or afterward—not during. Save that for your "autopsy" meeting. (That's when you discuss later what you did right, where you went wrong, and how you can fix it the next time.)

Don't burn your bridges with these people. An enemy today may be a helper tomorrow. The people you will be meeting with are just doing their jobs. If they don't want to give you what you want, if they disagree with your whole premise, it's nothing personal. It's just business.

They may get angry and holler at you. (That's "saber rattling," a common technique to intimidate people.) Or they may think that once you're there, they'll tell you what's what. (That's known as the "king holding court.") But you can't be intimidated or made to feel inferior if you decide you won't be.

• *Keep your expectations reasonable.* Part of being prepared is knowing what's reasonable to expect. We knew when we arranged a meeting with one influential pediatrician that we could expect that for most of one hour he would tell us all the things wrong with our project. And he did. He certainly met our expectations. However, we did squeeze in an explanation of our project from our point of view.

As it turned out, this particular doctor was helpful later in making some of the very changes we had suggested. No, it's not always going to work out that way. But it's important to remember that the people you are trying to persuade are looking at the issues from a different perspective. Don't take your marbles and go home just because they disagree with you. There are always areas of disagreement.

• *Don't go alone to any meeting.* Pad your delegation. If possible, have more people on your side than they have on theirs. Presidents of big companies travel with a regular entourage of people. You can do the same. You'll automatically be perceived as more important. Have all members prepared—if only to remain silent observers.

• *Know their deadlines* (and use them to your advantage). Before the hospital here could begin construction on their new maternity unit, they had to get an okay from the state. Consequently, we knew the hospital's deadline was the final state hearing. Because we were invited to testify at that hearing, it was important to the hospital that we be in agreement with them on the plans. When we next met with the administrators, they had to make concessions to us.

- *Go on the offensive in meetings.* Bring up your own issues, your own agenda. For instance, if you want to talk about special arrangements for cesarean mothers, say so. Don't expect them to say, "Now, what's on your mind?" They'll be busy bringing up their own issues instead.

- *Be a good saleswoman,* not an apologizer. Present your project in the best light. If you're convinced that women want maternity options your hospital doesn't now offer, be enthusiastic. Be unafraid to represent all women. All women do want individualized care. A hospital that offers women alternatives meets the needs of all women.

- *Use the "broken record" technique* if it helps you get where you're going. Sometimes it's clear that the administrators don't want you to give them the facts. Their minds are made up, and they don't want to be confused with the facts. Then use the "broken record" technique. When they tell you that they can't change the hospital policy to allow fathers in the cesarean operating room, just keep repeating the same phrase, "It's very important to cesarean mothers that their husbands be present at the birth." They may tell you that the anesthesiologists refuse or that the obstetricians refuse. You just keep repeating your original sentence. It's not your problem that the administrator might have some difficulty in making this policy change. That's his problem. He's paid to solve problems.

12. *Develop staying power.* Changemaking is a process, not a single event. To be successful, you must let them know that the issue will not go away. Send regular reports to people at every level. Schedule meetings. Tell the other side you look forward to continued review of this project with them.

   Part of staying power is follow-up. One West Coast hospital gathered a full day's worth of speakers to discuss what hospital-maternity-care options women wanted. However, for all the talk that day, no changes were made. A follow-up would have indicated a meeting with administrators to discuss *which* options would be added and *when.*

How long do you have to last? Your timetable may be different from ours, but two years passed from our first conversation about doing a survey until the hospital policies and blueprints contained all the major preferences of women.

No, you don't have to work on this project all the time, every day. But you must keep abreast of the issues. Do take care of yourselves, too. Because you're dealing with a serious issue, you'll find you need a balance—time to laugh and have some fun. Keep in touch with your network of supporters. Don't lose heart. There will be pitfalls. You'll make mistakes. You'll be criticized. That's okay. Develop a watchdog committee to monitor the hospital after changes are made, or the hospital will predictably lapse back to former policies. Above all, persevere.

STRATEGIES TO GUARD AGAINST

Bureaucracies don't like outsiders trying to rock the boat. That's understandable. If you were in their shoes, you wouldn't like it either. So what the hospital will do in response is what just about anyone in a position of power will try. You may find that not all of these steps are used against you, but if some are, you'll be forewarned and forearmed, so that they won't deflect you from your goals.

Hospital administrators, doctors, nurses, and board directors aren't bent on frustrating you, so don't take it personally. They're just doing the job they're hired to do. And they do it very well. Here's what they'll do—how they sock it to you:

1. *They'll ignore you.* An effective technique, guaranteed to weed out the faint of heart. You'll write a letter and get no response. Your phone calls won't be returned. You'll present a proposal, and they'll smile and say, "Thank you, the committee will consider it." Months will go by before you find out from a friend who's on the staff that it never came before the committee. Or it was voted down in the last two and a half minutes of the November meeting. We circulated 125 copies of our survey to every doctor, health-care agency, hospital adminis-

trator, and nurse having anything to do with birth or babies in our community and asked each for a response. Out of 125 copies circulated, we got zero responses. Frankly, being ignored makes you feel like a balloon that just got stuck with a pin. We thought we had finished the job by circulating the survey, but we were wrong. Oh, you faint of heart. It was just the beginning.

You do the obvious then. Refuse to be ignored. Contact people. We decided who the opinion leaders were (one obstetrician, one pediatrician, one hospital administrator) and arranged to meet with them individually. When it seemed the information still wasn't going places, we went to the top. We wrote a letter to the chairman of the board summarizing in one page what women wanted. We asked other agencies to send a similar letter, using ours as a model. Many did, which forced the hospital to realize we were determined to be visible. So, keep plugging. Make phone calls. Write letters. Solicit support from others. Do not accept silence as the final response. Never go away.

2. *You'll be told, "Don't call us, we'll call you."* When we first began our survey, we kept the original hospital administrator we worked with informed of what was happening—not to ask permission, remember, just to keep him informed. We had not been invited to do this project, but we were always open to talking about it. As a matter of fact, in the first conversation, he told us we didn't need to go to "all that trouble." "You and some of the girls could come in, and we could all just sit down and chat about it," he said. We thanked him kindly for his suggestion and went on with the survey.

Later, when we discussed the questionnaire with him, he complained about some of the questions asked. He said we had no business asking women questions about procedures that only doctors should decide.

Incidentally, in other cities when groups (such as childbirth educators) begin to make noises about wanting changes at the hospital, more than one group has been called in for a meeting, usually 7:30

A.M.—good for doctors, not so good for mothers with young children—and has been told, "Don't call us, we'll call you" (which translates to "when it's too late for your input to matter" or "never").

Remember, when you accept their timetable, you have totally given away yours.

3. *They'll find flaws.* When our survey was hot off the press, and we had found a way to get them to talk to us about it, we were told we had gone about it all wrong. "You only interviewed mountain hippies," one doctor said. Another told us the survey was heavily biased. Disappointed, we could have accepted their verdict. We could have nitpicked details, whined a little, and said, "Well, we did the best we could." But the issue (always remember your goal) was not defending *how* we did the survey. The issue was what options do women want. We said, "You may not have confidence in our methods, but are you saying that you don't think this is what women want?" Now what could they say? No one else had ever asked women what they wanted, so how could our detractors know? Doctors told us that their patients didn't tell them that they wanted these options. But women often don't tell their doctors what they like or don't like.

When your "fatal flaws" are pointed out, remember—it's a sign of success. You're getting somewhere. It's usually the next step after being ignored. If you've done your homework well, and your project is well thought out, you're not likely to have a genuine "fatal flaw." Stick to the real business at hand—your goals.

4. *They'll placate you, even excite you, with their interpretation of what you want.* They'll use words like "homelike delivery" or "birth room" and you'll think it's music to your ears. What's homelike to many hospital personnel (who live in a world of rules and regulations and gray-green paint) may be just a splash of color, a rug on the floor, a comfortable chair, and, the ultimate ruse, a cheerful bedspread. Is that what you really wanted when you said you wanted a "homelike delivery?"

Specify exactly what changes you want a hospital to make. Follow up with a letter. Be specific and definite. State: "Most postpartum rooms need to be private, so that women may more easily have their babies with them," *not* "Women want more contact with their babies." State: "Based on survey results, two of the four planned delivery rooms should have the flexibility of labor and delivery in the same bed," *not* "Women want an alternative birth situation." Vagueness allows the hospital to interpret as they wish.

5. *They'll appeal to your logic.* They'll say . . . "The doctors won't use a birth center, no sense in putting one in" . . . "You may want to do that, but it's not safe" . . . "It's not financially possible" . . . "It's not structurally possible" . . . "It's just not reasonable; be logical." In a world where books of rules and regulations are inches thick and numerous enough to line a wall, it's easy to pull a book out, open to almost any page, and find a reason why you can't do something. Keep repeating what you want. Stick to your goals. Don't let their version of logic sidetrack you.

6. *They'll refuse you access to the facts,* and then tell you your information isn't good enough. When we questioned an administrator about a government procedure, he said, "Well, it's so complicated, you wouldn't understand." The initial refusal to disclose facts is often just that—the first response. Keep asking. If you're still refused, try something else. Ask, "If you can't help me, who can?" You are signaling to them that you can't be put off. (We finally contacted the government agency ourselves for the information.)

We were refused the use of patient names from hospital records for our survey. We found another source (all the while keeping the administration informed). Naturally, they told us our results would not be valid. Remember, they'll find flaws.

7. *They'll keep you an "outsider."* They won't let you into the system, because they know that you will disrupt their comfortable routine. That's fair. It's their football, and if you don't play the game they want to play, they can take their ball home. They

don't have to let you serve on the hospital obstetrics committee, for example. It's composed of eight men and only one woman—and it's in the business of providing health care for women. But it certainly isn't discrimination: nine out of ten doctors are men.

So go with what is. Make sure that you contact individual members of this committee and tell them what women say they want. Do not always rely on hospital-appointed go-betweens to keep committee members informed.

8. *They'll appoint someone to listen to you, raise your hopes, and they'll make sure that person is powerless.* They'll send a head nurse on the maternity floor, or the director of public relations. Yes, you finally get someone to listen to you, and though he or she will write reports or whatever, there will still be no change.

A group on the West Coast was told to take their requests to the head nurse. They did. Months passed, nothing happened. Finally, they asked the nurse, "What's going to happen?" "Nothing," was the reply. The head nurse this group spoke to had no power to change anything.

Don't quit talking to nurses, though. They're key to getting the maternity care women want. Nurses are on the front line. They can either help wonderfully or sabotage changes thoroughly every day they're at work on the floor. But don't stop with nurses. Make an appointment with the hospital administrator. Always start at the top. If you're denied access, try again. Use another tactic. Call a member of the board of directors, explain who you are, what you want to do. Board members represent the public—that's you. Once you have the board's ear, the administrator will probably be available, too.

9. *They'll act as if they're playing along.* Ah, this is so effective. This is not usually immediately obvious. One changemaking group had drawn up their own list of needed maternity options. Then came one of those 7:30-in-the-morning meetings with doctors. Told "Thanks for coming, meeting with us, and giving us input. We'll take care of it," the women

went home excited about their "partnership" meeting. Nine months later, there were no changes in sight.

Another example is one of our own. Our group was told that our input on the kind of bed used in the birth center would be welcomed. However, only a short time later we discovered that the budget for the hospital—which is established six to twelve months in advance—already had another kind of bed planned for and ordered. And it sure wasn't the one we wanted. We goofed! When making requests for certain kinds of equipment, ask what the status of the budget is. How much money is allocated for equipment, when could it be bought, what is the timetable for purchase?

10. *They'll get frustrated and start retaliating.* Name-calling and sabotage are the two most popular ways to retaliate. Be ready to grow a thick skin for name-calling. You need to respond swiftly to sabotage. Nurses can be skilled at sabotage, and it doesn't always have to be intentional. In one hospital, the nursing staff reluctantly followed a new policy that allowed siblings to visit their moms on the maternity floor. But in complying with the new policy, they sabotaged an old one that permitted mom to keep her baby during visiting hours if she had no visitors herself. Here's where you change-makers need to stay on top of things. This contradiction was pointed out right away to the director of nursing, who showed the staff a way to include both policies.

Another obvious retaliation is plain old lying, missed deadlines, or statements like, "Gee, didn't I tell you about that?"

11. *They'll try to make you feel guilty.* This can easily come from an ally. As a matter of fact, men have never intentionally or unintentionally used this strategy with us. It's always been other women.

An up-to-then-supportive board member accused us of "ruining the whole project and making mothers suffer yet another summer in that sweatbox of a hospital" because our testimony at a preliminary government agency hearing might have delayed the project.

Another time a fellow worker in the Perinatal Council told us that we were causing trouble for people like her, who worked regularly with the hospital. She didn't feel as welcome there as she used to and suggested it was all our fault.

Your first response might be an anxious, "Who me?" Accept that momentary twinge of anxiety and realize that this tactic is used on all persons who try to change the system. Remember, it gets easier with practice to accept the grievance for what it is, one person's opinion.

You may not have all these tactics used against you. But when any one of them is used, pat yourself and your fellow changemakers on the back. You are right on schedule.

What's in it for you to be a changemaker? You'll use up your own resources—money, time, and emotion. But you'll also feel a sense of accomplishment. You'll develop your creative powers to a new level. You'll permanently share mutual respect with "the other side." You'll be able to get what you want in other areas in the future.

And the ultimate success? If you've done your job well, the "other side" will take credit for it when the project is completed.

Nobel peace laureate Betty Williams told us, "It is within the power of any individual to fight for what is right and to change the course of events." She was talking about achieving peace. But the fight for humane maternity care is just as important—perhaps the beginning of all other issues. And change doesn't happen just because the cause is right. Families are the backbone of every culture. Why not become a change-maker yourself and give families the best of starts by getting maternity care that women want for good and safe births.

READER QUESTIONNAIRE

Readers are invited to complete this questionnaire or use it for their own local surveys. You may wish to photocopy this or simply answer on a fresh sheet with reference to the question number.

1. Rate your satisfaction with your most recent birth experience. (Circle one.)

Completely satisfied   Mostly satisfied   Satisfied
Unsatisfied   Mostly unsatisfied   Completely unsatisfied

2. What would you have changed about your prenatal care, your labor, your birth, or your hospital postpartum stay?

3. Where was your baby born? (Circle one.)
Traditional hospital unit   Birth room
ABC (Alternative birth center in the hospital)
Out-of-hospital birth center   Home   Other (Describe.)

4. Who was your primary birth attendant? (Circle one.)
Obstetrician   Family practitioner   Nurse-midwife
Direct-entry midwife   Other (Describe.)

5. Who is the caregiver for your baby? (Circle one.)
Pediatrician   Family practitioner
Pediatric nurse practitioner   Other (Describe.)

6. What interventions were used in your birth?

7. What complications did you have?

8. What complications did your baby have?

9. If your baby had to stay in the hospital or be rehospitalized, please explain.

10. Did you have a doula or monitrice present during your labor? (Please circle which one.) Was this person helpful?
Doula   Monitrice

11. Did you attend childbirth preparation classes? _____Yes
_____No
If you did, were they helpful? _____Yes _____No

If you did, what kind of class was it? (Lamaze, Bradley, etc.)

Who sponsored the class? (Circle one.)
My doctor   My hospital   The childbirth teacher
Don't know   Other (Describe.)

Do you wish you had been given any additional information?
If so, what?

12. Circle which of the following were helpful to you with
breastfeeding.
Friends   Hospital nurses   La Leche League
Childbirth educator   Family   Obstetrician
Pediatrician   Family practitioner   Books/publications
Midwife   Pediatric nurse practitioner
Other (Describe.)

Circle which of the following were *not* helpful to you with
breastfeeding.
Friends   Hospital nurses   La Leche League
Childbirth educator   Family   Obstetrician   Pediatrician
Family practitioner   Books/publications   Midwife
Pediatric nurse practitioner   Other (Describe.)

13. Did you attend La Leche League meetings or have personal or phone contact with an LLL leader? (Circle which one.)
Meetings   Phone
Do you wish you had been given any additional information?
_____Yes   _____No   If so, what?

14. What information in this book helped you the most?

15. What information in this book was not helpful?

16. What information was missing in this book?

17. Anything else you'd like to tell us? (Birth stories are welcome.)

18. Please give your name, address, and phone number in case we decide to ask for additional information. (Omit if you prefer.) Send to: Diana Korte and Roberta Scaer; %Bantam Books, 666 Fifth Avenue, New York, New York 10103.

THE THREE SURVEYS

The three surveys of American women, asking what options they wanted in their hospital maternity care, were conducted in Boulder, Colorado, in 1976; in Wenatchee, Washington, in 1978; and in Baltimore, Maryland, in 1979. The first, the Boulder survey, was the impetus and model for the others.

The M.O.M. Survey; Boulder, Colorado

Boulder is an attractive college town of eighty-five thousand, in the foothills of the Rocky Mountains, thirty miles northwest of Denver. Many residents are highly educated, white-collar workers. The city is home to high-technology government research programs and private business. Most of the citizens think of Boulder as a progressive place. For example, 84 percent of new mothers breastfeed their babies (many of them in public).

The survey started with our concern that women weren't being asked for input into plans for the local hospital's new maternity wing. We didn't know what a radical idea that was; it seemed logical to us. And so the M.O.M. (Maternity Options for Mothers) Survey was developed, with a network of women friends and health professionals.

We are longtime leaders in the worldwide breastfeeding organization, La Leche League. We knew from our many years of working with mothers that many women were frustrated about the care given to them when their babies were born. So we knew there were things that hospitals could and should be doing differently. We were also mothers ourselves, so we had some ideas on how things could have been different for us.

We got together a proposal and the assistance of forty-two volunteers, and applied to the Northern Colorado Chapter of the March of Dimes for a grant to cover the costs of computer-assisted analysis of data and publication of survey results. With the grant approved, over a period of four weeks, we were able to contact and survey 694 women from a master list of 906 names. Three groups of women were surveyed: nearly 100 percent of the Boulder Area La Leche League Women (240 women), a sample of women attending childbirth classes (205 women), and a random sample taken from newspaper birth announcements over a one-year period (210 women). All three groups totaled 694 women surveyed by means of a telephone interview. Only 24 women refused to participate. The survey took about fifteen minutes, but some women stayed on the line another half hour or more. Once started, they wanted to talk more about their birth experience.

The women were asked to indicate their preferences ("strongly agree, agree, disagree, strongly disagree") on thirty-eight maternity care options. We were greeted with great enthusiasm from the moms, and a willingness to cooperate. One of our surveyors said: "This is an experience many women feel strongly about, but have no convenient way to get their opinions to the proper people." When the results of the survey were published early in 1977, it was a first—not only for Boulder, but for the nation, and for the American health-care system. Never had health consumers been so approached.

The Mothers' Survey; Wenatchee, Washington

Wenatchee is another attractive city, with a population of nearly twenty thousand. It is located in the rolling hills of apple-growing country in eastern Washington State. Wenatchee residents are mostly blue-collar workers, with high-school educations.

The Mothers' Survey in Wenatchee was the result of the "radicalization" of one woman. Here's her story:

"I was angry!" says Shannon Pope of Wenatchee, in reply to why she was the first person to duplicate the M.O.M. Survey. "When I was pregnant with my first child, I knew just what I wanted, and I kept telling my ob what I wanted at each visit, as he was rushing out the door. I knew the risks of anesthesia to the baby, and I wanted a natural childbirth. When I got to the hospital in labor, I found out that my doctor wasn't on call. I had to argue all over again for everything I wanted. I thought everything went well, until I got my bill and discovered I had been charged for a pudendal block. I had been given this without being asked. I hadn't wanted it and didn't need it. The doctor had exposed my unborn baby to anesthesia completely against my wishes. I was still upset months later when I came across an article in *McCall's* about the M.O.M. Survey and knew I had to do something."

Shannon went directly to the top and made an appointment with the hospital administrator. He suggested that the M.O.M. Survey represented women only in Boulder and asked her to do a similar survey and present the information to the doctors. After getting a copy of the M.O.M. Survey and consulting with Roberta Scaer by phone, Shannon did the second maternity-options survey. Central Washington Hospital of Wenatchee contributed money and staff time for the study. In a random sample of 173 women who were mailed questionnaires, 68 replied. As in Boulder, they expressed definite opinions about what they wanted in maternity care.

Committee on Maternal Alternatives; Baltimore, Maryland

Baltimore, with 1.6 million people, is one of the oldest cities in America. It is a port city famed for its Chesapeake Bay seafood, its rich immigrant culture traditions, its professional sporting teams, and its famed Johns Hopkins Hospital. In the fall of 1978, just as the Wenatchee survey was being completed on the other side of the country, Bobbi Seabolt and her committee were hard at work putting the finishing touches on the third and most extensive questionnaire of women's preferences in maternity care ever done. Bobbi, too, had read of the M.O.M. Survey in *McCall's*. She wrote us for a copy of the survey results and the M.O.M. questionnaire and passed it around her group of volunteers (who call themselves the Committee on Maternal Alternatives or COMA). Bobbi, like Shannon Pope, consulted with Roberta Scaer before doing the survey. Her group received some funds from the Baltimore Childbirth Education Association and the March of Dimes, but, as in Boulder, it was a huge volunteer effort that enabled them to get the job done. A total of six thousand questionnaires was distributed by the Nu-Dy-Per Baby Service to all women using their diaper service in the greater Baltimore area. Responses came in from 1,345 women, who told of their preferences in their birthing experience. In addition, they replied to a whole new section asking what kinds of medical interventions were used in their births, and what their opinions of those interventions were. A complete report, first published in the fall of 1979 by the Committee on Maternal Alternatives, is available for nineteen dollars from Bobbi Seabolt; 1822 Notre Dame Avenue; Lutherville, Maryland 21093.

• APPENDIX D •

YOUR LIST OF HELPERS

These organizations are mostly national and occasionally regional, and a few are located in Canada, England, and Australia where we have readers. Many fine local childbirth teachers and groups are not listed (though the national organizations that are included can give you referrals). That's because many of these local listings would be out of date by the time you read them.

However, you can call the reference room of your local library or contact your local United Way office for leads to groups and contacts in your city. You can also call these places if you find that one of the following listings is now out of date, too. Every listing in this appendix has been confirmed by mail or phone at least once, and often the wording used is what the organization gave us. The listing of any person or organization in this directory, however, is not an endorsement by us.

When requesting information from these organizations (with the exception of the mail-order companies), please send a stamped, self-addressed, business-size envelope.

INDEX

Birth Centers (Free-standing)
Birth Defects
Breastfeeding/Lactation Consultants
Childbirth Organizations (General)
Cesarean Birth
Circumcision
Doulas (Birth Assistants and mother-helpers)
Education (Childbirth)
Home Birth
Midwifery
Miscarriage, Stillborn, and Newborn Deaths

Mothering Organizations and Publications
Newborn Care
Other Publications, Videos, Cassettes, and Supplies
Premature Birth
Research Service
SIDS (Sudden Infant Death Syndrome)
Twins, Triplets, and Quads
Underwater Birth

BIRTH CENTERS (FREE-STANDING)

National Association of Childbearing Centers
Eunice K.M. Ernst, C.N.M., M.P.H., Director
R.D. #1, Box #1
Perkiomenville, PA 18074
(215) 234-8068

Provides referrals to consumers for more than 130 birth centers, publications including newsletter.

BIRTH DEFECTS

March of Dimes Birth Defects Foundation
National Headquarters
1275 Mamaroneck Avenue
White Plains, NY 10605
(914) 428-7100

Provides materials on healthy childbearing, birth defects and their prevention with information sheets on individual birth defects, such as club foot, Tay Sachs and sickle-cell anemia.

BREASTFEEDING/LACTATION CONSULTANTS

La Leche League International, Inc.
P.O. Box 1209
9616 Minneapolis Avenue
Franklin Park, IL 60131-8209
(312) 455-7730 or 1-800-La-Leche
(9am-3pm CST, M-F)

Provides mother-to-mother breastfeeding information worldwide to one million mothers annually. Publications, including information sheets, newsletters, and books for both consumers and health-care professionals, and catalog of publications. Also tapes and braille for the visually impaired regarding pregnancy, childbirth, and breastfeeding. Send for name of nearest LLL counselor.

International Lactation Consultant Association
Jeanine Klaus, President
P.O. Box 4031, University of Virginia Station
Charlottesville, VA 22903
(404) 381–5127

Provides professional association for lactation consultants. Quarterly publication, *Journal of Human Lactation,* and annual conferences.

CHILDBIRTH ORGANIZATIONS (GENERAL)

American Foundation for Maternal and Child Health
Doris Haire, President
439 East 51st Street
New York, NY 10022
(212) 759–5510

Promotes unmedicated childbirth by sponsoring research and seminars, publishing literature, and exerting pressures on national and state legislators and agencies.

National Association of
  Parents and Professionals
  for Safe Alternatives (NAPSAC)
Dave and Lee Stewart, Directors
P.O. Box 646
Marble Hill, MO 63764-9726
(314) 238–2010

Promotes education about all childbirth alternatives. Newsletter, books, and other publications, including alternative birth directory. Active in legislative reform and political action.

CESAREAN BIRTH

Cesarean Prevention Movement (CPM)
Esther Zorn, President
P.O. Box 152, University Station
Syracuse, NY 13210
(315) 424–1942

Provides information on cesarean prevention and VBAC (vaginal birth after cesarean); sixty-five local chapters; book catalog, quarterly newsletter.

C/Sec, Inc. (Cesareans/Support, Education and Concern)
Norma Shulman
22 Forest Road
Framingham, MA 01701
(508) 877–8266

Provides support and information on cesarean childbirth, cesarean prevention, and vaginal birth after cesarean (VBAC).

Conscious Childbearing
Lynn Baptisti Richards
59 Royden Drive E.
North Merrick, NY 11566
(516) 781–0785

Provides workshops, counseling, and hot line for avoiding cesareans and having a VBAC in hospital or at home; also provides referral list of professionals who support VBACs. Call during school hours (9 A.M.–3 P.M.) or late evening (9 P.M.–10 P.M.). Write for a free pamphlet.

Public Citizen's Health Research Group
Department PR, Room 700
2000 P Street, N.W.
Washington, DC 20036

Sells report, *Unnecessary Cesarean Sections: A Rapidly Growing National Epidemic*. $10 for consumers, twenty dollars for physicians and hospitals.

VBAC (Vaginal Birth after Cesarean)
Nancy Wainer Cohen
10 Great Plain Terrace
Needham, MA 02192
(617) 449–2490

Provides VBAC information and counseling.

CIRCUMCISION

Childbirth Education Foundation
P.O. Box 5
Richboro, PA 18954

Provides information about avoiding circumcision, including a variety of publications, as well as pamphlets about other childbirth issues.

National Organization of Circumcision
  Information Resource Centers (NO-CIRC)
Marilyn Milos
731 Sir Francis Drake Boulevard
San Anselmo, CA 94960
(415) 454–5669

Provides information about avoiding circumcision; publications, including newsletter and pamphlet, *Circumcision Why?*

Peaceful Beginnings
Rosemary R. Wiener
13020 Homestead Court
Anchorage, AK 99510–7741
(206) 671–9335

Provides information about avoiding circumcision; publications, including book, *Circumcision: The Painful Dilemma.*

Tree of Life
Lynn Reed
1118 Azalea Drive
Augusta, GA 30904
(404) 733–7666

Provides support and information to Jewish parents who choose not to have their sons circumcised.

DOULAS (BIRTH ASSISTANTS AND MOTHER-HELPERS)

National Association of Postpartum Care Services
Diane McQuiston
4414 Buxton Court
Indianapolis, IN 46254
317-293-7763

Provides referrals to consumers for more than 60 individuals or companies who provide mother-to-mother help after the baby is born. Publications, including quarterly newsletter, and national conventions for providers of these services.
  The following three organizations provide birth-assistant training through workshops and publications:

Association of Professional Birth Assistants
P.O. Box 1304
Ashland, OR 97520
(503) 482–8881

Informed Homebirth/Informed Birth and Parenting (IH/IBP)
P.O. Box 3675
Ann Arbor, MI 48106
313-662-6857

National Association of Childbirth Assistants
219 Meridian Avenue
San Jose, CA 95126
(408) 225–9167

EDUCATION (CHILDBIRTH)

Academy of Certified Birth Educators
Sally Riley
11011 King, Suite 111
Overland Park, KS 66210
(913) 451–0915; or (800) 444–8223

Provides certification course for childbirth educators, including a three-day course specializing in adult education, curriculum development, relaxation, labor and support techniques, teaching skills, and teen pregnancy.

American Academy of Husband-Coached Childbirth
Jay and Marjie Hathaway, Directors
P.O. Box 5224
Sherman Oaks, CA 91413
(800) 42-BIRTH (in California); (800) 423–2397 (national); (818) 788–6662

Certifies and trains instructors in Bradley method of childbirth education. Publications and videos.

American Society for Psychoprophylaxsis
 in Obstetrics (ASPO)
1840 Wilson Blvd. Suite 204
Arlington, VA 22201
202-783-7050 or 1-800-368-4404

Certifies and trains instructors in Lamaze method and provides information for consumers, including referrals to instructors, books about childbirth and family-centered maternity care, and magazines, including *Lamaze Parents Magazine* and *Genesis*. Videos about parenting are available through ASPO instructors.

Birth Works
CPM, Inc.
P.O. Box 152
Syracuse, NY 13210
(315) 424–1942

Combines traditional childbirth education classes with prevention of unnecessary cesareans.

Childbirth Without Pain Education Association
20134 Snowden
Detroit, MI 48235

Offers classes to expectant parents and certifies and trains instructors in the Lamaze method of painless childbirth. Publications and films.

Gamper International, Inc. (formerly
  Midwest Parentcraft Center)
627 Beaver Road
Glenview, IL 60025

Teaches Gamper method of childbirth education. Numerous groups in the greater Chicago area, publications, quarterly newsletter, *Heir Raising News*, $15 / year.

International Childbirth Education Association
P.O. Box 20048
Minneapolis, MN 55420

Gathers together parents and professionals interested in family-centered maternity care. Classes for both parents and childbirth educators; national and regional meetings; local chapters; publications, including the *International Journal of Childbirth Education*; and films.

Read Natural Childbirth Foundation, Inc.
Margaret B. Farley, R.P.T.
P.O. Box 956
San Rafael, CA 94915
(415) 456–8462

Provides a program to prepare expectant parents for a more satisfying pregnancy, labor, and postpartum birth experience.

HOME BIRTH

American College of Home Obstetrics
P.O. Box 25
River Forest, IL 60305

Provides information for physicians who cooperate with couples choosing a home birth.

Association for Childbirth at Home, International
116 South Louise
Glendale, CA 91250
(213) 667–0839

Provides information and support for home birth, including publications. They also have in-house birth center at this location.

Birth at Home League
Marilyn Moran
P.O. Box 6223
Leawood, KS 66206

Provides information and support for do-it-yourself wife/husband home birthing, including the newsletter, *The New Nativity*.

Birth Day
P.O. Box 388
Cambridge, MA 02138
(617) 259–0362

Provides alternative childbirth classes, referrals, and certified teacher training programs.

The Birthing Circle
303 E. Main Street
Burkittsville, MD 21718
Robyn Molloy (301) 834–8142
Diane Younkins (301) 662–0176
Rose Gerstner (304) 876–6392

Provides referrals to expectant parents for all birth alternatives.

Homebirth Australia
Hilda Bastian
P.O. Box 107
Lawson, NSW 2783 (AUSTRALIA)
 or Rose Fleming
8 Busby Street
O'Connor ACT 2601 (AUSTRALIA)
062–473257

Provides information, support, and referrals for home birth in Australia; publications, including quarterly newsletter and books; annual conference (SASE in international postage).

Informed Homebirth/Informed Birth
Rahima Baldwin, Ute Beck
P.O. Box 3675
Ann Arbor, MI 48106
(313) 662–6857

Trains and certifies home-birth teachers and attendants; offers classes
for couples planning home births. Publications, including newsletter,
books. Also cassettes.

MIDWIFERY

American College of Nurse-Midwives (ACNM)
1522 K Street, NW
Suite 1000
Washington, DC 20005
(202) 289-0171

Provides certification of nurse-midwives, referrals for consumers, and
publications, including brochures, fact sheets, and a pregnancy
calculator (a gestational wheel that estimates due date and includes
other information, too, for $2.50).

Apprentice Academics
Carla Hartley
3805 Mosswood
Conroe, TX 77302–1176
(409) 273–5175

Provides midwifery education, teaching aids, midwifery gifts, creative
childbirth education seminars, quarterly newsletter.

Association of Ontario Midwives
P.O. Box 85
Postal Station C
Toronto, Ontario, CANADA MBJ 3M7

Provides consumer referrals for midwives in this area.

Association of Radical Midwives
Ishbel Kargar
62 Greetby Hill, Ormskirk, Lancs
L39 2DT ENGLAND
0695–72776

Provides study and support for midwives and mothers, and information on choices in childbirth.

Fellowship of Christian Midwives
Renee Stein
7661 Deertrail Drive
Parker, CO 80134

Provides information and support for Christian midwives through
newsletters and referrals.

"Midwifery and the Law" Booklet *Mothering* Magazine

Provides current legal status and contracts in each state. (See *Mothering* Magazine listing for address.)

Midwives of North America (MANA)
P.O. Box 5337
Cheyenne, WY 82003

Provides support for all midwives and makes referrals to midwives in
your home state.

Seattle Midwifery School
JoAnne Myer-Ciecko
2524 Sixteenth Avenue, South #300
Seattle, WA 98144
(206) 322–8834

Certifies direct-entry midwives and offers continuing education, labor
support course, obstetrics and gynecology nurse-practitioner course,
and other lectures and workshops.

MISCARRIAGE, STILLBIRTH, AND NEWBORN DEATHS

AMEND
Maureen J. Connelly
4324 Berrywick Terrace
Saint Louis, MO 63128
(314) 487–7528

Provides one-on-one contact with parents who lose a baby through
miscarriage, stillbirth, or shortly after delivery.

Bereavement Magazine
Andrea Gambill, Editor
350 Gradle Drive
Carmel, IN 46032
(317) 846–9429

Publishes full-service magazine that comprehensively covers grief
issues, including miscarriage, stillbirth, and neonatal death. There are

features for widows, bereaved parents, children, and generally bereaved individuals. Published nine times/year, $22/year.

HOPING
Judy Boomer, R.N., and Sandy Cruz, R.N.
3288 Moanalua Road
Kaiser Hospital
Honolulu, HI 96819
(808) 834–5333, ext. 9903

Provides a perinatal loss support group for parents; lending library; newsletter; parent-to-parent phone support and group meetings.

Intensive Caring Unlimited
Carol Randolph, President
910 Bent Lane
Philadelphia, PA 19118
(609) 848–1945

Provides information and support for those women who have a high-risk pregnancy; who have experienced a miscarriage, stillbirth, or death of a child; who have a hospitalized child and/or want to breastfeed a hospitalized child; or who have a child with a birth defect or who is developmentally delayed.

The Compassionate Friends, Inc.
Therese Goodrich
P.O. Box 3696
Oak Brook, IL 60522–3696
(312) 990–0010

Provides support to parents who have experienced the death of a child. Hundreds of local chapters. Publications, book list, newsletter.

Perinatal Loss
2443 N.E. Twentieth Avenue
Portland, OR 97212

Publishes booklet of suggestions for grieving parents.

Pregnancy and Infant Loss Center (PILC)
1415 E. Wayzata Boulevard
Suite 22
Wayzata, MN 55391
(612) 473–9372

Provides referrals to support groups nationwide; publications including literature on pregnancy and infant loss, quarterly newsletter, *Loving Arms;* lending library; educational programs for parents and care providers; consultation for professional care providers.

PRIDE (Parents Resolving Infant Death Experiences)
Kate Luscombe, R.N.
Jersey Shore Medical Center—1945 Route 33
Neptune, NJ 07754
(201) 776-4349

Provides self-help and support groups for parents who have lost an infant for any reason or who had experienced pregnancy loss.

Reach Out to the Parents of an Unknown Child, Inc.
Kathy Geldart, President
555 North County Road
Saint James, NY 11780
(516) 584-5525; or (516) 862-6743

Provides support for families experiencing the death of a child due to miscarriage, stillbirth, or early infant death. Quarterly newsletter, perinatal bereavement cards, etc.

SHARE National Office
Sister Jane Marie Lamb
Saint Elizabeth's Hospital
211 South Third Street
Belleville, IL 62222
(618) 234-2415

Provides mutual help for parents of miscarriage, stillbirth, or newborn death; local groups; publications, including bimonthly newsletter, manual for farewell rituals, and book on starting your own group.

Shattered Dreams
Cathy McDiarmid
21 Potsdam Road, #61
Downsview, Ontario, CANADA M3N IN3
(416) 663-7143

Quarterly newsletter offering support, information, sharing, and hope for the future to parents experiencing miscarriage.

The Southern California Pregnancy
    and Infant Loss Center
c/o Marie Teague
5505 E. Carson Street, Suite 215
Lakewood, CA 90713
(213) 425-4889

Provides support, resources, information, and education on miscarriage, stillbirth, and infant death. Makes referrals to "Hoping and Sharing," as well as other parent support groups. Offers a monthly newsletter, lending library, and subsequent pregnancy support.

MOTHERING ORGANIZATIONS AND PUBLICATIONS

The Compleat Mother
P.O. Box 399
Mildmay, Ontario, CANADA NOG 2J0
(519) 367-2394

Provides quarterly magazine about pregnancy, birth, and breastfeeding. $10/year.

The Doula
P.O. Box 71
Santa Cruz, CA 95063–0071
(408) 423–5056

Provides women and their families with support, inspiration, and resources to foster an emotionally satisfying pregnancy, birth, and mothering experience.

FEMALE (Formerly Employed Mothers at Loose Ends)
Joanne Brundage
P.O. Box 31
Elmhurst, IL 60126
(312) 279–8862

Provides support through publications.

FOCUS
Nancy S. Inui
509 Tenth Avenue E.
Seattle, WA 98102
(206) 329–7918

Provides information on work-schedule options such as part-time, job sharing, flextime, temporary, and free-lance work; addresses work/family issues.

Healthy Mothers, Healthy Babies
Lori Cooper, Executive Director
409 Twelfth Street S.W.
Washington, DC 20024–2188
(202) 863–2458

Provides coalition that coordinates national activities of member and state groups to promote quality health care and education for mothers and children. Publications in English and Spanish.

Mothering Magazine
P.O. Box 1690
Albuquerque, NM 87504
(505) 984-8116

Provides magazine that celebrates the experience of mothering and fathering, advocates the needs and rights of the child, empowers decision making that will embrace the needs of all family members, recognizes the parents as experts, and provides truly helpful information on which parents can base informed choices. 1 year (4 issues), $15; Canada, $18; overseas, $20.

Mothers at Home
Deanne Dixon, President
P.O. Box 2208
Merrifield, VA 22116
(703) 352–2292

Provides educational support and advocacy for mothers who are at home. Monthly magazine, *Welcome Home.*

Mothers' Center Development Project
Lorraine Slepian/Linda Landsman
129 Jackson Street
Hempstead, NY 11550
(800) 645–3828; (516) 486–6614 in New York State

Provides a community program where women meet to explore the experience of becoming and being mothers. Together with social work consultants, they design programs and services to meet the needs of women and their families. Contact them for location of sixty local groups, or how to start a center in your area.

Mothers' Home Business Network
Georganne Fiumara
P.O. Box 423
East Meadow, NY 11554
(516) 997–7394

Provides information for mothers who want to work at home. Publications, including newsletter, *Kids and Career—New Ideas and Options for Mothers,* $6 / year. Sample issue $1.

New Ways to Work
149 Ninth Street
San Francisco, CA 94103
(415) 552–1000

Provides clearinghouse for work-time alternatives, such as job sharing, permanent part-time, flextime, etc. Publications, including newsletter.

Pacific Postpartum Support Society
Christine Bender
#104–1416 Commercial Drive
Vancouver, British Columbia, CANADA V55 431
(604) 255–7999

Provides treatment program for mothers suffering postpartum depression and educational materials on PPD; including the handbook, *Post Partum Depression and Anxiety: A Self-Help Guide for Mothers*, for $7.95, plus $1.00 postage.

Sidetracked Home Executives, Inc.
DeeAnne Cloke
401 N.W. Overlook Drive
Vancouver, WA 98665
(206) 696–1716

Provides information on getting home and life organized: books, tapes, card file, newsletter.

Spiritual Mothering Journal
Rene Knightweiler
P.O. Box 213
Lyle, WA 98635
(509) 395–2288

Quarterly publication dedicated to the raising up of peaceful humanity.

Woman's Workshop
Christine Donovan and Deborah Dawson
P.O. Box 843
Coronado, CA 92118

Newsletter to help at-home mothers explore outside interests and plan for life after motherhood. $16 / 4 issues.

WOTO—Women on Their Own
Maxine Karelitz
P.O. Box O, Department W
Malaga, NJ 08328
(609) 728–4071

Provides advocacy, networking, loans, workshops, newsletter for women raising children on their own (divorced, separated, widowed, single).

OTHER PUBLICATIONS, VIDEOS, CASSETTES, AND SUPPLIES

Birth and Life Bookstore, Inc.
Lynn Moen
P.O. Box 70625
Seattle, WA 98107
(206) 789–4444

Sells full range of mail-order birth, child-care, and health books.

Birth Journal
Blackwell Scientific Publications
Three Cambridge Center
Suite 208
Cambridge, MA 02142

Provides quarterly journal about birth issues for nurses, consumers, midwives, childbirth educators, and physicians. $20/year, single issues $5.

The Birth Gazette
Ina May Gaskin
42, The Farm
Summertown, TN 38483
(615) 964–2519

Quarterly magazine for midwives, physicians, childbirth educators, parents, breastfeeding counselors, and health planners and legislators.

Childbirth Alternatives Quarterly
327 Glenmount Drive
Solana Beach, CA 92075
(619) 481–7065

Newsletter about alternative birth and maternal/child issues. $20/ year. Also slides, books, postcards, and art prints.

Childbirth Graphics
Jamie Bolane, President
P.O. Box 20540
Rochester, NY 14602–0540
(716) 272–0300 FAX (716) 272–0716

Catalog sales for childbirth education materials. Books, posters, pamphlets, cassettes, and videos.

Educational Graphic Aids
7762 Brentwood Court
Arvada, CO 80005
(303) 424–9221

Sells mail-order books, publications, films, slides, and videocassettes.

Maternity Center Association/Publications
Elizabeth Haak
48 E. Ninety-second Street
New York, NY 10128
(212) 369–7300

Provides free catalog of publications available. MCA sells books; pamphlets; charts; slides; videotapes for prospective parents and health-care professionals, parent educators, and others interested in improving maternal, infant, and family health.

Michael Anderson
402 San Francisco Boulevard
San Anselmo, CA 94960
(415) 454–8099

Sells video (or 16 mm film), *Midwife*.

Midwifery Today
Box 2672
Eugene, OR 97402

Publishes fifty-two-page magazine quarterly, $20/year. For and by birth practitioners, childbirth educators, midwives, mothers, doctors, and nurses. Includes twenty regular features.

Minot Childbirth Information Project
Jody Mclaughlin
Box 3154
Minot, ND 58702
(701) 852–2822

Provides information on pregnancy, birth, and infant care especially nutrition, vertical/active birth, cesarean prevention, breastfeeding.

M.O.M. Magazine (Mothers and Others for Midwives)
Anne Cleary Sommers
P.O. Box 3164
Huntington Beach, CA 92647
(714) 893–4687

Provides magazine, as well as alternative birth referrals.

Nicholas J. Kaufman Productions
14 Clyde Street
Newtonville, MA 02160
(617) 964–4466

Sells video, *Once a Cesarean: Vaginal Birth after Cesarean*. This
shows a VBAC with supportive people.

Pennypress, Inc.
Penny Simkin
1100 Twenty-third Avenue E.
Seattle, WA 98112

Publishes and sells mail-order material on childbearing and parenting,
including a birth plan.

People's Productions
2115 Pearl Street
Boulder, CO 80302
(303) 449–6086

Sells video, *Special Delivery*. This presents options of hospital birth,
free-standing birth center, and home birth.

Perinatal Loss
Kay Mulligan, Managing Editor
5275 F Street
Sacramento, CA 95819
(916) 733–1750

Publishes nonaffiliated, nonprofit newsletter designed for those dedicated to improving the health care of the pregnant woman, fetus, and
newborn. Subscription $17.50/year.

Spirit-Led Childbirth
Kathy Arns
6413 N. Lunar Court
Parker, CO 80431
(303) 226–5079

Provides midwifery and parenting supplies, childbirth education
supplies, and free catalog.

WishGarden Herbs
Catherine Hunziker
Box 1304
Boulder, CO 80306
(303) 665–9508

Provides quality herbal preparations for childbearing and general health; free catalog; regular field trips offered to Rocky Mountains and Southwestern desert.

PREMATURE BIRTH

Children in Hospitals, Inc.
31 Wilshire Park
Needham, MA 02192

Provides information about the need for ample contact between children and parents when either is hospitalized. Encourages hospitals to adopt flexible visiting and living-in policies. Publications, including *The Consumer Directory of Massachusetts Hospital Policies*.

RESEARCH SERVICE

The Health Resource
Janice R. Guthrie
209 Katherine Drive
Conway, AR 72032

Provides customized, thorough information on your medical problem, including reasons for and side effects from cesareans, with reports averaging 40–100 pages. Request copy of complimentary newsletter.

SIDS (SUDDEN INFANT DEATH SYNDROME)

Counseling and Research Center for Sudden Infant Death
Kris Polzer, R.N.
9000 W. Wisconsin Avenue
P.O. Box 1997
Milwaukee, WI 53226
(414) 266–2SID (2734)

Provides counseling and support for families that have experienced a sudden unexpected infant death. Publications.

Illowa Guild for Infant Survival
Melanie Pangbuin
P.O. Box 3586
Davenport, IA 52808
(319) 322–4870

Raises funds for research toward the prevention of SIDS. Offers support to the families of SIDS victims, educates the public, and supports families using in-home monitors.

National Sudden Infant Death Syndrome Clearinghouse
8201 Greensboro Drive, Suite 600
McLean, VA 22102
(703) 821–8955

Provides publications about SIDS, apnea, apnea monitoring, grief/
bereavement, current research. Makes referrals to national and local
parent support organizations.

National Sudden Infant Death Syndrome Foundation
Mitchell Stoller
National SIDS Foundation
8200 Professional Place
Suite 104
Landover, MD 20785
(301) 459–3388

Provides peer counseling for SIDS families; education for SIDS
families, general public, related professionals; promotion of research
on SIDS and related issues.

TWINS, TRIPLETS, AND QUADS

Center for Study of Multiple Births
Linda Neglia
333 E. Superior Street, Suite 476
Chicago, IL 60611
(312) 266–9093

Provides information for parents of twins, triplets, and quadruplets.
Publications, including mail-order books.

Double Talk
Mary Hurlburt
P.O. Box 412
Amelia, OH 45102
(513) 753–7117

Provides resource center for parents of twins, triplets, or more.
Newsletter.

National Organization of Mothers
   of Twins Clubs, Inc.
Lois Gallmeyer, Executive Secretary
12404 Princess Jeanne N.E.
Albuquerque, NM 87112–0955

Offers opportunity for mothers of multiples to share information, concerns, and advice. Information sheets, quarterly newspapers, chapter development kit.

Parents of Multiple Births Association
   of Canada, Inc.
Sherly McInnes
P.O. Box 2200
Lethbridge, Alberta, CANADA T1J 4K9
(403) 328–9165

Provides referral to local clubs, newsletter, mail-order literature service, research.

The Triplet Connection
Janet Bleyl, President
8900 Thornton Road, #25
P.O. Box 99571
Stockton, CA 95209
(209) 474–0885

Provides information to families expecting triplets, or more, as well as encouragement, information, resources, and networking for parents of larger multiples. Newsletter.

Twinline, Services for Multiple Birth Families
Patricia M. Malmstrom, Executive Director
P.O. Box 10066
Berkeley, CA 94709
(415) 644–0861

Provides services, publications, resource referral, and advocacy for families with twins, triplets, quadruplets, and quintuplets. Hot line: (415) 644–0863, Monday-Friday 10 A.M.–4 P.M. PST.

Twins Magazine
Barbara C. Unell, Editor
P.O. Box 12045
Overland Park, KS 66212
(913) 722–1090

Bimonthly, national magazine offers a wide variety of viewpoints on twins, triplets, and more with research-based child development and family-living guidance written by health-care authorities, as well as multiples and parents themselves. $21/year.

UNDERWATER BIRTH

Point of View Productions
2477 Folsom Street
San Francisco, CA 94110
(415) 821–0435

Rents and sells video, *Water Baby: Experiences of Water Birth,* which was filmed in a birth center with Dr. Michel Odent.

Underwater Birth Exchange
Nancy Taylor
P.O. Box 5152
Gainesville, FL 32602–5152
(904) 373–3824

Provides underwater birth information, including resource packet, slide set, VHS video.

▪ APPENDIX E ▪

BIBLIOGRAPHIC REFERENCES

(By Chapter)

Introduction to the Revised Edition

Areskog, B. and others. "Experience of Delivery in Women with and without Antenatal Fear of Childbirth," *Gynecological and Obstetrical Investigations* 16:1, 1983

Freudenheim, Milt. "Health Insurers Rebound as Rates Increase." *The New York Times*, March 6, 1989

Hartford, Robert B. "The Ease of the Elusive Infant Mortality Rate," *Population Today*, May 1984

Kramon, Glenn. Employees Paying Ever-Bigger Share of Medical Costs." *The New York Times*, November 22, 1988

Lumley, Judith. "Assessing Satisfaction with Childbirth," *Birth* 12:3, Fall 1985

Malone, Theresa. "American and Dutch Women Differ on Expectation of Pain During Childbirth," *The American College of Obstetricians and Gynecologists News Release*, May 24, 1988

Melzack, Ronald. "The Myth of Painless Childbirth," *Pain*, 19, 1984

National Center for Health Statistics. "Advance Report of Final Natality Statistics, 1987," *Monthly Vital Statistics Report* 38:3 Supplement, June 29, 1989

Oakley, Ann. "Doctors, Maternity Patients and Social Scientists," *Birth* 12:3, Fall 1985

Rhundle, Rhonda L. "Insurers Step Up Efforts to Reduce Use of Free-Choice Health Plans." *The Wall Street Journal*, May 11, 1988

Rooks, Judith P., and others. "Outcomes of Care in Birth Centers. The National Birth Center Study." *The New England Journal of Medicine*, 321:26 (December 28, 1989)

Sargent, Carolyn, and Nancy Stark. "Surgical Birth: Interpretations of Cesarean Delivery Among Private Hospital Patients and Nursing Staff," *Social Science Medicine* 25:12, 1987

Senden, I.P.M., and others. "Labor Pain: A Comparison of Parturients in a Dutch and an American Teaching Hospital," *Obstetrics and Gynecology* 71, April 1988.

"Seventy Percent Would Consider Having a Child Alone," *Glamour*, January 1986

Thomson, Molly, and James Hanley. "Factors Predisposing to Difficult

Labor in Primiparas," *American Journal of Obstetrics and Gynecology* 158:5, May 1988

I ▪ What Women Want

Anderson, Sandra F., R.N., M.S., and Leta J. Brown, R.N., C.C.E. "A Scientific Survey of Siblings at Birth," *Compulsory Hospitalization or Freedom of Choice in Childbirth?* Vol. 3, David Stewart, Ph.D., and Lee Stewart, C.C.E., eds., Marble Hill, Mo.: NAPSAC Reproductions, 1979

COMA, The Committee on Maternal Alternatives. *How Women Want to Have Their Babies*, Baltimore: self-published, 1980

Eisenstein, Mayer, M.D. "Homebirth and the Physician," *Safe Alternative in Childbirth*, David Stewart, Ph.D., and Lee Stewart, C.C.E., eds., Chapel Hill, N.C.: NAPSAC, 1976

Ericson, Avis J., Pharm.D., ed. *Medications Used During Labor and Birth*, Milwaukee: ICEA, 1977

Hathaway, Marjie and Jay, AAHCC, and Kids. *Children at Birth*, Sherman Oaks, Ca.: Academy Publications, 1978

Kennell, John, M.D. "Are We in the Midst of a Revolution?" *Am. J. Dis. Child*, Vol. 134, March 1980

Klaus, Marshall, M.D., et al. "Maternal Attachment," *The New England Journal of Medicine* 286:9:460–463, 1972

———, and John H. Kennell, M.D. *Parent-Infant Bonding*, St. Louis: C.V. Mosby, 1982

La Leche League, *The Womanly Art of Breast-feeding*, Franklin Park, Ill.: La Leche League International, 1987

Montagu, Ashley, Ph.D. *Touching*, New York and London: Columbia University Press, 1971

Newton, Niles, Ph.D. "Trebly Sensuous Woman," *Psychology Today*, July 1971

———, and Michael Newton, M.D. "Psychologic Aspects of Lactation," *The New England Journal of Medicine* 277:22:1179–1188, 1967

Phillips, Celeste R. Nagel, R.N., B.S.N., M.S. "Neonatal Heat Loss in Heated Cribs vs. Mothers' Arms," *JOGN Nursing*, Vol. 3, No. 6, Nov.–Dec. 1974

Pitt, Jane, M.D. Phone interview, November 14, 1979

Pittenger, James E., and Jane G. "The Perinatal Period: Breeding Ground for Marital and Parental Maladjustment," *Keeping Abreast Journal* 1:18–29, 1977

Reader questionnaire responses, 1984–1989

"Regionals Can Prolong Labor," *Medical World News*, October 15, 1971

Sander, Louis W., M.D., et. al. "Early Mother-Infant Interaction and 24-Hour Patterns of Activity and Sleep," *Journal of the American Academy of Child Psychiatry* 9:103–123, 1970

Shearer, Beth. "Forced Cesareans: The Case of the Disappearing Mother," *International Journal of Childbirth Education*, February, 1989

Sugarman, Muriel, M.D. "Review of Maternal-Infant Attachment Literature," presented at ICEA Eastern-Southeastern Regional Conference, 1977

Tanzer, Deborah, Ph.D. "Natural Childbirth: Pain or Peak Experience?" *Psychology Today,* October 1968

Thoman, Mark, M.D. Personal interviews, July and November 1979

Wernick, Robert, and the Editors of Time-Life Books. *The Family,* New York: Time-Life Books, 1974

2 ▪ The Pleasure Principle

Baldwin, Rahima. "The New Homebirth," *Informed Homebirth Newsletter,* September 1978

Bing, Elisabeth, and Libby Colman. *Making Love During Pregnancy,* New York: Bantam, 1977

Birch, Elizabeth R. "The Experience of Touch Received During Labor," *Journal of Nurse Midwifery* 31:6, November/December 1986

Brewin, C., and C. Bradley. "Perceived Control and the Experience of Childbirth," *British Journal of Clinical Psychology* 21:4, November, 1982

Chute, Owen E. "Expectation and Experience in Alternative and Conventional Birth," *Journal of Obstetrical, Gynecological, and Neonatal Nursing,* January/February 1985

Cogan, Rosemary, Ph.D., and Evelyn P. Edmunds. "The Unkindest Cut?" *Contemporary Ob/Gyn,* April 1977

Hall, Elizabeth. "Mining New Gold for Old Research," *Psychology Today,* February 1986

Haney, Daniel Q. "Runner's High Has Chemical Basis, Research Shows," *Boulder Daily Camera,* September 3, 1981

Hartman, Rhondda Evans, R.N., M.A. Interview, January 1983

Hodnett, Ellen D., and Daryl A. Simmons-Tropea. "The Labour Agentry Scale: Psychometric Properties of an Instrument Measuring Control during Childbirth," *Research in Nursing and Health* 10, 1987

Huston, Barbara. "Seattle Obstetrician Advocates Return to Nature's Painkiller," *Seattle Post-Intelligencer,* February 8, 1981

Masters, William, M.D. and Virginia Johnson, D.Sc. *Human Sexual Response,* Boston: Little, Brown, 1966

———, and Virginia Johnson-Masters, D.Sc. Interview, July 1979

Newton, Niles, Ph.D. "Psychologic Factors in Birth and Breastfeeding," LLLI Northwest Area Conference, Seattle, Wash., September 28, 1979

———. *Maternal Emotions,* New York: Paul B. Hoeber, Inc., 1955

———. "Trebly Sensuous Woman," *Psychology Today,* July 1971

———. "Interrelationships between Sexual Responsiveness, Birth, and Breastfeeding," *Contemporary Sexual Behavior, Critical Issues For the 1970s,* J. Zubin and John Money, eds., Baltimore: Johns Hopkins University Press, 1973

———. "The Role of the Oxytocin Reflexes in the Three Interpersonal Reproductive Acts: Coitus, Birth, and Breastfeeding," a paper given at Serono Symposia, Siena, Italy, December 2, 3, and 4, 1976

O'Connell, M.L. "Locus of Control Specific to Pregnancy," *Journal of Obstetrics and Gynecological Nursing* 12:3, May/June 1983

Pert, Agu. "The Body's Own Tranquilizers," *Psychology Today*, September 1981

Sherfey, Mary Jane, M.D. *The Nature and Evolution of Female Sexuality*, New York: Random House, Vintage Books, 1973

Tanzer, Deborah, Ph.D. "Natural Childbirth: Pain or Peak Experience?" *Psychology Today*, October 1968

Zweig, S., and others. "Patient Satisfaction with Obstetric Care," *Journal of Family Practice* 23:2, August 1986

3 ▪ If You Don't Know Your Options, You Don't Have Any

Ashford, Janet Isaacs, ed. "Midwifery Task Force in Ontario," *Childbirth Alternatives Quarterly* 8:3:14, Spring, 1987

Bajo, Kathleen, director, Ross Marketing Associates. Interview, December, 1988

Ballard, Roberta, M.D., F.A.A.P., et al. "Safety of a Hospital-Based Alternative Birth Center (ABC)," American Academy of Pediatrics Plenary Session, undated

Barber, Rebecca A., C.N.M. "Renaissance in Birthing: The American Nurse-Midwife," *Journal of the Colorado Institute of Transpersonal Psychology*, Summer, 1984

Bennetts, Anita B., C.N.M., Ph.D., and Ruth Watson Lubic, C.N.M., Ed. D. "The Free-Standing Birth Centre," *Lancet* 1:8268:378–380, February 13, 1982

Berman, Salee, C.N.M. and Berman, Victor, M.D. *The Birth Center*, New York: Prentice Hall, 1986

Berman, Vic, M.D. Letter with NACHIS statistics, December 3, 1981, and update on first 1,000 births, September 25, 1982

"Birthing: Home's as Good as the Hospital" (Missouri Department of Health Study), *Hippocrates*, January/February, 1988

Bond, Enriqueta, Ph.D., research scientist, National Academy of Science. Phone interviews, July and August 1982

Branca, Paul, M.D. "Forum of Health Policy Issues of the Freestanding Birth Center; If It Is Safe, What Makes It Safe?" *NACC News* 2:1:3, Spring, 1984

Burnett, Claude A. III, M.D., M.P.H., et al. "Home Delivery and Neonatal Mortality in North Carolina," *JAMA* 244:24:2741–2745, December 19, 1980

Campbell, Rona, speaker. Homebirth Conference, London, October, 1987
———, and Alison Macfarlane. "Place of Delivery: A Review," *British Journal of Obstetrics and Gynaecology* 93:675–683, July, 1986
———, and Alison Macfarlane. *Where to Be Born*, Oxford: National Perinatal Epidemiology Unit, Radcliffe Infirmary, 1987

Clark, Linda, C.N.M., in group practice with Richard B. Stewart, M.D. Phone interview, October 6, 1982

COMA (The Committee on Maternal Alternatives). *How Women Want to Have Their Babies*, Baltimore: self-published, 1980

Cranch, Gene, C.N.M., Ph.D., Maternity Center Association, NYC. Phone interview, January 1982

Denver Birth Center. Open house, November 1977

Editors of Heron House. *The Odds*, New York: G.P. Putnam's Sons, 1980

Ernst, Eunice K.M. "Outcomes of 20,000 Women Who Sought Freestanding Birth Center Care: A National Collaborative Study," *Eighth Birth Conference*, San Francisco, March, 1989

Eshelman, Michael, M.D. Personal Interview, January 1980

Feldman, Elizabeth, M.D., and Marsha Hurst, Ph.D. "Outcome and Procedures in Low Risk Birth: A Comparison of Hospital and Birth Center Settings," *Birth* 14:1:18–24, March, 1987

Feldman, Silvia, Ph.D. *Choices in Childbirth*, New York: Bantam, 1980

Ferguson, Patty, administrative assistant, Denver Birth Center. Interview, December, 1988

Gaskin, Ina May. "The Farm: A Living Example of the Five Standards," *The Five Standards for Safe Childbearing*. David Stewart, Ph.D., ed., Marble Hill, Mo: NAPSAC International, 1981

————speaker. Homebirth Conference, London, October, 1987

————"International Conferences," *Birth Gazette* 4:2:37–38, Winter, 1988

Goodlin, Robert C. "Low Risk Obstetric Care for Low Risk Mothers," *Lancet* I (8176):1017–1019, May 10, 1980

Harness, Barbara, director, Section for Maternal and Child Health, American Hospital Association. Interview, December, 1988

Health Science Center, ob/gyn department, Denver. Phone interview, November 1981

Hinds, M. Ward, M.D., M.P.H., et al. "Neonatal Outcome in Planned v. Unplanned Out-of-Hospital Births in Kentucky," *JAMA* 253:11: 1578–1582, March 15, 1985

Honton, Margaret, ed. "Contemporary Obstetric Design," *Perspectives in Perinatal and Pediatric Design*, Columbus, Ohio: Ross Planning Associates, Ross Laboratories, 1988

Hope, Jenny. "No Place Like Home," London *Daily Mail*, March 29, 1989

Hosford, Betty, R.N., C.N.M., and Ruth Watson Lubic, C.N.M, Ed. D. "Childbearing and Maternity Centers—Alternatives to Homebirth and Hospital," *Safe Alternatives in Childbirth*, David Stewart, Ph.D. and Lee Stewart, C.C.E., eds., Chapel Hill, N.C.: NAPSAC, 1976

Huey, Kenneth, C.E.O., Longmont United Hospital. Interview, May, 1989

Ivory, Loretta, C.N.M., Director, Denver Birth Center. Personal interviews, November 6, 1981, March, 1989

Kerner, John, M.D., F.A.C.O.G., and Carolyn Bailey Ferris, R.N. "An Alternative Birth Center in a Community Teaching Hospital," *Obstetrics and Gynecology* 51:3:371–373, March 1978

Kitzinger, Shelia. "Why Home Birth," London Homebirth Conference, October, 1987

Klass, Kay, B.S.N., and Kay Capps, R.N. "Nine Years' Experience with Family-Centered Maternity Care in a Community Hospital," *Birth* 7:3:175–180, Fall 1980

Korte, Diana. "Birth Once Again a Family Affair," Boulder *Daily Camera, Focus*, November 26, 1978

Levy, Barry S., M.P.H., et al. "Reducing Neonatal Mortality Rate With Nurse-Midwives," *American Journal of Obstetrics and Gynecology* 109:1:50–58, January 1, 1971

Lubic, Ruth Watson, C.N.M., Ed.D. "Midwifery: An Extended Role in Nursing Practice," Maternity Center Association, undated

————, and Eunice K.M. Ernst, C.N.M. "The Childbearing Center: An Alternative to Conventional Care," *Nursing Outlook* 26:12:754–760, December 1978

Lumley, Judith, M.A., M.B., B.S., Ph.D., and Brian A. Davey, B.S., M.S., Ph.D. "Do Hospitals with Family-centered Maternity Care Policies Have Lower Intervention Rates?" *Birth* 14:3:132–134, September, 1987

Mehl, Lewis E., M.D., Ph.D. "Home Delivery Research Today: A Review," presented at the annual meeting of the American Foundation for Maternal and Infant Health, New York City, November 15, 1976

Moran, Marilyn. *Birth and the Dialogue of Love,* Leawood, Kans.: New Nativity Press, 1981

Nelson, Linda P., M.Ed.N., B.Sc., S.C.M. (London). "Results of the First 124 Deliveries in the Birth Room at Roosevelt Hospital in New York City," *Birth* 6:2:97–102, Summer 1979

"Nurse-Midwives See Growing Role in U.S. Care System," *American Medical News,* February 26, 1982

Ozerkis, Robin, C.N.M., Natural Childbirth Institute. Interview, March, 1989

Palmarini, Terra, midwife, coauthor *Pregnant Feelings.* Interview, March, 1989

Perez, Polly, R.N., B.S.N. "Hospital Birth Centers versus Single Room Labor-Delivery Units," Eighth Birth Conference, San Francisco, March, 1989

"Perinatal Care: Organization and Outcome," *The Lancet,* April 5, 1986

Petty, Roy. *Home Birth,* Chicago and New York: Domus Books, 1979

Polomeno, Viola. "Birthing Rooms in Canada," *International Journal of Childbirth Education,* May 1986

Poppema, Suzanne, M.D. Interview, January 1980

Porter, Gail. "Research Needs Described for Evaluating Birth Settings," summary of *Research Issues in the Assessment of Birth Settings,* communication dated January 5, 1983

Schlinger, Hilary, midwife. Personal communication, July, 1984

Schmidt, Judith, R.N., M.S. "The First Year of Stanford University's Family Birth Room," *Birth* 7:3:169–174, Fall 1980

Scupholme, A., et al. "A Birth Center Affiliated with a Tertiary Care Center," *Obstet Gynecol* 67:4:598, April, 1986, abstracted in *Birth* 13:4:276, December, 1986

Shearer, Madeleine H. "Editor's Reply," *Birth* 6:3:205, Fall 1979

Sheehy, Gail. *Passages,* New York: E.P. Dutton, 1976

Stewart, David, Ph.D. "The Philosophy of Proponents of Home Birth," paper given at District IV Conference, The Nurses Association and Junior Fellow Division of ACOG, November 9, 1977

————. "Skillful Midwifery: The Highest and Safest Standard," *The Five Standards for Safe Childbearing,* David Stewart, Ph.D., ed. Marble Hill, Mo.: NAPSAC International, 1981

————, and Lee Stewart, C.C.E. Phone interviews, September 23, 1982, December 5, 1988

Stewart, Richard B., M.D., F.A.C.O.G., in group practice with four midwives. Phone interview, October 8, 1982

————, and Linda Clark, C.N.M., M.N. "Nurse-Midwifery Practice in an In-Hospital Birthing Center: 2050 Births," *Journal of Nurse-Midwifery* 27:3:21–26, May/June 1982

————, Asher Galloway, M.D., and Linda Goodman, C.N.M., "An In-Hospital Birthing Room: One Year's Experience," *Compulsory Hospitalization or Freedom of Choice in Childbirth,* Vol. 1, David Stewart, Ph.D., and Lee Stewart C.C.E., eds., Marble Hill, Mo.: NAPSAC Reproductions, 1979

Strickhouser, Margaret, C.N.M., Decator/Douglasville Nurse Midwifery Service. Phone interview, April, 1989

Sullivan, Deborah A., Ph.D., and Ruth Beeman, R.N., C.N.M., M.P.H. "Four Years' Experience with Home Birth by Licensed Midwives in Arizona," *American Journal of Public Health* 73:6:641–645, June, 1983

Sumner, Philip E., M.D., F.A.C.O.G., and Celeste R. Phillips, R.N., M.S. *Birthing Rooms Concept and Reality,* St. Louis, Toronto, and London: C.V. Mosby, 1981

Testimony of American College of Nurse-Midwives before the Subcommittee on Oversight and Investigation of the House Interstate and Foreign Commerce Committee," Record of Testimony, December 18, 1980

Tew, Marjorie. "Place of Birth and Perinatal Mortality," *Journal of the Royal College of General Practitioners* 35:390–394, August, 1985

————. "Do Obstetric Intranatal Interventions Make Birth Safer?" *British Journal of Obstetrics and Gynaecology* 93:659–674, July, 1986

————, speaker. Homebirth Conference, London, October, 1987

Torrington, Judy L., R.N., and James R. Dingfelder, M.D. "Recent Surveys of Parental Attitudes and Preferences in Childbirth," paper presented at NAPSAC conference, Atlanta, May 1978

Wagner, Marsden, M.D., speaker. Homebirth Conference, London, October, 1987

Ward, Charlotte and Fred. *The Home Birth Book,* Garden City, N.Y.: Doubleday, Dolphin Books, 1977

Wilf, Ruth, C.N.M., Ph.D. "Alternatives: Booth Maternity Center in Philadelphia," Booth Maternity Center, March 1977

————. "Fulfilling the Needs of Families in a Hospital Setting: Can It Be Done?" *21st Century Obstetrics Now!* Vol. 1, David Stewart, Ph.D., and Lee Stewart, C.C.E., eds., Chapel Hill, N.C.: NAPSAC, Inc., 1977

————, C.N.M., Ph.D. Interview, March, 1989

Wilner, Susan, M.S., M.P.H., et al. "Comparison of the Quality of Maternity Care Between a Health Maintenance Organization and Fee-for-Service Practices," *New England Journal of Medicine* 304:13:784–787, March 26, 1981

World Health Organization, "Appropriate Technology for Birth," *Lancet,* August 24, 1985, pp. 436–437

Youcha, Geraldine, and Sharon Youcha. "Where Should Baby Be Born? A Guide to Today's Options in Childbirth," *Woman's Day,* April 7, 1981

4 • Understanding Doctors

AMA/Specialty Society Medical Liability Project. "Medical Groups Offer Proposal to Resolve Malpractice Crisis," *American Medical Association,* January 13, 1988

"Bendectin Production Ends," *Science News* 123:25, June 18, 1983

Bogdanich, Walt, and others. "Hospitals That Need Patients Pay Bounties for Doctors' Referrals," *The Wall Street Journal,* February 27, 1989

Boone, Richard W., J.D., Michael D. Roth, J.D., and John W. Scanlon, M.D. "What Every Perinatologist Should Know about Medicolegal Problems," *Contemporary Ob/Gyn,* Vol. 18, October 1981

Brown, Stephen W., Ph.D. "How Physicians See Themselves," *Medical Marketing & Media* 17:2, February 1982

Califano, Joseph A., Jr. "Billions Blown on Health," *The New York Times,* April 12, 1989

Center for Health Policy Research. "Projected Active U.S. Physician Population, 1986–2010," *American Medical Association Demographic Model of the Physician Population,* 1988

Cousins, Norman. "Internship: Preparation or Hazing?" *JAMA* 245:4, January 23–30, 1981

———. "Malpractice Backlash," *Saturday Review,* May 1980

———. "The Malpractice Crisis—Winner: The Lawyer, Loser: The Patient," *The Female Patient* 6:8, August 1981

Davis-Floyd, Robbie E. "Obstetric Training as a Rite of Passage," *Medical Anthropology Quarterly* 1:3, September 1987

"Doctors' Earnings: On the Rise Again/New Continuing Survey Figures," *Medical Economics,* September 1987

Donnelly, Julie C., Ed.D. "Management Report: Understanding Physicians: Stresses of Internship Can Have Adverse Effects on Doctors," *Hospital Management Quarterly,* Fall 1981/Winter 1982

Eichna, Ludwig W., M.D. "Medical-School Education, 1975–1979," Special Article, *The New England Journal of Medicine* 303:31, September 25, 1980

Emerson, Ralph S., M.D. "Trends in Professional Liability," *Bulletin of the American College of Surgeons,* March 1981

Eshelman, Michael, M.D. Interview, January 1980

"Excess Marks the Spot—The FDA Blows the Whistle on Abuses in New-Drug Ads," *Time,* September 27, 1982

French, Howard W. "In Overhaul of Hospital Rules, New York Slashes Interns' Hours," *The New York Times,* July 3, 1989

Freudenheim, Milt. "Doctors' Concerns: Fixing Prices and Price Fixing," *The New York Times,* December 18, 1988

Fuchs, Victor R., Ph.D. "Who Shall Live?" *Rochester Review,* Spring 1978

Glandon, Gerald L., and Roberta J. Shapiro, eds., Department of Economic Research. "Profile of Medical Practice—1981," Center for Health Research and Development, American Medical Association

"GMENAC Predicts Physician Surplus," *Health Resources Administration,* Department of Health and Human Services, November 1980

Goodman, Ellen. "Doctors Take the Rap for Public Uncertainties," *Boulder Daily Camera,* January 5, 1979

Harrison, Michelle, M.D. *A Woman in Residence*, New York: Random House, 1982

"Interview with Richard Selzer, M.D.," *East West Journal*, November 1980

Kirchner, Merian. "Doctor Surplus—What 1990 Will Look Like," *Medical Economics*, September 29, 1980

———. "Non-Surgical Practice: What's The Key to Higher Earnings," *Medical Economics*, February 16, 1981

Kramon, Glenn. "Employees Paying Ever-Bigger Share of Medical Costs," *The New York Times*, November 22, 1988

Lurie, Nicole, and others. "How Do House Officers Spend Their Nights?" *The New England Journal of Medicine* 320:25 June 22, 1989

Malcolm, Andrew H. "Fear of Malpractice Suits Leading Some Doctors to Quit Obstetrics," *The New York Times*, February 12, 1985

Mawardi, Betty Hosmer, Ph.D. "Satisfactions, Dissatisfactions, and Causes of Stress in Medical Practice," *JAMA* 241:14, April 6, 1979

McCall, T.B. "No Turning Back: A Blueprint for Residency Reform." *Journal of the American Medical Association* 261, 1989

"M.D.'s Seek to Stifle Competition," *ABCC News* (Alternative Birth Crisis Coalition), Vol. 1, November 1981

"Medicine: Business or Charity? A Los Angeles M.D. Stirs Debate," *American Medical News*, October 5, 1979

Obstetrician-gynecologist, anonymous. Interview, January 1983

Pagliuso, James J., J.D. "Situations to Avoid If You Don't Want to Be Sued," *Contemporary Ob/Gyn*, March 1982

"Phone Calls That Are Shortening My Career," *Medical Economics*, February 16, 1981

"Physicians Miseducated, Hearing Told," *The U.S. Journal*, January 1980

"Professional Liability and its Effects: Report of a 1987 Survey of ACOG's Membership," *American College of Obstetricians and Gynecologists*, March 1988

Raffenach, Glenn. "Medical Tests Go under the Microscope," *The Wall Street Journal*, February 7, 1989

Rhundle, Rhonda L. "Insurers Step up Efforts to Reduce Use of Free-Choice Health Plans," *The Wall Street Journal*, May 11, 1988

Savage, Wendy D., and Pat Tate. "Medical Students' Attitudes Towards Women: A Sex-Linked Variable?" *Medical Education* 17:15, 1983

Schwartz, William B., M.D., Joseph P. Newhouse, Ph.D., Bruce W. Bennett, Ph.D., and Albert P. Williams, Ph.D. "The Changing Geographic Distribution of Board-Certified Physicians," *New England Journal of Medicine*, October 30, 1980

Scully, Diana. *Men Who Control Women's Health: The Miseducation of Obstetricians-Gynecologists*, Boston: Houghton-Mifflin, 1980

Shearer, Madeleine H. "The Effects of Regionalization of Perinatal Care on Hospital Services for Normal Childbirth," *Birth* 4:4, Winter 1977

Shell, Ellen R. "Doctors and Drugs," *Atlantic*, August 1988

Siu, Albert, and others. "Use of the Hospital in a Randomized Trial of Prepaid Care," *JAMA* 259:9, March 4, 1988

"This Is What You Thought About Doctors' Attitudes," *Glamour*, October 1981

"Why More Doctors Won't Mean Lower Bills," *Business Week*, May 11, 1981

Wolff, Sidney. "If You Can't Find the Patients, You Can Always Find the Doctors: Hospitals Are Filling Beds by Buying Physicians," *The Washington Post,* October 26, 1987

5 ▪ Finding Dr. Right

"An Overview of Ultrasound: Theory, Measurement, Medical Applications, and Biological Effects," *U.S. Department of Health and Human Services,* July 1982

Bakketeig, L.S., and others. "Randomised Controlled Trial of Ultrasonographic Screening in Pregnancy," *Lancet* 2, July 28, 1984

Barber, Hugh R.K., M.D. "High-Risk Pregnancy—Part 1," *The Female Patient* 7:7, July 1982

Bernaschek, G., and others. "Vaginal Sonography Versus Serum Human Chorionic Gonadotropin in Early Detection of Pregnancy," *American Journal of Obstetrics and Gynecology* 158:1, March 1988

Bloom, Stephen G. "As for Male Gynecologists . . ." *Chicago Tribune,* November 5, 1987

Brien, Monica, and others. "How Lamaze-Prepared Expectant Parents Select Obstetricians," *Research in Nursing and Health* 6, 1983

Challacombe, Christine B. "Do Women Patients Need Women Doctors?" *The Practioner* 227, May 1983

Check, William A. "Question of Risk Still Hovers Over Routine Prenatal Use of Ultrasound," *JAMA* 247:16, April 23–30 1982

Chitkara, U., and others. "Twin Pregnancy: Routine Use of Ultrasound Examinations in the Prenatal Diagnosis of Intrauterine Growth Retardation and Discordant Growth." *American Journal of Perinatology* 2:1, January 1985

Cogan, Donna R. "Women in Medicine: Australia, New Zealand, Canada, and United States," *Women and Health* 7:1, Spring 1982

De Muylder, X., and others. "Obstetrical Profile of Twin Pregnancies: A Retrospective Review of Eleven Years (1969–1979) at Hospital Notre-Dame, Montreal Canada," *Acta Geneticae Medicae et Gemellologiae (Roma)* 31:3–4, 1982

"Doctors, Lawyers, Birth Rooms, Courts," *NAPSAC News* 7:1, Spring 1982

Feletti, G., and others. "Patient Satisfaction with Primary-Care Consultations," *Journal of Behavioral Medicine* 9:4, August 1986

Field, Tiffany, and others. "Effects of Ultrasound Feedback on Pregnancy Anxiety, Fetal Activity, and Neonate Outcome," *Obstetrics and Gynecology* 66:4, October 1985

Freeman, Roger K., M.D., and Susan Pescar. *Safe Delivery: Protecting Your Baby During Pregnancy,* New York: Facts on File, 1982

Haire, Doris. "Fetal Effects of Ultrasound: A Growing Controversy," *Journal of Nurse-Midwifery* 29:4, July/August 1984

Irwin, Susan, and Brigitte Jordan. "Knowledge, Practice and Power: Court-Ordered Cesarean Sections," *Medical Anthropology Quarterly* 1:3, September 1987

Johnson, C.G., and others. "Does Physician Uncertainty Affect Patient Satisfaction?" *Journal of General Internal Medicine* 3:2, March/April 1988

Jordon, Brigitte, and Susan Irwin. "The Ultimate Failure: Court-Ordered Cesarean Sections," *New Approaches to Human Reproduction: Social and Ethical Decisions,* Linda Whiteford and Marilyn Poland, eds., Boulder, Colo.: Westview Press, 1988

Jurow, Ronna, and Richard H. Paul. "Cesarean Delivery for Fetal Distress without Maternal Consent," *Obstetrics and Gynecology* 63:4, April 1984

Kolder, Veronika E.B., and others. "Court-Ordered Obstetrical Interventions," *The New England Journal of Medicine* 316:19, May 7, 1987

Lazare, Aaron. "Shame and Humiliation in the Medical Encounter," *Archives of Internal Medicine* 147, September 1987

Lebrow, Morton. "Court Ordered Treatment Rarely Justified for Obstetrical Care," *American College of Obstetricians and Gynecologists News Release,* August 11, 1987

Li, T.C., and others. "Data Assessing the Usefulness of Screening Obstetrical Ultrasonography for Detecting Fetal and Placental Abnormalities in Uncomplicated Pregnancy: Effects of Screening a Low-Risk Population," *Medical Decision Making* 8:1, January/March 1988

Liebeskind, Doreen, and others. "Morphological Changes in the Surface Characteristics of Cultured Cells after Exposure to Diagnostic Ultrasound," *Radiology* 138:2, February 1981

McElhinney, Susan, J.D., and Stuart McElhinney. "The Legal Rights of Parents," *ABCC News* (Alternative Birth Crisis Coalition), undated

Nelson, Lawrence J., and Nancy Milliken. "Compelled Medical Treatment of Pregnant Women," *JAMA* 259:7, February 19, 1988

"New York Law Requires Disclosure Risks of OB Drugs," *NAPSAC News,* September 1979

Orleans, Miriam, and Albert D. Haverkamp. "Appropriate Technology in Perinatal Medicine," *WHO: Health for All 2000,* March 1, 1987

"Patient Choice: Maternal-Fetal Conflict," *American College of Obstetricians and Gynecologists,* March 3, 1987

Peterson, I. "Ultrasound Safety and Collapsing Bubbles," *Science News* 130, December 13, 1986

Shapiro, M.C., and others. "Information Control and the Exercise of Power in the Obstetrical Encounter," *Social Science Medicine* 17:3, 1983

Shepard, Mary Jo, and others. "An Evaluation of Two Equations for Predicting Fetal Weight by Ultrasound," *American Journal of Obstetrics and Gynecology* 142, January 1, 1982

Stark, C., and others. "Short and Long-Term Risks After Exposure of Diagnostic Ultrasound in Utero," *Obstetrics and Gynecology* 63:2, February 1984

Stewart, H.F., and M.E. Stratmeyer. "An Overview of Ultrasound: Theory, Measurement, Medical Applications, and Biological Effects," *Bureau of Radiological Health, Food and Drug Administration,* July 1982

Stewart, Nancy. "Women's Views of Ultrasonography in Obstetrics," *Birth* 13, December 1986

Thacker, Stephen B. "Quality of Controlled Clinical Trials. The Case of Imaging Ultrasound in Obstetrics: A Review," *British Journal of Obstetrics and Gynaecology* 92, May 1985

"The Pregnant Patient's Bill of Rights," *Journal of Nurse-Midwifery,* Vol. 20, No. 4, Winter 1975

Webster, M.A., and others. "Obstetric High Risk Screening and Prediction of Neonatal Morbidity," *Australian Journal of Obstetrics and Gynaecology* 28:1, February 1988

Yoder, Marilyn. "Finding Out Your Hospital Options," *Leader Line* (a La Leche League area newsletter), September 1980

Ziskin, M.C., and Diana Petitti. "Epidemiology of Human Exposure to Ultrasound: A Critical Review," *Ultrasound in Medicine and Biology* 14:2, 1988

Zweig, S., and others. "Patient Satisfaction with Obstetric Care," *Journal of Family Practice* 23:2, August 1986

6 ▪ Obstetricians' Beliefs about a "Safe Birth"

"ACOG Official: Home Delivery 'Maternal Trauma, Child Abuse,'" *Ob/Gyn. News,* October 1, 1977

Alderman, Mary M., ed. "Childbirth at Home? U.S. experts: Safety vs. Sentiment," *Patient Care,* November 15, 1977

Anderson, Sandra F., R.N., M.S. "Childbirth as a Pathological Process: An American Perspective," *The American Journal of Maternal Child Nursing,* July/August 1977

Ashford, Janet Isaacs. "Unjustified Empires, Marjorie Tew's Campaign for the Truth about Birth Safety," *Childbirth Alternatives Quarterly* 8:3:18–19, Summer, 1987

———. "The U.S. is Still Declining in World Infant Mortality Ranking," *Childbirth Alternatives Quarterly* 9:2:12, Winter, 1988

Aubry, Richard, M.D. "The American College of Obstetrician and Gynecologists (ACOG): Standards for Safe Childbearing," *21st Century Obstetrics Now!* Vol. 1, Lee Stewart, C.C.E., and David Stewart, Ph.D., eds., Chapel Hill, N.C.: NAPSAC, 1977

Beard, Richard. "Childbirth at Home? Mother's Wishes vs. Doctor's Duties," *Patient Care,* November 15, 1977

Campbell, Rona, and Alison Macfarlane. "Place of Delivery: A Review," *British Journal of Obstetrics and Gynaecology* 93:675–683, July, 1986

Cardwell, Jewell. "Doctor Decries Trend Toward At-Home Delivery of Babies," Boulder *Daily Camera,* August 26, 1982

Chalmers, Iain, and Martin Richards. "Intervention and Causal Inference in Obstetric Practice," *Benefits and Hazards of the New Obstetrics,* Tim Chard and Martin Richards, eds., London: William Heinemann Medical Books; Philadelphia: J.B. Lippincott, 1977

Chalmers, Iain, M.B., B.S., M.Sc., D.C.H. "Minimizing Harm and Maximizing Benefit during Innovation in Health Care: Controlled or Uncontrolled Experimentation?" *Birth* 13:3:155–164

Corea, Gena. *The Hidden Malpractice,* New York: Jove Publications, 1977

"Do Most Obstetricians Really Care About Family Centered Programs?" *NAPSAC News,* Vol. 3, No. 1, Winter 1978

Erickson, J. David, Ph.D., and Tor Bjerkedal, M.D. "Fetal and Infant Mortality in Norway and the United States," *Journal of the*

American Medical Association 247:7:987–1028, February 19, 1982

Haire, Doris, D.M.S. "Maternity Practices Around the World: How Do We Measure Up?" *Safe Alternatives in Childbirth*, David Stewart, Ph.D., and Lee Stewart, C.C.E., eds., Chapel Hill, N.C.: NAPSAC, 1976

Knox, G. Eric, M.D., et al. "Management of Prolonged Pregnancy: Results of a Prospective Randomized Trial," *American Journal of Obstetrics and Gynecology* 134:4:376–384, June 15, 1979

Lake, Alice. "Childbirth in America," *McCall's*, January 1976

Loudon, Irvine. "Medical History—Obstetric Care, Social Class, and Maternal Mortality," *British Medical Journal* 293:606–608, September 6, 1986

Maurer, Jeff, M.S., Mortality Statistics Branch, Division of Vital Statistics, National Center for Health Statistics, phone interview, October 23, 1989

McCormick, Marie C., M.D., Sc.D. "The Contribution of Low Birth Weight to Infant Mortality and Childhood Morbidity," *The New England Journal of Medicine* 312:2:82–89, January 10, 1985

McCoy, Jan. "County Officials Troubled by CU Hospital Limitations," Boulder *Daily Camera*, August 12, 1982

Miller, C. Arden, M.D. *Maternal Health and Infant Survival*, Washington, D.C.: National Center for Clinical Infant Programs, July, 1987

" 'Natural' Childbirth Decried; High Mortality Rates Cited," *Convention Reporter*, Vol. 11, No. 30, November 1981, reprinted in *NAPSAC News*, Vol. 7, No. 1, Spring 1982

Obstetrical Practices in the United States, U.S. Senate Subcommittee on Health, 95th Congress, 2nd Session, April 17, 1978

Paneth, Nigel, M.D., M.P.H., et al. "Newborn Intensive Care and Neonatal Mortality in Low-Birth-Weight Infants, *The New England Journal of Medicine* 307:3:149–155, July 15, 1982

Pearse, Warren, M.D. "Home Birth Crisis," *ACOG Newsletter*, July 1977

Placek, Paul, J., Ph.D., National Center for Health Statistics. Phone interview, April 3, 1989

Poppema, Suzanne, M.D. Personal interview, January 1980

Ratner, Herbert, M.D. "History of the Dehumanization of American Obstetrical Practice," *21st Century Obstetrics Now!* Vol. 1, David Stewart, Ph.D., and Lee Stewart, C.C.E., eds., Chapel Hill, N.C.: NAPSAC, 1977

Shearer, Madeleine H. "The Effects of Regionalization of Perinatal Care on Hospital Services for Normal Childbirth," *Birth* 4:4:139–151, Winter 1977

Steward, Marsh, M.D., ed. "Consumerism and the Malpractice Problem," *CAOG Newsletter*, Vol. 3, No. 3, November 1981, reprinted in *NAPSAC News*, Vol.7, No. 1, Spring 1982

Tew, Marjorie. "Obstetricians Over-ruled: The Myth of Hospital Safety," *Association for Improvements in Maternity Services (AIMS) Quarterly Journal*, Spring, 1984

———. "Place of Birth and Perinatal Mortality," *Journal of the Royal College of General Practitioners* 35:390–394, August, 1985

———. "Do Obstetric Intranatal Interventions Make Birth Safer?" *British Journal of Obstetrics and Gynaecology* 93:659–674, July, 1986

Wagner, Marsden. "The Epidemiology of Ourselves: A Light in a Dark Tunnel," *The Birth Gazette* 4:3:21–22, Spring 1988
———. "Testimony before the U.S. Commission to Prevent Infant Mortality," *The Birth Gazette* 4:3:12–17, Spring, 1988
World Health Organization. "Appropriate Technology for Birth," *The Lancet*, August 24, 1985, pp. 436–437

7 ▪ The Obstetrician's Black Bag of Interventions

A Review of Research Literature and Federal Involvement Relating to Selected Obstetric Practices, United States General Accounting Office, September 24, 1979
Banta, H. David, M.D., M.P.H., and Stephen B. Thacker, M.D. *Costs and Benefits of Electronic Fetal Monitoring: A Review of the Literature*, National Center for Health Services Research (NCHSR), Research Report Series, DHEW Publication No. (PHS) 79–3245, April 1979
———, and Stephen B. Thacker, M.D. "The Risks and Benefits of Episiotomy," *Birth* 9:1:25–30, Spring, 1982
Berman, Salee. C.N.M., and Victor Berman, M.D. *The Birth Center*, New York: Prentice Hall, 1986
Billingsley, Johanna. "Fasting in Labor," *Aims Quarterly Journal* 1:1:25, 1989
Brackbill, Yvonne. Ph.D. "Lasting Behavioral Effects of Obstetric Medication on Children," testimony before the U.S. Senate Subcommittee on Health and Scientific Research, April 17, 1978, reprinted in *Compulsory Hospitalization or Freedom of Choice in Childbirth?* Vol. 1, David Stewart, Ph.D., and Lee Stewart, C.C.E., eds., Marble Hill, Mo.: NAPSAC Reproductions, 1979
Brazelton, T. Berry, M.D. "Phychophysiologic Reaction in the Neonate, II. Effect of Maternal Medication on the Neonate and His Behavior," *Pediatrics* 58:4:513–518, April 1961
———. "What Childbirth Drugs Can Do to Your Child," *Redbook*, February 1971
Caldeyro-Barcia, Roberto. M.D. "Some Consequences of Obstetrical Interference," *Birth* 2:2:34–38, Spring 1975
———. "The Influence of Maternal Position on Time of Spontaneous Rupture of the Membranes, Progress of Labor and Fetal Head Compression," *Birth* 6:1:7–15, Spring 1979
Carr, Katherine Camacho. C.N.M., M.S. "Obstetric Practices Which Protect Against Neonatal Morbidity: Focus on Maternal Position in Labor and Birth," *Birth* 7:4:249–254, Winter 1980
Cesarean Childbirth, Consensus Development Conference, Bethesda, Md.: NIH Publication No. 82–2067, October, 1981
Chalmers, Iain. and Martin Richards. "Intervention and Casual Inference in Obstetric Practice," *Benefits and Hazards of the New Obstetrics*, Tim Chard and Martin Richards, eds., London: Wm. Heinemann Medical Books; Philadelphia: J.B. Lippincott, 1977
Cogan, Rosemary. Ph.D., and Evelyn P. Edmunds. "The Unkindest Cut?" reprint from author, undated.
Conway, Esther. and Yvonne Brackbill. "Delivery Medication and Infant

Outcome: An Empirical Study," *The Effects of Obstetrical Medication on Fetus and Infant,* by Watson A. Bower, Jr., et al., Monographs of the Society for Research in Child Development, Serial No. 137, Vol. 35, No. 4, June 1970

Curtis, Peter, M.D., and Norma Safransky. "Rethinking Oxytocin Protocols in the Augmentation of Labor," *Birth* 15:4:199–202, December, 1988

"DGH Birth Surge 'Courts Disaster,' " *The Denver Post,* April 27, 1978

Dunn, P. "Obstetric Delivery Today: For Better or for Worse?" *Lancet,* 7963:790–793, April 19, 1976, abstract from *Birth,* 3:3:141, 1976

"Electronic Fetal Monitoring Takes More Professional Time, Not Less," *NAPSAC News,* Vol. 6, No. 3, Fall 1981

Elsberry, Dixie, C.N.M., M.S.N., Director, Midwifery Services, North Central Bronx Hospital, phone interviews, September 22 and 26, 1989

Ettner, Frederic M., M.D. "Comparative Study of Obstetrics," *Safe Alternatives in Childbirth,* David Stewart, Ph.D., and Lee Stewart, C.C.E., eds., Chapel Hill, N.C.: NAPSAC, Inc., 1977

———. "Hospital Obstetrics: Do the Benefits Outweigh the Risks?" *21st Century Obstetrics Now!* Vol. 1, David Stewart, Ph.D., and Lee Stewart, C.C.E., eds., Chapel Hill, N.C.: NAPSAC, 1977

Floyd, Cathy. R.N., M.S., A.C.C.E. "Epidural Anesthesia: Use or Abuse?" *Genesis,* August/September, 1984

Friedman, Emanuel. M.D., Sc.D. "The Obstetrician's Dilemma: How Much Fetal Monitoring and Cesarean Section is Enough?" *The New England Journal of Medicine,* 315:10:641–643, September 4, 1986

Glassman, Judith. "The Changing World of Childbirth," *Cosmopolitan,* April 1981

Gordon, H., and M. Logue. "Perineal Muscle Function after Childbirth," *Lancet* 2(8447):123–125, July 20, 1985

Gray, Ann. "FDA Reviews Brackbill-Broman Research on OB Drugs," *NAPSAC News,* Vol. 4:2, 1979

Haire, Doris, D.M.S. *The Cultural Warping of Childbirth,* International Childbirth Education Association, 1972

———. "Maternity Practices around the World: How Do We Measure Up?" *Safe Alternatives in Childbirth,* David Steward, Ph.D., and Lee Stewart, C.C.E., eds., Chapel Hill, N.C.: NAPSAC, 1976

———. "Safety of Drugs—How Safe is 'Safe'?" American Foundation for Maternal and Child Health, 30 Beekman Pl., N.Y.C., undated

———. Testimony before Senate Health Subcommittee on April 17, 1978

Havercamp, Albert D., M.D., FACOG. "Oxytocin, Neonatal Seizures, and Other Insights Derived from the Dublin Trial," *Birth* 13:3:188–189, September, 1986

Havercamp, Albert, M.D., et al. "A Controlled Trial of the Differential Effects of Intrapartum Fetal Monitoring," *American Journal of Obstetrics and Gynecology* 134:4:399–412, June 15, 1979

———. "The Evaluation of Continuous Fetal Heart Rate Monitoring in High-Risk Pregnancy," *Am. J. Obstet. Gynecol* 125:3:310–317, June 1, 1976

Hellman, Louis M., and Jack A. Pritchard, *Williams Obstetrics,* 14th ed. New York: Appleton-Century-Crofts, 1971

Hughes, Richard. "Infant Brain Damage Linked to Delivery Drugs—Study's Author Charges U.S. Delaying Release," *Valley News,* January 14, 1979

"ICEA Position Paper: Epidural Anesthesia for Labor," International Childbirth Education Association, November, 1987

Kitzinger, Sheila. "Episiotomy," *ICEA Review* 9:2:1–2, August, 1985

Lake, Alice. "Childbirth in America," *McCall's*, January 1976

Leveno, Kenneth, M.D., et al. "A Prospective Comparison of Selective and Universal Electronic Fetal Monitoring in 34,995 Pregnancies," *The New England Journal of Medicine* 315:10:615–619

Levy, H., et al. "Umbilical Cord Prolapse," *Obstetrics and Gynecology* 64:4:499, October, 1984, abstracted in *Birth* 12:1:65, Spring, 1985

Lumley, Judith, Ph.D. "The Irresistible Rise of Electronic Fetal Monitoring, *Birth* 9:3:150–152, Fall 1982

MacDonald, D., et al. "The Dublin Randomized Controlled Trial of Intrapartum Fetal Heart Rate Monitoring," *American Journal of Obstetrics and Gynecology* 152:5:524–539, 1985

Martell, M., et al. "Blood Acid-Base at Birth in Neonates from Labors with Early and Late Rupture of Membranes," *Journal of Pediatrics* 6:963–7, December 1976 abstract in *Birth* 4:2:87, Summer 1977

McKay, Susan, R.N., Ph.D., A.C.C.E., and Charles Mahan, M.D., FACOG. "How Can Aspiration of Vomitus in Obstetrics Best Be Prevented?" *Birth* 15:4:222–228, December, 1988

Mehl, Lewis E., M.D., Ph.D. "Home Delivery Research Today: A Review," paper from author presented at the annual meeting of the American Foundation for Maternal and Infant Health, N.Y.C., N.Y., November 15, 1976

————. Research on Obstetric Procedures and Neonatal Outcome reported in *The Five Standards for Safe Childbearing*, by David Stewart, Ph.D., Marble Hill, Mo.: NAPSAC, Int'l, 1981

Minkoff, Howard L., M.D., and Richard H. Schwarz, M.D. "The Rising Cesarean Section Rate: Can It Safely Be Reversed?" *Obstetrics and Gynecology* 56:2:135–145, August 1980

Moore, W.M.O. "The Conduct of the Second Stage," *Benefits and Hazards of the New Obstetrics*, Tim Chard and Martin Richards, eds., London: Wm. Heinemann Medical Books; Philadelphia: J.B. Lippincott, 1977

Newcombe, R.G. "Reversal of Changes in Distribution of Gestational Age and Birth Weight among Firstborn Infants of Cardiff Residents," *British Medical Journal* 287(6399):1095, October 15, 1983, abstracted in *Birth,* 11:1:67. Spring, 1984

Phillipson, E.H., et al. "Maternal, Fetal, and Neonatal Lidocaine Levels Following Local Perineal Infiltration," *American Journal of Obstetrics and Gynecology* 149:403:404, June 15, 1984, abstracted in *Birth* 11:4:269, Winter, 1984

Prentice, A., and T. Lind. "Fetal Heart Rate Monitoring during Labor— Too Frequent Intervention, Too Little Benefit?" *The Lancet,* December 12, 1987, pp. 1375–1377

Raymond, Janice. "Healthy Women in a High Tech Era," *International Journal of Childbirth Education* 3:4:9–12, November, 1988

Read, John A., Lt. Col., M.C., U.S.A., et al. "Randomized Trial of Ambulation Versus Oxytocin for Labor Enhancement: A Preliminary Report," *American Journal of Obstetrics and Gynecology* 139:6:669–672, March 15, 1981

Richards, M.P.M., and J.F. Bernal. "Effects of Obstetric Medication on Mother-Infant Interaction and Infant Development," *Psychoso-*

matic Medicine in Obstetrics and Gynecology, pp. 303–307, 3rd Int. Congr., London, 1971

Shearer, Madeleine H., R.P.T. "Auscultation is Acceptable in Low Risk Women," editorial, *Birth* 6:1:3–5, Spring 1979

———. "Fetal Monitoring: For Better or Worse?" *Compulsory Hospitalization, Freedom of Choice in Childbirth,* Vol. 1, David Stewart, Ph.D., and Lee Stewart, C.C.E., eds., Marble Hill, Mo.: NAPSAC Reproductions, 1979

Simkin, Penny, P.T. "Is Anyone Listening? The Lack of Clinical Impact of Randomized Controlled Trials of Electronic Fetal Monitoring," *Birth* 13:4:219–220, December, 1986

"Statement of Fetal Heart Rate Monitoring," *ACOG Newsletter,* November, 1988

Stimeling, Gary. "Will Common Delivery Techniques Soon Become Malpractice?" *The Journal of Legal Medicine,* May 1975

"Study: Labor Pain Killers Associated with Drug Addiction," *The Clarion-Ledger/Jackson Daily News,* July 12, 1987, reprinted in *NAPSAC News* 12:3:19, Fall, 1987

Thacker, Stephen, and David Banta. "Benefits and Risks of Episiotomy: An Interpretative Review of the English Language Literature 1860–1980," *Obstetrics and Gynecology Survey* 38:6:322–338

Thomas, Mark, M.D. Personal interviews, July and November, 1979

Thorp, John M., Jr., M.D., and Watson A. Bowes, Jr., M.D., "Episiotomy: Can Its Routine Use Be Defended?" *American Journal of Obstetrics and Gyecology,* May, 1989, Volume 160, Number 5, Part 1, abstracted in *The Birth Gazette* 5:4:18–19, Fall, 1989

"Trauma at Birth Associated with High Suicide Rates in Young Adults," *The Denver Post,* July 11, 1987

Wood, C., et al. "A Controlled Trial of Fetal Heart Rate Monitoring in a Low Risk Obstetric Population," *Am. J. Obstet. Gynecol.* 141(5):527, November 1, 1981, abstract from *Birth,* 9:3:211, Fall 1982

8 • The Cesarean Epidemic

"Advance Report on Final Natality Statistics, 1986," *Monthly Vital Statistics Report* 37:3 Supplement, July 12, 1988

Alvarez, Piera Maghella. "Birth Is Not an Illness: Fifteen Recommendations from the World Health Organization," *Association for Improvements in the Maternity Services (AIMS),* 40 Kingswood Avenue, London NW6, undated reprint

Banta, H. David, M.D., M.P.H., and Stephen Thacker, M.D. *Costs and Benefits of Electronic Fetal Monitoring: A Review of the Literature,* Washington D.C.: DHEW Publications No. (PHS) 70-3245, April 1979

Boylan, Peter, M.B., D.C.H., M.A.O., M.R.C.O.G., M.R.C.P.I. "Failure in Active Management of Labor: Accounting for Different Cesarean Rates in Dublin, Dallas, and London Trials," Eighth Birth Conference, San Francisco, March, 1989

Brice, John E. H., and Colin H. M. Walker. "Changing Pattern of

Respiratory Distress in Newborns," *Lancet* 2:8041:752–754, October 8, 1977

Bruce, Gene. "So You Want to be a Mid-Life Mom?" *East West,* January, 1987

Burkhard, Nancy. "Group Advocates Birth at Home," *Denver Post,* January 19, 1979

Cesarean Childbirth, Consensus Development Conference, Bethesda, Md.: NIH Publication No. 82–2067, October 1981

"Cesareans Increasing but Few Study Related Maternal Deaths," *Ob/Gyn News,* July 1, 1980

Chalmers, Iain, and Martin Richards. "Intervention and Causal Inference in Obstetric Practice," *Benefits and Hazards of the New Obstetrics,* Tim Chard and Martin Richards, eds., London: William Heinemann Medical Books; Philadelphia, J. B. Lippincott, 1977

Cohen, Wayne R., M.D. "Influence of the Duration of Second Stage Labor on Perinatal Outcome and Puerperal Morbidity," *Obstetrics and Gynecology* 49:3:266–269, March 1977

Coleman, Cheryl H. "Fetal Stress Response in Labor," *International Journal of Childbirth Education,* August, 1986

Collea, Joseph V., M.D., et al. "The Randomized Management of Term Frank Breech Presentations: A Study of 208 Cases," *American Journal of Obstetrics and Gynecology* 137:2:235–244, May 15, 1980

COMA (The Committee on Maternal Alternatives), *How Women Want to Have Their Babies,* Baltimore: self-published, 1980

"Consensus Conference Report: Indications for Cesarean Section: Final Statement of the Panel of the National Consensus Conference on Aspects of Cesarean Birth," *Canadian Medical Association Journal* 134:1348–1352, June 15, 1986

Conway, D. I., et al. "Management of Spontaneous Rupture of the Membranes in the Absence of Labor in Primagravid Women at Term," *American Journal of Obstetrics and Gynecology* 150:8:947, December, 1984, abstracted in *Childbirth Alternatives Quarterly* 6:4:11, Summer, 1985

Cook, William A., M.D. *Natural Childbirth: Fact and Fallacy,* Chicago: Nelson Hall, 1982

Corea, Gena. "The Cesarean Epidemic; Who's Having This Baby, Anyway—You or the Doctor?" *Mother Jones,* July 1980

Corey, Lawrence, M.D. "The Diagnosis and Treatment of Genital Herpes," *JAMA* 248:9:1041–1050, September 3, 1982

"Correcting a Breech Presentation," *Informed Homebirth Newsletter,* January–February 1978

Correspondence regarding Leveno, et al. and Haynes de Reght, et al. *New England Journal of Medicine* 316:8:480–483, February 19, 1987

Cox, Janice P. "Delivery Alternatives in the Term Breech Pregnancy," *International Journal of Childbirth Education* 12:4:21–29, November, 1988

Cruz, Amelia C., M.D. "Postmaurity: Fact or Fiction?" *Contemporary Ob/gyn,* March, 1982

"Cuomo Vetoes Women's Right to Know," *Childbirth Alternatives Quarterly* 9:1:14, Fall, 1987

Danforth, David N., M.D. "Cesarean Section," *Journal of the American Medical Association* 253:6:811–818, February 8, 1985

Daniels, Kari. *Water Baby: Experiences of Water Birth,* video distributed by Point of View Productions, 2477 Folsom Street, San Francisco, CA 94110

Davis, M. Edward, M.D. "The Expectant Mother: What Does 'Due Date' Really Mean?" *Redbook,* August, 1965

Doering, Susan G., Ph.D. "Unnecessary Cesareans: Doctor's Choice, Parent's Dilemma," *Compulsory Hospitalization or Freedom of Choice in Childbirth,* Vol. 1, David Stewart, Ph.D., and Lee Stewart, C.C.E., eds., Marble Hill, Mo.: NAPSAC Reproductions, 1979

Evrard, John R., M.D., M.P.H., F.A.C.O.G., and Edwin M. Gold, M.D., F.A.C.O.G. "Cesarean Section and Maternal Mortality in Rhode Island, Incidence and Risk Factors, 1965–1975," *Obstetrics and Gynecology* 50:5:594–597, November 1977

Feldman, Silvia, Ph.D. "Cesarean Deliveries/When and Why are They Justified," *Self,* May 1979

———. *Choices in Childbirth,* New York; Bantam, 1980

"Fetal 'Distress' as a Positive Sign," *East West,* 1986

Frechette, Alfred L., M.D., M.P.H., and Pearl K. Russo. "A Comparison of the Quality of Maternity Care between a Health Maintenance Organization and Fee-For-Service Practices," *The New England Journal of Medicine* 304:13:784–787, March 26, 1981

Friedman, Emanuel, M.D., Sc.D. "The Obstetrician's Dilemma: How Much Fetal Monitoring and Cesarean Section is Enough?" *New England Journal of Medicine* 315:10:641–643, September 4, 1986

Frye, Anne. "How Do You Handle Risks When Your Water Breaks?" *Special Delivery,* Summer, 1986

Gibbs, C.E., M.D. "Planned Vaginal Delivery Following Cesarean Section," *Clinical Obstetrics and Gynecology* 23:2:507–515, June 1980

Gleicher, Norbert, M.D. "Cesarean Section Rates in the United States: The Short-term Failure of the National Consensus Development Conference in 1980," *Journal of the American Medical Association* 252:23:3273–3276, December 21, 1984

Gluck, Lewis, M.D. Quoted from "current issue" of *Hospital Practice* in *Tallahassee Democrat,* April 7, 1977

Goer, Henci, A.C.C.E. "Are Cesareans Saving Babies? A Review of the Medical Literature," *Childbirth Alternatives Quarterly* 7:4:9–12, Summer, 1986

Goyert, Gregory L., M.D., et al. "The Physician Factor in Cesarean Birth Rates," *New England Journal of Medicine* 320:11:706–709, March 16, 1989

Graves, William, M.D., F.A.C.O.G. "Breech Delivery in Twenty Years of Practice," *American Journal of Obstetrics and Gynecology* 137:2:229–234, May 15, 1980

"Guidelines for Vaginal Delivery after a Previous Cesarean Birth," ACOG Committee Opinion, October, 1988

Halperin, Mary E., M.D., and Murray Enkin, M.D. "Induction of Labor in Postterm Pregnancy," *ICEA Review* 12:1:23–26, February, 1988

Havercamp, Albert, M.D., et al. "A Controlled Trial of the Differential Effects of Intrapartum Fetal Monitoring," *American Journal of Obstetrics and Gynecology* 134:4:399–408, June 15, 1979

————. "Does Anyone Need Fetal Monitors?" testimony before the U.S. Senate Sub-Committee on Health, April 17, 1978, reprinted in *Compulsory Hospitalization or Freedom of Choice in Childbirth*, Vol. 1, David Stewart, Ph.D., and Lee Stewart, C.C.E., eds., Marble Hill, Mo.: NAPSAC Reproductions, 1979

Havercamp, Albert D., M.D. "How to Keep Cesarean Rates Below 10% in a High Risk Population," Third Birth Conference, San Francisco, October, 1984

Haynes de Reght, Roberta, M.D., et al. "Relation of Private or Clinic Care to the Cesarean Birth Rate," *New England Journal of Medicine* 315:10:619–624, September 4, 1986

Heilman, Jean Rattner. "Breaking the Cesarean Cycle," *New York Times Magazine*, September 7, 1980

Hellman, Louis M., and Jack A. Pritchard. *Williams Obstetrics*, 14th ed., New York: Appleton-Century-Crofts, 1971

"Hospital Disclosures to Maternity Patients Now Required in Massachusetts," *Childbirth Alternatives Quarterly* 7:2:16, Winter, 1986

Johnson, John W. C., M.D., et al. "Premature Rupture of the Membranes and Prolonged Latency," *Obstetrics and Gynecology* 57:5:547–556, May 1981

Jones, M. Douglas Jr., et al. "Failure of Association of Premature Rupture of Membranes with Respiratory-Distress Syndrome," *New England Journal of Medicine* 292:24:1253–1292, June 12, 1975

Kappy, Kenneth A., M.D., et al. "Premature Rupture of the Membranes: A Conservative Approach," *American Journal of Obstetrics and Gynecology* 134:6:655–661, July 15, 1979

Kaye, Edward M., M.D., and Elizabeth C. Dooling, M.D. "Neonatal Herpes Simplex Meningoencephalitis Associated with Fetal Monitor Scalp Electrodes," *Neurology* 31:1045–1047, August 1981

Klaus, Marshall H., M.D. "The Houston Randomized Controlled Trial of Effects of a Continuous Supportive Companion in Labor: A Significant Aspect of the Management of Labor," Eighth Birth Conference, San Francisco, March, 1989

Lagercrantz, Hugo, and Theodore A. Slotkin. "The 'Stress' of Being Born," *Scientific American* 254:4:100–107, April, 1986, abstracted in *Childbirth Alternatives Quarterly* 7:3:13, Spring, 1986

Lenihan, J. P. "Relationship of Antepartum Pelvic Examination to Premature Rupture of the Membranes," *Obstetrics and Gynecology* 83(1):33, January, 1984, abstracted in *Birth*, 11:2:137, Summer, 1984

Leveno, Kenneth J., et al. "A Prospective Comparison of Selective and Universal Electronic Fetal Monitoring in 34,995 Pregnancies," *New England Journal of Medicine* 315:10:615–619, September 4, 1986

Marieskind, Helen A., Dr. P.H. *An Evaluation of Cesarean Section in the United States*, Washington D.C.: Department of Health, Education and Welfare, June 1979

Myers, Stephen A., and Norbert Gleicher. "A Successful Program to Lower Cesarean-Section Rates," *New England Journal of Medicine* 319:23:1511–1540, December 8, 1988

Notzon, Francis C., M.S., et al. "Comparisons of National Cesarean Section Rates," *New England Journal of Medicine* 316:7:386–389, February 12, 1987

Nouhan, Joseph, M.D. Personal interview, March 17, 1989

Odent, Michel. "Birth under Water," *Lancet* December 24/31, 1983

O'Driscoll, Kieran, M.D., and Michael Foley, M.D. "Correlation of Decrease in Perinatal Mortality and Increase in Cesarean Section Rates," *Obstetrics and Gynecology* 61:1:1–5, January, 1983

Perez, Polly, R.N., A.C.C.E. "Avoiding the 'High-Risk' Label," *Genesis,* June/July, 1985

———. "Nurturing Laboring Women in a High-Tech Town," *Childbirth Alternatives Quarterly* 6:3:9–10, Spring, 1985

Placek, Paul J., et al. "The Cesarean Future," *American Demographics,* September, 1987

Placek, Paul J., Ph.D., and Selma M. Taffel, B.B.A. "Recent Patterns in Cesarean Delivery in the United States," *Obstetrics and Gynecology Clinics of North America* 15:4:607–627, December, 1988

———, and Selma Taffel, B.B.A. "Vaginal Birth after Cesarean (VBAC) in the 1980s," *American Journal of Public Health* 78:5:512–515, May, 1988

Placek, Paul J., Ph.D., National Center for Health Statistics. Telephone interview, April 3, 1989

Porreco, Richard, M.D., F.A.C.O.G. "How Well Can Education Contain the Cesarean Birth Rate? Outcome of a Program," Eighth Birth Conference, San Francisco, March, 1989

Porreco, Richard, M.D., F.A.C.O.G., et al. "Roundtable: The U.S. Cesarean Birth Rate is 25% and Rising. How Can We Reverse the Rise?" Eighth Birth Conference, San Francisco, March, 1989

"Pregnancy Is Safe for Women over Thirty-five," *Childbirth Alternatives Quarterly* 5:1:16, Fall, 1983

Prober, Charles G., M.D., et al. "Low Risk of Herpes Simplex Virus Infections in Neonates Exposed to the Virus at the Time of Vaginal Delivery to Mothers with Recurrent Genital Herpes Simplex Virus Infections," *New England Journal of Medicine* 316:5:240–244, January 27, 1987

Randal, Judith. "Doctors: First Cesarean Section Needn't Start Pattern," *New York Daily News,* reprinted in *Boulder Daily Camera,* February 25, 1982

Richart, Ralph M., M.D., "Turn a Breech and Prevent a Cesarean," *Contemporary Ob/Gyn,* March 1982

Rosen, M. G., et al. "The Effect of Delivery Route on Outcome in Breech Presentation," *American Journal of Obstetrics and Gynecology* 148:909, April, 1984, abstracted in *Childbirth Alternatives Quarterly* 6:2:10, Winter, 1985

Rubin, George, M.D., et al. "The Risk of Childbearing Re-Evaluated," *American Journal of Public Health* 71:7:712–716, July 1981

Saunders, M.C., et al. "The Effects of Hospital Admission for Bed Rest on the Duration of Twin Pregnancy: A Randomized Trial," *Lancet* 1985(2):793, abstracted in *Birth* 13:2:141–142, June, 1986

Savage, Beverly, and Diana Simkin. *Preparation for Birth: The Complete Guide to the Lamaze Method,* New York: Ballantine Books, 1987

Shearer, Madeleine H., R.P.T. "Complications of Cesarean to Infant," *Birth,* 4:3:105, Fall 1977

———. "Complications of Cesarean to Mothers," *Birth* 4:3:103–104, Fall 1977

Shearer, Madeleine H., R.P.T., and Milton Estes, M.D., F.A.B.F.P., "A

Critical Review of the Recent Literature on Postterm Pregnancy and a Look at Women's Experiences," *Birth* 12:2:95–111, Summer, 1985

Showstack, Jonathon A., M.P.H., et al. "The Role of Changing Practices in the Rising Costs of Hospital Care," *New England Journal of Medicine* 313:19:1201–1207, November 1, 1985

Silberner, Joanne. "What Nationality Means to the Fine Art of Healing," *U.S. News and World Report*, December 26, 1988/January 2, 1989

Silver, Lynn, M.D., M.P.H., and Sidney Wolfe, M.D. *Unnecessary Cesarean Sections: How to Cure a National Epidemic*, Public Citizen Health Research Group, Dept. PR, 2000 P St., NW, Room 700, Washington, DC 20036

"Summary Report," Joint Interregional Conference on Appropriate Technology for Birth, Fortaleza, Brazil, April 22–26, 1985, English version, June 10, 1985

Sumner, Philip E., M.D., and Celeste R. Phillips, R.N., M.S. *Birthing Rooms*, Saint Louis, Toronto, London: C.V. Mosby, 1981

Szczepaniak, Jane C. "Issues in Breech Births," *International Journal of Childbirth Education*, November, 1986

Taffel, Selma M., B.B.A., et al. "Trends in the United States Cesarean Rate and Reasons for the 1980–85 Rise," *American Journal of Public Health* 77:8:955–959, August, 1987

Taffel, Selma M., B.B.A., National Center for Health Statistics, Telephone interview. October 27, 1989

Thorp, James, M.D., F.A.C.O.G. "Effects of Epidural on the Incidence of Cesarean Section for Dystocia in First Labors," Eighth Birth Conference, San Francisco, March, 1989

———. Personal interview regarding use of cesarean section for women with herpes simplex virus, March 16, 1989

Trathen, William T., M.D. "Management of Labor Following Rupture of Membranes," *ICEA Review* 8:3:1–7, December, 1984

Weston, Marianne Brorup. "Postmaturity and Induction of Labor," *Maternal Health News*, March, 1987

White, E., et al. "An Investigation of the Relationship between Cesarean Section Birth and Respiratory Distress Syndrome of the Newborn," *Am J Epidemiol* 121 (5):651, May, 1985, abstracted in *Birth* 12:4:264, Winter, 1985

"Women Are the Recipients of Most Major Surgery," *East West*, August, 1988

Young, Diony. "Cesareans in the United States: A Sobering Situation," *ICEA News* 18:41:1, 1979

———, and Charles Mahan, M.D. *Unnecessary Cesareans*, ICEA, Minneapolis, 1980

———. "Crisis in Obstetrics—The Management of Labor," *International Journal of Childbirth Education*, August, 1987

9 ▪ Having a Cesarean Is Having a Baby

Botlos, Kate. "Birth Dis-Illusions," *Mothering*, Summer 1979

Clark, Carol. "Vaginal Birth after Cesarean Section," *ICEA Review* 11:3:21–27, November, 1987

————. "Use of Oxytocins and Epidural Anesthesia in VBAC," *International Journal of Childbirth Education*, November, 1986

Cohen, Nancy. Interview, September 18, 1982

"Guidelines for Vaginal Delivery after a Previous Cesarean Birth," ACOG Committee Opinion Paper, October, 1988

Klaus, Marshall H., and John H. Kennell. *Parent-Infant Bonding*, Saint Louis: C.V. Mosby, 1982

"Medical Journal References—1986–1988, Vaginal Birth after Cesarean," by C/Sec, Inc., reprinted by ICEA, undated

Meier, Paul R., M.D., and Richard P. Porreco, M.D. "Trial of labor following cesarean section: A two-year experience," *American Journal of Obstetrics and Gynecology* 144:6:671–678, November 15, 1982

"Multiple C-sections Not a Labor Waiver," *Science News*, August 27, 1988

Myers, Stephen A., and Norbert Gleicher. "A Successful Program to Lower Cesarean Section Rates," *New England Journal of Medicine* 319:23:1511–1516, December 8, 1988

Once a Cesarean: Vaginal Birth after Cesarean, video distributor: Nicolas J. Kaufman Productions, 14 Clyde Street, Newton, MA 02160

Perez, Polly. "VBAC: The Possible Dream," *Childbirth Alternatives Quarterly* 9:1:9, Fall, 1987

Placek, Paul J., Ph.D., National Center for Health Statistics, Room 144, Federal Center Bldg. Phone interview, April 3, 1989

Placek, Paul J., et al. "1986 C-Sections Rise; VBACs Inch Upward," *American Journal of Public Health* 78:5:562–563, May, 1988

Placek, Paul J., Ph.D., and Selma Taffel, B.B.A. "Vaginal Birth after Cesarean (VBAC) in the 1980s," *American Journal of Public Health* 78:5:512–515, May, 1988

Porreco, Richard P., M.D. Phone Interview, October 1983; personal communication, Feb. 15, 1989

Pruett, Kathleen M., et al. "Is Vaginal Birth after Two or More Cesareans Safe?" *Obstetrics and Gynecology* 72:2:163–165, August, 1988

"Repeat Cesareans Births No Longer the Norm," ACOG News Release, October 26, 1988

Shearer, Elizabeth Conner, M.Ed., M.P.H. "Education for Vaginal Birth after Cesarean," *Birth* 9:1:31–34, Spring 1982

Syed, Christiana. "Working for a Positive Birth," *New Beginnings*, November-December, 1988

Weston, Marianne Brorup, et al. "Vaginal Birth after Cesarean," reprint, Pennypress, Inc., 1987

Zorn, Esther, president, Cesarean Prevention Movement. "Cesarean and VBAC Rates? Responses," *C/Sec Newsletter* 13:3:2, third quarter, 1987

————. Interview, November 9, 1988

10 ▪ Understanding Your Feelings

Affonso, Dyanne D., R.N., M.S. "Missing Pieces, A Study of Postpartum Feelings," *Birth* 4:4, Winter 1977

Buesching, Don P., and others. "Progression and Depression in the

Prenatal and Postpartum Periods," *Women and Health* 11:2, Summer 1986

Cooper, Peter J. "Non-Psychotic Psychiatric Disorder after Childbirth: A Prospective Study of Prevalence, Incidence, Course and Nature," *JAMA* 260:22, December 9, 1988

Dimitroyvsky, L., and others. "Depression During and Following Pregnancy: Quality of Family Relationships," *Journal of Psychology* 121:3, 1987

Gottlieb, S.E., and D.E. Barrett. "Effects of Unanticipated Cesarean Section on Mothers, Infants, and Their Interaction in the First Month of Life," *Journal of Developmental and Behavioral Pediatrics* 7:3, June 1986

Halas, Celia, Ph.D., and Roberta Matteson, Ph.D. *I've Done So Well— Why Do I Feel So Bad?* New York: Macmillan, 1978; London: Collier Macmillan, 1978

Hobfoll, Stevan E., and others. "Satisfaction with Social Support during Crisis: Intimacy and Self-Esteem as Critical Determinants," *Journal of Personality and Social Psychology* 51:2, August 1986

Kendell, R.E., and others. "Day-to-Day Mood Changes after Childbirth: Further Data," *British Journal of Psychiatry* 145, December 1984

Kendell, R.E., and others. "Epidemiology of Puerperal Psychoses," *British Journal of Psychiatry* 150, May 1987

Kitzsinger, Sheila. "Brief Encounters: Effects of Induction on the Mother-Baby Relationship," *Practitioner*, 1976.

Lang, Raven. "Delivery In the Home," *Maternal Attachment and Mothering Disorders: A Round Table*, Marshall H. Klaus, M.D., Treville Leger, and Mary Ann Trause, Ph.D., eds., Johnson and Johnson, 1975

Loftus, Elizabeth. *Memory—Surprising New Insights into How We Remember and Why We Forget*, Reading, Mass.: Addison-Wesley, 1980

Lozoff, Betsy, M.D. "Birth in Non-Industrial Societies," *Birth, Interaction and Attachment: Exploring the Foundations for Modern Perinatal Care*, Marshall Klaus, M.D., and Martha Oschrin Robertson, eds., Johnson and Johnson, 1982

Morgan, B.M., and others. "Analgesia and Satisfaction in Childbirth (The Queen Charlotte's 1000 Mother Survey)," *Lancet* 2, October 9, 1982

Morrison, C.E., and others. "Pethidine Compared with Meptazinol during Labour. A Prospective Randomised Double-Blind Study in 1100 Patients," *Anaesthesia* 42:1, January 1987

Moss, Peter, and others. "The Hospital Inpatient Stay: The Experience of First-Time Parents," *Child: Care, Health and Development* 13, 1987

Newton, Niles, Ph.D. Address reported in *News from H.O.M.E. (Home Oriented Maternity Experience)*, 1977

————. *Maternal Emotions*, New York: Paul B. Hoeber, 1955

Peterson, Gayle, *Birthing Normally: A Personal Growth Approach to Childbirth*, Berkeley, Calif.: Mindbody Press, 1981

Quadagno, D.M., and others. "Postpartum Moods in Men and Women," *American Journal of Obstetrics and Gynecology* 154:5, May 1986

Rothman, Barbara Katz. *In Labor: Women and Power in the Birthplace*, New York: W. W. Norton, 1982

Sandelowski, Margarete. "Expectations for Childbirth versus Actual Experiences: The Gap Widens," *Maternal Child Nursing* 9, July/August 1984

Scarf, Maggie. *Unfinished Business: Pressure Points in the Lives of Women,* Garden City, N.Y. Doubleday, 1980

Stern, G., and L. Kruckman. "Multi-Disciplinary Perspectives on Post-Partum Depression: An Anthropological Critique," *Social Science Medicine* 17:15, 1983

Stewart, David, Ph.D., ed. *Five Standards for Safe Childbearing,* Marble Hill, Mo.: NAPSAC Reproductions, 1981

Stolte, Karen. "A Comparison of Women's Expectations of Labor with the Actual Event," *Birth* 14:2, June 1987

———. "Postpartum 'Missing Pieces': Sequela of a Passing Obstetrical Era?" *Birth* 13:2, June 1986

Yarrow, Leah. "When My Baby Was Born," *Parents,* August 1982

11 • Your Supporters

Bradley, Robert, M.D. *Husband-Coached Childbirth,* New York: Harper & Row, 1981

Copstick, S.M., and others. "Partner Support and the Use of Coping Techniques in Labour," *Journal of Psychosomatic Research* 30:4, 1986

Dick-Read, Grantly, M.D. *Childbirth without Fear: The Principles and Practices of Natural Childbirth,* New York: Harper & Row, 1974

Gunn, T.R. "Antenatal Education: Does It Improve the Quality of Labour and Delivery?" *New Zealand Medical Journal* 96:724, January 26, 1983

Karmel, Marjorie. *Thank You, Dr. Lamaze: A Mother's Experience in Painless Childbirth,* New York: Doubleday, 1965

Kennell, John H., M.D. "Are We in the Midst of a Revolution?" *Am. J. Dis. Child,* Vol. 134, March 1980

———. "The Physiologic Effects of a Supportive Companion (Doula) during Labor," *Birth, Interaction and Attachment: Exploring the Foundations for Modern Perinatal Care,* Marshall Klaus, M.D., and Martha Oschrin Robertson, eds., Johnson and Johnson, 1982

Klaus, Marshall H., M.D., and John H. Kennell, M.D. *Parent-Infant Bonding,* Saint Louis: C.V. Mosby, 1982

Lozoff, Betsy, M.D. "Birth in Non-Industrial Societies," *Birth, Interaction and Attachment: Exploring the Foundations for Modern Perinatal Care,* Marshall Klaus, M.D., and Martha Oschrin Robertson, eds., Johnson and Johnson, 1982

Maloney, R. "Childbirth Education Classes: Expectant Parents' Expectations," *Journal of Obstetrics, Gynecology and Neonatal Nursing* 14:3, May/June 1985

McNatt, Nona L., R.N., C.N.M. "A Lesson in Empathy," *Obstetrics and Gynecology* 56:1, July 1980

Nevin, C., and K. Gijsbers. "A Study of Labour Pain Using the McGill Pain Questionnaire," *Social Science Medicine* 19:12, 1984

Patton, L.L., and others. "Childbirth Preparation and Outcomes of Labor and Delivery in Primiparous Women," *Journal of Family Practice* 20:4, April 1985

Raphael, Dana, Ph.D. *The Tender Gift*, Englewood Cliffs, N.J.: Prentice Hall, 1973

Shearer, Madeleine H., and Nenelle Bunnin. "Childbirth Educators in the 1980's: A Survey of Twenty-five Veterans," *Birth* 10:4, Winter 1983

Simkin, Penny, R.P.T. Interview, December 1982

Sosa, Roberto, M.D., John Kennell, M.D., Marshall Klaus, M.D., and Juan Urrutia, M.D. "The Effect of a Supportive Woman on Mothering Behavior and the Duration and Complications of Labor. Abstracted," *Pediatr Res* 13:338, 1979

———, John Kennell, M.D., Marshall Klaus, M.D., Steven Robertson, Ph.D., and Juan Urrutia, M.D. "The Effect of a Supportive Companion on Perinatal Problems, Length of Labor, and Mother-Infant Interaction," *The New England Journal of Medicine* 303:11, September 11, 1980

Sumner, Philip E., M.D., and Celeste R. Phillips, R.N. *Birthing Rooms: Concept and Reality,* Saint Louis: C.V. Mosby, 1981

Tanzer, Deborah, Ph.D. "Natural Childbirth: Pain or Peak Experience?" *Psychology Today,* October 1968

Waletzky, Lucy R., M.D. "Husbands' Problems with Breastfeeding," *Amer. J. Orthopsychiat.* 49(2), April 1979

Yarrow, Leah. "Fathers Who Deliver," *Parents*, June 1981

12 ▪ How to Have a Normal Vaginal Birth

"A Warning to Drinking Moms-to-Be," *Boulder Daily Camera,* November 20, 1988

"Aspirin Causes Unusual Bleeding in Mothers and Their Newborns," Boulder *Daily Camera,* October 7, 1982

Berman, Salee, C.N.M. "How Mother's Smoking Affects Her Child," NACHIS, undated

Berman, Salee, C.N.M., and Victor Berman, M.D. "Preparation of the Perineum," *The Birth Center,* New York: Prentice Hall, 1986

Brewer, Gail Sforza, with Tom Brewer, M.D. *What Every Pregnant Woman Should Know,* New York: Random House, 1977

Butler, Hilary. "Delayed Cord Clamping," *Mothering,* Fall, 1986

Carr, Daniel B., M.D., et al. "Physical Conditioning Facilitates the Exercise-Induced Secretion of Beta-Endorphins and Beta-Lipotropin in Women," *New England Journal of Medicine* 305:10:560–562, September 3, 1981

Cassel, Eric J., M.D. "The Nature of Suffering and the Goals of Medicine," *New England Journal of Medicine,* Special Article, 306:11:639–645, March 18, 1982

Cogan, Rosemary. "Comfort during Prepared Childbirth as a Function of Parity, Reported by Four Classes of Participant Observers," *Journal of Psychosomatic Research,* Vol. 19, pp. 37–39, 1975

Cox, Janice. "Effect of Warm Tub Baths during Labor," *International Journal of Childbirth Education,* November, 1988

"Crib Deaths, Moms' Smoking Linked," *Boulder Daily Camera*, February 24, 1984

Enkin, M. W., M.D., "Changing Attitudes toward Childbirth Need Not Create Patient-Physician Conflict," brief, *Postgraduate Medicine*, Vol. 71, No. 1, January 1982

Ewy, Donna and Rodger. *Guide to Family Centered Childbirth*, New York: E. P. Dutton, 1981

————. *Preparation for Childbirth: A Lamaze Guide*, Boulder, Colo.: Pruett, 1970

"FDA Urges Label Forbidding Aspirin Use Late in Pregnancy," *The Denver Post*, November 18, 1988

Forman, Michele R., Ph.D., et al. "Delayed Childbearing in Sweden," *Journal of the American Medical Association* 252:22:3135–3139

Gamper, Margaret, R.N. *Preparations for the Heir Minded*, Chicago, self-published, 1971

Gillett, Jane. "Childbirth in Pithiviers, France," *Lancet* 2:8148:894–896, October 27, 1979

Gunn, Gordon C., M.D. "Premature Rupture of the Fetal Membranes," *American Journal of Obstetrics and Gynecology* 106:3:469–483, 1970

Haire, Doris, D.M.S. Comments at La Leche League International Conference, Chicago, July 1981

Hartman, Rhondda Evans, R.N. *Exercises for True Natural Childbirth*, New York: Harper & Row, 1975

Keppel, Kenneth G., and Selma M. Taffel. "Maternal Smoking and Weight Gain in Relation to Birth Weight and the Risk of Fetal and Infant Death," *Smoking and Reproductive Health*, Littleton, Mass.: PSG Publishing Company, undated reprint from author

Klaus, Marshall, M.D., and Martha Oschrin Robertson, eds. *Birth, Interaction and Attachment*, Johnson and Johnson, 1982

KuroKawa, Jude, R.N., B.S.N., and Mark Zilkoski, M.D. "Adapting Hospital Obstetrics to Birth in the Squatting Position," *Birth* 12:2:87–90, Summer 1985

Lappe, Frances Moore. *Diet for a Small Planet*, New York: Ballantine Books, 1975

Lieberman, Adrienne B. *Easing Labor Pain*, Garden City, NY: Doubleday, 1987

McNeal, Chuck, O.C., and Ramona McNeal. "The Neurophysiology of Letting Go," *Special Delivery*, Spring 1980

Melzak, R., et al. "Severity of Labour Pain: Influence of Physical as Well as Psychological Variables," *Canadian Medical Association Journal* 130:5:579, March 1, 1984, abstracted in *Birth* 11:2:136, Summer 1984

Newton, Niles, Ph.D. "The Fetus Ejection Reflex Revisited," *Birth* 14:2:106–108, June 1987

Noble, Elizabeth, R.P.T. *Essential Exercises for the Child Bearing Years*, Boston: Houghton Mifflin, 1982

Odent, Michel, M.D. *Birth Reborn*, New York: Pantheon, 1984

————. "The Evolution of Obstetrics at Pithiviers," *Birth* 8:1:7–15, Spring 1981

————. "The Fetus Ejection Reflex," *Birth* 14:2:104–105, June, 1987

————. "The Milieu and Obstetrical Positions during Labor. A New

Approach from France," reprint from Marshall Klaus, M.D., undated

"Perineal Massage," Denver Birth Center reprint, undated

Pietz, Carol. "Weight Gain, Nutrition and High Risk Pregnancy," *International Journal of Childbirth Education*, August 1986

Roberts, Joyce, R.N., C.N.M., Ph.D., et al. "The Effects of Maternal Position on Uterine Contractility and Efficiency," *Birth* 10:4:243–249, Winter 1983

Roberts, Joyce, and Donna van Lier. "Debate: Which Position for the Second Stage?" *Childbirth Educator*, Spring 1984

Romond, Janis Loomis, and Irene Taylor Baker. "Squatting in Childbirth: A New Look at an Old Tradition," *Journal of Obstetric, Gynecologic and Neonatal Nursing*, September/October 1985, pp. 406–11, abstracted in *Childbirth Alternatives Quarterly* 8:1:10, Fall 1986

Sagen, N., et al. "Maternal Hemoglobin Concentration Is Closely Related to Birthweight in Normal Pregnancies," *Acta Obstet Gynecol Scand* 63:3:245, 1984, abstracted in *Birth* 11:4:266, Winter 1984

Scott, Rebecca Lovell, ed. "Alcohol and Pregnancy," *ICEA Review* 8:2:1–7, August 1984, reprint

Shearer, Madeleine H., R.P.T. "Malnutrition in Middle Class Pregnant Women," *Birth* 7:1:27–35, Spring 1980

"Smoking and Childbearing," *ICEA Review* 10:2:1R–8R, August 1986, reprint

"Study Shows Smoking Increases Fetal and Maternal Risks," *Genesis*, December/January 1981

Taffel, Selma M., B.B.A. "Association between Maternal Weight Gain and Outcome of Pregnancy," *Journal of Nurse-Midwifery* 31:2:78–86, March/April 1986

Taffel, Selma M., B.B.A., and Kenneth G. Keppel, Ph.D. "Advice about Weight Gain during Pregnancy and Actual Weight Gain," *American Journal of Public Health* 76:12:1396–1399, December 1986

———. "Implications of Mother's Weight Gain on the Outcome of Pregnancy," paper from authors presented at the American Statistical Association Philadelphia meeting, August 1984

Tanzer, Deborah, Ph.D. "Natural Childbirth: Pain or Peak Experience?" *Psychology Today*, October 1968

"Unclamped Cord Seen as Mother's Helper," *Medical World News*, March 14, 1969

Vincent, Peggy, R.N. Review of *Spiritual Midwifery*, *Birth* 4:2:81–82, Summer 1977

White, Gregory, M.D. *Emergency Childbirth*, Franklin Park, Ill.: Police Training Foundation, 1958

"Will My Drinking Hurt My Baby?" March of Dimes/Birth Defects Foundation, 1984

13 ▪ The Nurse

Collins, B.A. "The Role of the Nurse in Labor and Delivery as Perceived by Nurses and Patients," *Journal of Obstetrical, Gynecological, and Neonatal Nursing* 15:5, September/October 1986

Fowler, Elizabeth M. "A Program to Recruit More Nurses," *The New York Times,* April 11, 1989

Gardner, Sandra L., P.N.P. "Mothering: The Unconscious Conflict Between Nurses and New Mothers," *Keeping Abreast, Journal of Human Nurturing* 3:3, July–September 1978

Gartner, Lawrence M., M.D. "Facts And Fantasies About Neonatal Jaundice," address, 10th Annual Seminar for Physicians on Breastfeeding, La Leche League International, Las Vegas, July 15 and 16, 1982

Hillard, Paula J. Adams, M.D. "When an Obstetrician Has a Baby," *The Female Patient* 6:8, August 1981

Holcomb, Betty. "Nurses Fight Back," *Ms.,* June 1988

Klass, Kay, B.S.N., and Kay Capps, R.N. "Nine Years' Experience With Family-Centered Maternity Care in A Community Hospital," *Birth* 7:3, Fall 1980

Meara, Hanna, Ph.D. "A Key to Successful Breastfeeding in a Non-Supportive Culture," *Journal of Nurse Midwivery,* Vol. XXI:1, Spring 1976

Moss, P., and others. "The Hospital Inpatient Stay: The Experience of First-Time Parents," *Child Care and Health Development* 13:3, May/June 1987

Myers, Sheila Taylor. "Nurses' Responses to Changes in Maternity Care, Part II. Technologic Revolution, Legal Climate, and Economic Changes," *Birth* 14:2, June 1987

Stolte, Karen. "Nurses' Responses to Changes in Maternity Care, Part I. Family-Centered Changes and Short Hospitalization," *Birth* 14:2, June 1987

Tompson, Marian. "The Effectiveness of Mother-to-Mother Help—Research on the La Leche League International Program," *Birth* 3:4, 1976

Tregarthen, Timothy. "This Nursing Shortage Is Different," *The Wall Street Journal,* November 11, 1987

14 ▪ Your Baby Doctor

Bedell, Richard, M.D. Interview, October, 1982

Bell, Edward F., M.D., et al. "Combined Effect of Radiant Warmer and Phototherapy on Insensible Water Loss in Low-Birth-Weight Infants," *Journal of Pediatrics* 94:5, May 1979

Bell, T. A., and others. "Comparison of Ophthalmic Silver Nitrate Solution and Erythromycin Ointment for Prevention of Natally Acquired Chlamydia Trachomatis," *Sexually Transmitted Diseases* 14:4, October/December 1987

Bergevin, Y., M. Kramer, and C. Dougherty. "Do Infant Formula Samples Affect the Duration of Breastfeeding?" abstract presented at Annual Meeting of Ambulatory Pediatric Association, May 1981

"Birth Defects from PHisoHex Higher Than First Expected," *Boulder Daily Camera,* June 28, 1978

Blim, R. Don, M.D. "The President's Column—The 51st Year," *News and Comments* 31:11, American Academy of Pediatrics, November 1980

————. "The President's Column," *News and Comments,* September 1981

Boylan, P., M.B. "Oxytocin and Neonatal Jaundice," *British Medical Journal,* September 4, 1976

Brody, Jane E. "New Drug Therapy Blocks Severe Jaundice in Infants," *The New York Times,* April 12, 1988

Brown, Stephen W., Ph.D. "Survey Results: How Physicians See Themselves—and Their Image," *Medical Marketing Media* 17:2, February 1982

Buchan, Peter C. "Pathogenesis of Neonatal Hyperbilirubinaemia after Induction of Labour with Oxytocin," *British Medical Journal* 2(6200)1255–57, November 17, 1979

Butterfield, Perry M., et al. "Effects of Silver Nitrate on Initial Visual Behavior," *Am. J. Dis. Child* 132:426, April 1978

————. Phone interview, October 1983

Campbell, Neil, M.B., et al. "Increased Frequency of Neonatal Jaundice in a Maternity Hospital," *British Medical Journal,* June 7, 1975

Campbell, Priscilla, Academy of Pediatrics spokeswoman. Communication, quoting Edward J. Santzman, M.D., Hollywood, Florida, pediatrician who is chairman of the Provisional Committee on Practice and Ambulatory Medicine for the Academy of Pediatrics

"Canadian LLL," *News,* La Leche League, January–February 1981

Carmody, F., and others. "Follow Up of Babies Delivered in a Randomized Controlled Comparison of Vacuum Extraction and Forceps Delivery," *Acta Obstetricia et Gynecologica Scandanavica* 65:7, 1986

————. "Vacuum Extraction: A Randomized Controlled Comparison of the New Generation Cup with the Original Bird Cup," *Journal of Perinatal Medicine* 14:2, 1986

Chew, W.C., and I.L. Swann. "Influence of Simultaneous Low Amniotomy and Oxytocin Infusion and Other Maternal Factors on Neonatal Jaundice: A Prospective Study," *British Medical Journal,* January 8, 1977

Committee on Drugs, Committee on Fetus and Newborn, Committee on Infectious Diseases. "Prophylaxis and Treatment of Neonatal Gonococcal Infections," *Pediatrics* 65:5, May 1980

Committee on Nutrition. "Encouraging Breastfeeding," *Pediatrics* 65:3, March 1980

Cook, William A., M.D. *Natural Childbirth: Fact and Fallacy,* Chicago: Nelson-Hall, 1982

Costich, Timothy, M.D. Correspondence, 1981

Countryman, Betty Ann, R.N., M.S. "Breastfeeding and Jaundice," Information Sheet No. 10, La Leche League International, June 1978

Daystar, Paula, C.N.P. "Jaundice," Denver Birth Center, *News* 2:3, Fall 1981

Dharamraj, Claude, M.D., Concepcion G. Sia, M.D., Catherine M. P. Kierney, M.B., Ch.B., and Aruna Parekh. "Observations on Maternal Preference for Rooming-in Facilities," *Pediatrics* 67:5, May 1981

Drew, J. H., K. J. Marriage, V. V. Boyle, E. Bajraszewski, and J. M. McNamara. "Short and Long-Term Complications," *Archives of Disease in Childhood* 51:454, 1976

D'Souza, S.W., and others. "Oxytocin Induction of Labour: Hypona-traemia and Neonatal Jaundice," *European Journal of Obstetrics, Gynecology, and Reproductive Biology* 22:5, September 1986

Ellis, Judith. "Home Phototherapy for Newborn Jaundice," *Birth* 12:3, Fall 1985

Gartner, Lawrence, and Kathleen G. Auerbach. "Jaundice and Breastfeeding," *Mothering,* Fall 1986

Hammerschlag, Margaret R. "Efficacy of Neonatal Ocular Prophylaxis for the Prevention of Chlamydial and Gonococcal Conjunctivitis," *The New England Journal of Medicine* 320:12, March 23, 1989

Jacobs, Leonard. "Do Babies' Eyes Need Silver Nitrate?" *East West Journal,* August 1985

James, Frank E. "Pediatric Centers Spring Up to Provide Off-Hour Care," *The Wall Street Journal,* February 13, 1989

Jouppila, R., and others. "Effect of Segmental Epidural Analgesia on Neonatal Serum Bilirubin Concentration and Incidence of Neonatal Hyperbilirubinemia," *Acta Obstetricia et Gynecologica Scandanavica* 62:2, 1983

Khoury, Muin J., and others. "Recurrence Risk of Neonatal Hyperbilirubinemia in Siblings," *American Journal of Diseases of Children* 142, 1988

Laga, M., and others. "Prophylaxis of Gonococcal and Chlamydial Ophthalmia Neonatorum. A Comparison of Silver Nitrate and Tetracycline," *New England Journal of Medicine* 318:11, March 17, 1988

Lemons, James A. "What's New in the Newborn ICU?" *Perinatal Day* (Denver, Colo.), October 1984

Meyer, L., and others. "Maternal and Neonatal Morbidity in Instrumental Deliveries with the Kobayashi Vacuum Extractor and Low Forceps," *Acta Obstetricia et Gynecologica Scandinavica* 66:7, 1987

Paludetto, R., and others. "Moderate Hyperbilirubinemia Does Not Influence the Behavior of Jaundiced Infants," *Biology of the Neonate* 50:1, 1986

"Pediatrician Surplus Is Seen," *The New York Times,* July 14, 1987

Ramer, Cyril, M.D. Interview, October 1982

Rodriguez, E.M., and M.R. Hammerschlag. "Diagnostic Methods for Chlamydia Trachomatis Disease in Neonates," *Journal of Perinatology* 7:3, Summer 1987

Rosta, J., et al. "Delayed Meconium Passage and Hyperbilirubinemia," *Lancet* 2:1138, 23 November 1968

Rubin, Rosalyn A., et al. "Neonatal Serum Bilirubin Levels Related to Cognitive Development at Ages Four Through Seven Years," *Pediatrics* 94:4, April 1979

Scheidt, P.C., et al. "Toxicity to Bilirubin in Neonates: Infant Development during First Year in Relation to Maximum Neonatal Serum Bilirubin Concentration," *Journal of Pediatrics* 91:2, August 1977

Silverman, William A., M.D. *Retrolental Fibroplasia: A Modern Parable,* New York: Grune and Stratton, 1980, review in *Birth,* 8:3, Judith Lumley, Ph.D., Fall 1981

Simkin, P., P. A. Simkin, and Margot Edwards. "Neonatal Jaundice," *Birth* 6:1, Spring 1979

Speck, W. T., C. C. Chen, and H. S. Rosenkranz. "In Vitro Studies of

Effects of Light and Riboflavin on DNA and HeLa Cells," *Pediatr. Res.* 9:150, 1975

Stewart, David, Ph.D., ed. *The Five Standards for Safe Childbearing,* Marble Hill, Mo.: NAPSAC Productions, 1981

Taylor, Charles, M.D. Interview, January, 1980

Thomas, Howard P. "Considering Newborn Circumcision," *Intensive Caring Unlimited,* July/August 1988

Van Enk, A., and R. de Leeuw. "Phototherapy: The Hospital as Risk Factor," *British Medical Journal* 294:6574, March 21, 1987

Vecchi, C., and others. "Green Light in Phototherapy," *Pediatric Research* 17:6, June 1983

Vecchi, C., and others. "Phototherapy for Neonatal Jaundice: Clinical Equivalence of Fluorescent Green and 'Special' Blue Lamps," *Journal of Pediatrics* 108:3, March 1986

Whittaker, Nancy. "A Short Course on Neonatal Jaundice," *Mothering,* Summer 1982

Winfield, C. R., and R. MacFaul. "Clinical Study of Prolonged Jaundice in Breast- and Bottle-fed Babies," *Archives of Disease in Childhood* 53, 1978

▪ INDEX ▪

About the Authors

DIANA KORTE has won more than two dozen awards for health journalism in both print and radio, including the American Academy of Pediatrics Award. She has hosted public radio programs that focus on women's health and produced a thirty-minute documentary on birth, "A Woman's Hormones in a Man's World," which has aired on many U.S. stations. She is a frequent workshop leader and lecturer on health issues. A La Leche League leader for twenty years, she also served as a director of La Leche League's International Board. She has been a maternity care consultant to consumers, doctors, and hospitals and served on local and state health-related boards of directors. Based in Boulder, Colorado, she and her husband, parents of one daughter and three sons, recently spent about a year living in Europe. Her newest book is *Passages to Health* (Ballantine, 1991). This book describes dozens of women's health issues, including innovative options, and is based on information gathered from people in more than twenty countries.

ROBERTA SCAER is a maternity care advocate, breastfeeding counselor, lecturer, and workshop leader who has helped women as a La Leche League leader for twenty-four years. A Phi Beta Kappa graduate of the University of Rochester with a master's degree in social work, she initiated and coauthored the first survey of women's preferences in maternity care. Of her four children, three were born in hospital (two with the Bradley method), and one child was born at home with siblings present. She lives in Boulder, Colorado, with her husband, a physician whose specialties are neurology and rehabilitation.

We Deliver!
And So Do These Bestsellers.